ISBN 1595329021

9 781595 329028

50999

EAN

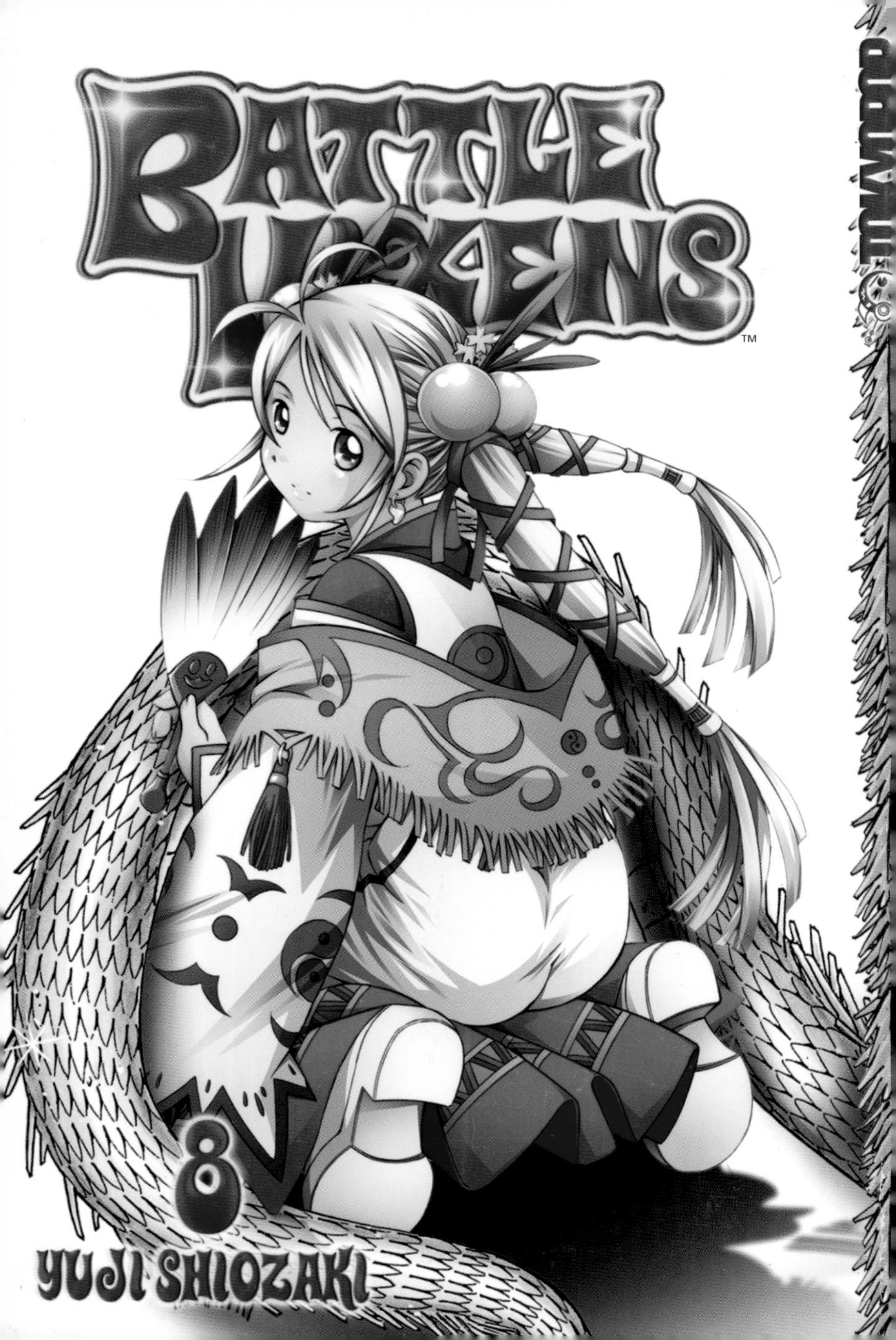
BATTLE VIXENS
™
8
YUJI SHIOZAKI

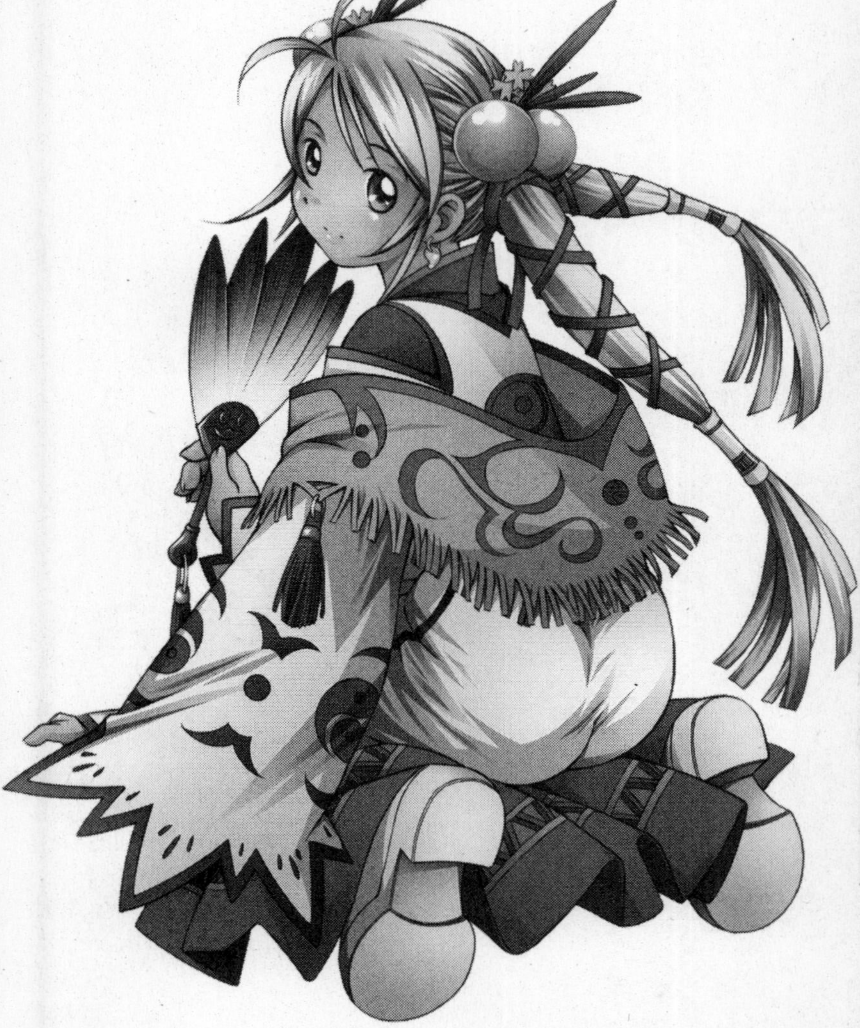

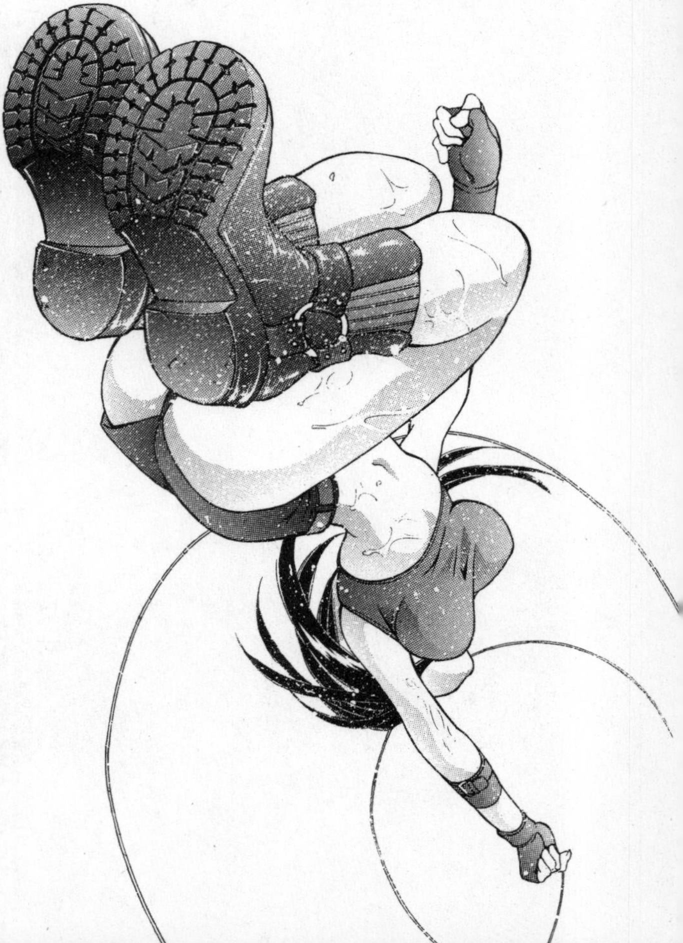

BATTLE VIXENS™

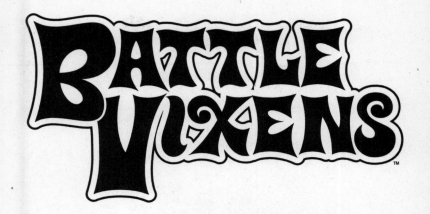

Battle Vixens Vol. 8
Created by Yuji Shiozaki

Translation - Louie Kawamoto
English Adaptation - Keith Giffen
Associate Editor - Troy Lewter
Copy Editors - Aaron Sparrow and Suzanne Waldman
Retouch and Lettering - William Suh
Production Artist - Chris Anderson
Cover Design - Christian Lownds

Editor - Rob Tokar
Digital Imaging Manager - Chris Buford
Production Managers - Jennifer Miller and Mutsumi Miyazaki
Managing Editor - Jill Freshney
VP of Production - Ron Klamert
Publisher and Editor-in-Chief - Mike Kiley
President and C.O.O. - John Parker
C.E.O. - Stuart Levy

A  Manga

TOKYOPOP Inc.
5900 Wilshire Blvd. Suite 2000
Los Angeles, CA 90036

E-mail: info@TOKYOPOP.com
Come visit us online at www.TOKYOPOP.com

ISBN: 1-59532-902-1

First TOKYOPOP printing: September 2005
10 9 8 7 6 5 4 3 2 1
Printed in Canada

BATTLE VIXENS™

Vol. 8

by
Yuji Shiozaki

TOKYOPOP®

HAMBURG // LONDON // LOS ANGELES // TOKYO

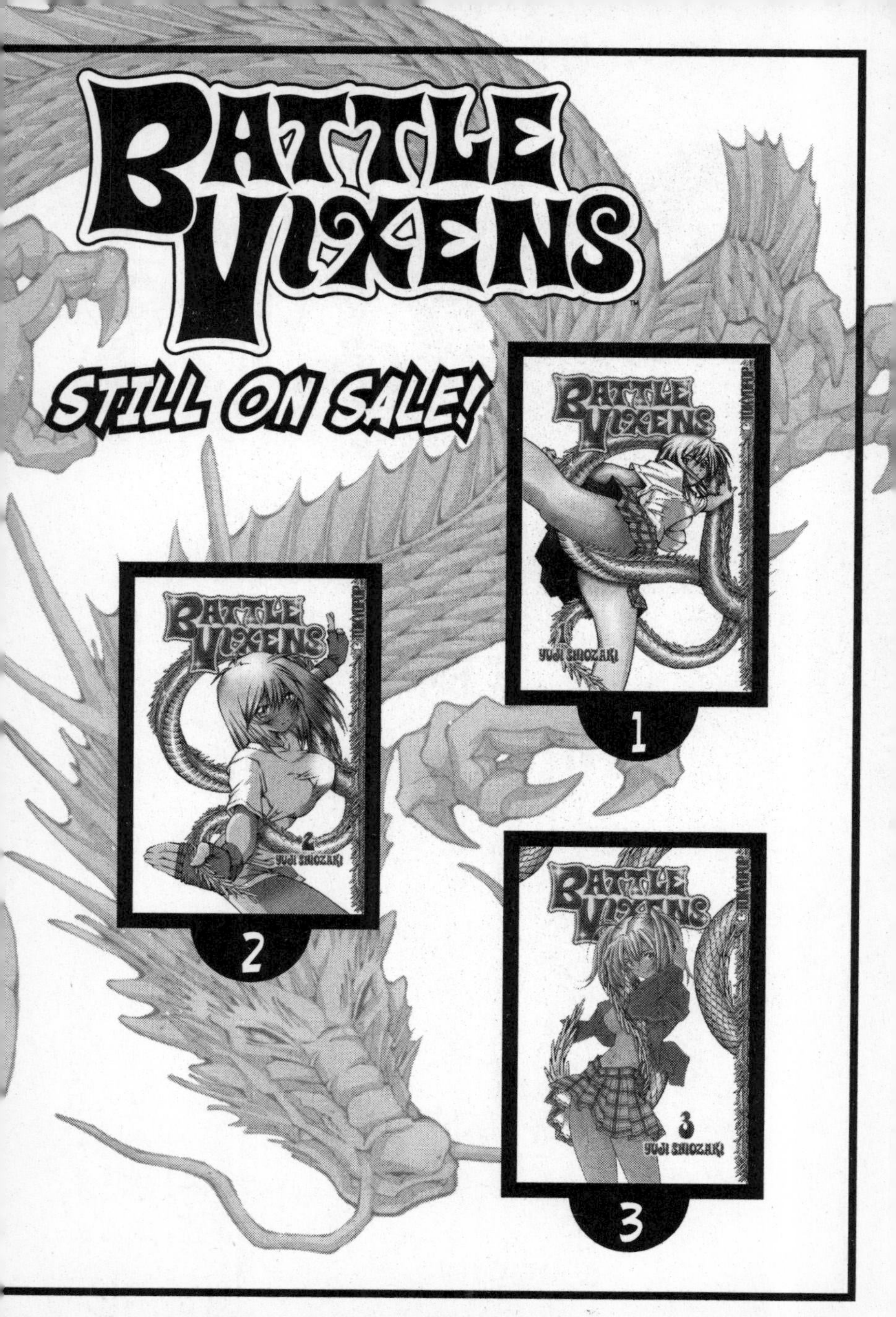
BATTLE VIXENS™
STILL ON SALE!
BATTLE VIXENS
1
YUJI SHIOZAKI
1
BATTLE VIXENS
2
YUJI SHIOZAKI
2
BATTLE VIXENS
3
YUJI SHIOZAKI
3

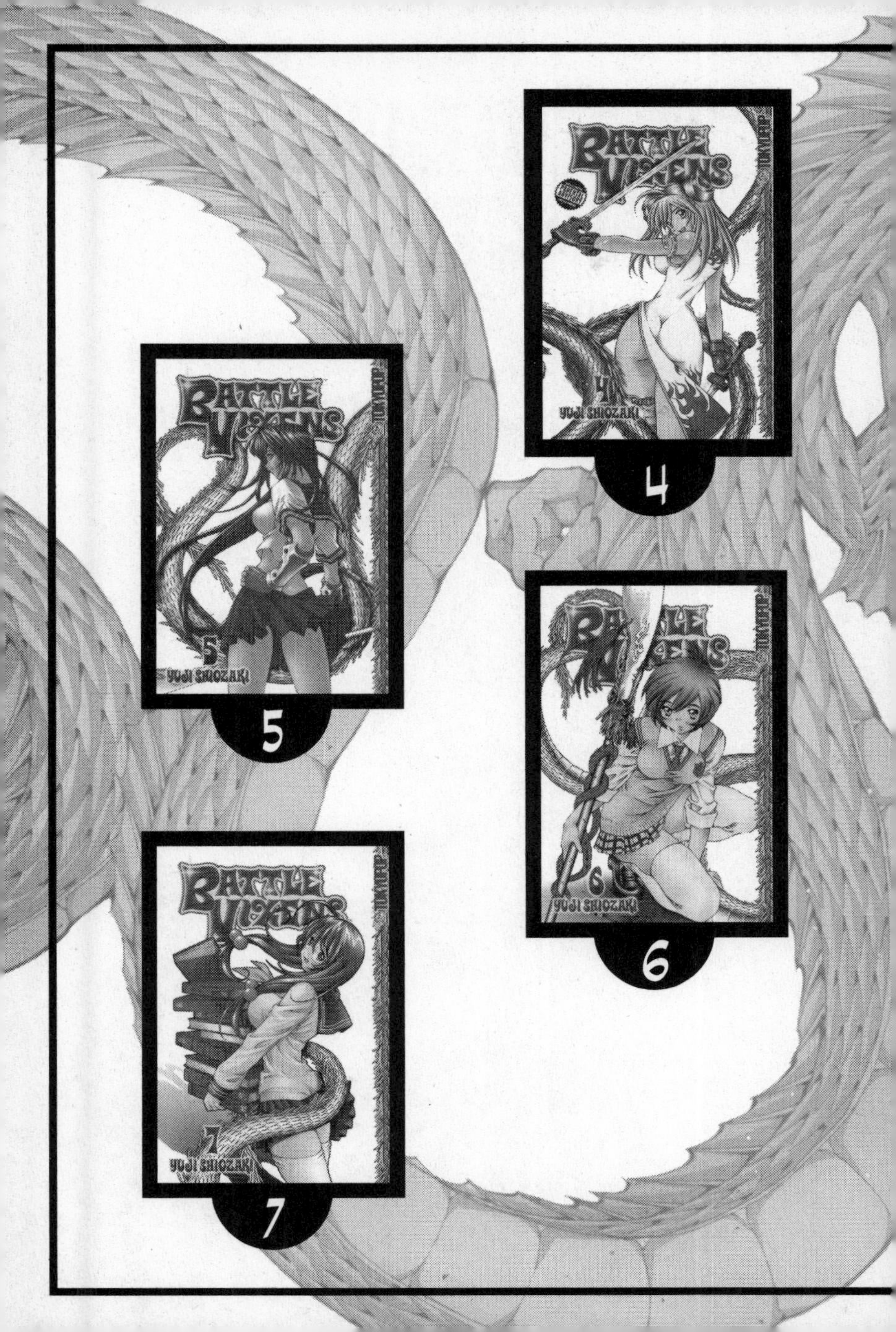
BATTLE VIXENS
4
YUJI SHIOZAKI
TOKYOPOP
4
BATTLE VIXENS
5
YUJI SHIOZAKI
TOKYOPOP
5
BATTLE VIXENS
6
YUJI SHIOZAKI
TOKYOPOP
6
BATTLE VIXENS
7
YUJI SHIOZAKI
TOKYOPOP
7

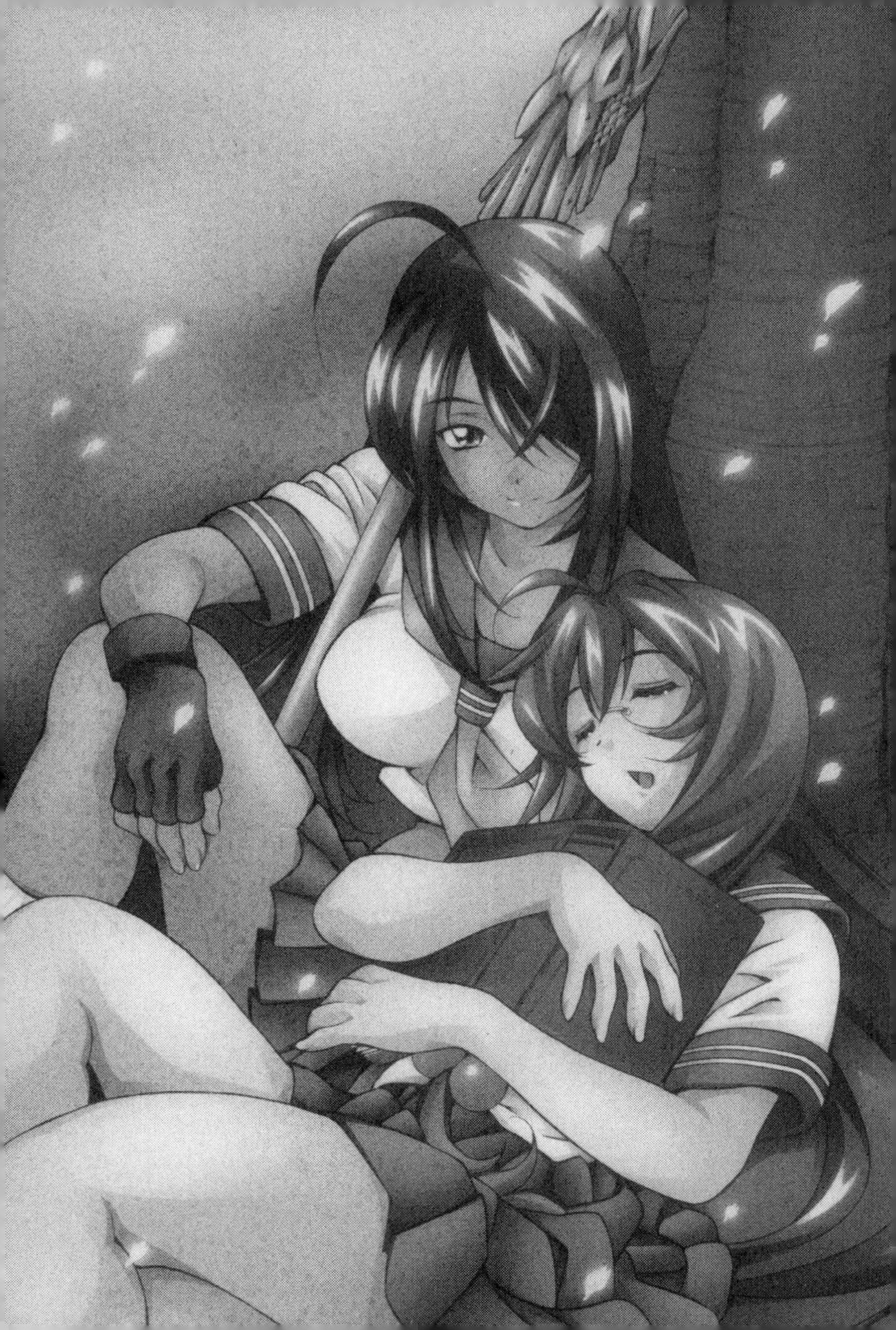

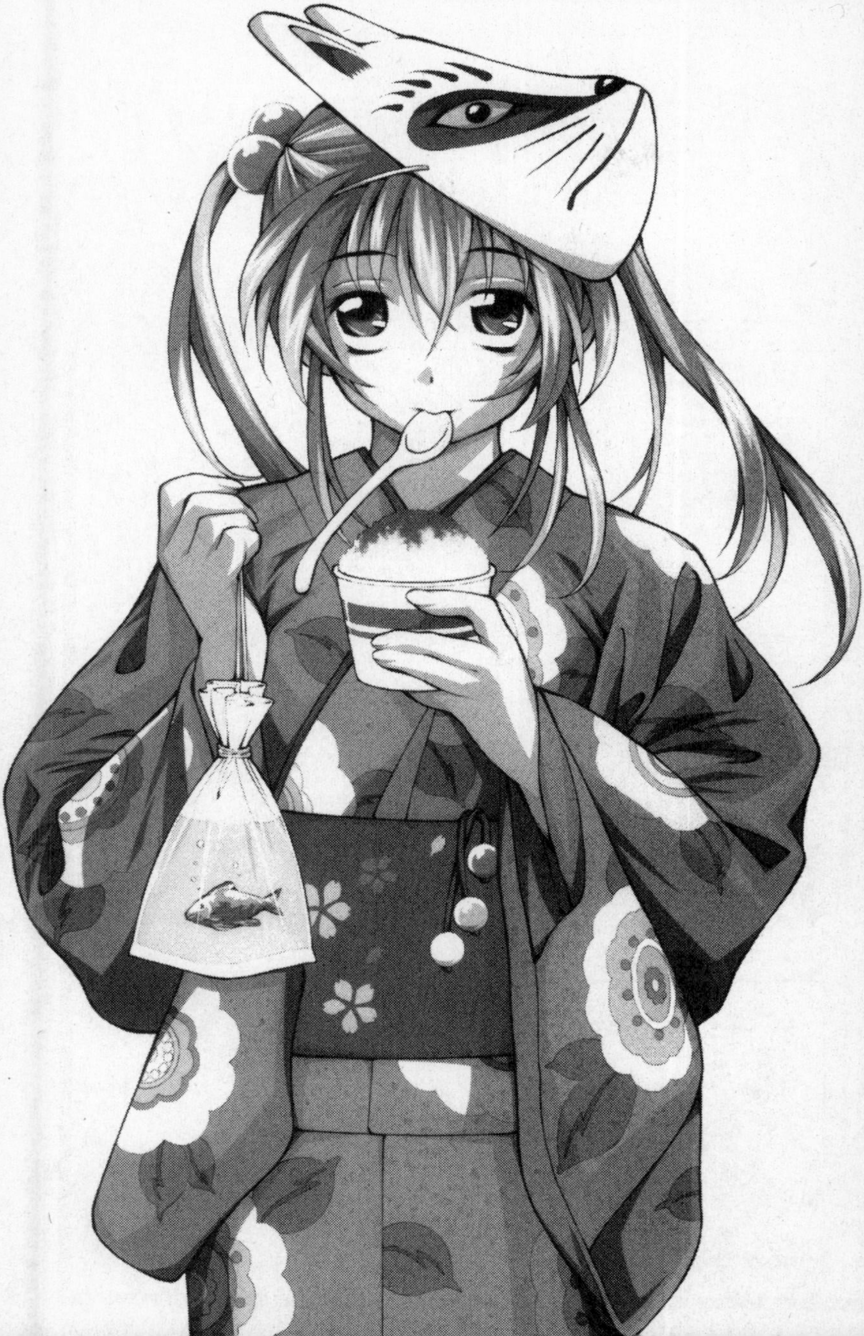

CAST

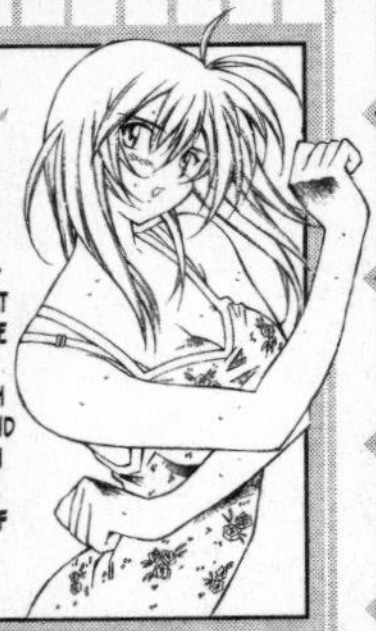

HAKUFU SONSAKU - DISPATCHED TO TOKYO BY HER MOTHER TO BETTER REALIZE HER FULL POTENTIAL, THIS BUSTY TOUSHI ARRIVED AT NANYO ACADEMY READY, WILLING AND ABLE. ALTHOUGH RANKED D, HER FIGHTING PROWESS FAR EXCEEDS THAT OF THE AVERAGE D-RANK. DID WE MENTION SHE HAS HUGE TITS? HAKUFU CURRENTLY ROOMS WITH HER COUSIN, SHYUYU KOUKIN, AND HAS RECENTLY HAD NIGHTMARISH HENTAI-LICIOUS DREAMS AFTER THE MYSTERIOUS APPEARANCE OF A SKULL-SHAPED TATTOO ON HER BODY.

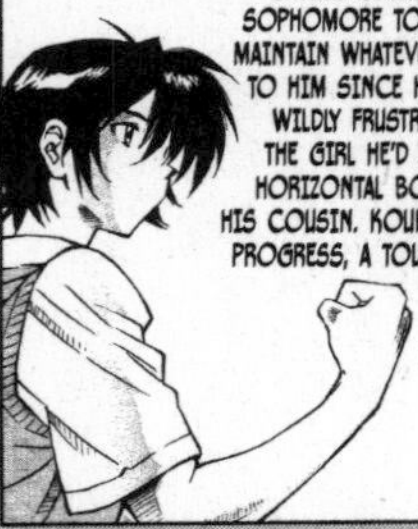

SHYUYU KOUKIN - A C-RANK SOPHOMORE TOUSHI TRYING TO MAINTAIN WHATEVER DECORUM LEFT TO HIM SINCE HAKUFU'S ARRIVAL. WILDLY FRUSTRATED BECAUSE THE GIRL HE'D MOST LIKE TO HORIZONTAL BOOGIE WITH IS HIS COUSIN. KOUKIN IS A WORK IN PROGRESS, A TOUSHI OF UNTAPPED POTENTIAL COMPROMISED BY LOW SELF-ESTEEM.

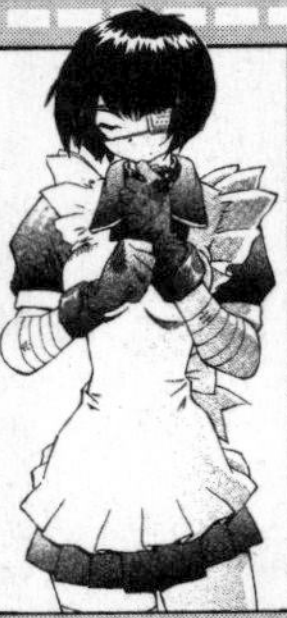

RYOMOU SHIMEI - A TOP-FOUR NANYO PLAYER SPECIALIZING IN JOINT/LIGAMENT STRESS ATTACK POINTS. SHIMEI'S LAID-BACK ATTITUDE STANDS IN DIRECT CONTRAST TO THE PSYCHO-SEXUAL FRENZY SHE EXHIBITS DURING COMBAT. SHIMEI IS RUMORED TO HAVE A "DEMON EYE" BENEATH HER EVER-PRESENT EYEPATCH.

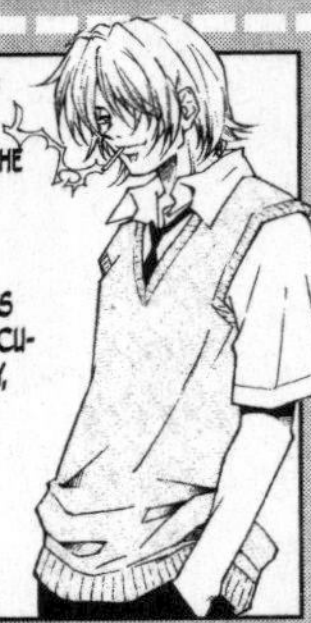

SAJI GENPOU - ONE OF THE PRIMARY PLAYERS AT NANYO. BEST KNOWN AS THE HENCHMAN OF CHOICE OF UNDISPUTED NANYO OVERLORD ENJUTSU. GENPOU'S TOUSHI RANK IS THE SUBJECT OF MUCH SPECULATION. NEEDLESS TO SAY, GENPOU'S NOT TALKING.

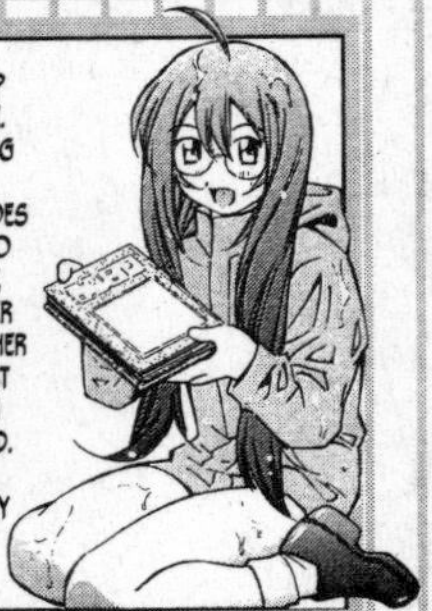

RYUBI GENTOKU - A TOP SEITO ACADEMY TOUSHI. RYUBI IS A WELL-MEANING BOOKWORM WHOSE INHERENT CLUMSINESS DOES LITTLE TO ENDEAR HER TO KANU. LOYAL TO A FAULT, RYUBI GOES OUT OF HER WAY TO ACCOMMODATE HER FRIENDS. BUT WATCH OUT WHENEVER THE DRAGON WITHIN HER IS AWAKENED. THEN SHE KNOWS NO FRIENDSHIP NOR LOYALTY AND WILL KILL ANY AND ALL.

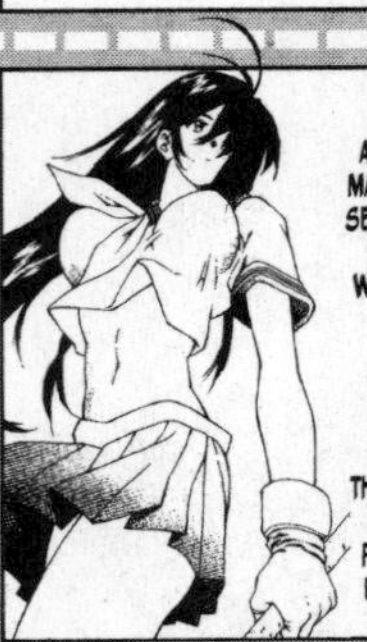

KANU UNCHOU - AN A-RANK SEITO ACADEMY MASTER. KANU WIELDS THE SEIRYU (DRAGON) SWORD KNOWN AS REIENKYO WITH LETHAL EFFICIENCY. KANU IS FEARED AND RESPECTED BY THE TOUSHI, HER COMBAT SKILLS HAVING OVERWHELMED MORE THAN A FEW OPPONENTS. KANU CONSIDERS PROTECTING RYUBI TO BE HER LIFE'S CALLING.

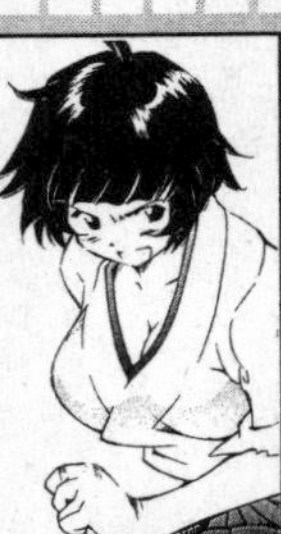

CHOUHI EKITOKU - A C-RANK SEITO ACADEMY FRESHMAN. CHOUHI PROTECTS (SOME WOULD SAY BABYSITS) RYUBI IN TANDEM WITH KANU. CHOUHI SERVES AS MAIDEN AT THE SHRINE, WHEREIN RYUBI IS DETAINED WHENEVER THE DRAGON WITHIN AWAKENS.

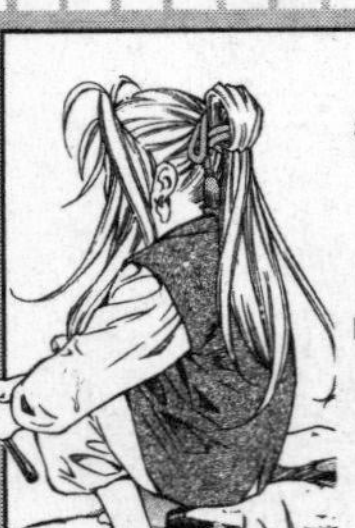

SHOKATSURYOU KOUMEI - A TOUSHI HARBORING "FUKU-RYU"; THE HIDDEN DRAGON (STOP SNICKERING, WE KNOW WHAT IT SOUNDS LIKE), HER ABILITIES AS TOUSHI ARE UNCONFIRMED BUT HER INTELLIGENCE IS EXCEPTIONAL. WE HAVE NO IDEA WHAT THAT IMPLIES.

BATTLE VIXENS

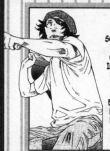

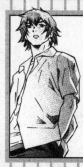

SOUSOU MOUTOKU - A KYOSHO HIGH B-RANK TOUSHI PRONE TO LENGTHY BOUTS OF DAYDREAMING. THE DAYDREAMS, FOR THE MOST PART, ARE ABOUT CONQUEST, CARNAGE, AND, KEEPING WITH THE SPIRIT OF THE SERIES, CAMEL-TOES AND EXPLODING SHIRTS.

KAKOUTON (TON-CHAN) GENJOU - A C-RANK SOPHOMORE AT THE SCHOOL OF CIVIL ENGINEERING (KYOSHO HIGH), TON-CHAN IS A STREET-FIGHTING PURIST WHOSE STRICT ADHERENCE TO TRADITION TENDS TO CONFUSE RATHER THAN ENLIGHTEN. LATELY, HE'S BEEN MORE THAN DISILLUSIONED BY THE APPALLING LACK OF HONOR DISPLAYED BY HIS SIDE IN BATTLE.

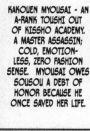

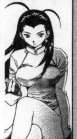

KAKOUEN MYOUSAI - AN A-RANK TOUSHI OUT OF KISSHO ACADEMY. A MASTER ASSASSIN; COLD, EMOTIONLESS, ZERO FASHION SENSE. MYOUSAI OWES SOUSOU A DEBT OF HONOR BECAUSE HE ONCE SAVED HER LIFE.

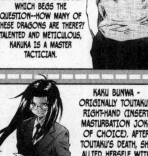

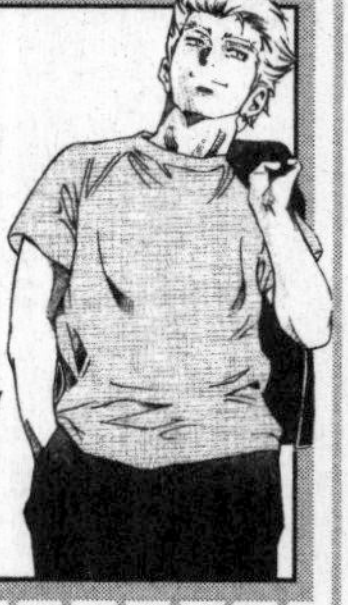

KAKUKA HOUKOU - A THIRD-YEAR TOUSHI OUT OF KYOSHO HIGH. SOUSOU'S RIGHT-HAND MAN. KAKUKA IS RESPONSIBLE FOR AWAKENING THE DRAGON SLEEPING WITHIN SOUSOU... WHICH BEGS THE QUESTION--HOW MANY OF THESE DRAGONS ARE THERE?! TALENTED AND METICULOUS, KAKUKA IS A MASTER TACTICIAN.

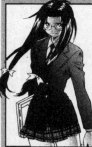

KAKU BUNWA - ORIGINALLY TOUTAKU'S RIGHT-HAND (INSERT MASTURBATION JOKE OF CHOICE). AFTER TOUTAKU'S DEATH, SHE ALLIED HERSELF WITH SOUSOU. ALTHOUGH DRAWN TO KAKUKA LIKE A MOTH TO A FLAME, KAKU'S TRUE FEELINGS REMAIN A MYSTERY.

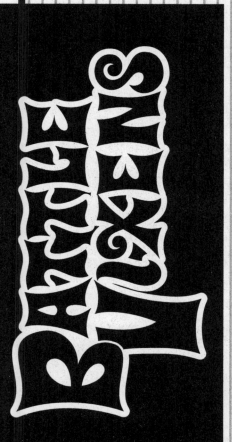

STORY THUS FAR...

AGES AGO, IN THE SANGOKU ERA, HEROES TRIED TO UNITE CHINA...AND FAILED. AFTER THEIR DEFEAT, THE HEROES' SPIRITS CAME TO REST IN JEWELS--KNOWN AS MAGATAMA--THAT CAN DRAW OUT THE FULL FIGHTING POTENTIAL OF THOSE WHO INHERIT THEM. HOW THE GEMS FOUND THEIR WAY TO JAPAN AND GOT DISSEMINATED IS, THANKFULLY, A STORY FOR ANOTHER DAY. THOSE WHO POSSESS THE MAGATAMA ARE CALLED TOUSHI (MINDS OUT OF THE GUTTER, PLEASE) AND, FUELED BY MAGATAMA-AMPLIFIED AGGRESSION, TOUSHI FIGHT--MOSTLY ONE ANOTHER--TO BECOME IKKI TOSEN: ONE WARRIOR WITH THE POWER OF ONE THOUSAND!

THE TOUSHI LEVELS RUN FROM THE EXPERT A-RANK TO THE NOVICE E-RANK AND EACH TOUSHI'S MAGATAMA IS COLORED TO INDICATE HIS/HER RANK. YEAH, WE KNOW IT'S A BLACK-AND-WHITE BOOK...JUST TAKE OUR WORD FOR IT, OKAY?

HAKUFU SONSAKU IS RELATIVELY NEW TO THE WHOLE TOUSHI SCENE, BUT SHE'S ALREADY CREATED PLENTY OF WAVES AT NANYO ACADEMY (A SCHOOL IN TOKYO POPULATED ENTIRELY BY TOUSHI), AS WELL AS AT NANYO'S RIVAL SCHOOLS. HAKUFU HAS EXHIBITED SOME INCREDIBLE ABILITIES THAT ARE WELL BEYOND HER D-RANK. SHE'S ALSO EXHIBITED A RAPTUR-OUS RACK THAT IS WELL BEYOND A D-CUP.

THE COMPLEX POLITICS OF THE TOUSHI WORLD CAN BE HARD FOR A NEWCOMER TO GRASP SO HAKUFU'S COUSIN/ROOMMATE--THE C-RANK TOUSHI KNOWN AS SHYUYU KOUKIN--TRIES TO KEEP HER OUT OF TROUBLE AS MUCH AS HE CAN. UNFORTUNATELY, KOUKIN CAN NO MORE KEEP HAKUFU'S IMPULSIVE NATURE IN CHECK THAN HE CAN KEEP HER ULTRA-SMOKIN' BOD OUT OF HIS MIND...AND BOTH SITUATIONS ARE DRIVING HIM CRAZY. AND DON'T EVEN GET US STARTED ABOUT KOUKIN AND HAKUFU'S MOM (A.K.A. AUNTS IN THE PANTS SYNDROME.) YEESH!

THOUGH SHE PASSED A CHALLENGE FROM TOUSHI MASTER CHOUSHOU, HAKUFU WAS UNABLE TO SAVE CHOUSHOU FROM A DEADLY ATTACK BY THE SELF-SLICING TOUTAKU. BUT BEFORE CHOUSHOU DIED SHE PASSED...SOMETHING...TO AN UNCONSCIOUS HAKUFU.
NOT LONG AFTERWARD, TOUTAKU, UNABLE TO BREAK THE TOUSHI "OUTCOMES ARE PREDES-TINED" CYCLE, COMMITTED SUICIDE RATHER THAN MEET HIS FATED MURDER AT THE HANDS OF RYOFU HOUSEN.

LATER, HAKUFU FOUGHT UKITSU--THE GIRL WHO IS MAGATAMA-DESTINED TO KILL HAKUFU. AFTER A BONE-CRUNCHING AND BONER-POPPIN' BRAWL, UKITSU GOT THE UPPER HAND AND WAS ABOUT TO FULFILL HER DESTINY WHEN KOUKIN ATTEMPTED TO BREAK UP THE FIGHT-ONLY TO GET HIS ASS KICKED BY UKITSU INSTEAD. THE SIGHT OF KOUKIN'S BRUISED AND BLOODIED BODY AWOKE THE DRAGON WITHIN HAKUFU, WHO INSTANTLY WENT FROM BUSTY YOUNG BABE TO SUPER-SCARY, BOOTY-BASHING BITCH FROM HELL.

AFTER BEATING UKITSU SENSELESS (AND SHREDDING ALL BUT THE TINIEST SCRAPS OF UKITSU'S CLOTHES), HAKUFU THE HORRIBLE PREPARED TO IMPALE HER OPPONENT WITH HYAKUHEKITOU (A MAGIC SWORD SHE'D RECEIVED FROM CHOUSHOW). APPARENTLY NOT HAVING LEARNED HIS LESSON EARLIER (OR MAYBE HE'S A SADOMASOCHISTIC FREAK-JOB), KOUKIN LEAPT BETWEEN THE GIRLS...AGAIN. THE RESULT? HAKUFU SKEWERS KOUKIN THROUGH THE CHEST.

HAKUFU, NOW BACK TO NORMAL (WHATEVER THAT IS), VISITED KOUKIN IN THE HOSPITAL. THERE SHE MANAGED TO USE HER KI (CHANNELED THROUGH HER BARE BAZONGAS) TO MIRACULOUSLY ACCELERATE KOUKIN'S HEALING PROCESS. HOWEVER, HAKUFU ACQUIRED A MYSTERIOUS SKULL-SHAPED MARK IN THE PROCESS THAT SEEMS TO BE AN INDICATOR OF SOME KIND OF CANCEROUS EVIL FORCE WITHIN HER (KINDA SIMILAR TO THE ONES MOST MODERN CELEBRITIES HAVE).

RYOFU ALSO FLIPPED DESTINY THE BIRD AND TOOK THE FIGHT TO SOUSOU AND HIS CREW. BAD IDEA. AS SHE LAY DYING, CHINKYU CAME TO HER AID--AND, IN A SELFLESS DISPLAY OF FRIENDSHIP AND HOT GIRL-ON-GIRL LOVIN', SACRIFICED HER OWN LIFE WHEN RYOFU DIED.

KANU UNCHOU AND CHOUHI EKITOKU, WHO ARE SWORN TO PROTECT MOUSEY BOOK-WORM RYUBI GENTOKU, FEND OFF ASSASINS WHILE RYUBI ESCAPES. BUT LOOKS DEFINITELY DECEIVE IN RYUBI'S CASE, FOR WITHIN HER DWELLS A POWERFUL DRAGON, A HARBINGER OF DEATH AND DESTRUCTION! (SURE, BUT IS IT LESS FILLING?)

SEVERAL TIT SHOTS LATER, KANU SEARCHES FOR SHOKATSURYOU KOUMEI, THE ONLY ONE WHO COULD POSSIBLY BRING BALANCE TO THE FORC--OOPS. WRONG STORY. DRAGON. SHOKATSURYOU CAN HELP RYUBI BALANCE THE POWER INSIDE HER. AHEM. ANYHOO...SHE ENCOUNTERS ZENFUKU, A CREEPY OLD MAN WHO LIKES EATING MUSHROOMS (AND NO, NOT THE TRIPPY, "THE WALLS ARE MELTING, MAN" KIND). THEY FIGHT BECAUSE, WELL, WHY THE HELL NOT?

MEANWHILE, IN HER FLIGHT TO SAFETY, RYUBI ENCOUNTERS SHOKATSURYOU FISHING BY A LAKE. SUDDENLY, SHOKATSURYOU IS YANKED INTO THE LAKE BY WHAT APPEARS TO BE A DRAGON. THE MENTAL MOUNT EVEREST THAT IS RYUBI JUMPS IN TO SAVE HER...THOUGH SHE HERSELF CAN'T SWIM. SHE BLACKS OUT...BUT AWAKENS SAFE AND SOUND ON THE BANK WITH A NOW UNCONSCIOUS SHOKATSURYOU.

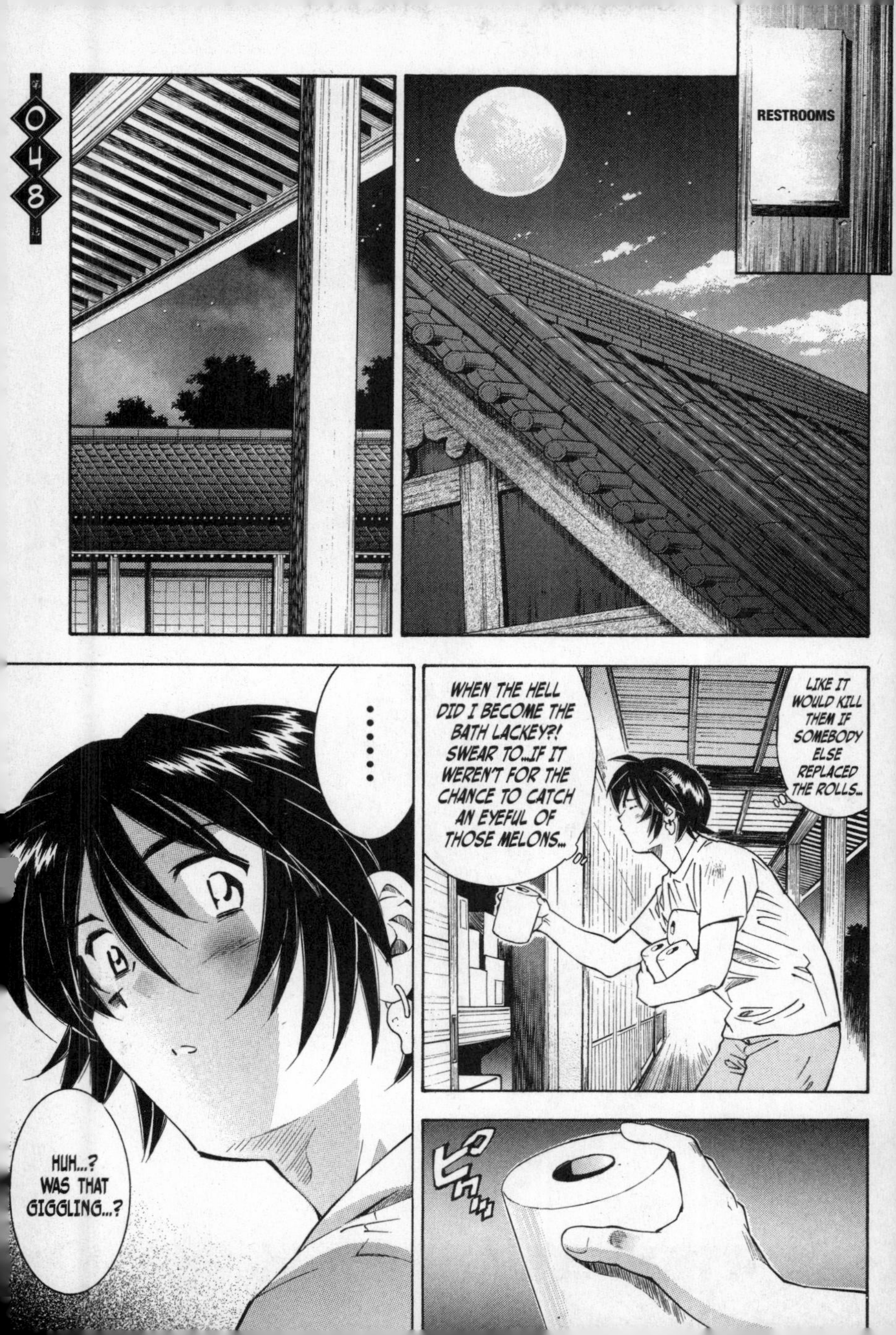
RESTROOMS
LIKE IT WOULD KILL THEM IF SOMEBODY ELSE REPLACED THE ROLLS...
WHEN THE HELL DID I BECOME THE BATH LACKEY?! SWEAR TO...IF IT WEREN'T FOR THE CHANCE TO CATCH AN EYEFUL OF THOSE MELONS...
ピクッ
......
HUH...? WAS THAT GIGGLING...?

OUIN SHISHI

OUIN WAS BORN INTO A FAMOUS FAMILY AND ACCLAIMED AS "OUSA NO SAI" (HAVING THE ABILITY TO SUPPORT HIS RULER). OUIN WAS TRUSTED BY TOUTAKU AND SERVED HIM WELL, BUT SECRETLY PLOTTED TO ASSASSINATE TOUTAKU (WHICH, PRETTY MUCH, INVALIDATED THE WHOLE "OUSA NO SAI" THING). OUIN SUCCEEDED IN ASSASSINATING TOUTAKU BY PLACING RYOFU IN "KANREN NO KEI" WHICH, DEPENDING ON THE DIALECT, WE BELIEVE ROUGHLY TRANSLATES TO "OUSA NO SAI MY ASS."

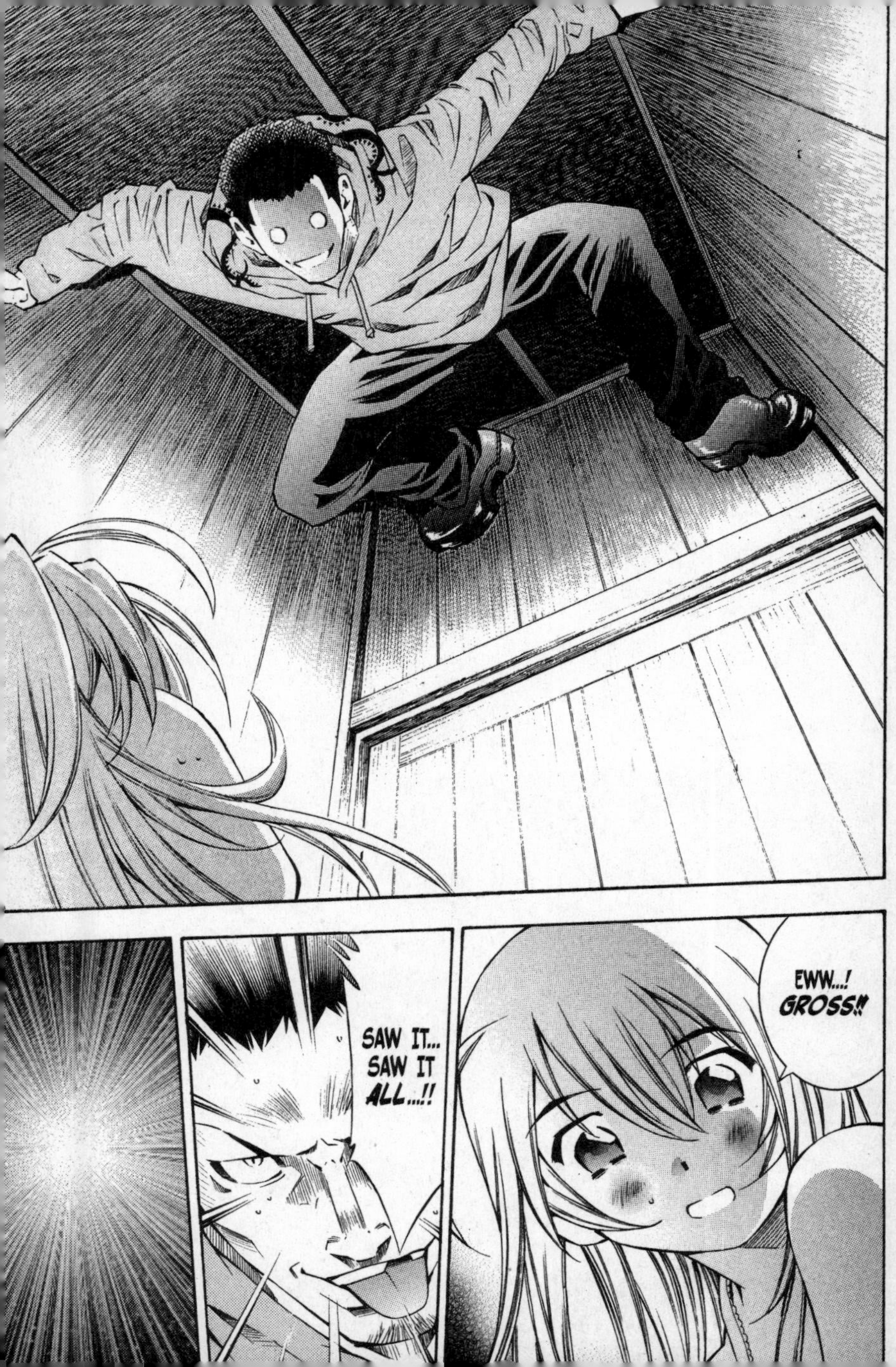
EWW...! GROSS!!
SAW IT... SAW IT ALL...!!

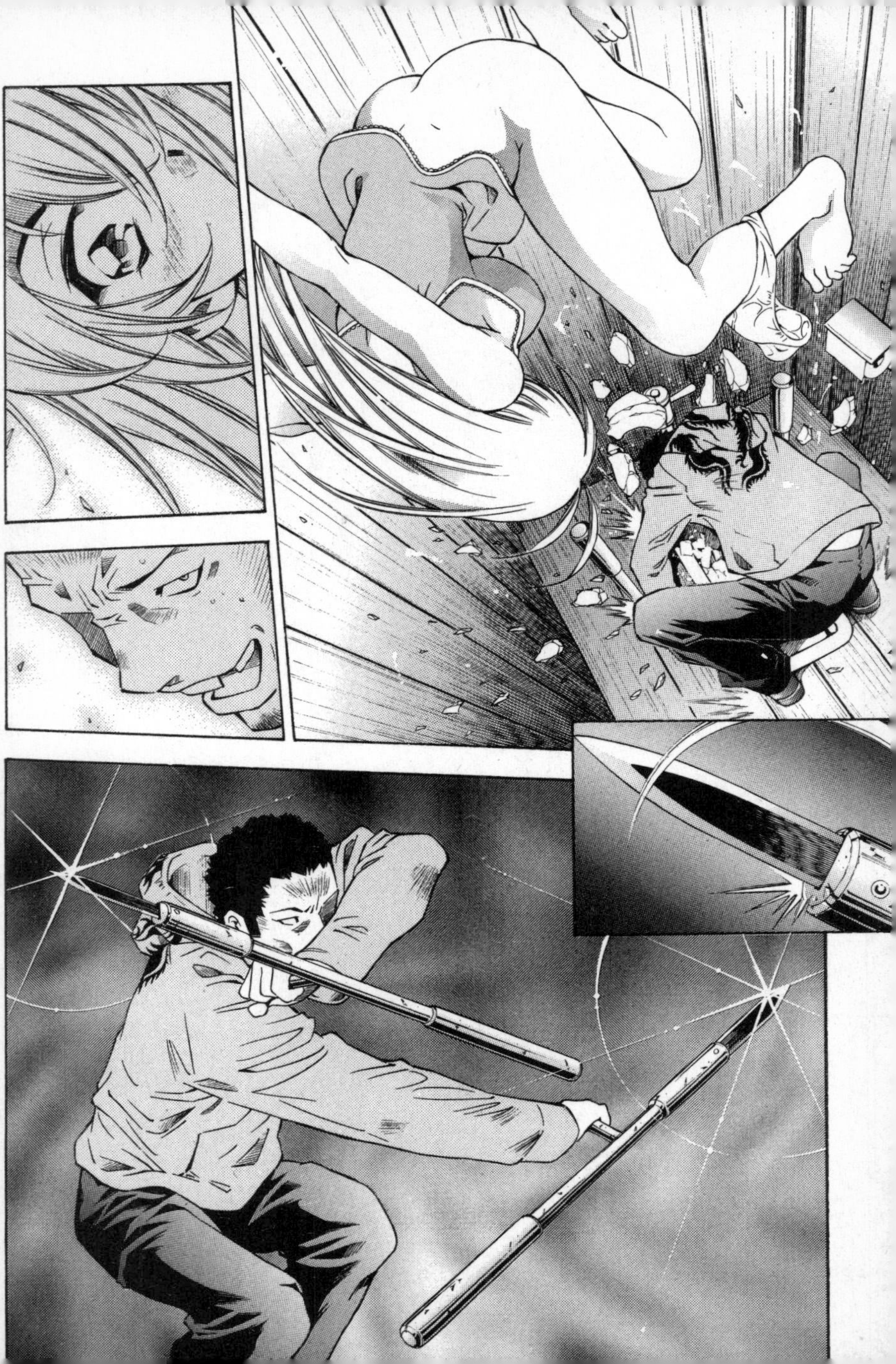

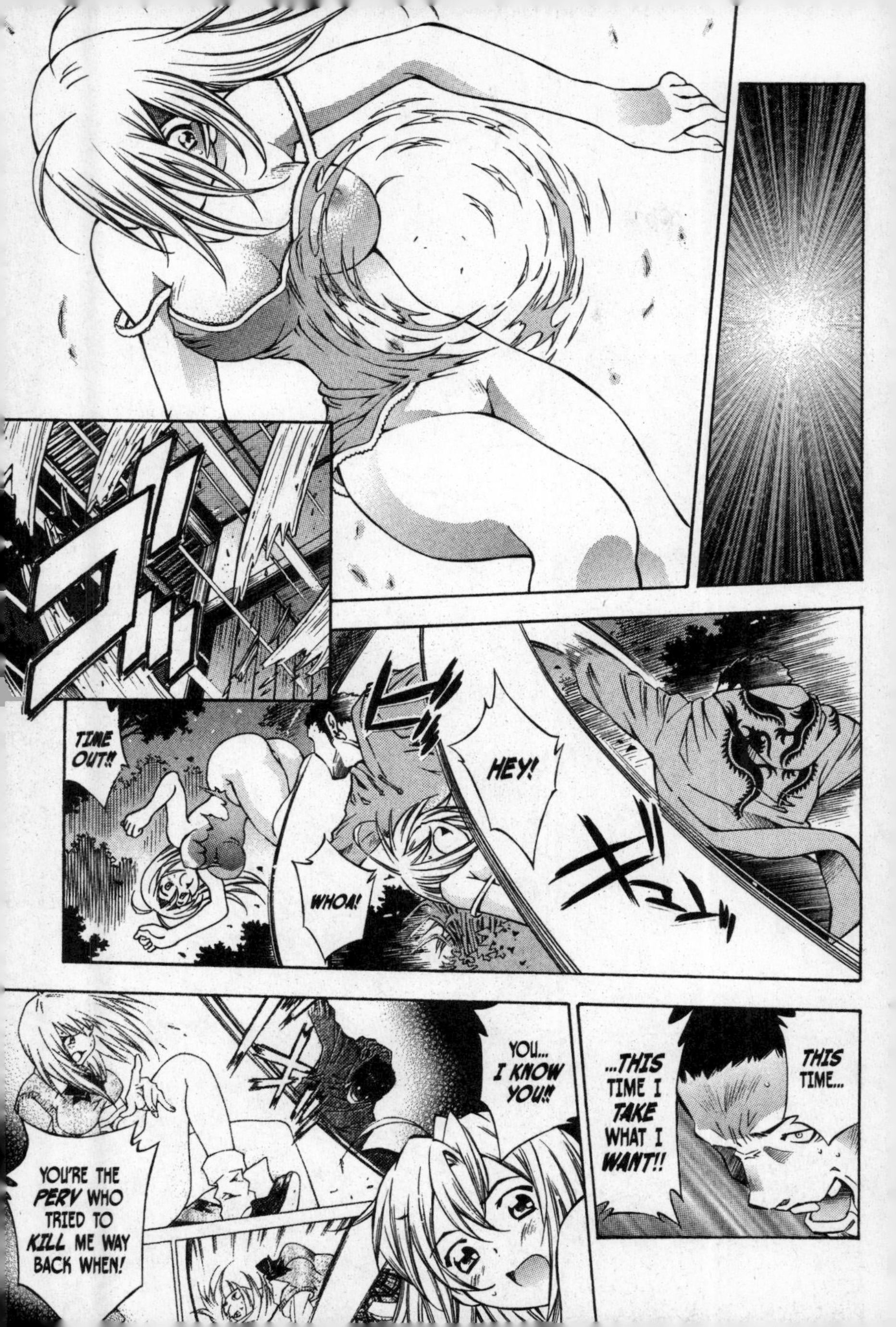
HEY!
TIME OUT!!
WHOA!
THIS TIME...
...THIS TIME I TAKE WHAT I WANT!!
YOU... I KNOW YOU!!
YOU'RE THE PERV WHO TRIED TO KILL ME WAY BACK WHEN!

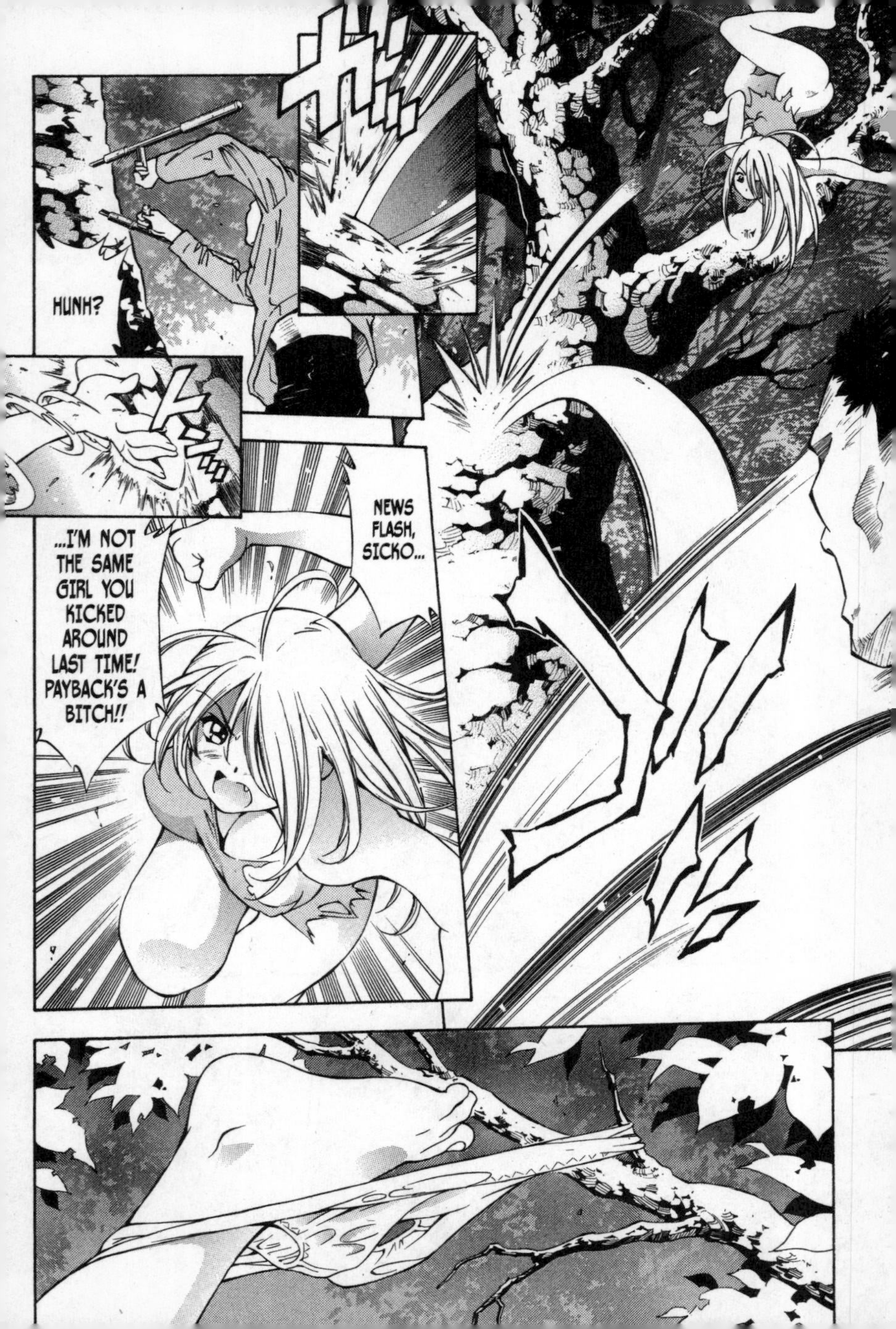
HUNH?
NEWS FLASH, SICKO...
...I'M NOT THE SAME GIRL YOU KICKED AROUND LAST TIME! PAYBACK'S A BITCH!!

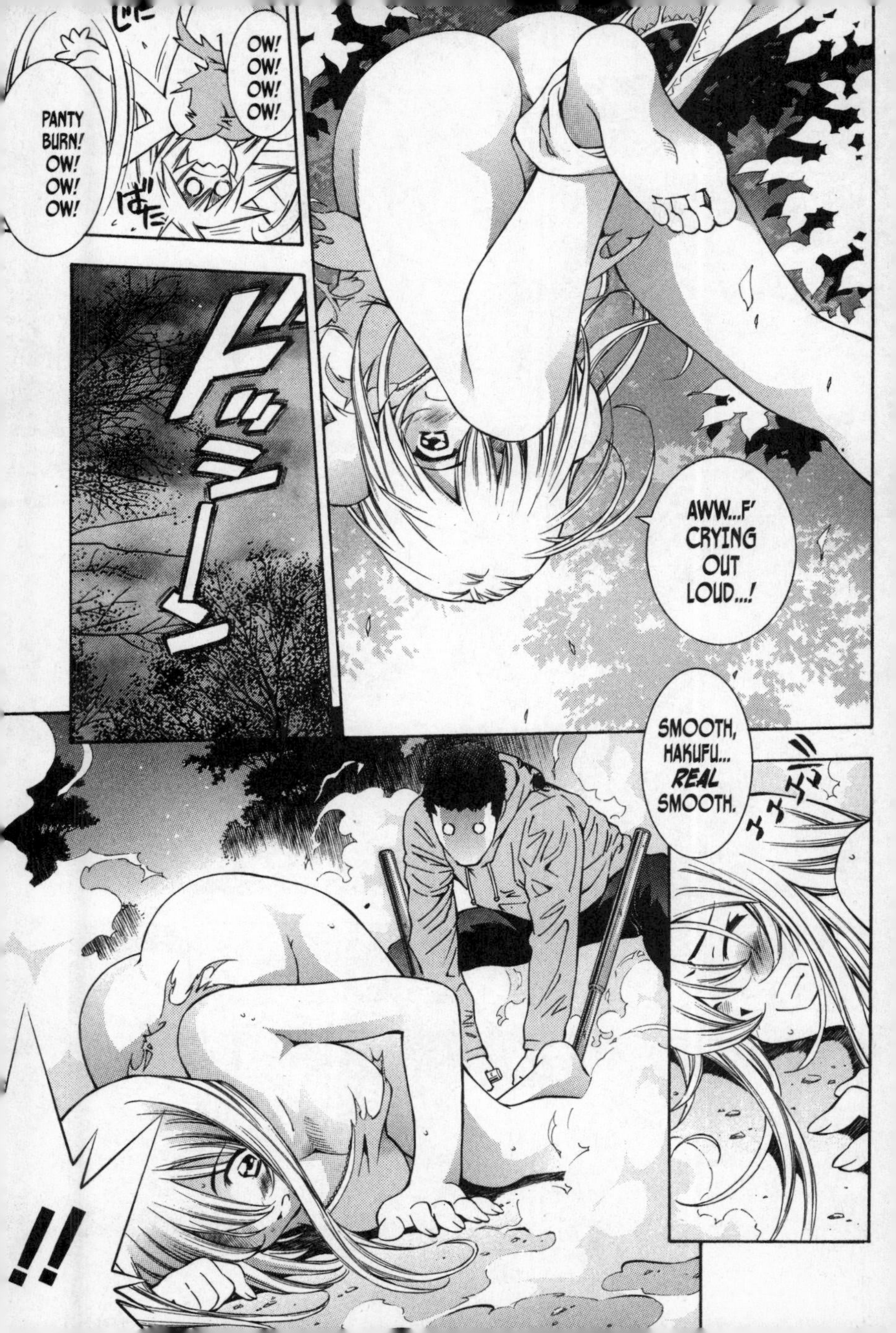
AWW...F' CRYING OUT LOUD...!
OW! OW! OW! OW!
PANTY BURN! OW! OW! OW!
SMOOTH, HAKUFU... *REAL* SMOOTH.
!!

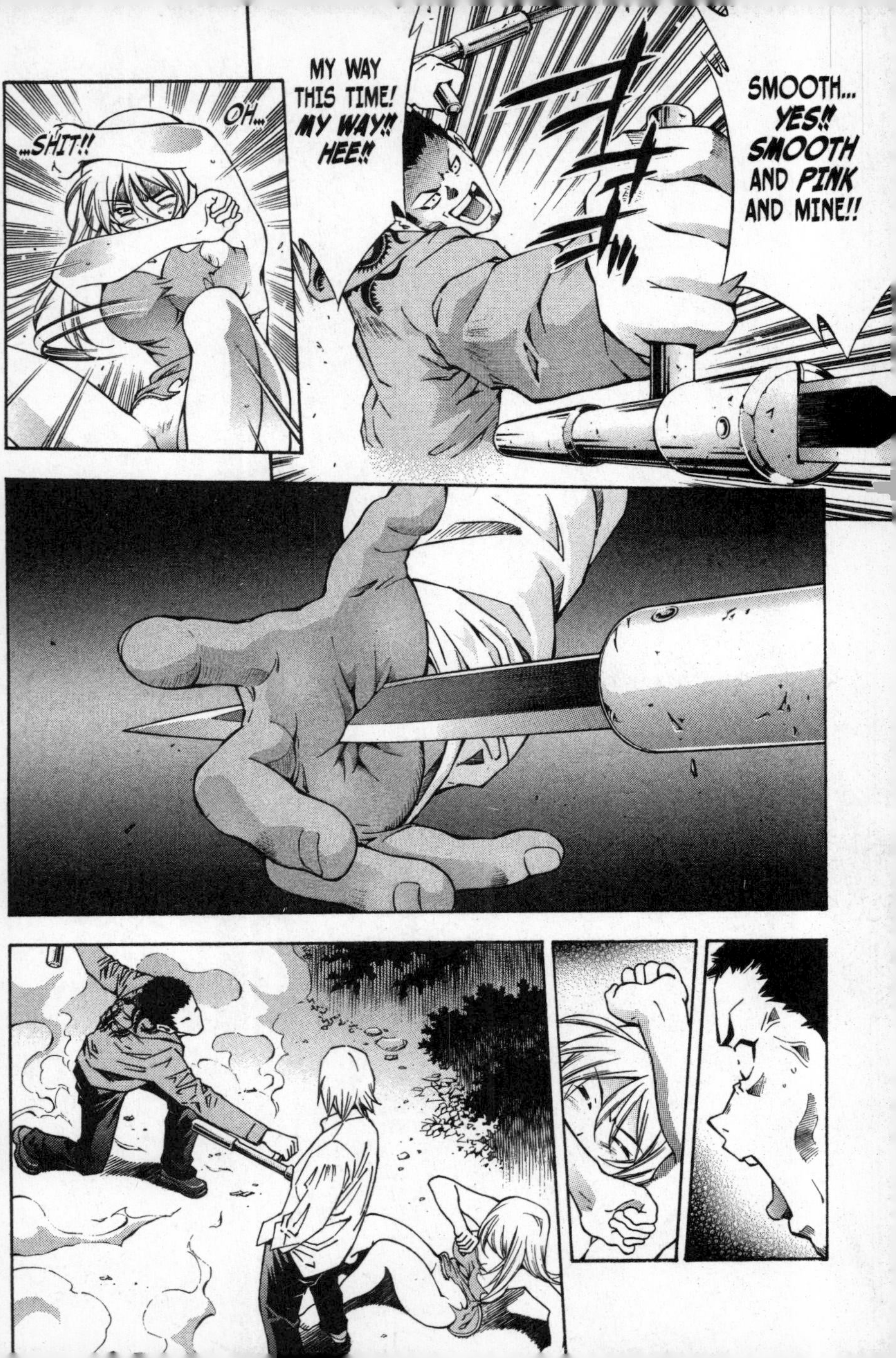
SMOOTH... YES!! SMOOTH AND PINK AND MINE!!
MY WAY THIS TIME! MY WAY!! HEE!!
OH...
...SHIT!!

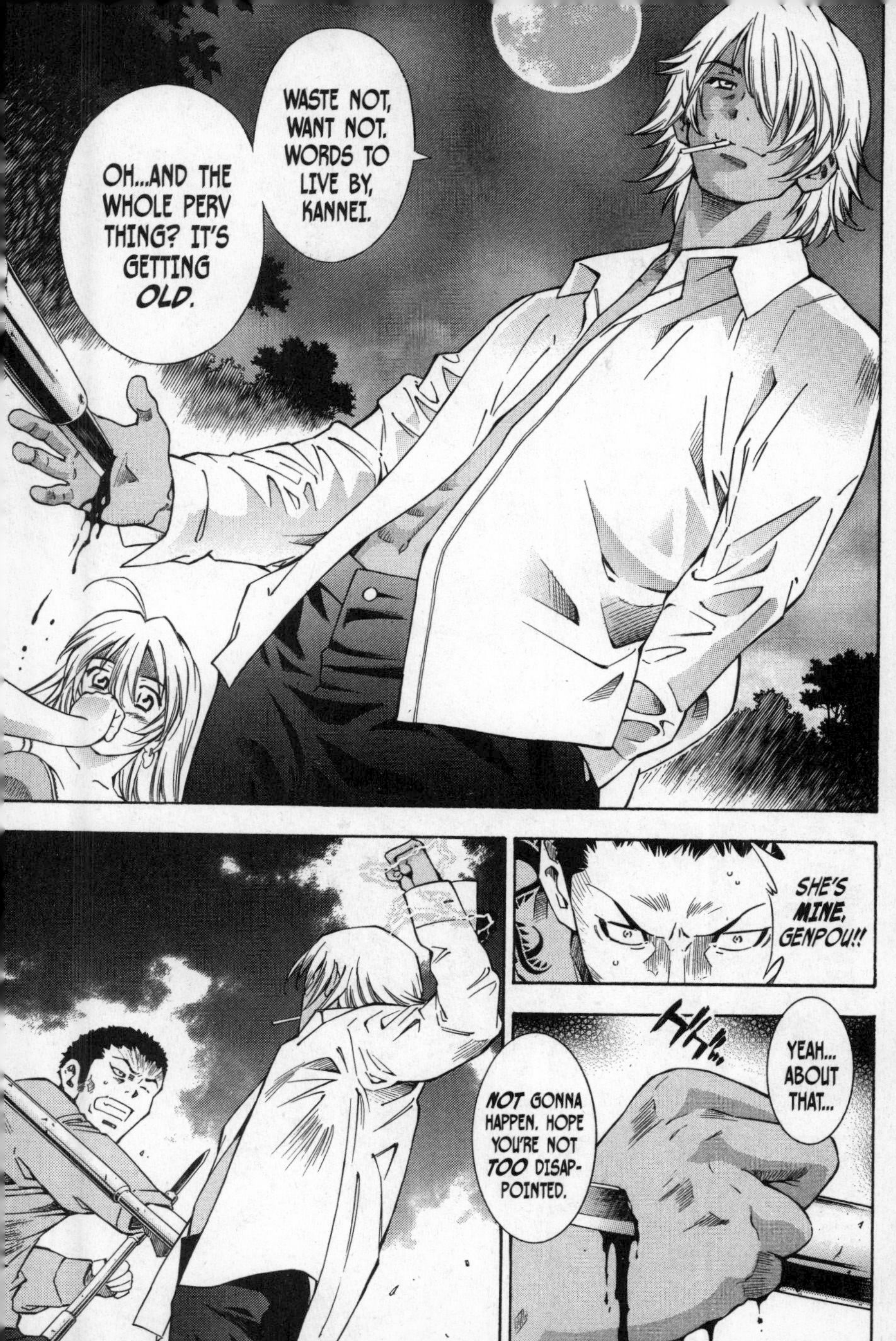
WASTE NOT, WANT NOT. WORDS TO LIVE BY, KANNEI.
OH...AND THE WHOLE PERV THING? IT'S GETTING OLD.
SHE'S MINE, GENPOU!!
YEAH... ABOUT THAT...
NOT GONNA HAPPEN. HOPE YOU'RE NOT TOO DISAP- POINTED.

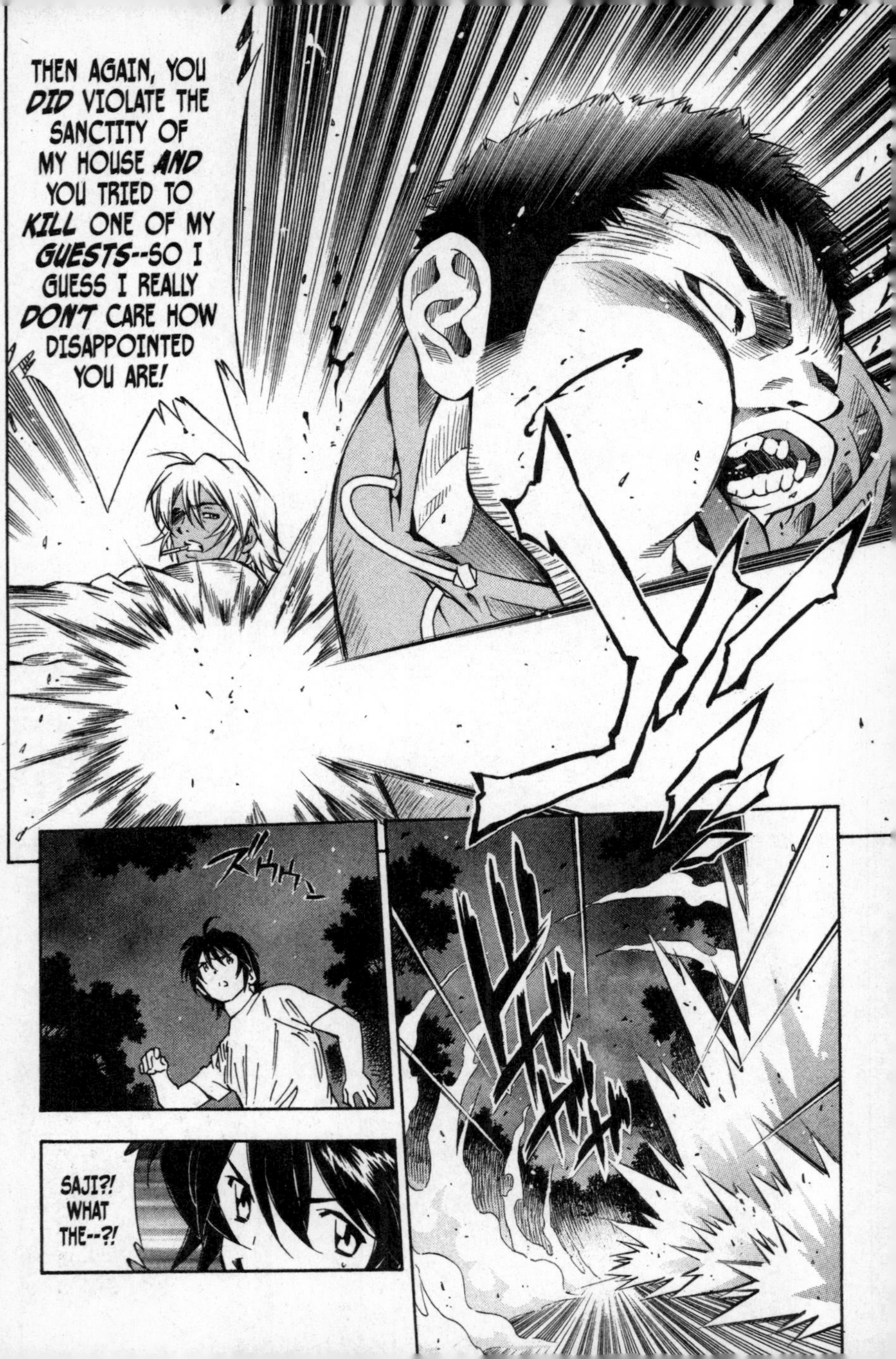
THEN AGAIN, YOU DID VIOLATE THE SANCTITY OF MY HOUSE AND YOU TRIED TO KILL ONE OF MY GUESTS--SO I GUESS I REALLY DON'T CARE HOW DISAPPOINTED YOU ARE!
SAJI?! WHAT THE--?!

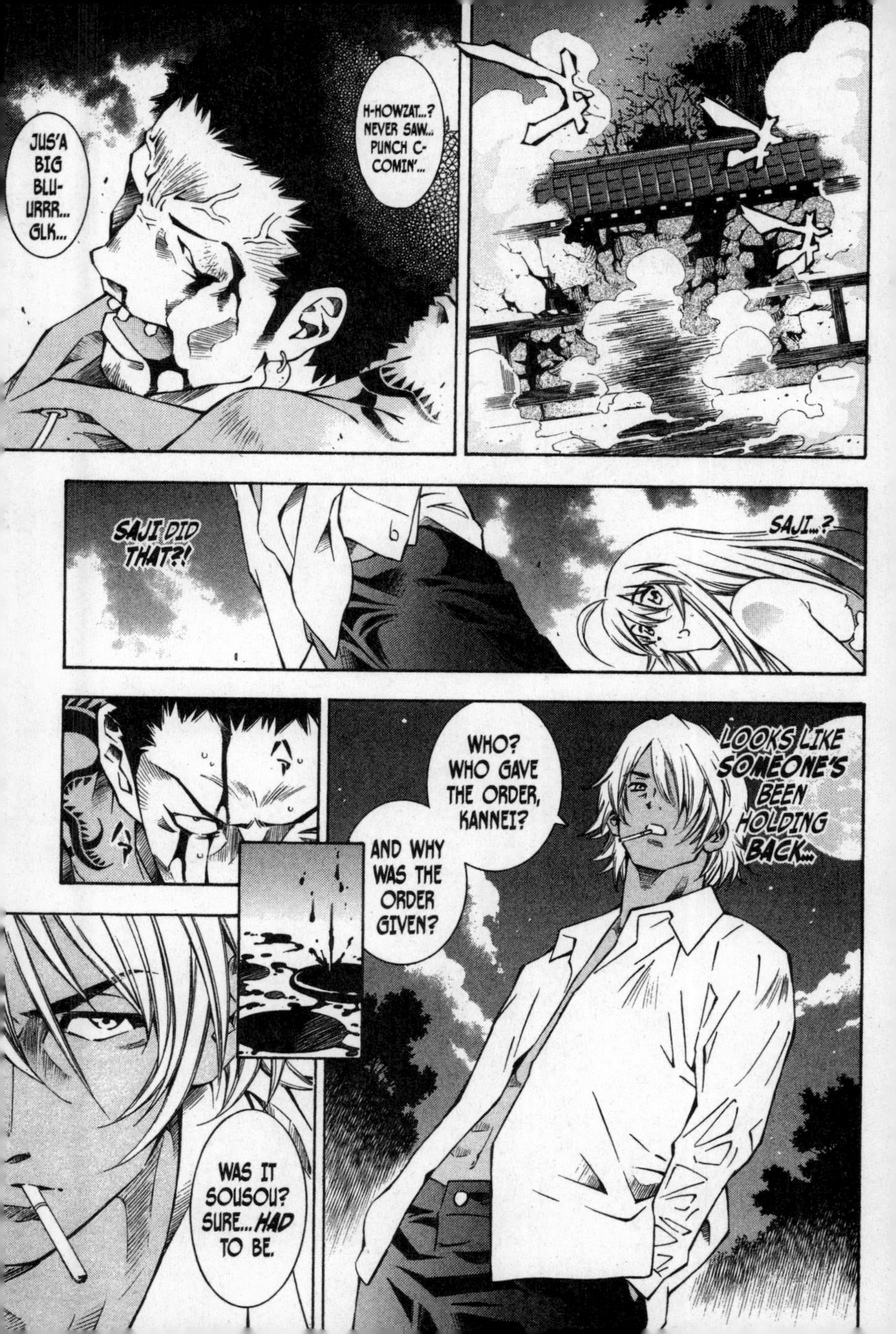
H-HOWZAT...? NEVER SAW... PUNCH C-COMIN'...
JUS'A BIG BLU-URRR... GLK...
SAJI...?
SAJI DID THAT?!
LOOKS LIKE SOMEONE'S BEEN HOLDING BACK...
WHO? WHO GAVE THE ORDER, KANNEI?
AND WHY WAS THE ORDER GIVEN?
WAS IT SOUSOU? SURE... *HAD* TO BE.

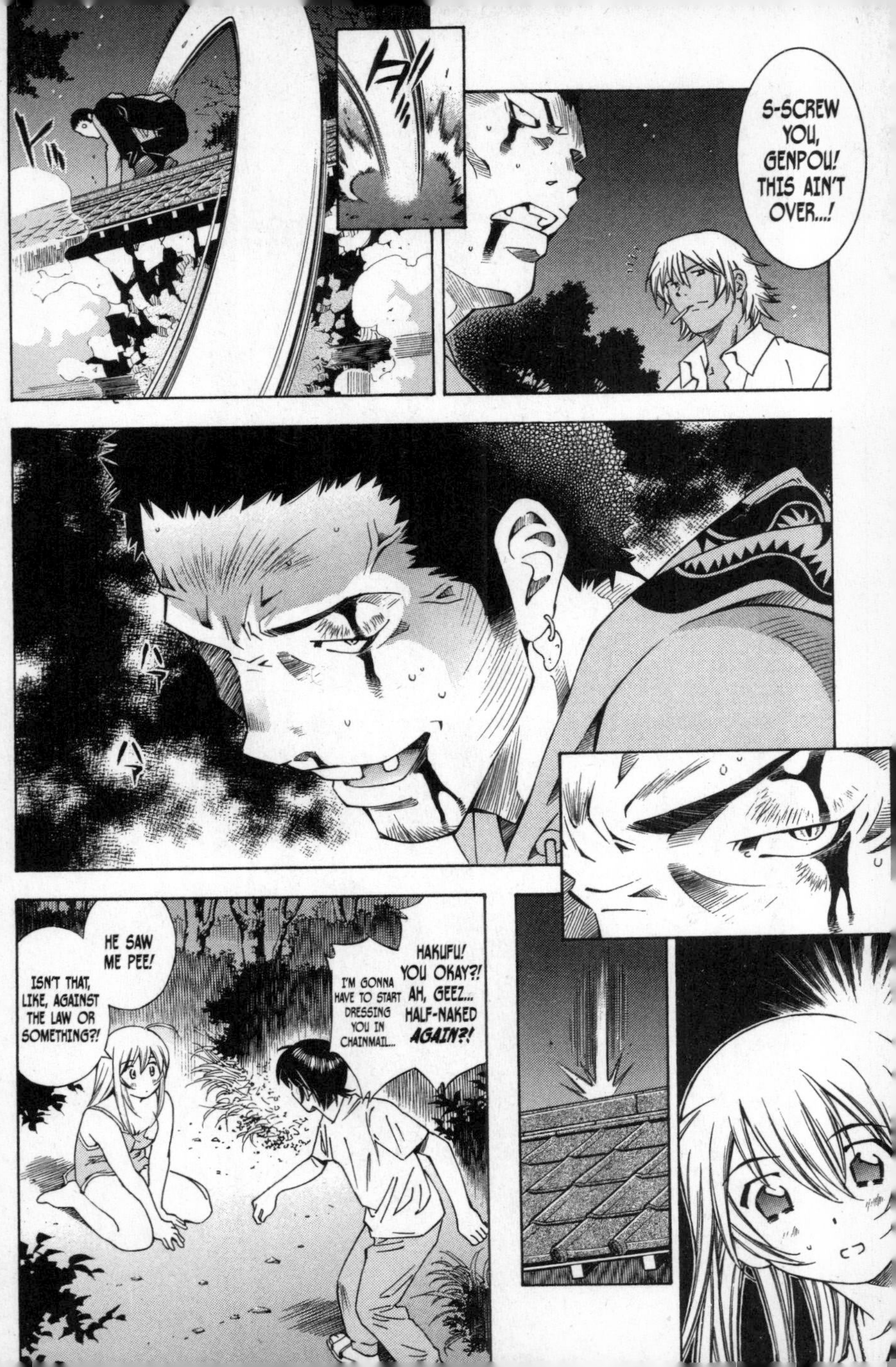
S-SCREW YOU, GENPOU! THIS AIN'T OVER...!
HAKUFU! YOU OKAY?! AH, GEEZ... HALF-NAKED *AGAIN?!*
I'M GONNA HAVE TO START DRESSING YOU IN CHAINMAIL...
HE SAW ME PEE!
ISN'T THAT, LIKE, AGAINST THE LAW OR SOMETHING?!

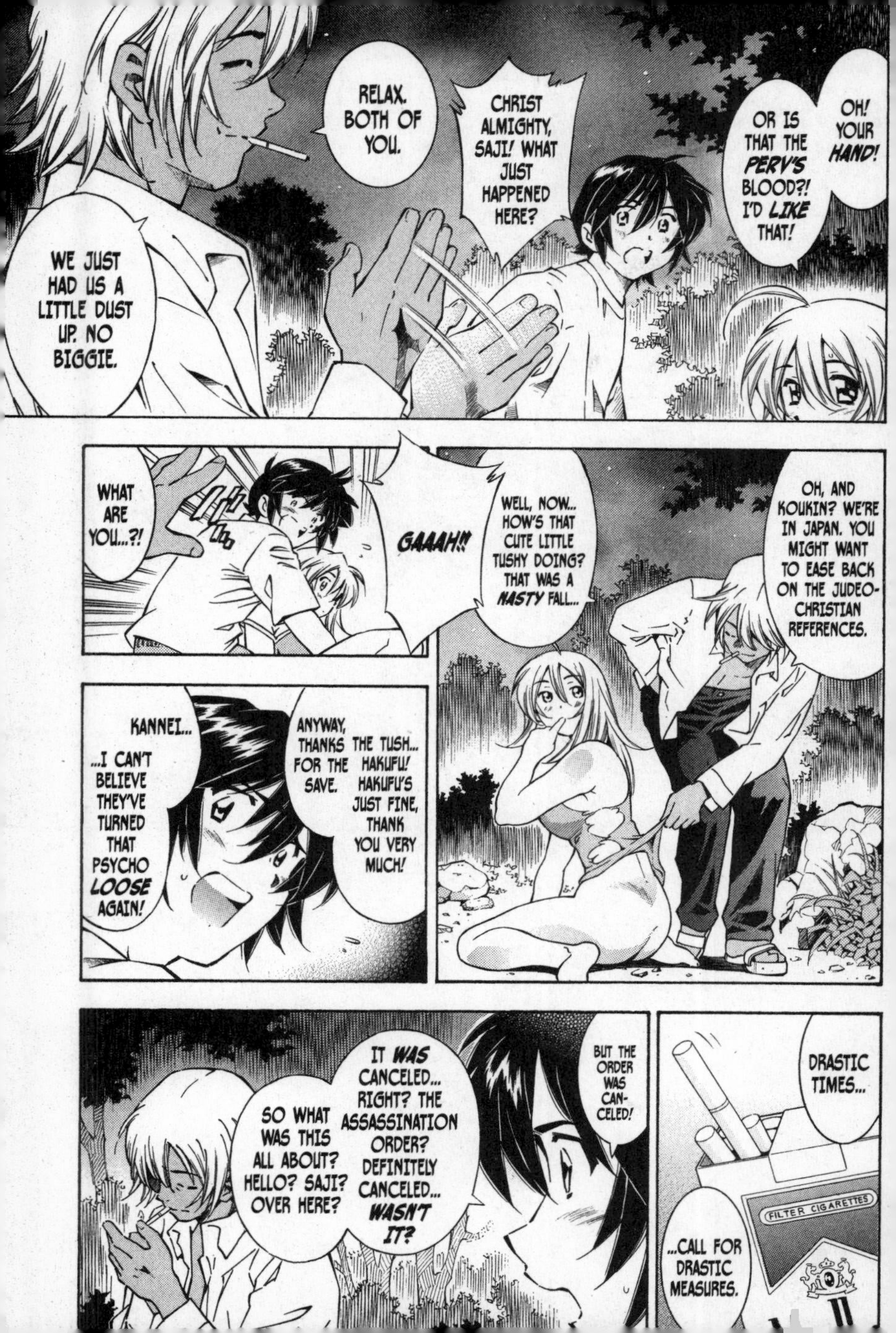
OH! YOUR HAND!
OR IS THAT THE PERV'S BLOOD?! I'D LIKE THAT!
CHRIST ALMIGHTY, SAJI! WHAT JUST HAPPENED HERE?
RELAX. BOTH OF YOU.
WE JUST HAD US A LITTLE DUST UP. NO BIGGIE.
OH, AND KOUKIN? WE'RE IN JAPAN. YOU MIGHT WANT TO EASE BACK ON THE JUDEO-CHRISTIAN REFERENCES.
WELL, NOW... HOW'S THAT CUTE LITTLE TUSHY DOING? THAT WAS A NASTY FALL...
GAAAH!!
WHAT ARE YOU...?!
THE TUSH... HAKUFU! HAKUFU'S JUST FINE, THANK YOU VERY MUCH!
ANYWAY, THANKS FOR THE SAVE.
KANNEI...
...I CAN'T BELIEVE THEY'VE TURNED THAT PSYCHO LOOSE AGAIN!
DRASTIC TIMES...
FILTER CIGARETTES
...CALL FOR DRASTIC MEASURES.
BUT THE ORDER WAS CAN-CELED!
IT WAS CANCELED... RIGHT? THE ASSASSINATION ORDER? DEFINITELY CANCELED... WASN'T IT?
SO WHAT WAS THIS ALL ABOUT? HELLO? SAJI? OVER HERE?

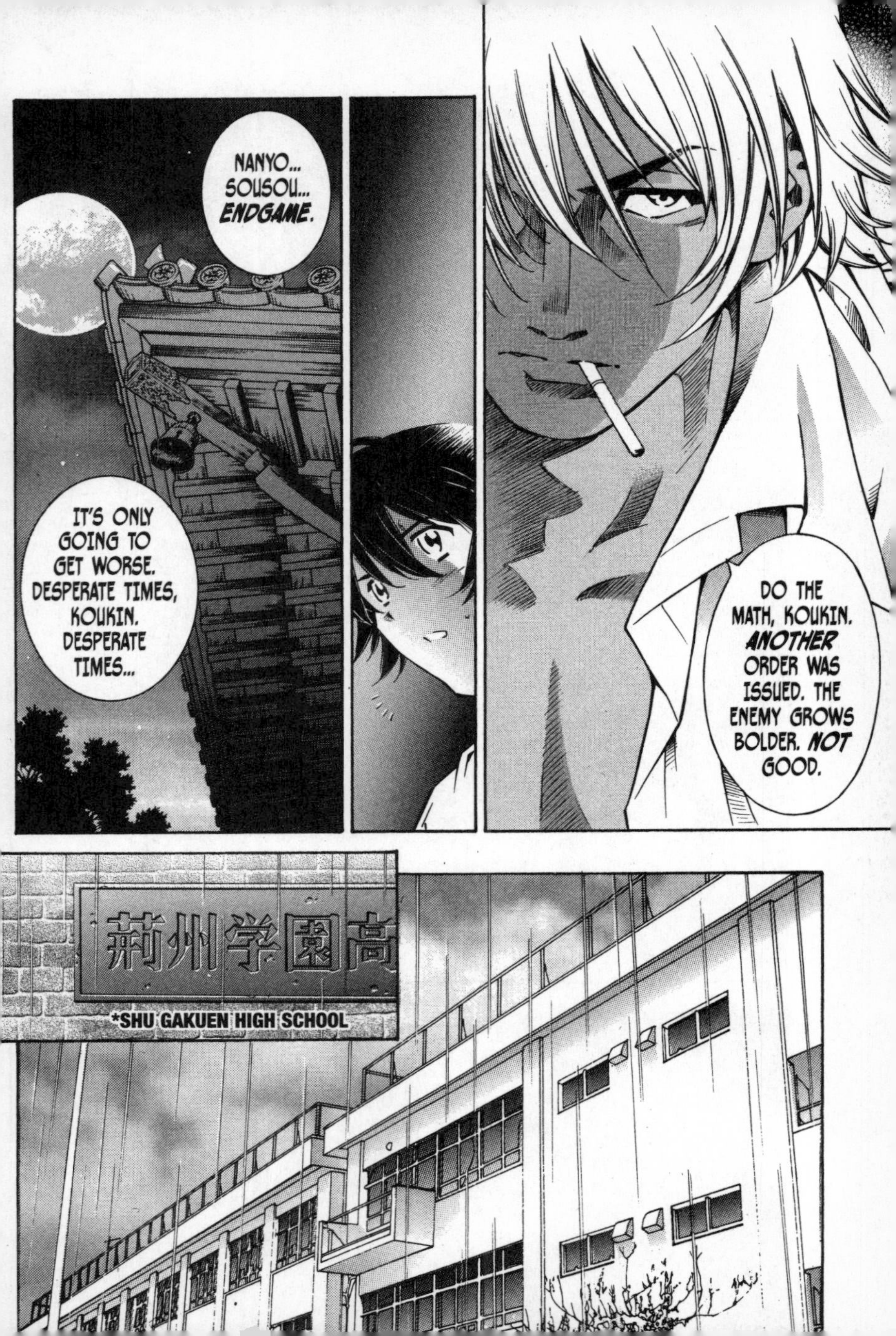
DO THE MATH, KOUKIN. ANOTHER ORDER WAS ISSUED. THE ENEMY GROWS BOLDER. NOT GOOD.
NANYO... SOUSOU... ENDGAME.
IT'S ONLY GOING TO GET WORSE. DESPERATE TIMES, KOUKIN. DESPERATE TIMES...
荊州学園高
*SHU GAKUEN HIGH SCHOOL

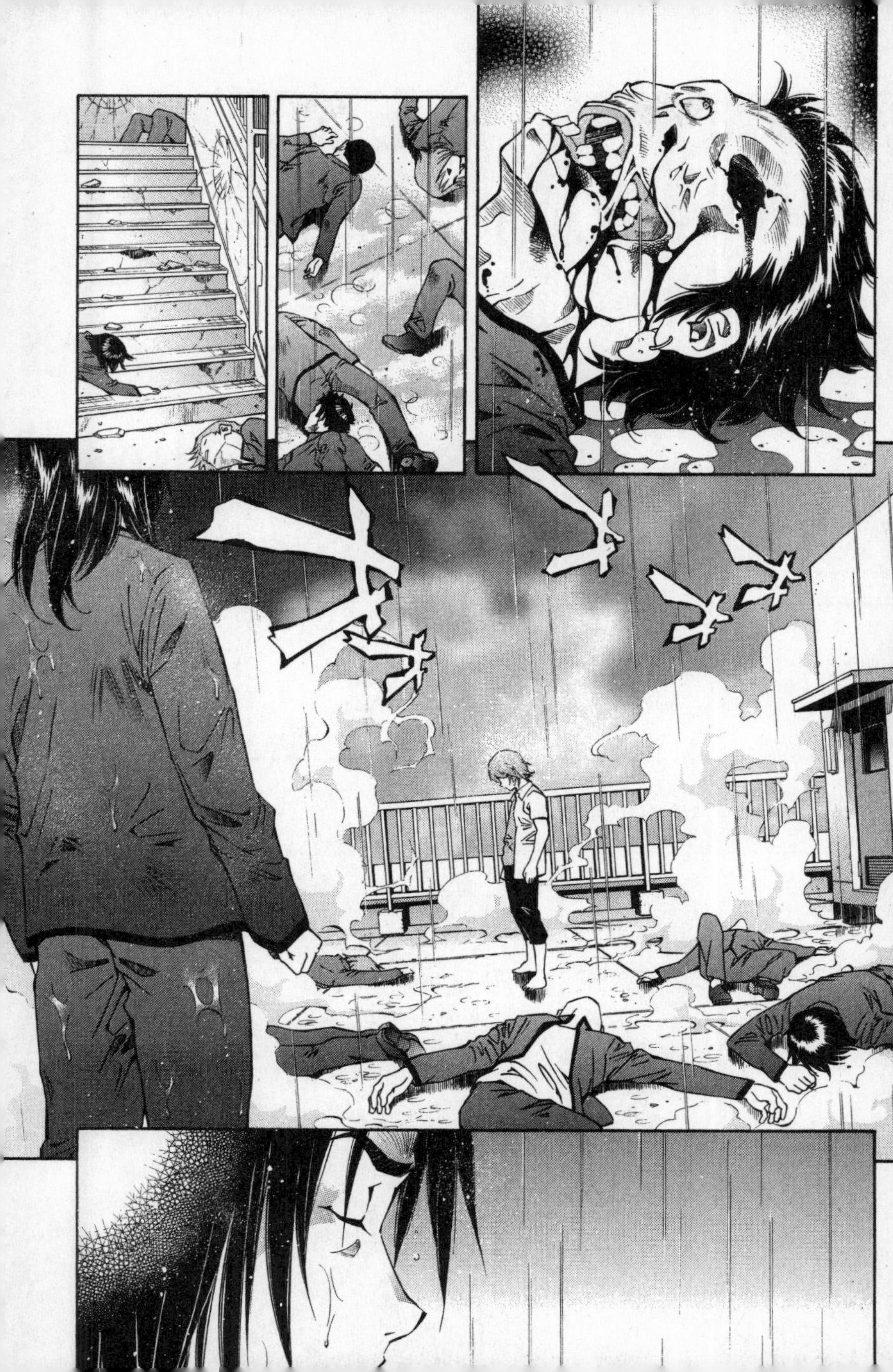

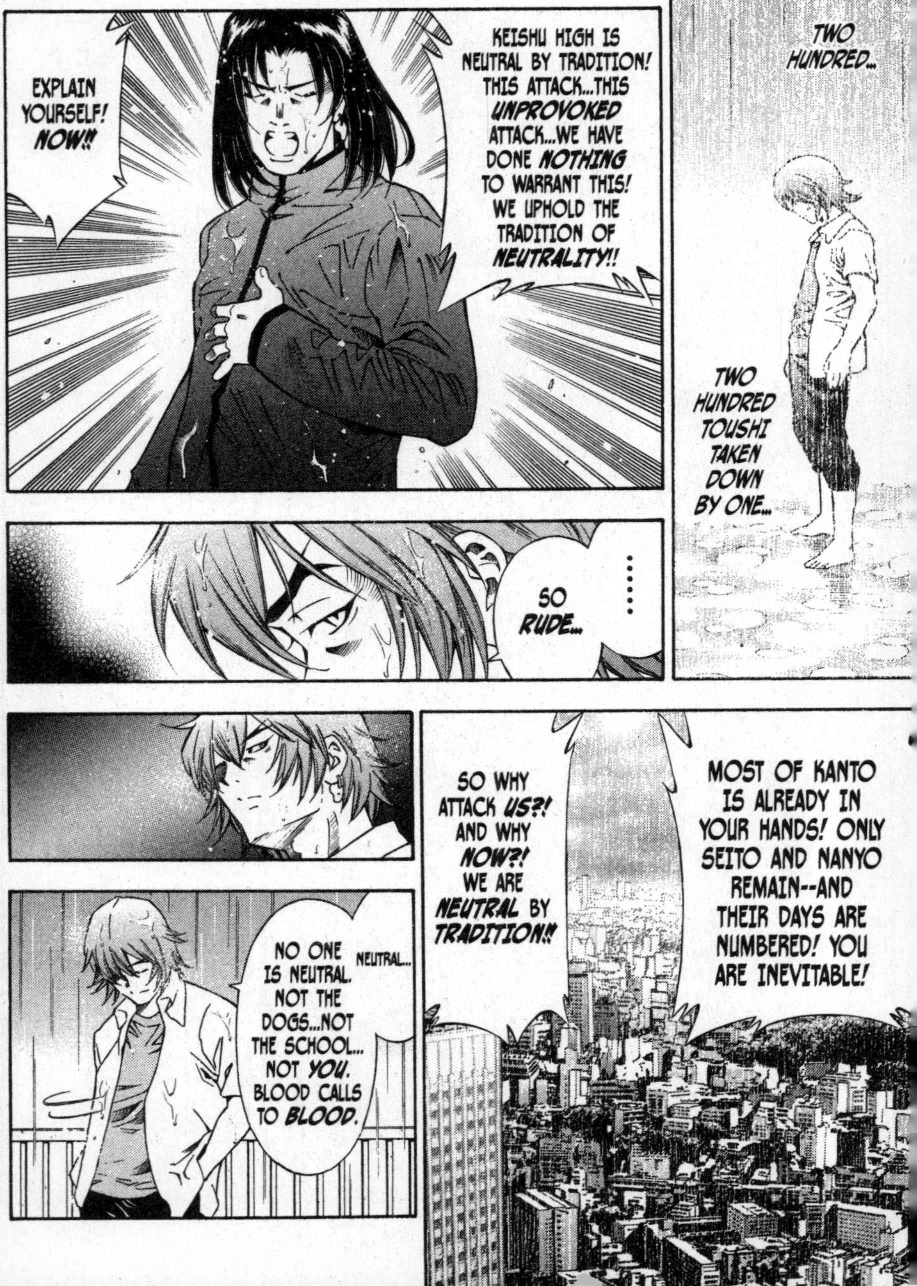
TWO HUNDRED...
TWO HUNDRED TOUSHI TAKEN DOWN BY ONE...
KEISHU HIGH IS NEUTRAL BY TRADITION! THIS ATTACK...THIS UNPROVOKED ATTACK...WE HAVE DONE NOTHING TO WARRANT THIS! WE UPHOLD THE TRADITION OF NEUTRALITY!!
EXPLAIN YOURSELF! NOW!!
......
SO RUDE...
MOST OF KANTO IS ALREADY IN YOUR HANDS! ONLY SEITO AND NANYO REMAIN--AND THEIR DAYS ARE NUMBERED! YOU ARE INEVITABLE!
SO WHY ATTACK US?! AND WHY NOW?! WE ARE NEUTRAL BY TRADITION!!
NEUTRAL...
NO ONE IS NEUTRAL. NOT THE DOGS...NOT THE SCHOOL... NOT YOU. BLOOD CALLS TO BLOOD.

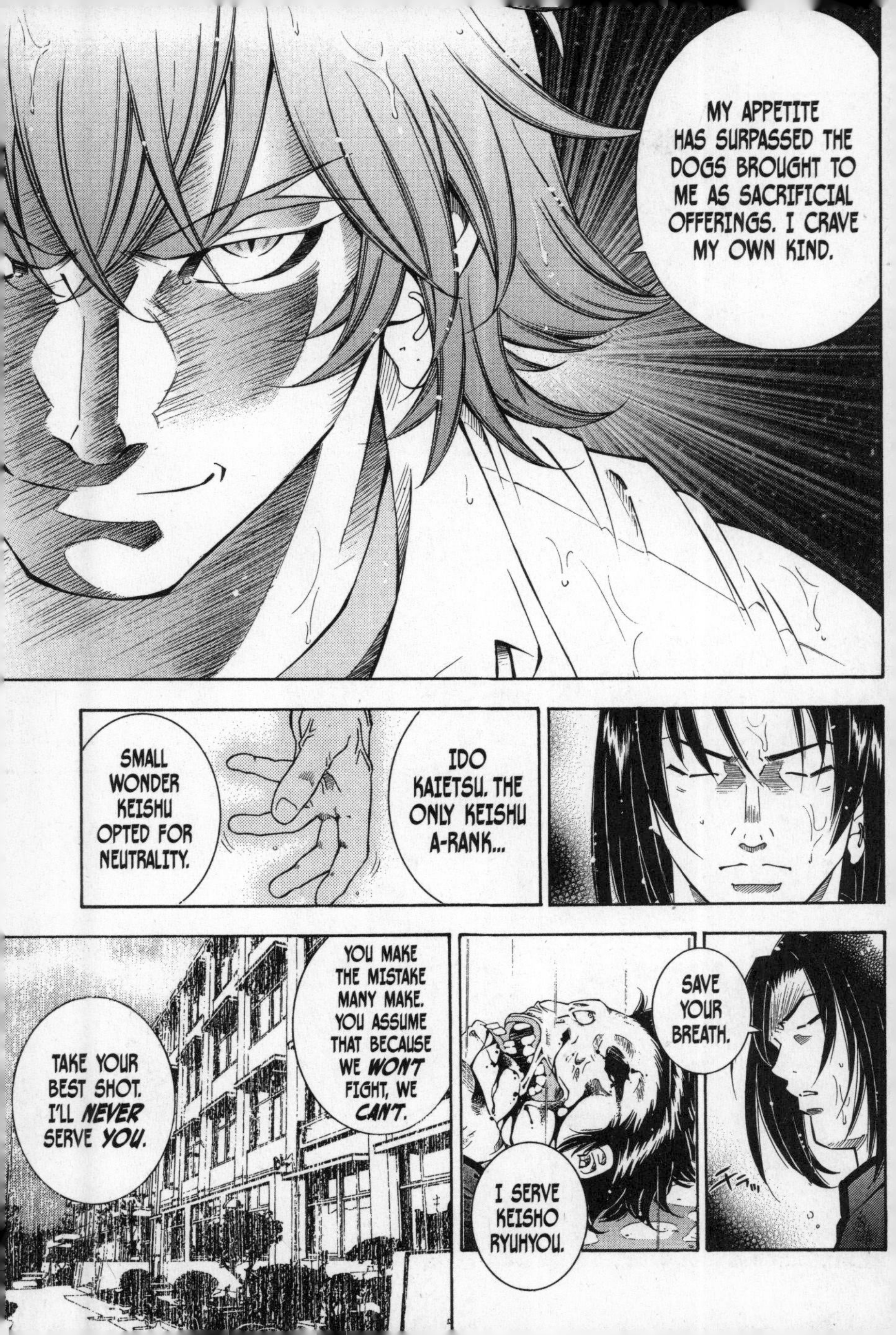
MY APPETITE HAS SURPASSED THE DOGS BROUGHT TO ME AS SACRIFICIAL OFFERINGS. I CRAVE MY OWN KIND.
IDO KAIETSU. THE ONLY KEISHU A-RANK...
SMALL WONDER KEISHU OPTED FOR NEUTRALITY.
SAVE YOUR BREATH.
I SERVE KEISHO RYUHYOU.
YOU MAKE THE MISTAKE MANY MAKE. YOU ASSUME THAT BECAUSE WE *WON'T* FIGHT, WE *CAN'T*.
TAKE YOUR BEST SHOT. I'LL *NEVER* SERVE *YOU*.

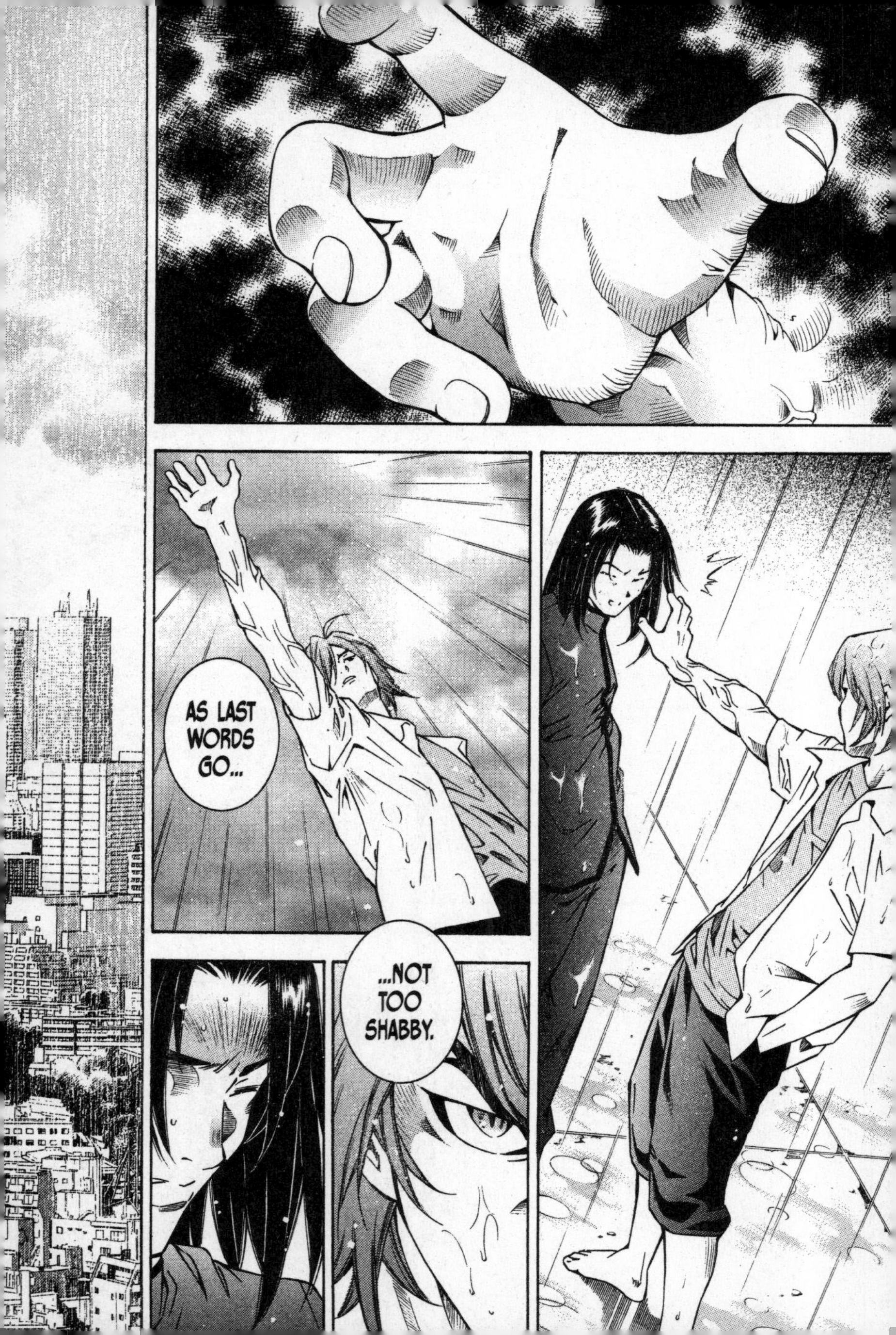
AS LAST WORDS GO...
...NOT TOO SHABBY.

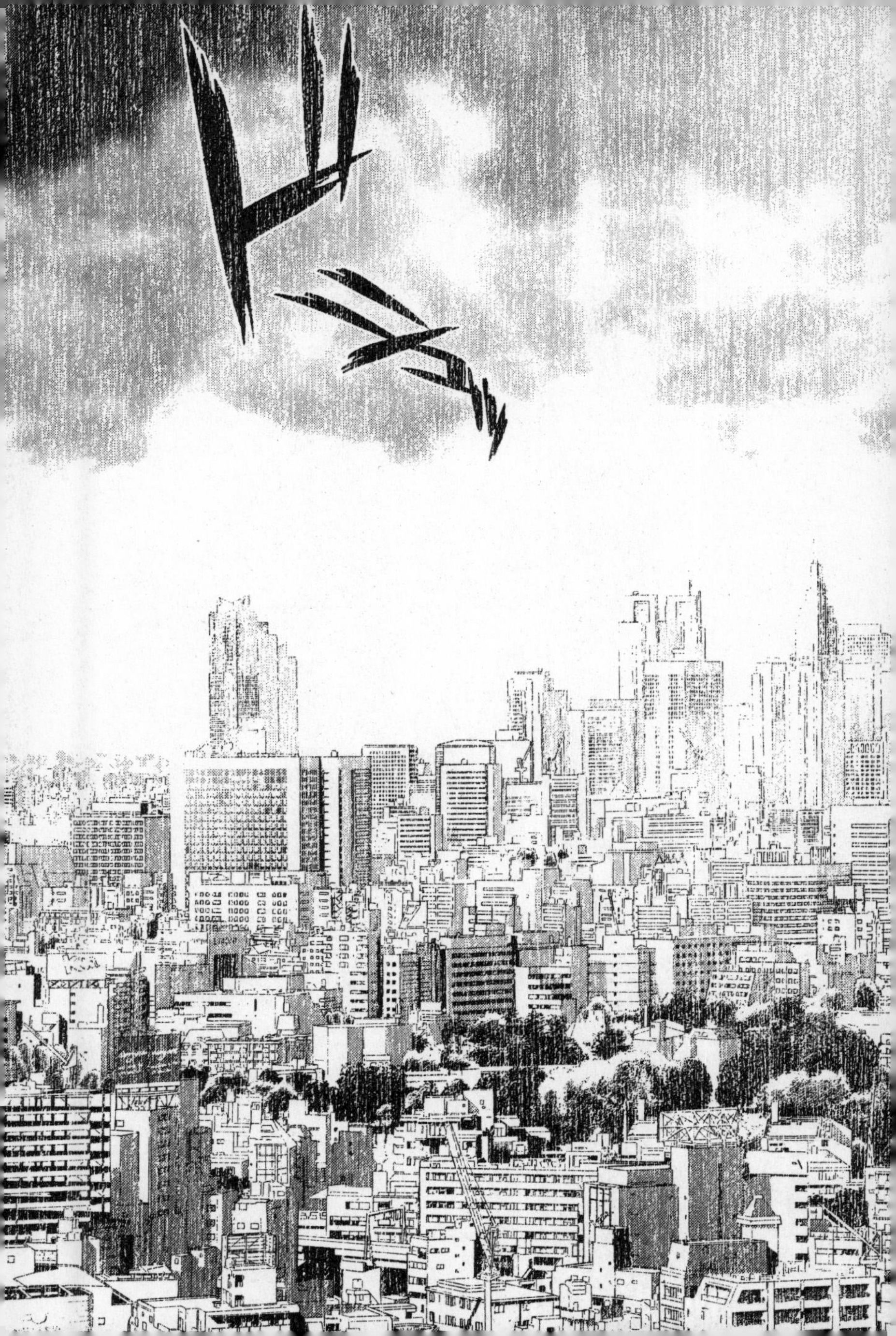

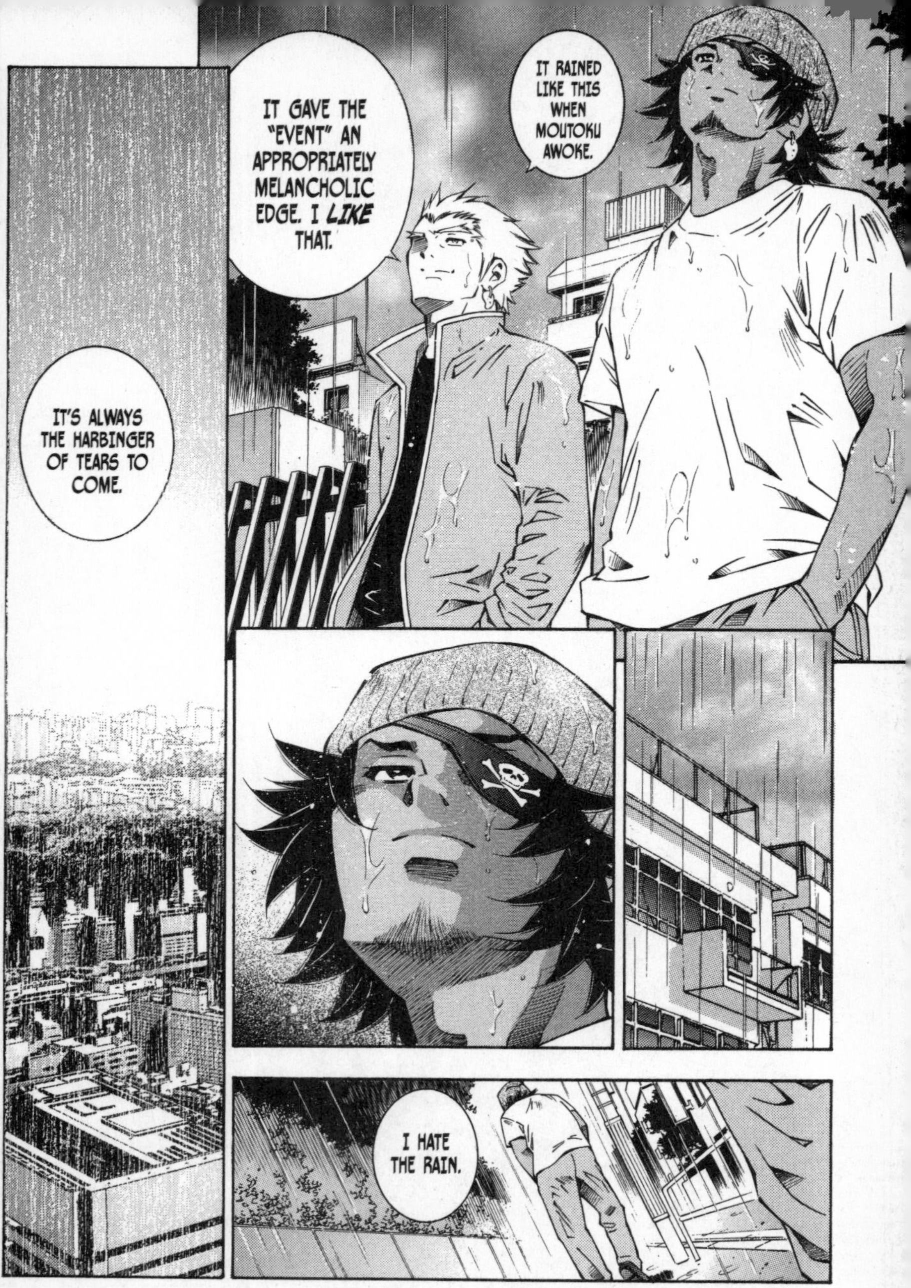
IT RAINED LIKE THIS WHEN MOUTOKU AWOKE.
IT GAVE THE "EVENT" AN APPROPRIATELY MELANCHOLIC EDGE. I *LIKE* THAT.
I HATE THE RAIN.
IT'S ALWAYS THE HARBINGER OF TEARS TO COME.

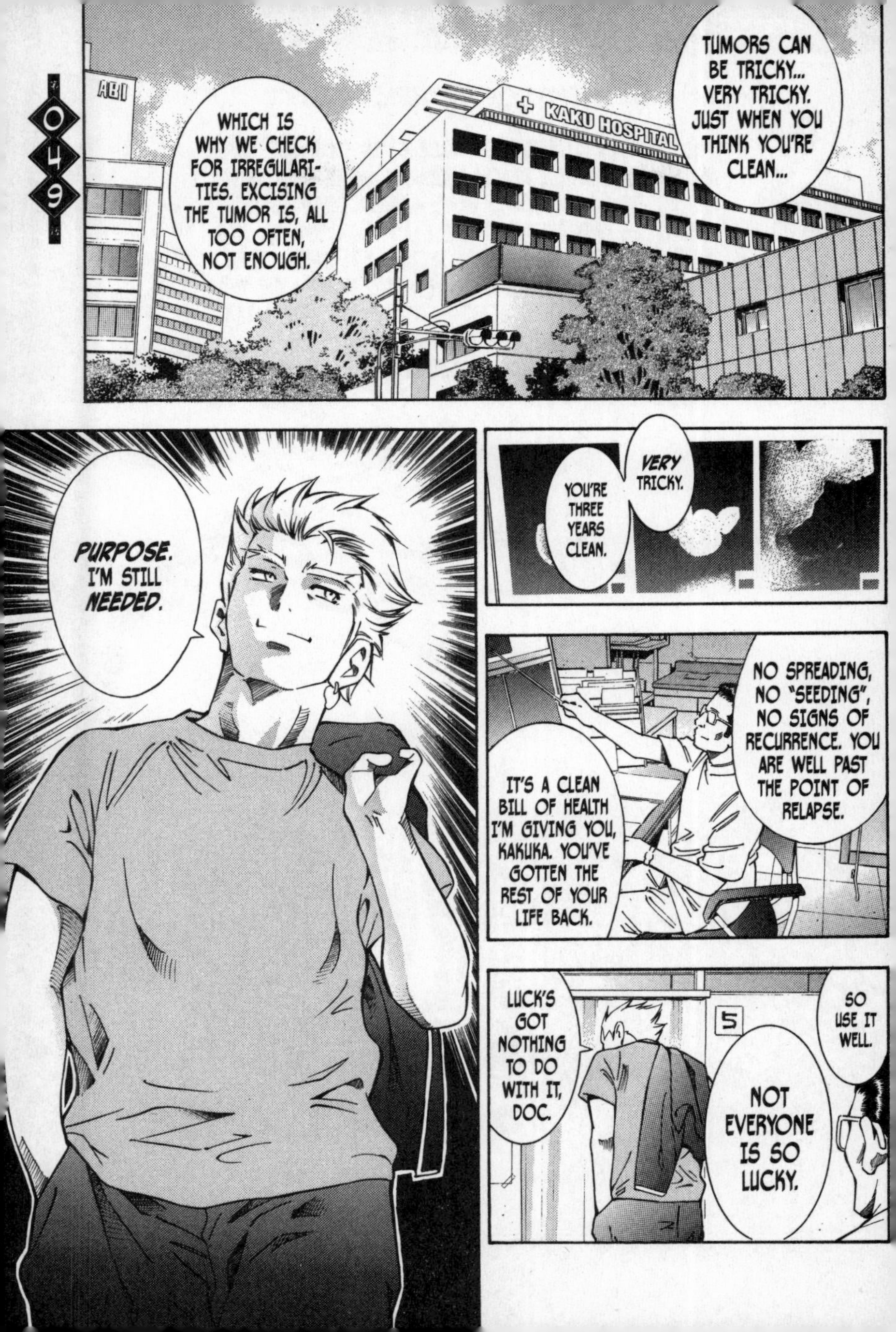
ABI
+ KAKU HOSPITAL
TUMORS CAN BE TRICKY... VERY TRICKY. JUST WHEN YOU THINK YOU'RE CLEAN...
WHICH IS WHY WE CHECK FOR IRREGULARITIES. EXCISING THE TUMOR IS, ALL TOO OFTEN, NOT ENOUGH.
VERY TRICKY.
YOU'RE THREE YEARS CLEAN.
NO SPREADING, NO "SEEDING", NO SIGNS OF RECURRENCE. YOU ARE WELL PAST THE POINT OF RELAPSE.
IT'S A CLEAN BILL OF HEALTH I'M GIVING YOU, KAKUKA. YOU'VE GOTTEN THE REST OF YOUR LIFE BACK.
SO USE IT WELL.
NOT EVERYONE IS SO LUCKY.
LUCK'S GOT NOTHING TO DO WITH IT, DOC.
PURPOSE. I'M STILL *NEEDED*.

第 049 話

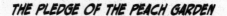

THE PLEDGE OF THE PEACH GARDEN

THIS REFERS TO A PLEDGE MADE BETWEEN RYUBI, KANU AND CHOUHI WHILE PEACH FLOWERS WERE BLOOMING. THEY DRANK WINE AND EXAGGERATED THEIR SEXUAL PROWESS AND PLEDGED THAT, EVEN THOUGH THEY DID NOT SHARE BIRTHDAYS, THEY WOULD ENDEAVOR TO ALL DIE ON THE SAME DAY OF THE SAME MONTH OF THE SAME YEAR. SEVERAL MORE BOTTLES OF WINE LATER, THEY FORGED A SIMILAR BLOOD-PACT WITH A SQUIRREL, THOUGH, BEING A SQUIRREL AND ALL, IT HAD NO IDEA WHAT THEY WERE TALKING ABOUT.

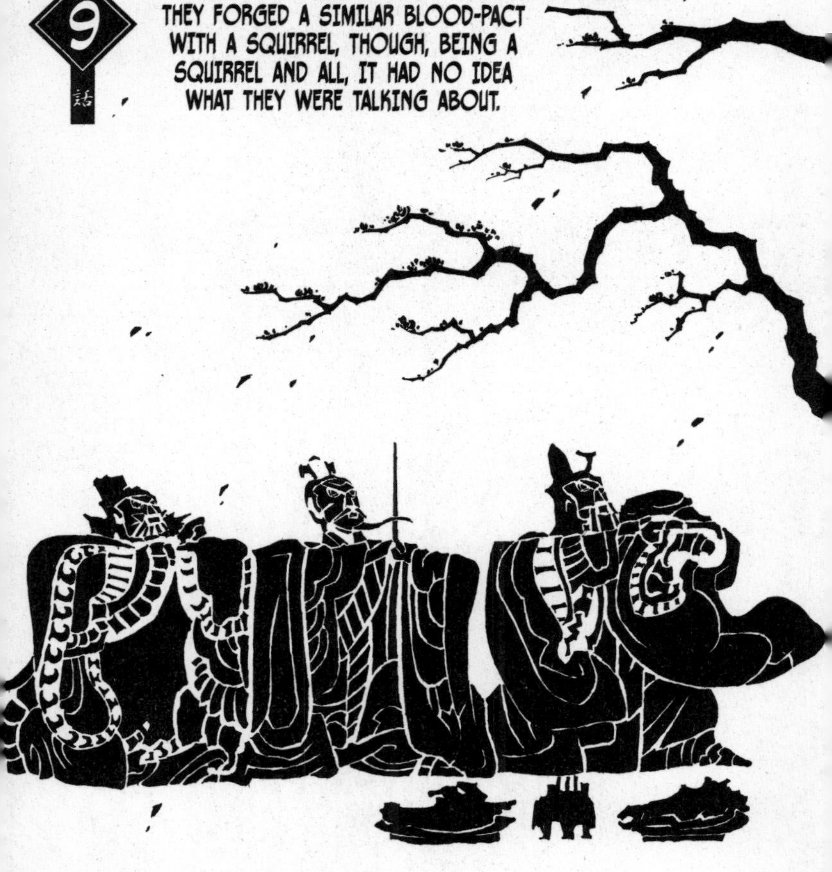

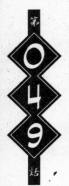

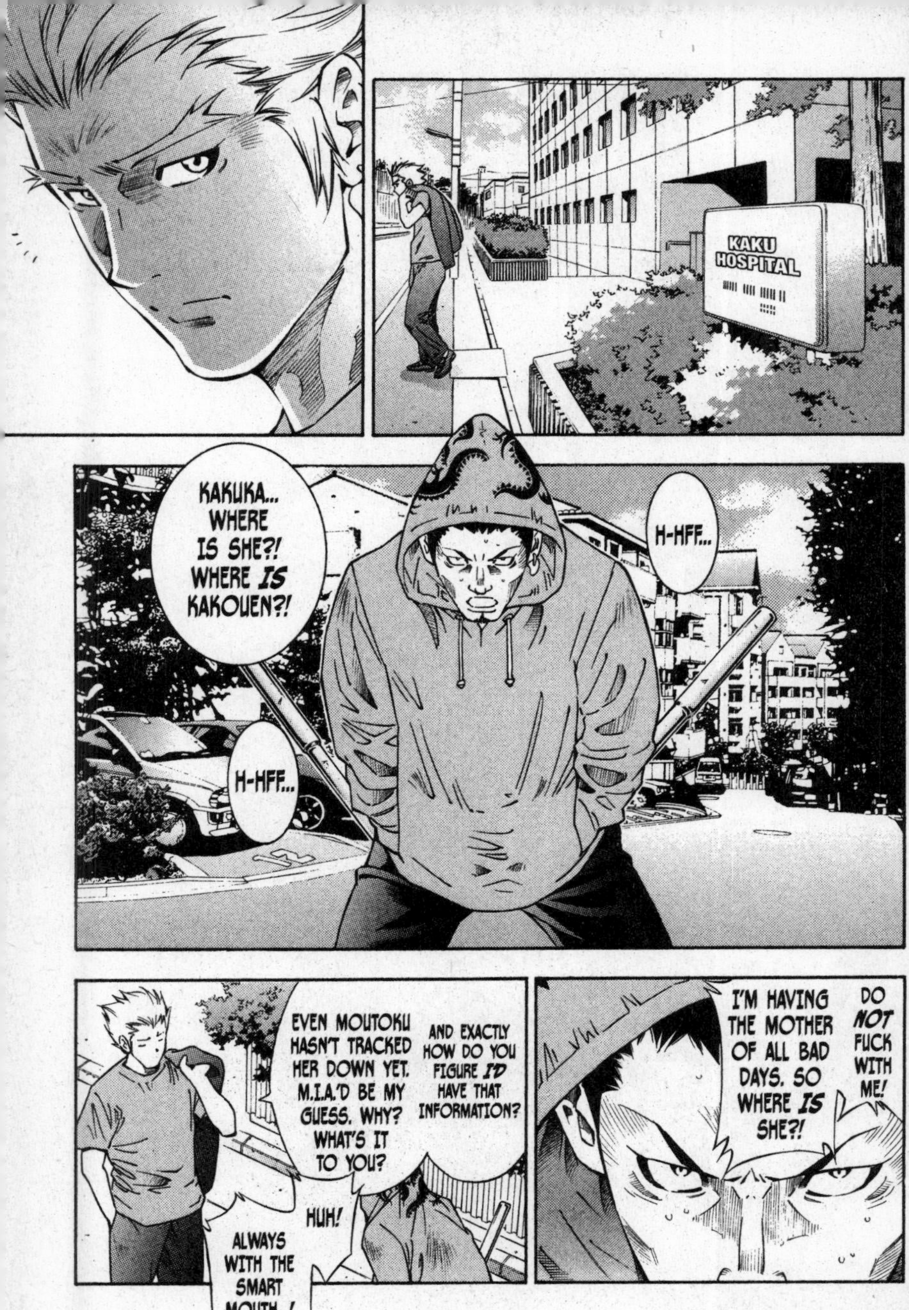
KAKU HOSPITAL
H-HFF...
KAKUKA... WHERE IS SHE?! WHERE *IS* KAKOUEN?!
H-HFF...
DO *NOT* FUCK WITH ME!
I'M HAVING THE MOTHER OF ALL BAD DAYS. SO WHERE *IS* SHE?!
AND EXACTLY HOW DO YOU FIGURE *I'D* HAVE THAT INFORMATION?
EVEN MOUTOKU HASN'T TRACKED HER DOWN YET. M.I.A.'D BE MY GUESS. WHY? WHAT'S IT TO YOU?
HUH!
ALWAYS WITH THE SMART MOUTH...!

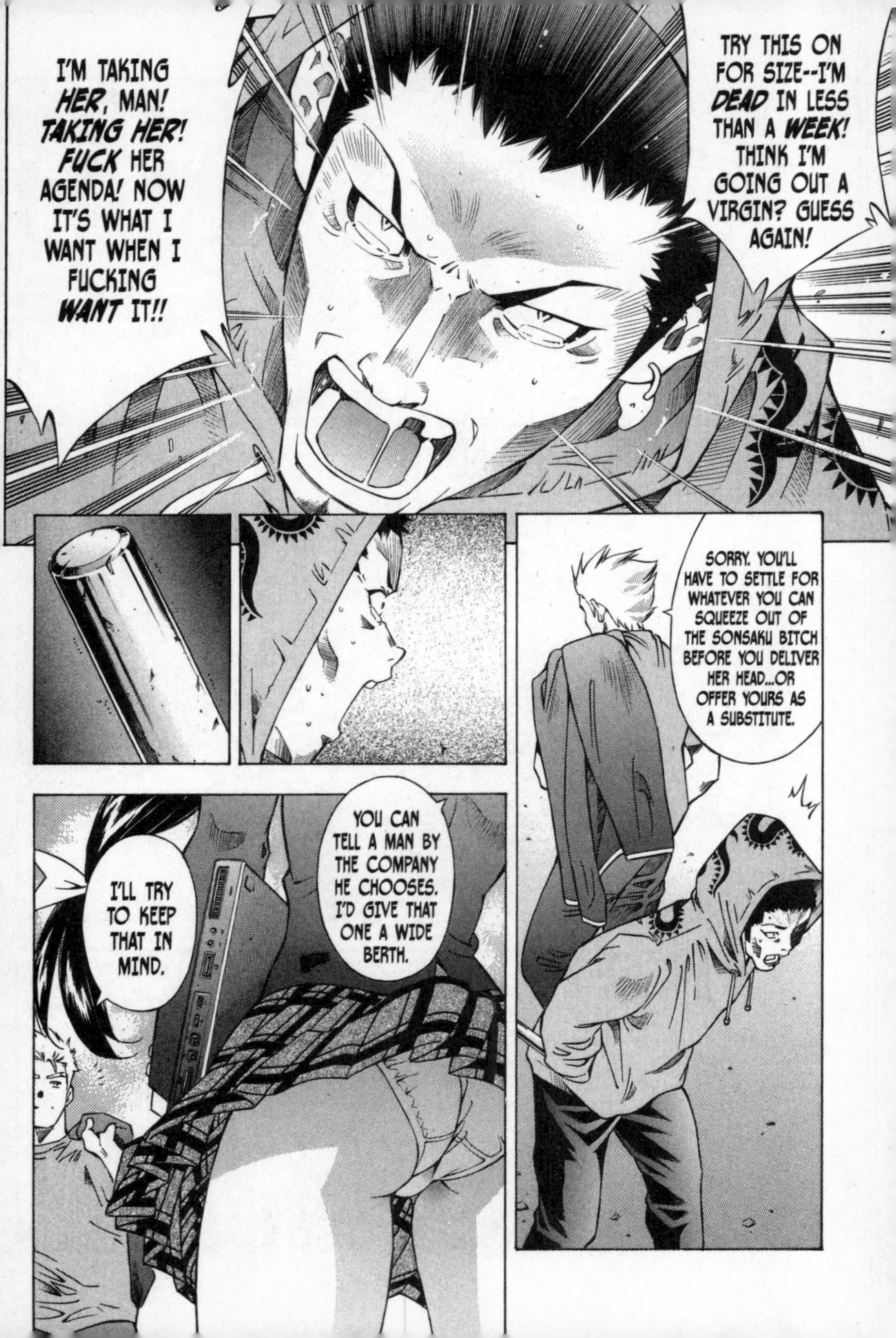
TRY THIS ON FOR SIZE--I'M DEAD IN LESS THAN A WEEK! THINK I'M GOING OUT A VIRGIN? GUESS AGAIN!
I'M TAKING HER, MAN! TAKING HER! FUCK HER AGENDA! NOW IT'S WHAT I WANT WHEN I FUCKING WANT IT!!
SORRY. YOU'LL HAVE TO SETTLE FOR WHATEVER YOU CAN SQUEEZE OUT OF THE SONSAKU BITCH BEFORE YOU DELIVER HER HEAD...OR OFFER YOURS AS A SUBSTITUTE.
YOU CAN TELL A MAN BY THE COMPANY HE CHOOSES. I'D GIVE THAT ONE A WIDE BERTH.
I'LL TRY TO KEEP THAT IN MIND.

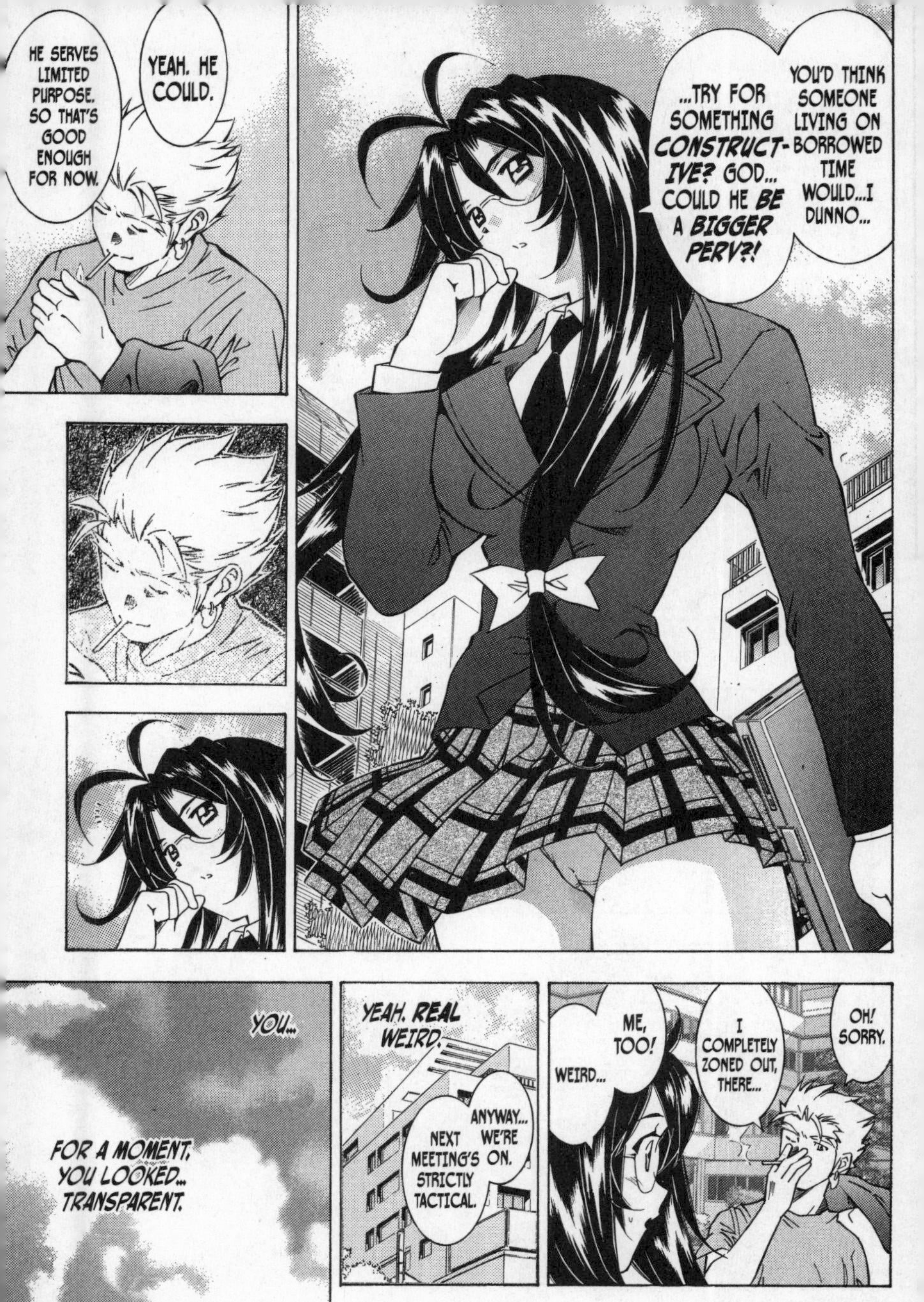
YOU'D THINK SOMEONE LIVING ON BORROWED TIME WOULD...I DUNNO...
...TRY FOR SOMETHING *CONSTRUCTIVE?* GOD... COULD HE *BE* A *BIGGER PERV?!*
YEAH. HE COULD.
HE SERVES LIMITED PURPOSE. SO THAT'S GOOD ENOUGH FOR NOW.
OH! SORRY.
I COMPLETELY ZONED OUT, THERE...
ME, TOO!
WEIRD...
YEAH. *REAL* WEIRD.
ANYWAY... WE'RE ON. NEXT MEETING'S STRICTLY TACTICAL.
YOU...
FOR A MOMENT, YOU LOOKED... TRANSPARENT.

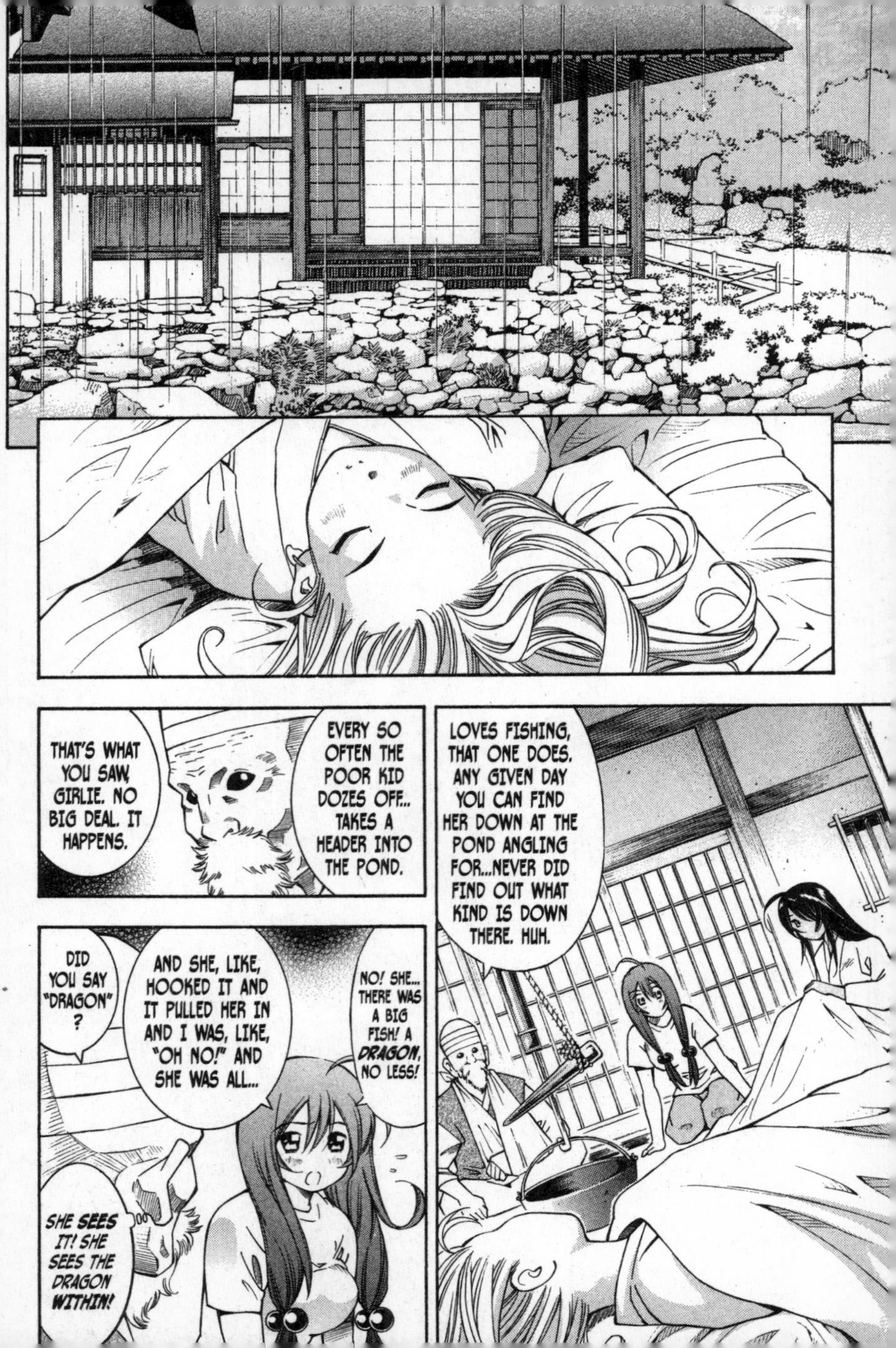
LOVES FISHING, THAT ONE DOES. ANY GIVEN DAY YOU CAN FIND HER DOWN AT THE POND ANGLING FOR...NEVER DID FIND OUT WHAT KIND IS DOWN THERE. HUH.
EVERY SO OFTEN THE POOR KID DOZES OFF... TAKES A HEADER INTO THE POND.
THAT'S WHAT YOU SAW, GIRLIE. NO BIG DEAL. IT HAPPENS.
NO! SHE... THERE WAS A BIG FISH! A DRAGON, NO LESS!
AND SHE, LIKE, HOOKED IT AND IT PULLED HER IN AND I WAS, LIKE, "OH NO!" AND SHE WAS ALL...
DID YOU SAY "DRAGON"?
SHE SEES IT! SHE SEES THE DRAGON WITHIN!

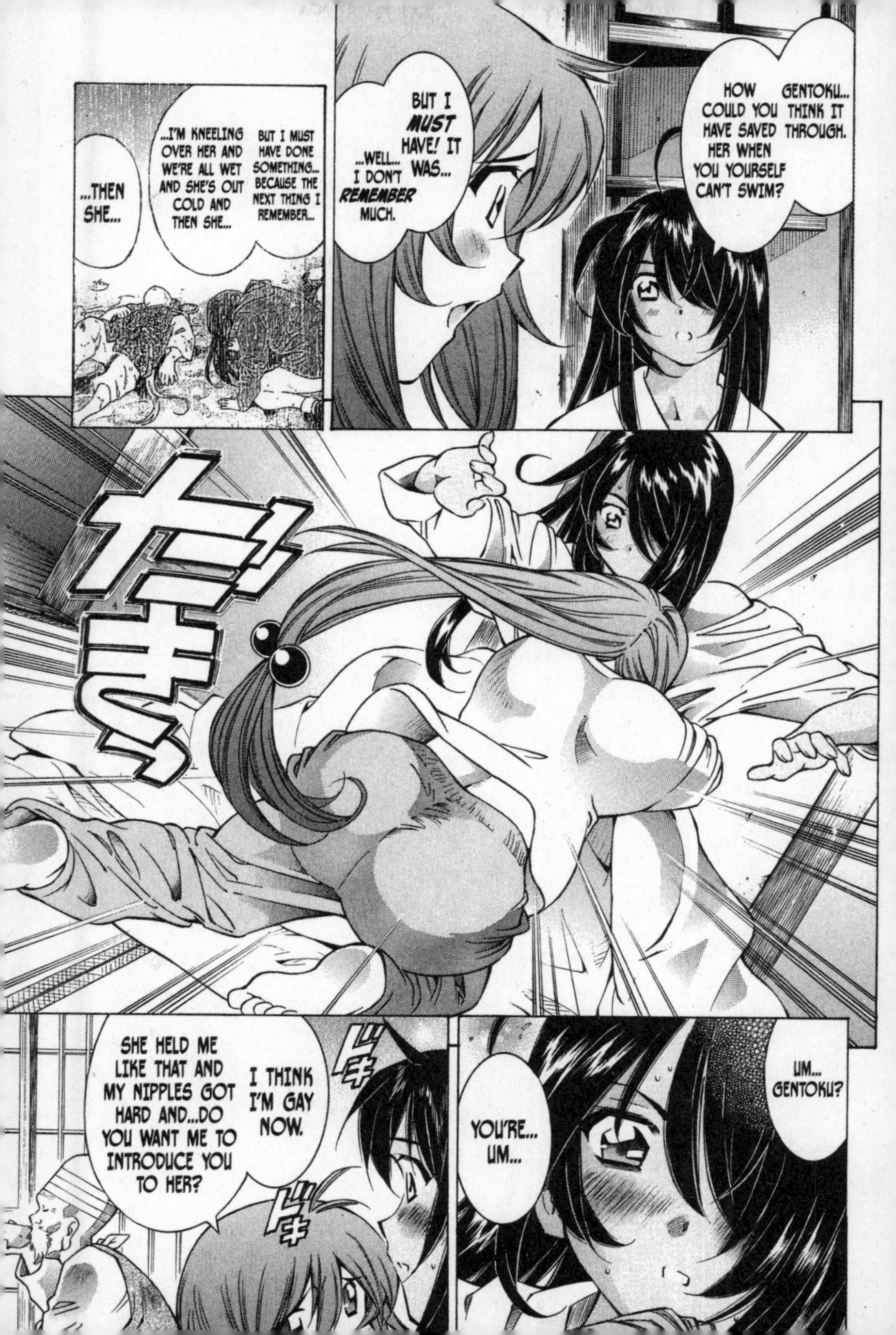
GENTOKU... THINK IT THROUGH.
HOW COULD YOU HAVE SAVED HER WHEN YOU YOURSELF CAN'T SWIM?
BUT I **MUST** HAVE! IT WAS...
...WELL... I DON'T **REMEMBER** MUCH.
BUT I MUST HAVE DONE SOMETHING... BECAUSE THE NEXT THING I REMEMBER...
...I'M KNEELING OVER HER AND WE'RE ALL WET AND SHE'S OUT COLD AND THEN SHE...
...THEN SHE...
UM... GENTOKU?
YOU'RE... UM...
ドキ
ドキ
I THINK I'M GAY NOW.
SHE HELD ME LIKE THAT AND MY NIPPLES GOT HARD AND...DO YOU WANT ME TO INTRODUCE YOU TO HER?

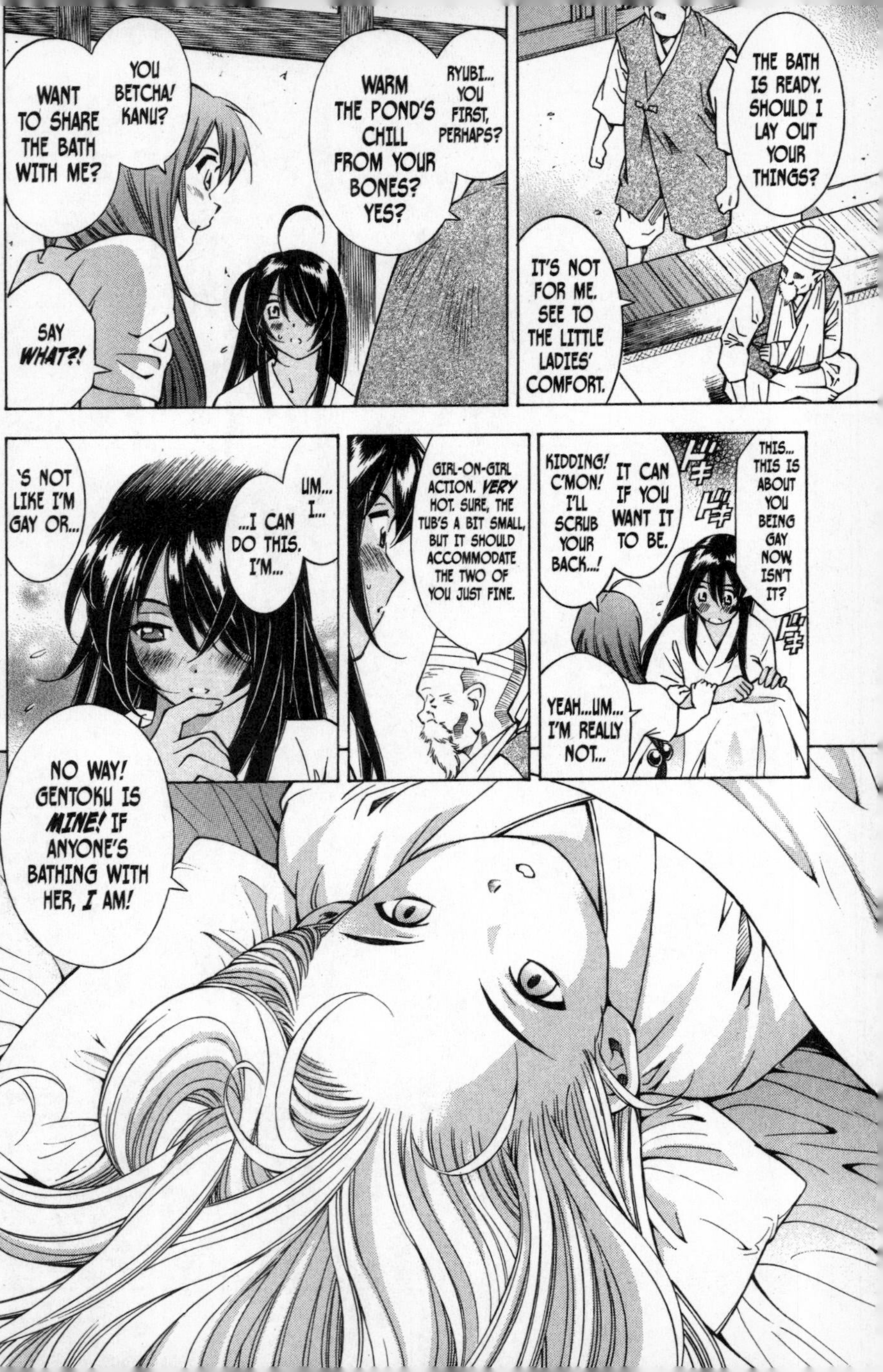
THE BATH IS READY. SHOULD I LAY OUT YOUR THINGS?
IT'S NOT FOR ME. SEE TO THE LITTLE LADIES' COMFORT.
RYUBI... YOU FIRST, PERHAPS?
WARM THE POND'S CHILL FROM YOUR BONES? YES?
YOU BETCHA! KANU?
WANT TO SHARE THE BATH WITH ME?
SAY *WHAT?!*
ドキ ドキ ドキ
THIS... THIS IS ABOUT YOU BEING GAY NOW, ISN'T IT?
IT CAN IF YOU WANT IT TO BE.
KIDDING! C'MON! I'LL SCRUB YOUR BACK...!
YEAH...UM... I'M REALLY NOT...
GIRL-ON-GIRL ACTION. *VERY* HOT. SURE, THE TUB'S A BIT SMALL, BUT IT SHOULD ACCOMMODATE THE TWO OF YOU JUST FINE.
UM... I...
...I CAN DO THIS. I'M...
'S NOT LIKE I'M GAY OR...
NO WAY! GENTOKU IS *MINE!* IF ANYONE'S BATHING WITH HER, *I* AM!

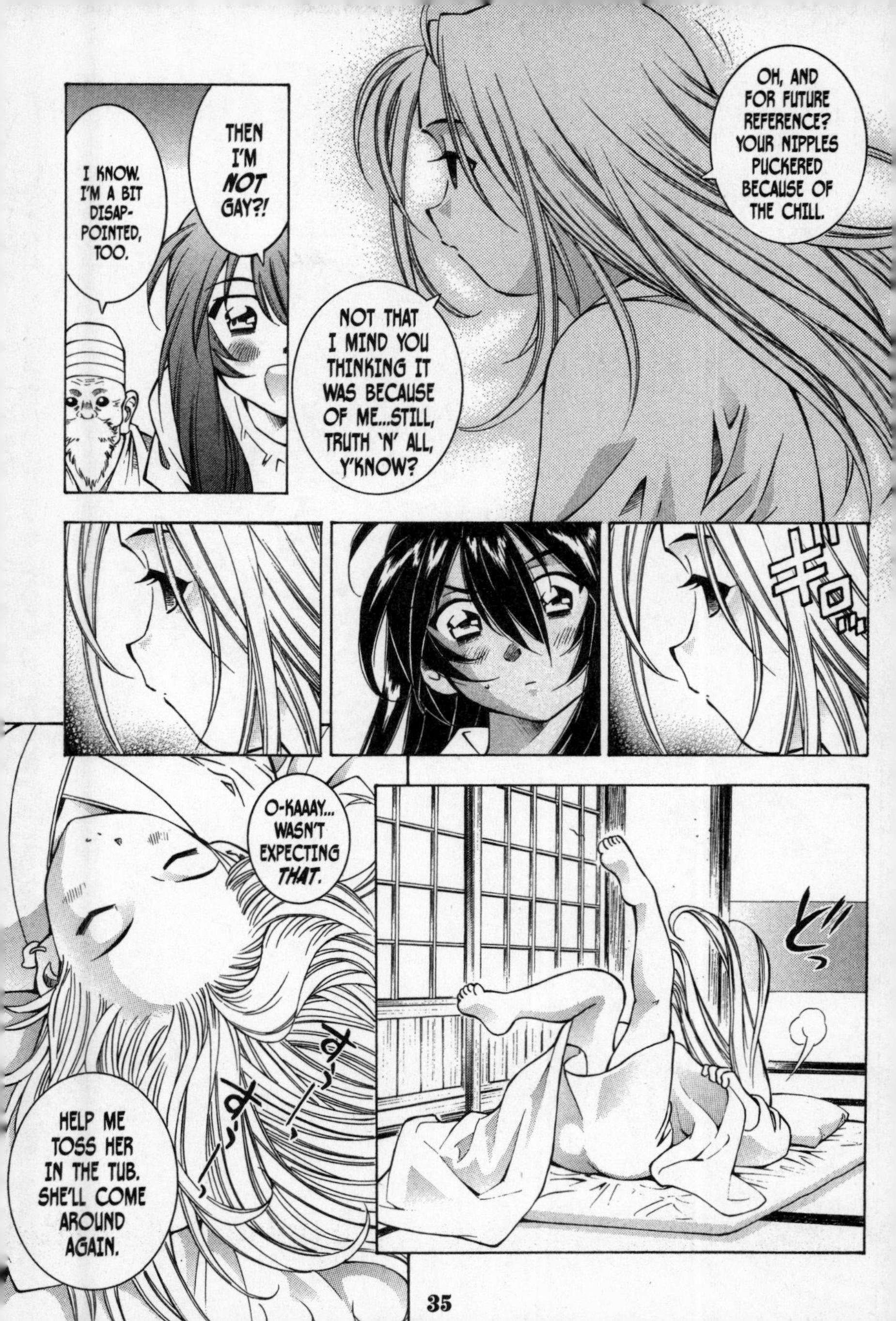
OH, AND FOR FUTURE REFERENCE? YOUR NIPPLES PUCKERED BECAUSE OF THE CHILL.
NOT THAT I MIND YOU THINKING IT WAS BECAUSE OF ME...STILL, TRUTH 'N' ALL, Y'KNOW?
THEN I'M *NOT* GAY?!
I KNOW. I'M A BIT DISAP-POINTED, TOO.
O-KAAAY... WASN'T EXPECTING *THAT*.
HELP ME TOSS HER IN THE TUB. SHE'LL COME AROUND AGAIN.

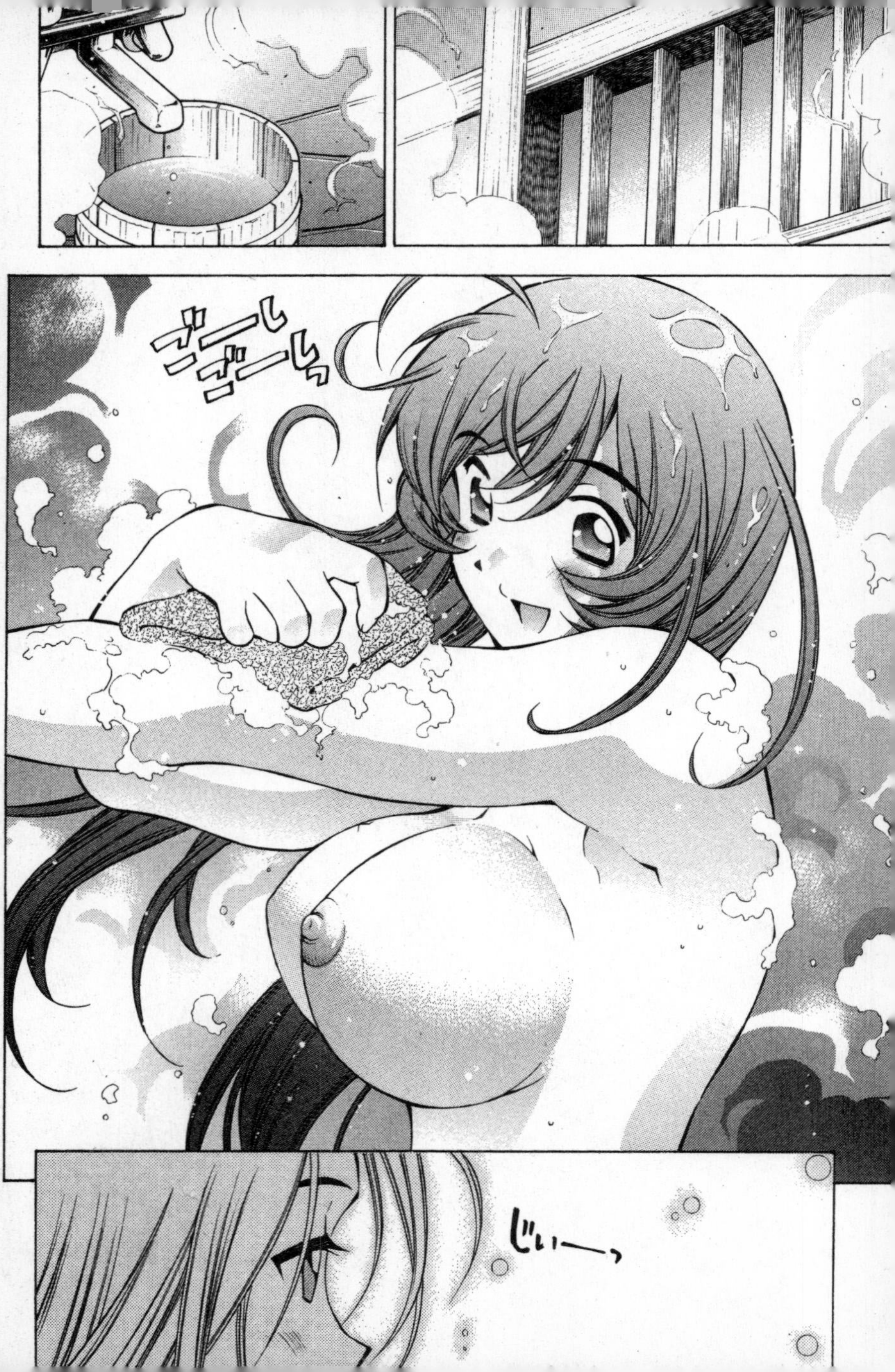
ゴーし
ゴーしっ
じぃーっ

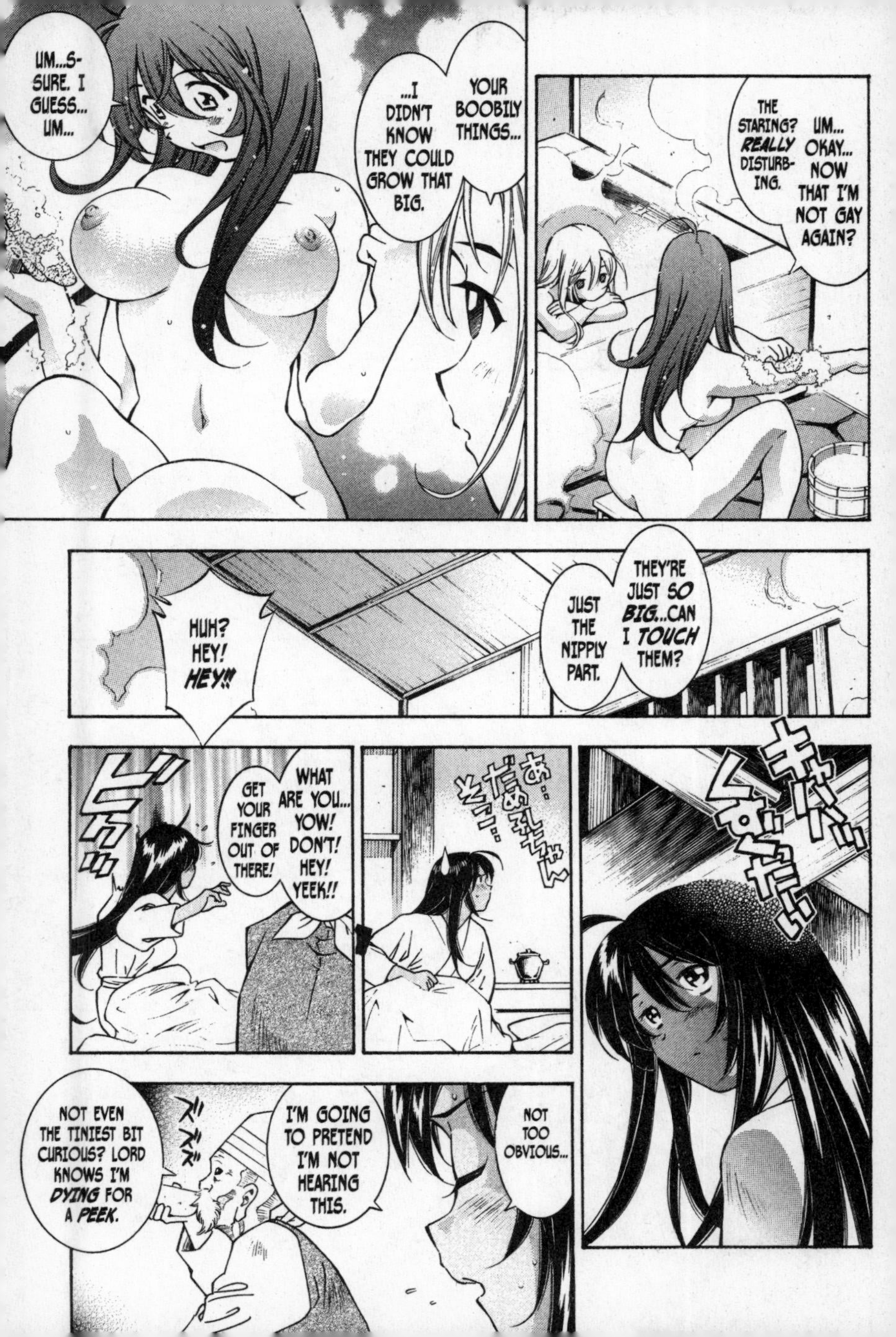
UM... OKAY... NOW THAT I'M NOT GAY AGAIN?
THE STARING? REALLY DISTURB-ING.
YOUR BOOBILY THINGS...
...I DIDN'T KNOW THEY COULD GROW THAT BIG.
UM...S-SURE. I GUESS... UM...
THEY'RE JUST SO BIG...CAN I TOUCH THEM?
JUST THE NIPPLY PART.
HUH? HEY! HEY!!
あ…だめえねえちゃん そこ…
WHAT ARE YOU... YOW! DON'T! HEY! YEEK!!
GET YOUR FINGER OUT OF THERE!
NOT TOO OBVIOUS...
I'M GOING TO PRETEND I'M NOT HEARING THIS.
NOT EVEN THE TINIEST BIT CURIOUS? LORD KNOWS I'M DYING FOR A PEEK.

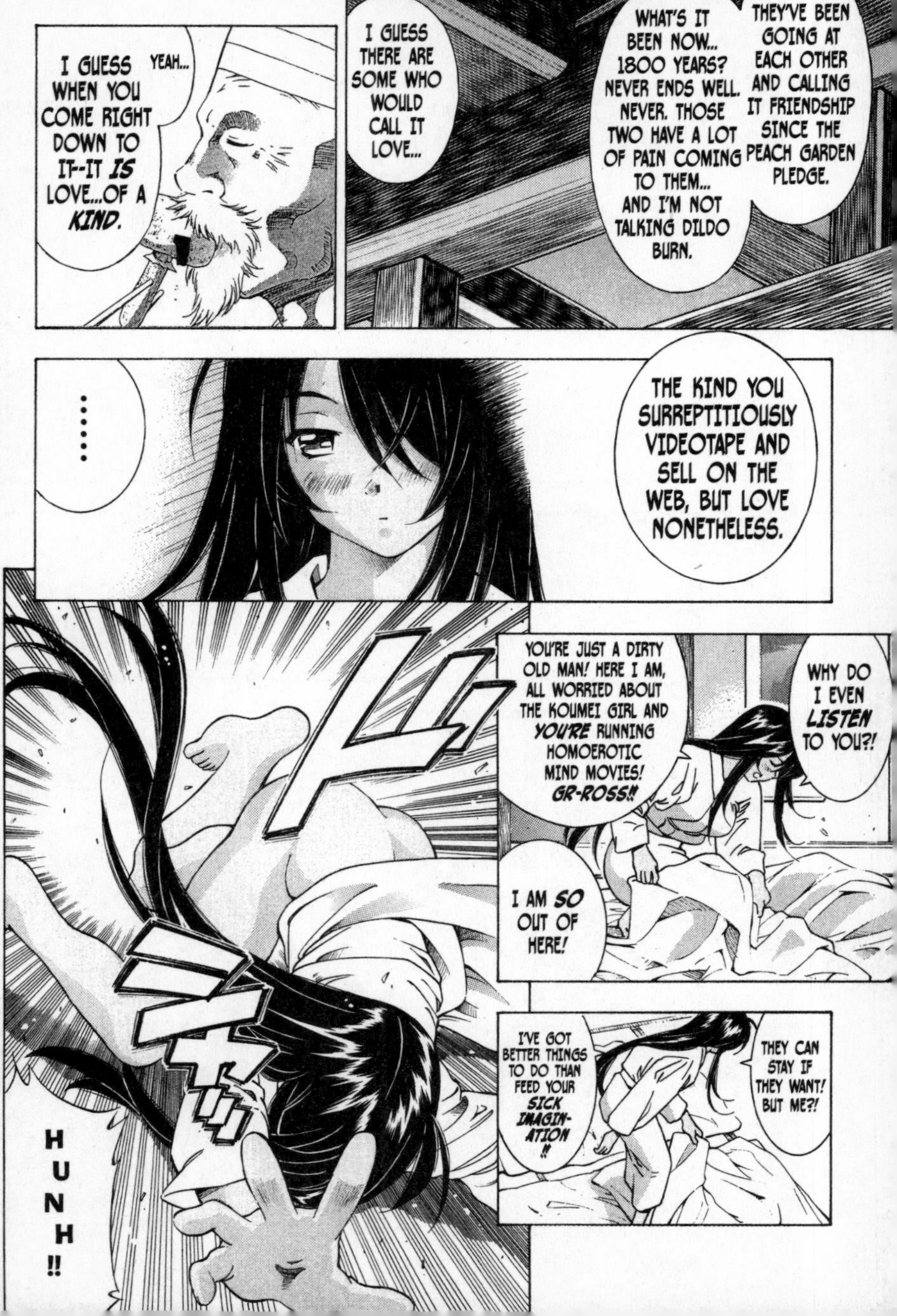
THEY'VE BEEN GOING AT EACH OTHER AND CALLING IT FRIENDSHIP SINCE THE PEACH GARDEN PLEDGE.
WHAT'S IT BEEN NOW... 1800 YEARS? NEVER ENDS WELL. NEVER. THOSE TWO HAVE A LOT OF PAIN COMING TO THEM... AND I'M NOT TALKING DILDO BURN.
I GUESS THERE ARE SOME WHO WOULD CALL IT LOVE...
YEAH...
I GUESS WHEN YOU COME RIGHT DOWN TO IT--IT *IS* LOVE...OF A *KIND*.
THE KIND YOU SURREPTITIOUSLY VIDEOTAPE AND SELL ON THE WEB, BUT LOVE NONETHELESS.
......
WHY DO I EVEN *LISTEN* TO YOU?!
YOU'RE JUST A DIRTY OLD MAN! HERE I AM, ALL WORRIED ABOUT THE KOUMEI GIRL AND *YOU'RE* RUNNING HOMOEROTIC MIND MOVIES! *GR-ROSS!!*
I AM *SO* OUT OF HERE!
THEY CAN STAY IF THEY WANT! BUT ME?!
I'VE GOT BETTER THINGS TO DO THAN FEED YOUR *SICK IMAGIN-ATION* !!
HUNH!!

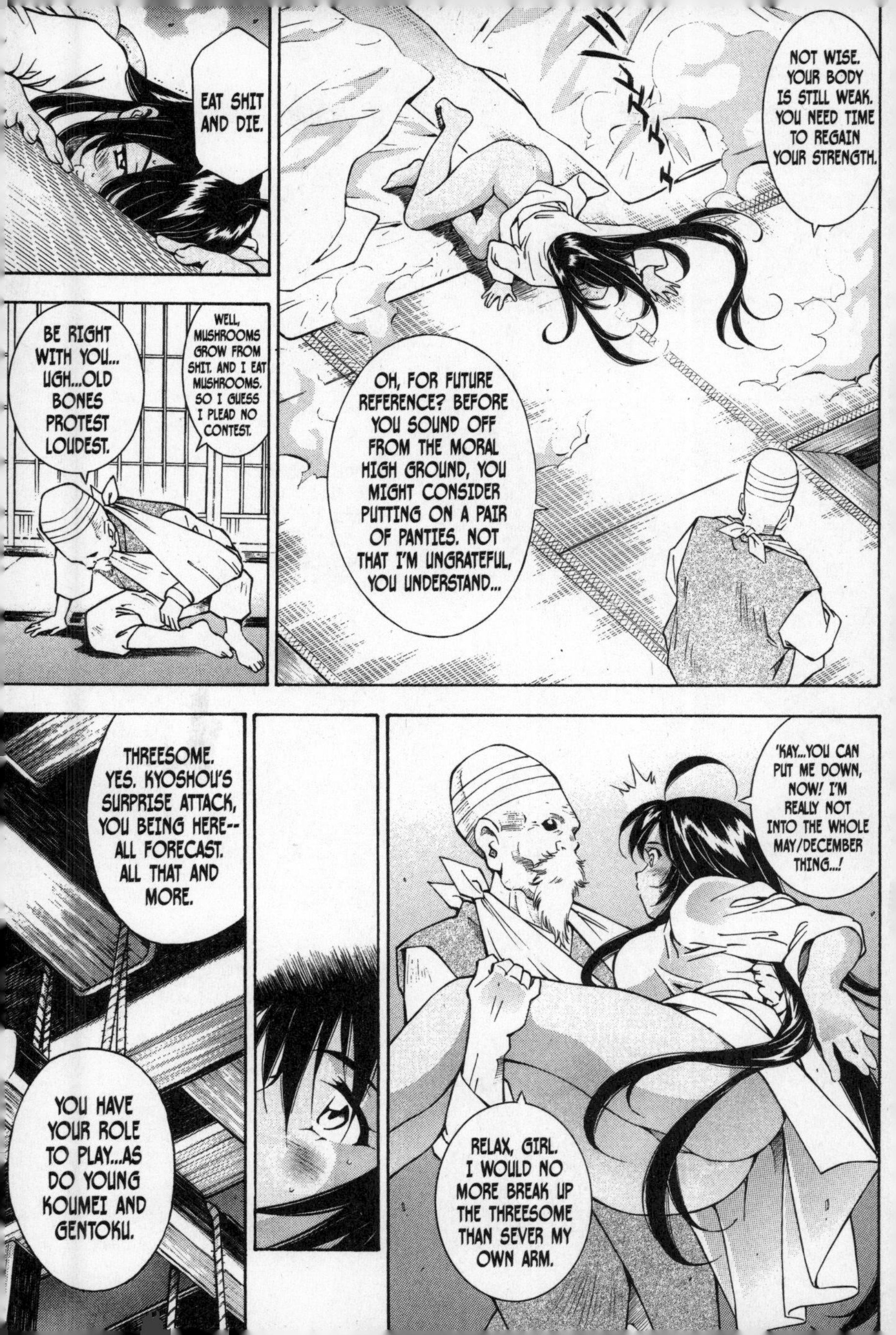
NOT WISE. YOUR BODY IS STILL WEAK. YOU NEED TIME TO REGAIN YOUR STRENGTH.
OH, FOR FUTURE REFERENCE? BEFORE YOU SOUND OFF FROM THE MORAL HIGH GROUND, YOU MIGHT CONSIDER PUTTING ON A PAIR OF PANTIES. NOT THAT I'M UNGRATEFUL, YOU UNDERSTAND...
EAT SHIT AND DIE.
WELL, MUSHROOMS GROW FROM SHIT. AND I EAT MUSHROOMS. SO I GUESS I PLEAD NO CONTEST.
BE RIGHT WITH YOU... UGH...OLD BONES PROTEST LOUDEST.
'KAY...YOU CAN PUT ME DOWN, NOW! I'M REALLY NOT INTO THE WHOLE MAY/DECEMBER THING...!
RELAX, GIRL. I WOULD NO MORE BREAK UP THE THREESOME THAN SEVER MY OWN ARM.
THREESOME. YES. KYOSHOU'S SURPRISE ATTACK, YOU BEING HERE--ALL FORECAST. ALL THAT AND MORE.
YOU HAVE YOUR ROLE TO PLAY...AS DO YOUNG KOUMEI AND GENTOKU.

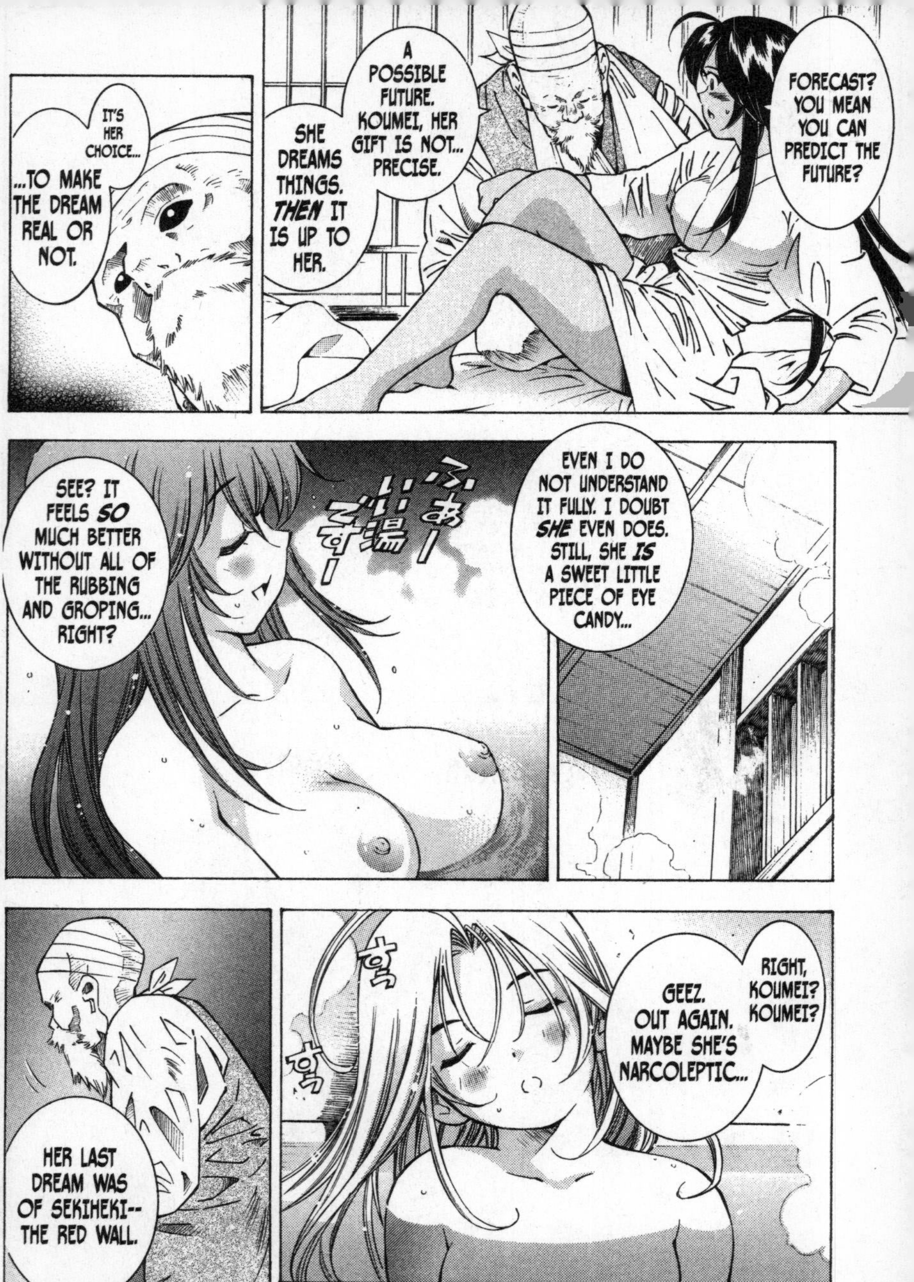
FORECAST? YOU MEAN YOU CAN PREDICT THE FUTURE?
A POSSIBLE FUTURE. KOUMEI, HER GIFT IS NOT... PRECISE.
SHE DREAMS THINGS. *THEN* IT IS UP TO HER.
IT'S HER CHOICE...
...TO MAKE THE DREAM REAL OR NOT.
EVEN I DO NOT UNDERSTAND IT FULLY. I DOUBT *SHE* EVEN DOES. STILL, SHE *IS* A SWEET LITTLE PIECE OF EYE CANDY...
ふぁー いい湯 ですー
SEE? IT FEELS *SO* MUCH BETTER WITHOUT ALL OF THE RUBBING AND GROPING... RIGHT?
RIGHT, KOUMEI? KOUMEI?
GEEZ. OUT AGAIN. MAYBE SHE'S NARCOLEPTIC...
HER LAST DREAM WAS OF SEKIHEKI-- THE RED WALL.

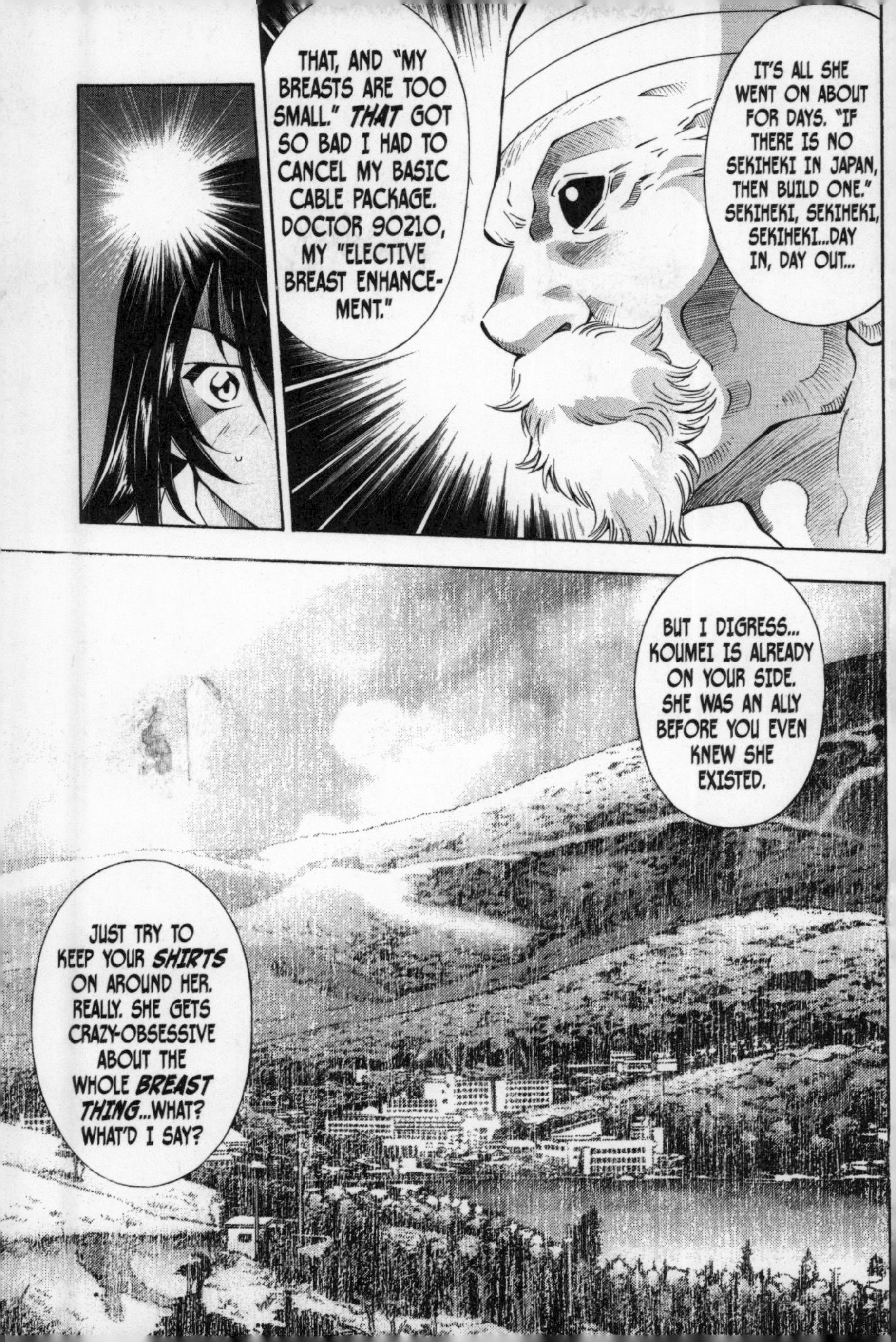
IT'S ALL SHE WENT ON ABOUT FOR DAYS. "IF THERE IS NO SEKIHEKI IN JAPAN, THEN BUILD ONE." SEKIHEKI, SEKIHEKI, SEKIHEKI...DAY IN, DAY OUT...
THAT, AND "MY BREASTS ARE TOO SMALL." *THAT* GOT SO BAD I HAD TO CANCEL MY BASIC CABLE PACKAGE. DOCTOR 90210, MY "ELECTIVE BREAST ENHANCE-MENT."
BUT I DIGRESS... KOUMEI IS ALREADY ON YOUR SIDE. SHE WAS AN ALLY BEFORE YOU EVEN KNEW SHE EXISTED.
JUST TRY TO KEEP YOUR *SHIRTS* ON AROUND HER. REALLY. SHE GETS CRAZY-OBSESSIVE ABOUT THE WHOLE *BREAST THING*...WHAT? WHAT'D I SAY?

303
KAKU
BEVEL flair
BIOPSY RESULTS
WBC 59 Hb 15.5 Fe
RBC 507 Ht 45.7 UIBC
血液 Eo Ba Mo Ly
血液像 NE
205 HDL-C 16
T-Cho 68 BUN
T-G 0.9 U-A
CRE 23 GPT
AL-P

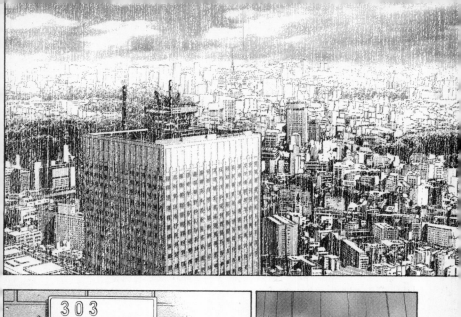

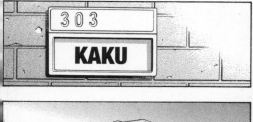

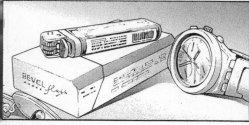

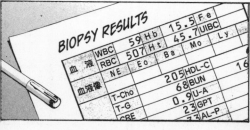

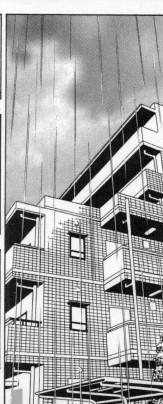

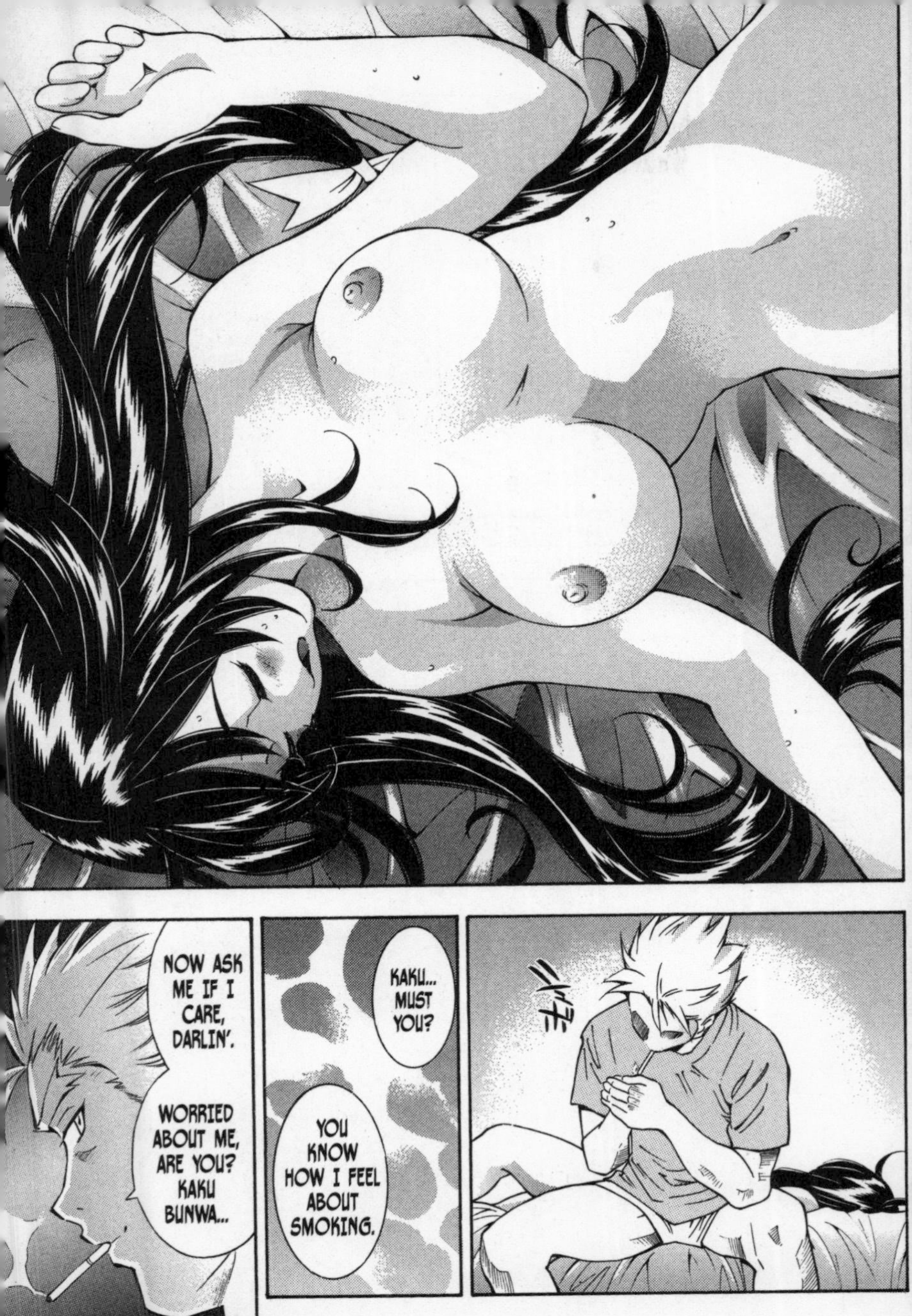
KAKU... MUST YOU?
YOU KNOW HOW I FEEL ABOUT SMOKING.
NOW ASK ME IF I CARE, DARLIN'.
WORRIED ABOUT ME, ARE YOU? KAKU BUNWA...

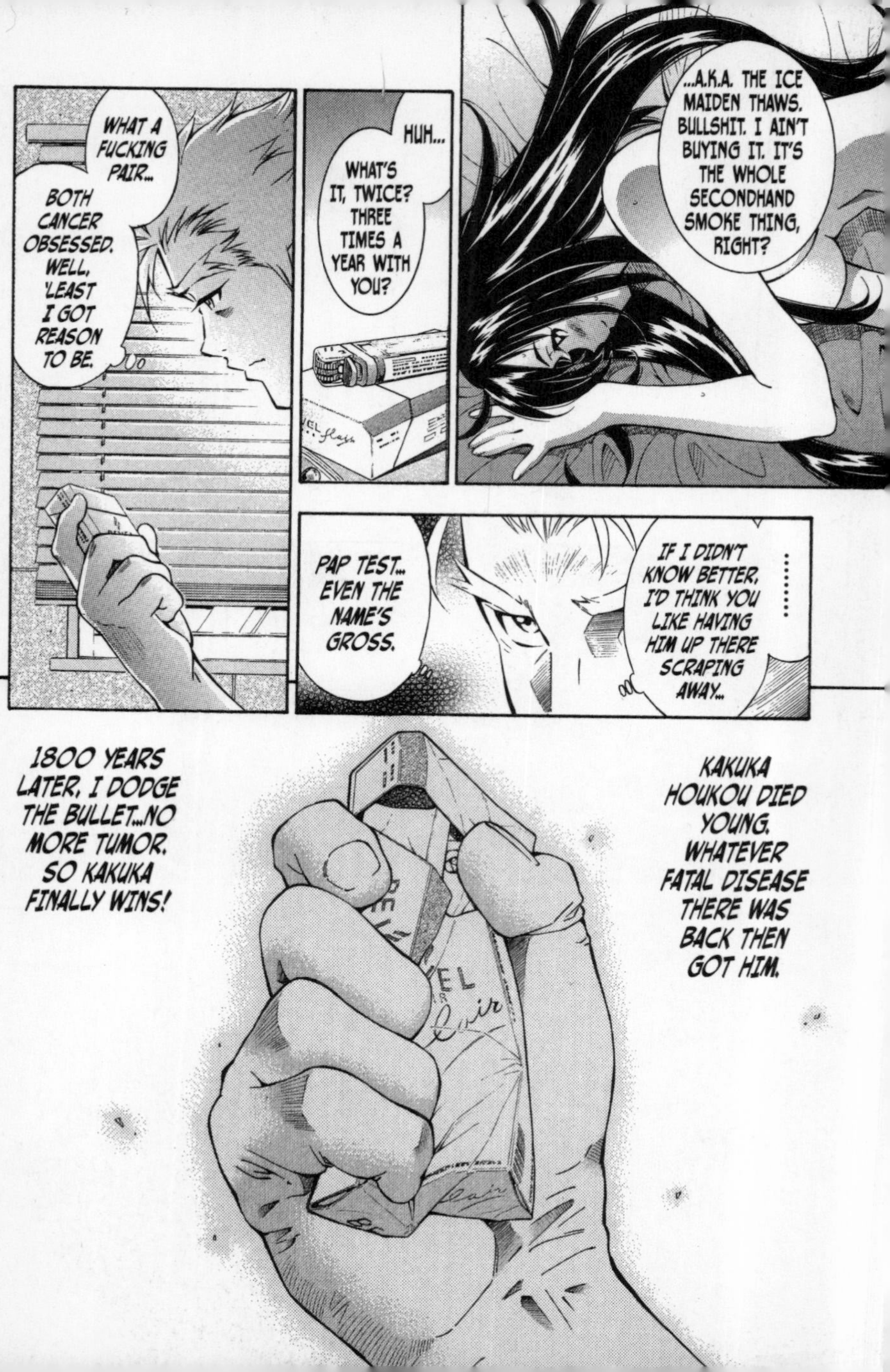
...A.K.A. THE ICE MAIDEN THAWS. BULLSHIT. I AIN'T BUYING IT. IT'S THE WHOLE SECONDHAND SMOKE THING, RIGHT?
HUH...
WHAT'S IT, TWICE? THREE TIMES A YEAR WITH YOU?
......
IF I DIDN'T KNOW BETTER, I'D THINK YOU LIKE HAVING HIM UP THERE SCRAPING AWAY...
PAP TEST... EVEN THE NAME'S GROSS.
WHAT A FUCKING PAIR...
BOTH CANCER OBSESSED. WELL, 'LEAST I GOT REASON TO BE.
KAKUKA HOUKOU DIED YOUNG. WHATEVER FATAL DISEASE THERE WAS BACK THEN GOT HIM.
1800 YEARS LATER, I DODGE THE BULLET...NO MORE TUMOR. SO KAKUKA FINALLY WINS!

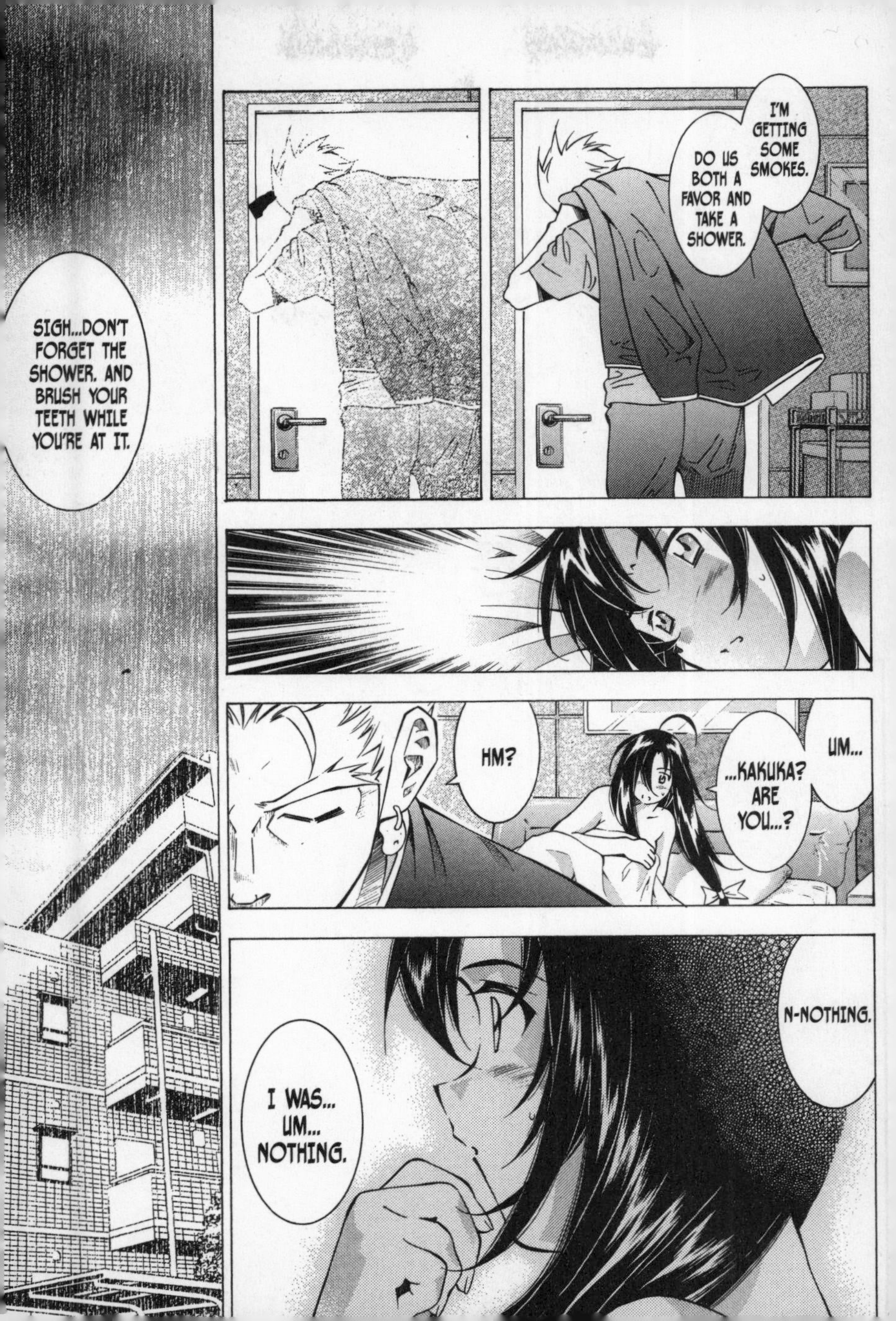
I'M GETTING SOME SMOKES.
DO US BOTH A FAVOR AND TAKE A SHOWER.
UM...
...KAKUKA? ARE YOU...?
HM?
N-NOTHING.
I WAS... UM... NOTHING.
SIGH...DON'T FORGET THE SHOWER. AND BRUSH YOUR TEETH WHILE YOU'RE AT IT.

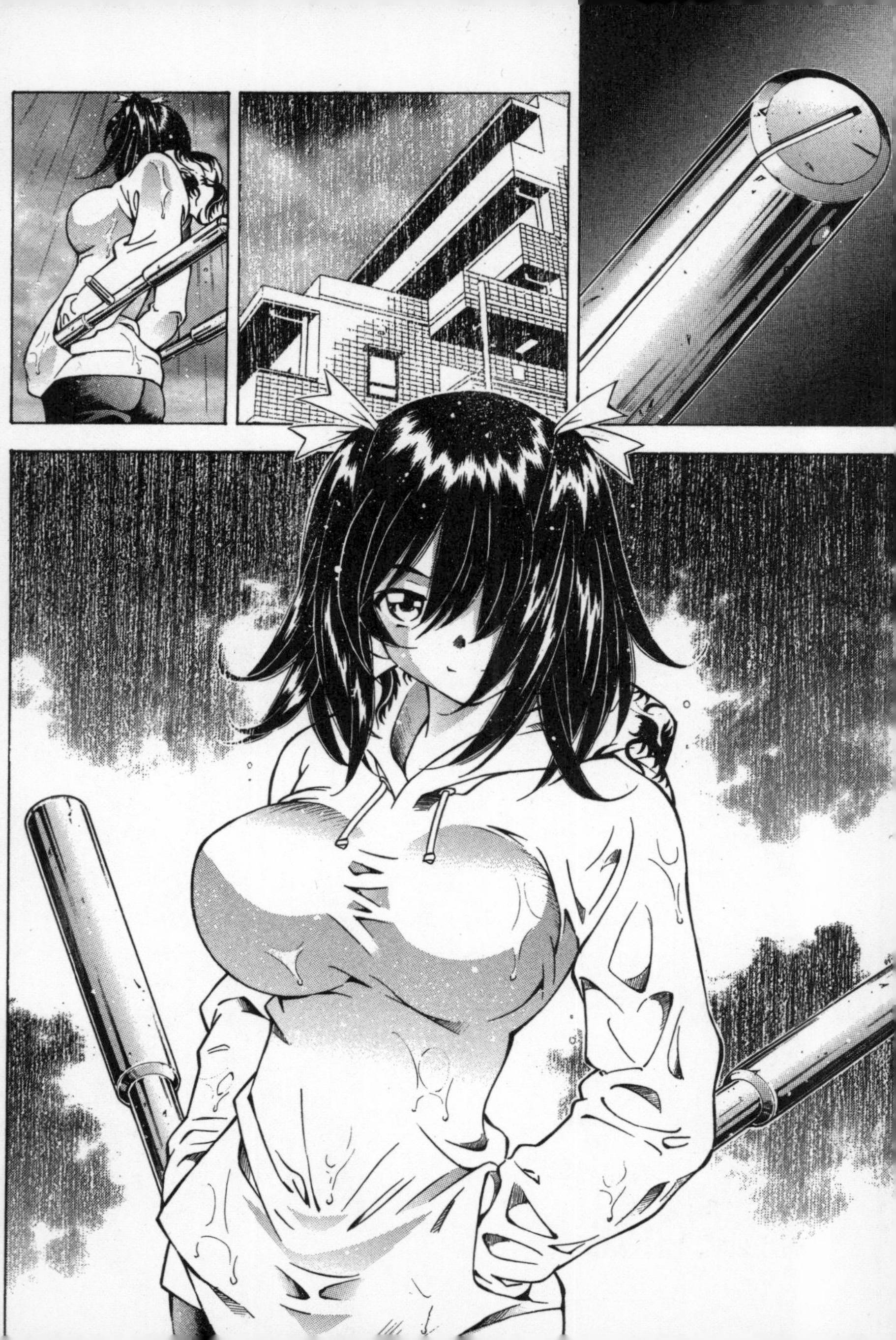

一騎当千

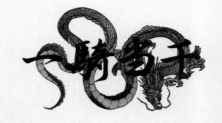

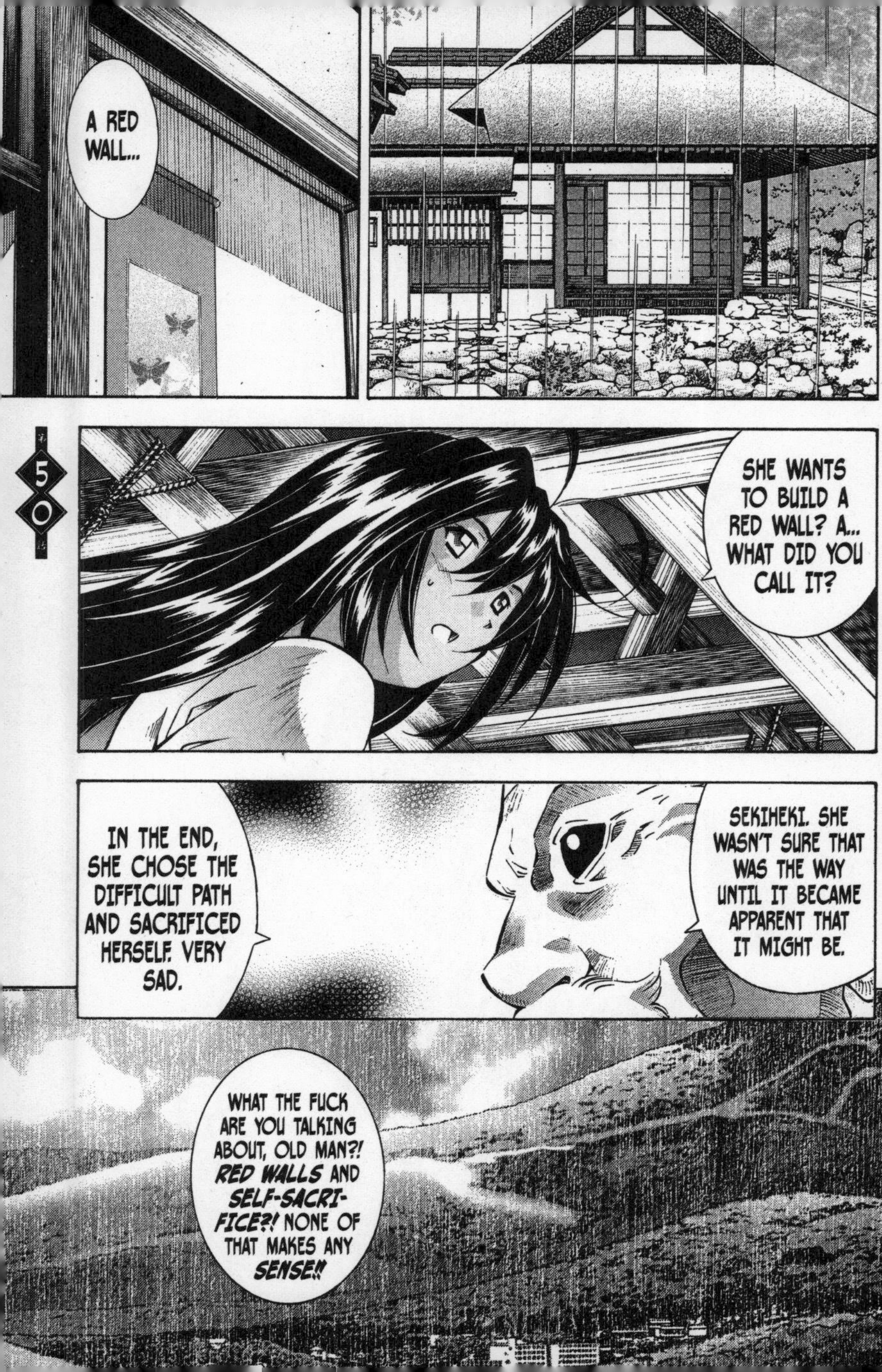
A RED WALL...
SHE WANTS TO BUILD A RED WALL? A... WHAT DID YOU CALL IT?
SEKIHEKI. SHE WASN'T SURE THAT WAS THE WAY UNTIL IT BECAME APPARENT THAT IT MIGHT BE.
IN THE END, SHE CHOSE THE DIFFICULT PATH AND SACRIFICED HERSELF. VERY SAD.
WHAT THE FUCK ARE YOU TALKING ABOUT, OLD MAN?! *RED WALLS* AND *SELF-SACRIFICE?!* NONE OF THAT MAKES ANY *SENSE!!*

BASHOKU YOUJYOU

BASHOKU WAS THE YOUNGER BROTHER OF BARYOU. SHOKATSURYO THOUGHT HIGHLY OF BASHOKU'S EXCEPTIONAL TALENTS, ESPECIALLY HIS ABILITY TO KEEP ALL TWELVE PLATES SPINNING SIMULTANEOUSLY. SHOKATSURYO AND BASHOKU ENGAGED IN PROLONGED DEBATES ABOUT MATTERS OF LITTLE IMPORTANCE--AND SO GREW CLOSER. SEEING THIS, RYUBI WARNED SHOKATSURYO THAT "BASHOKU IS ALL TALK AND NO ACTION." BASHUKO WAS LITTLE UTILIZED IN COMBAT WHICH, ONCE HE SAW THE GRIEVOUS WOUNDS COMING BACK FROM THE FRONT, SUITED HIM JUST FINE.

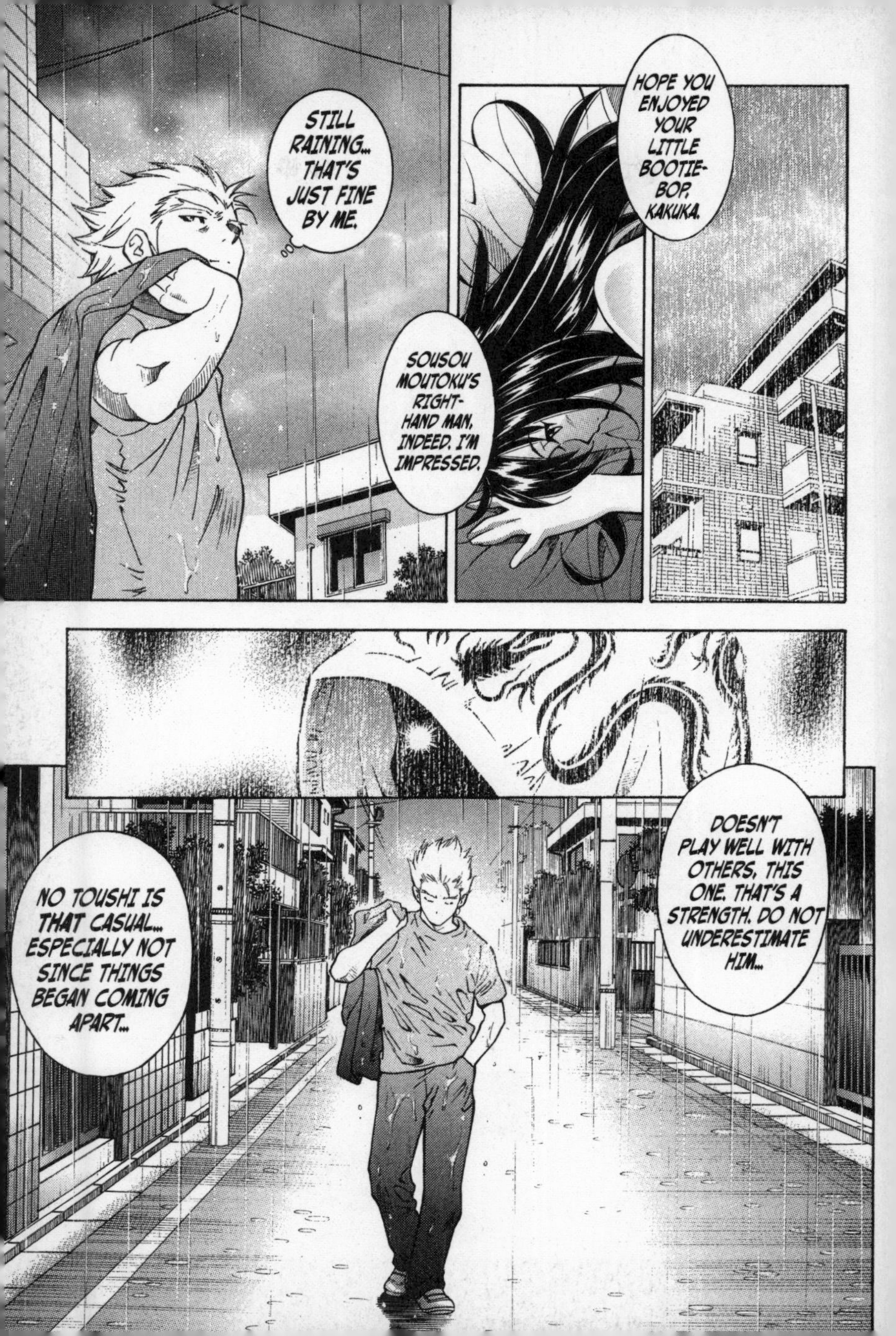
HOPE YOU ENJOYED YOUR LITTLE BOOTIE-BOP, KAKUKA.
SOUSOU MOUTOKU'S RIGHT-HAND MAN, INDEED. I'M IMPRESSED.
STILL RAINING... THAT'S JUST FINE BY ME.
DOESN'T PLAY WELL WITH OTHERS, THIS ONE. THAT'S A STRENGTH. DO NOT UNDERESTIMATE HIM...
NO TOUSHI IS THAT CASUAL... ESPECIALLY NOT SINCE THINGS BEGAN COMING APART...

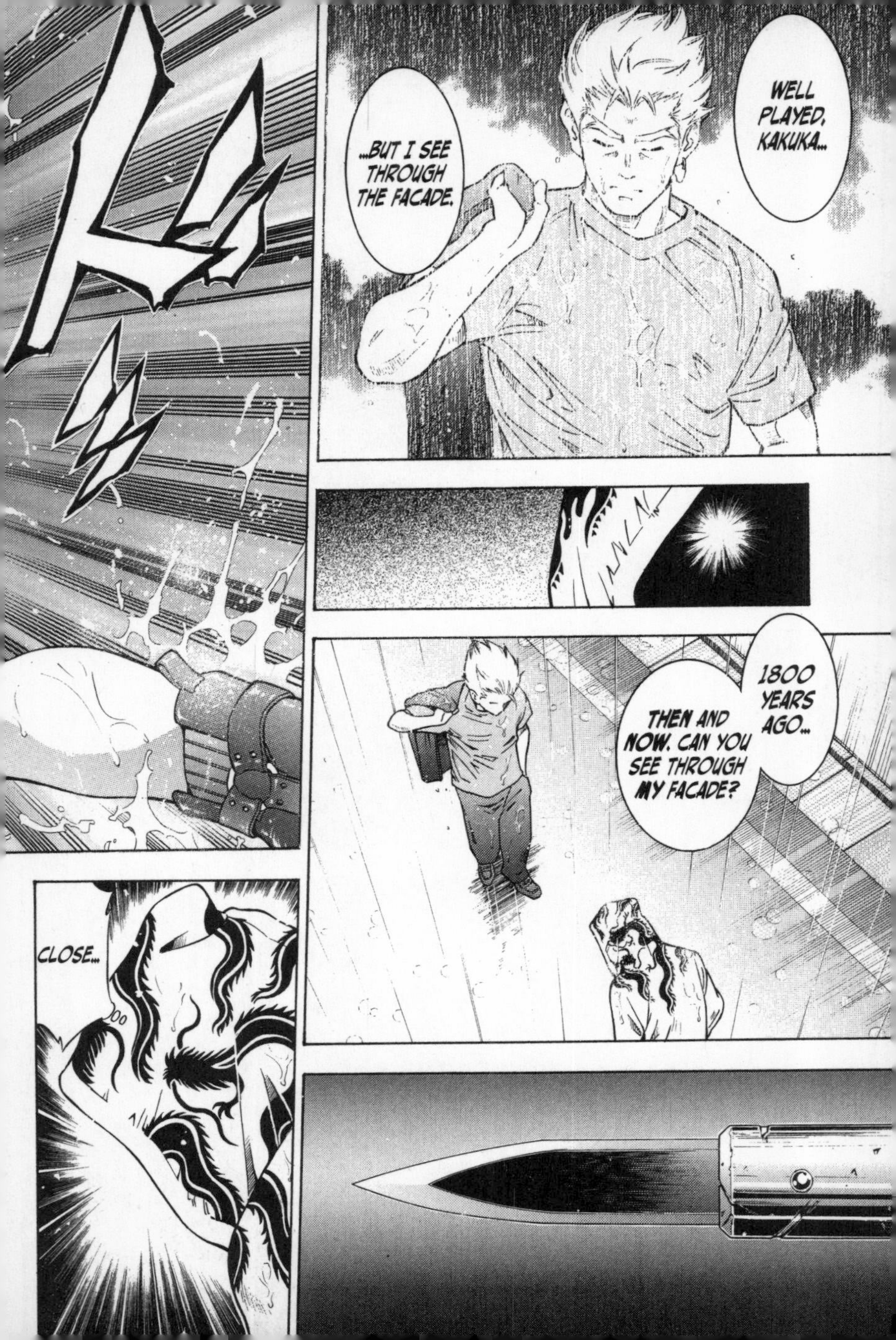
WELL PLAYED, KAKUKA...
...BUT I SEE THROUGH THE FACADE.
1800 YEARS AGO...
THEN AND NOW. CAN YOU SEE THROUGH MY FACADE?
CLOSE...

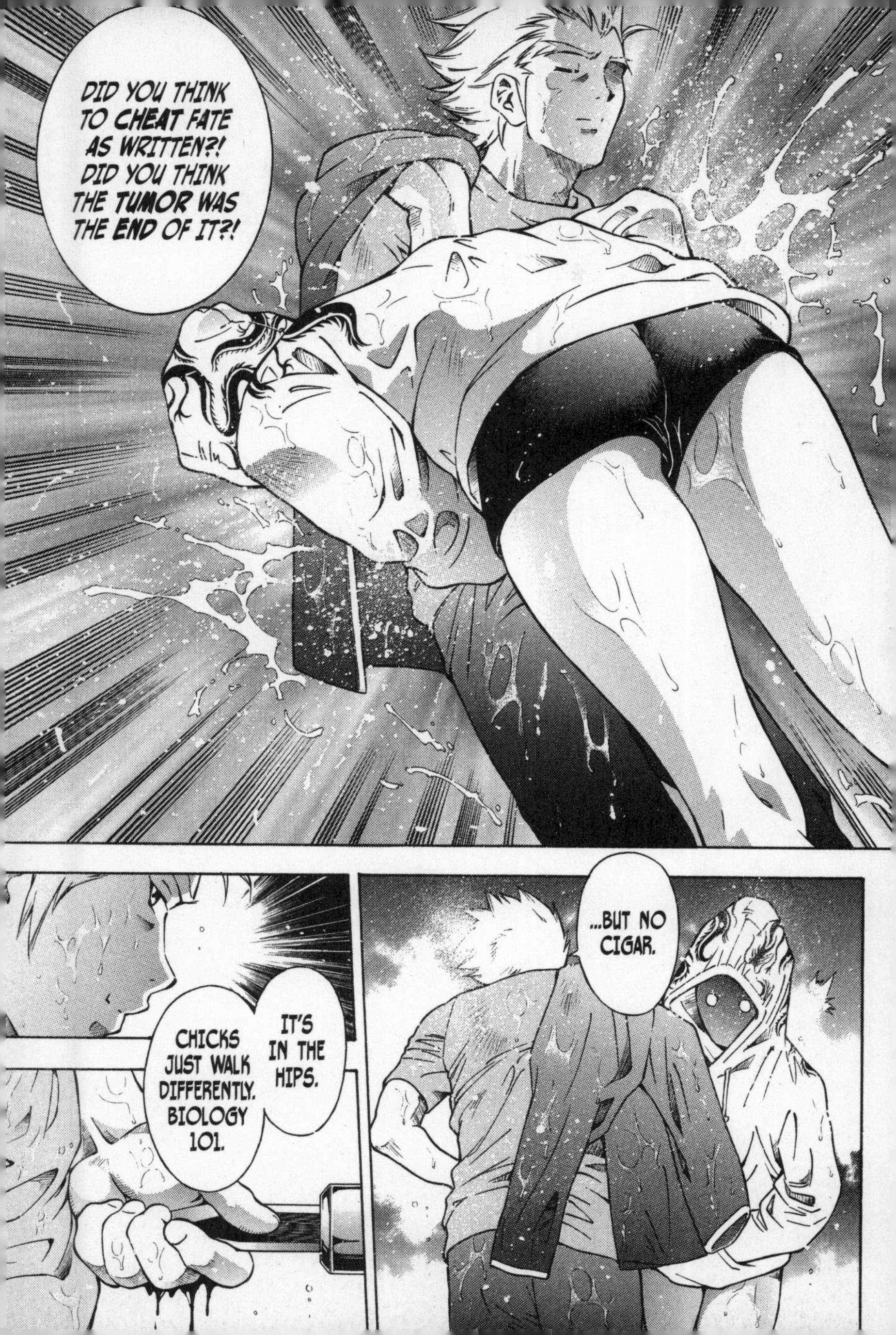
DID YOU THINK TO CHEAT FATE AS WRITTEN?! DID YOU THINK THE TUMOR WAS THE END OF IT?!
...BUT NO CIGAR.
IT'S IN THE HIPS.
CHICKS JUST WALK DIFFERENTLY. BIOLOGY 101.

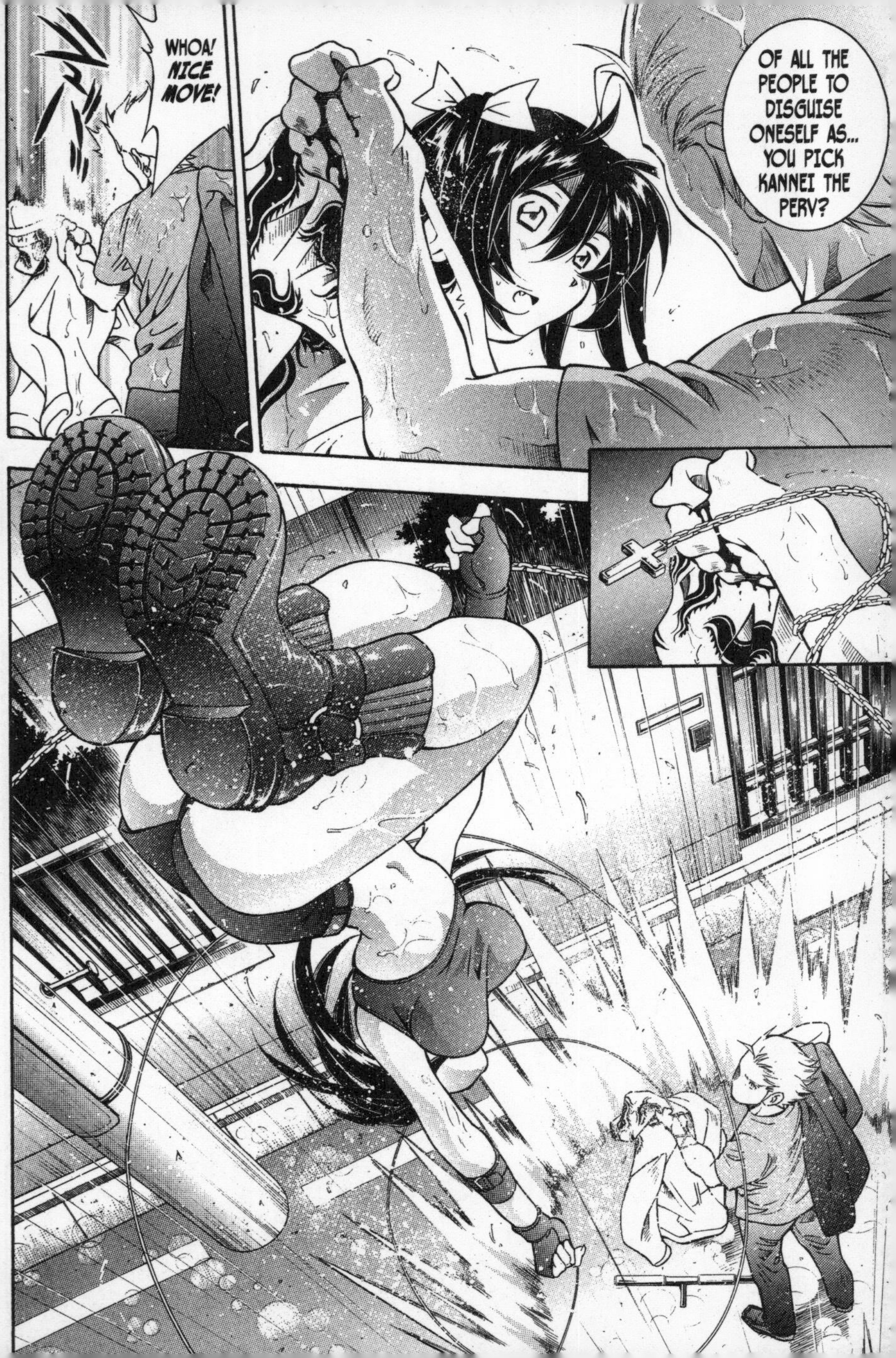
OF ALL THE PEOPLE TO DISGUISE ONESELF AS... YOU PICK KANNEI THE PERV?
WHOA! *NICE MOVE!*

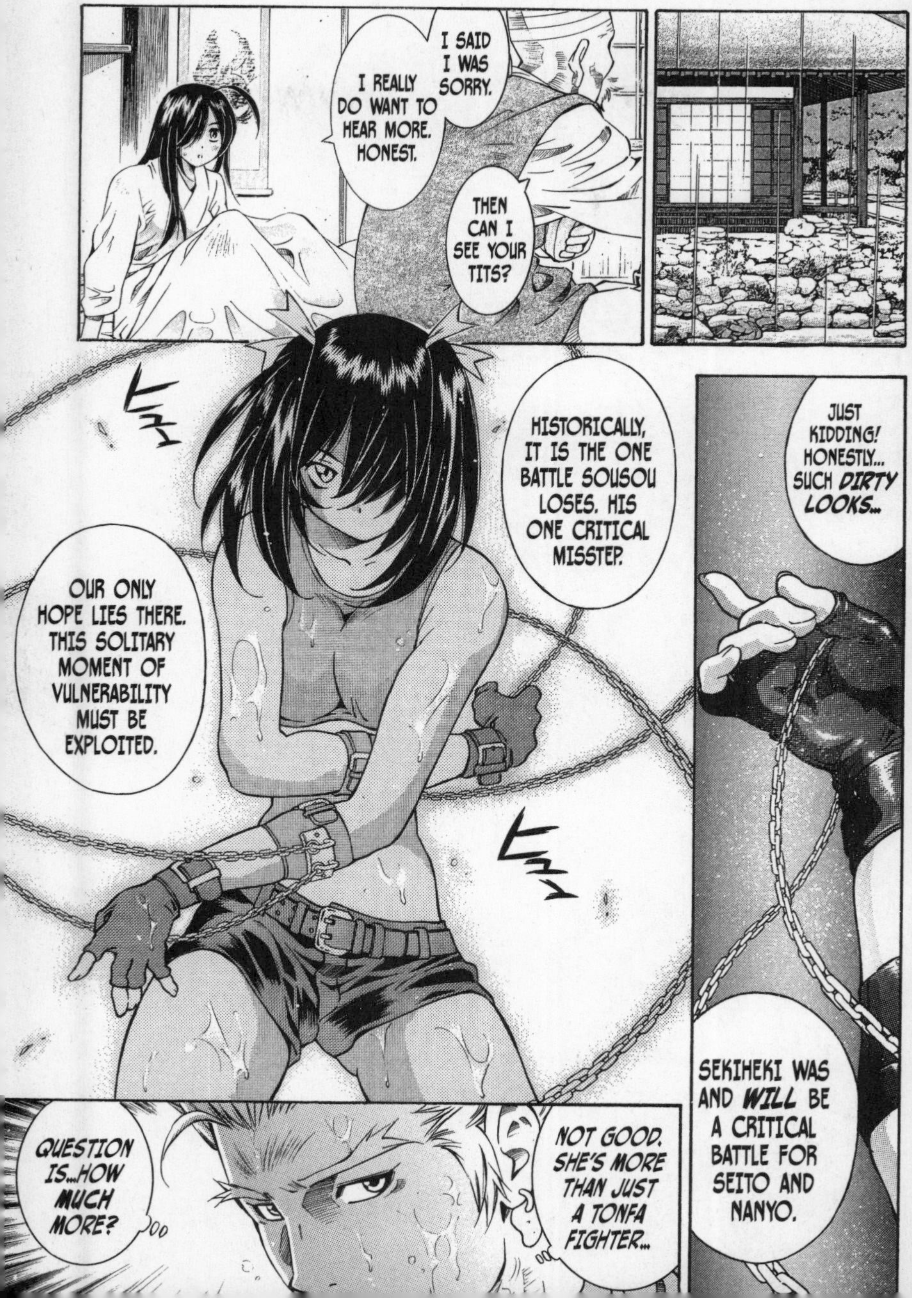
I SAID I WAS SORRY.
I REALLY DO WANT TO HEAR MORE. HONEST.
THEN CAN I SEE YOUR TITS?
JUST KIDDING! HONESTLY... SUCH *DIRTY LOOKS*...
SEKIHEKI WAS AND *WILL* BE A CRITICAL BATTLE FOR SEITO AND NANYO.
HISTORICALLY, IT IS THE ONE BATTLE SOUSOU LOSES. HIS ONE CRITICAL MISSTEP.
OUR ONLY HOPE LIES THERE. THIS SOLITARY MOMENT OF VULNERABILITY MUST BE EXPLOITED.
NOT GOOD. SHE'S MORE THAN JUST A TONFA FIGHTER...
QUESTION IS...HOW MUCH MORE?

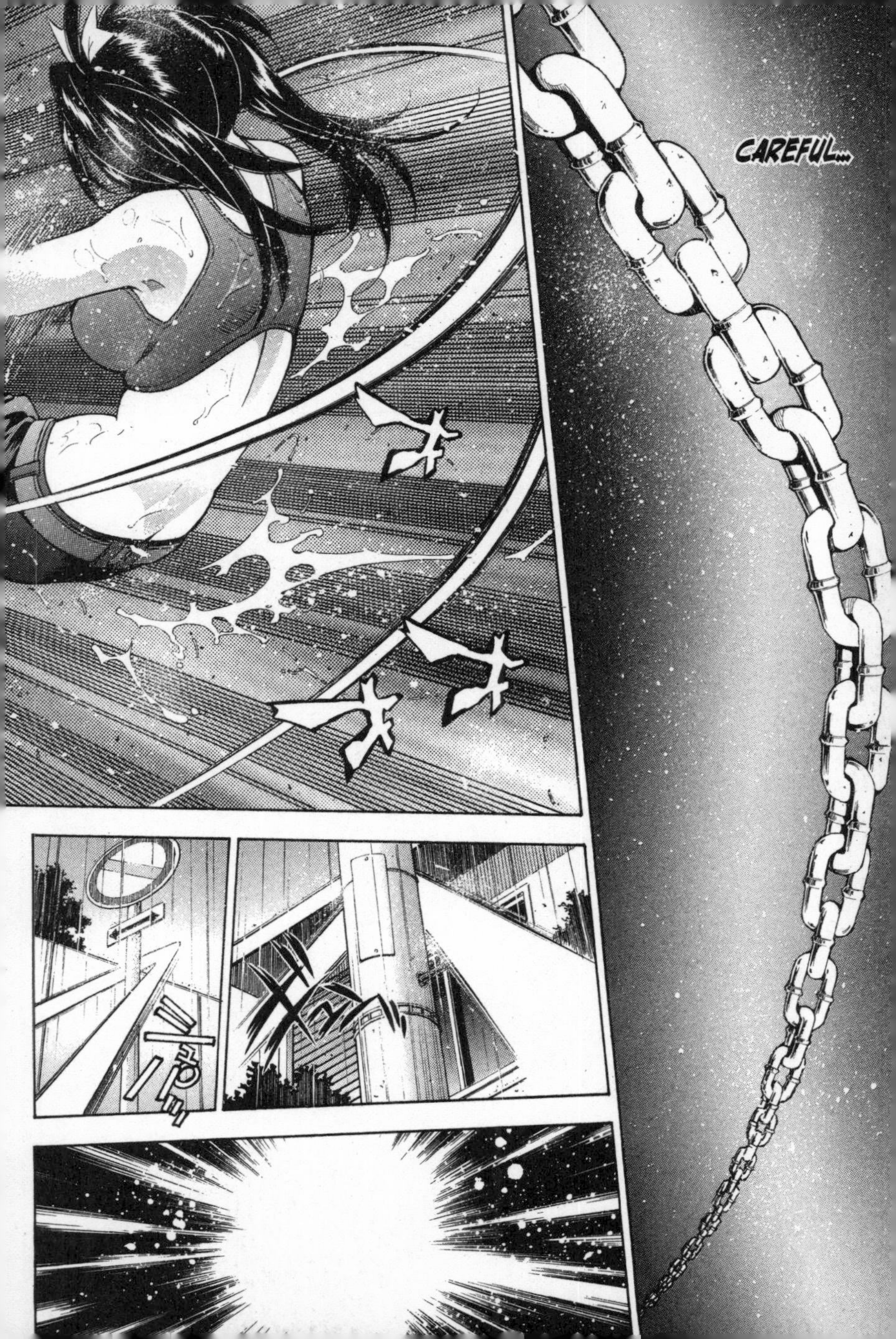
CAREFUL...

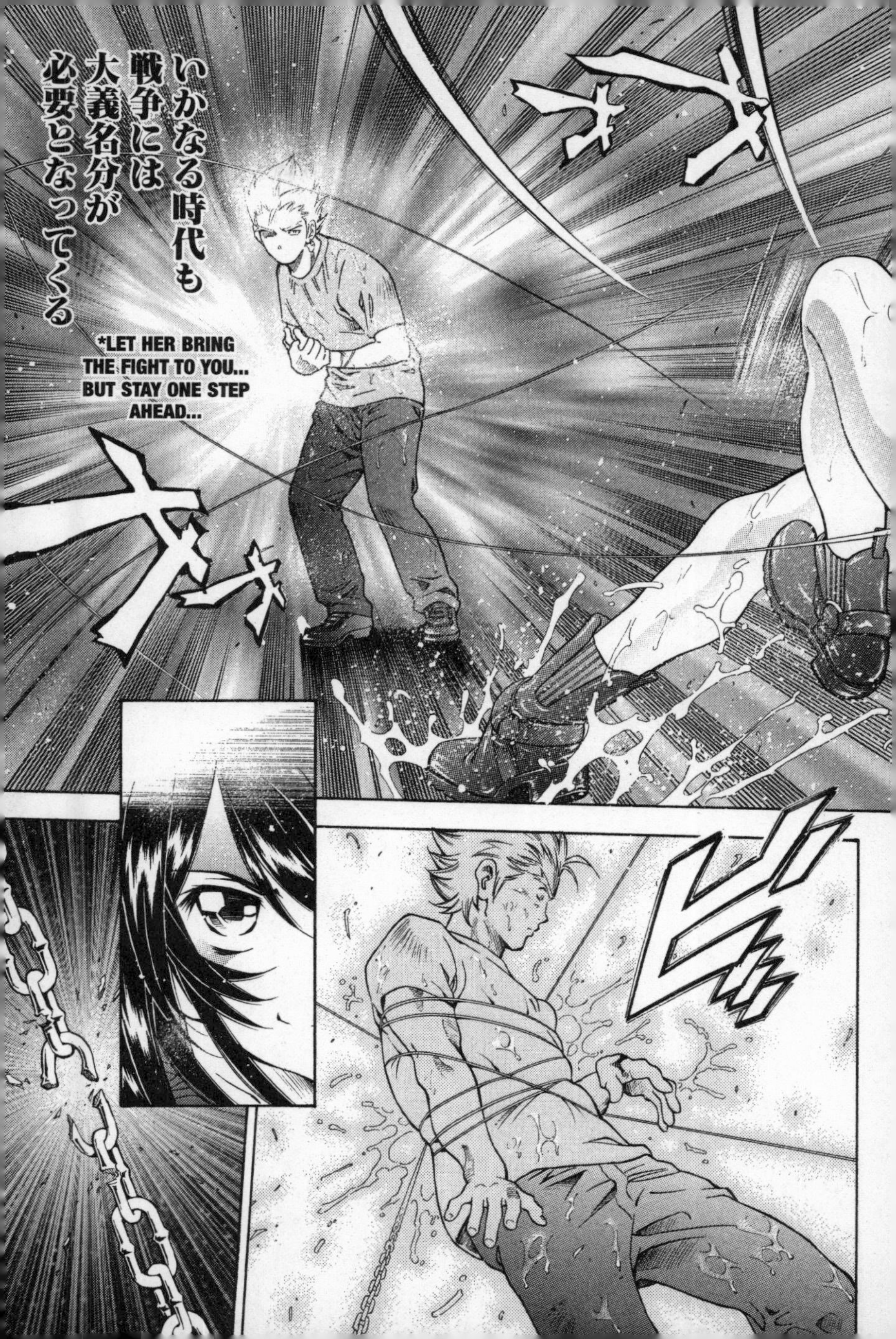
いかなる時代も
戦争には
大義名分が
必要となってくる
*LET HER BRING THE FIGHT TO YOU... BUT STAY ONE STEP AHEAD...

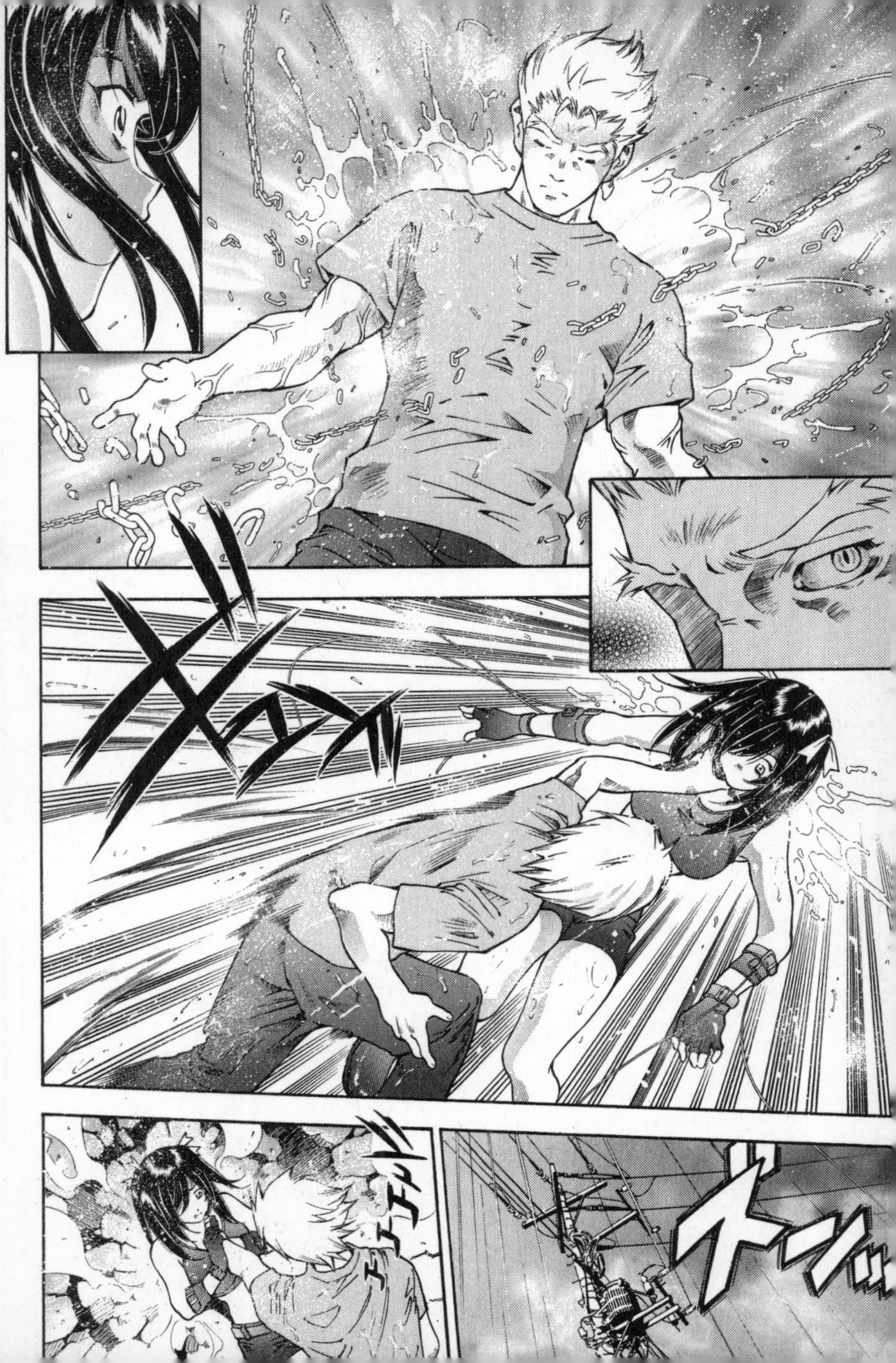

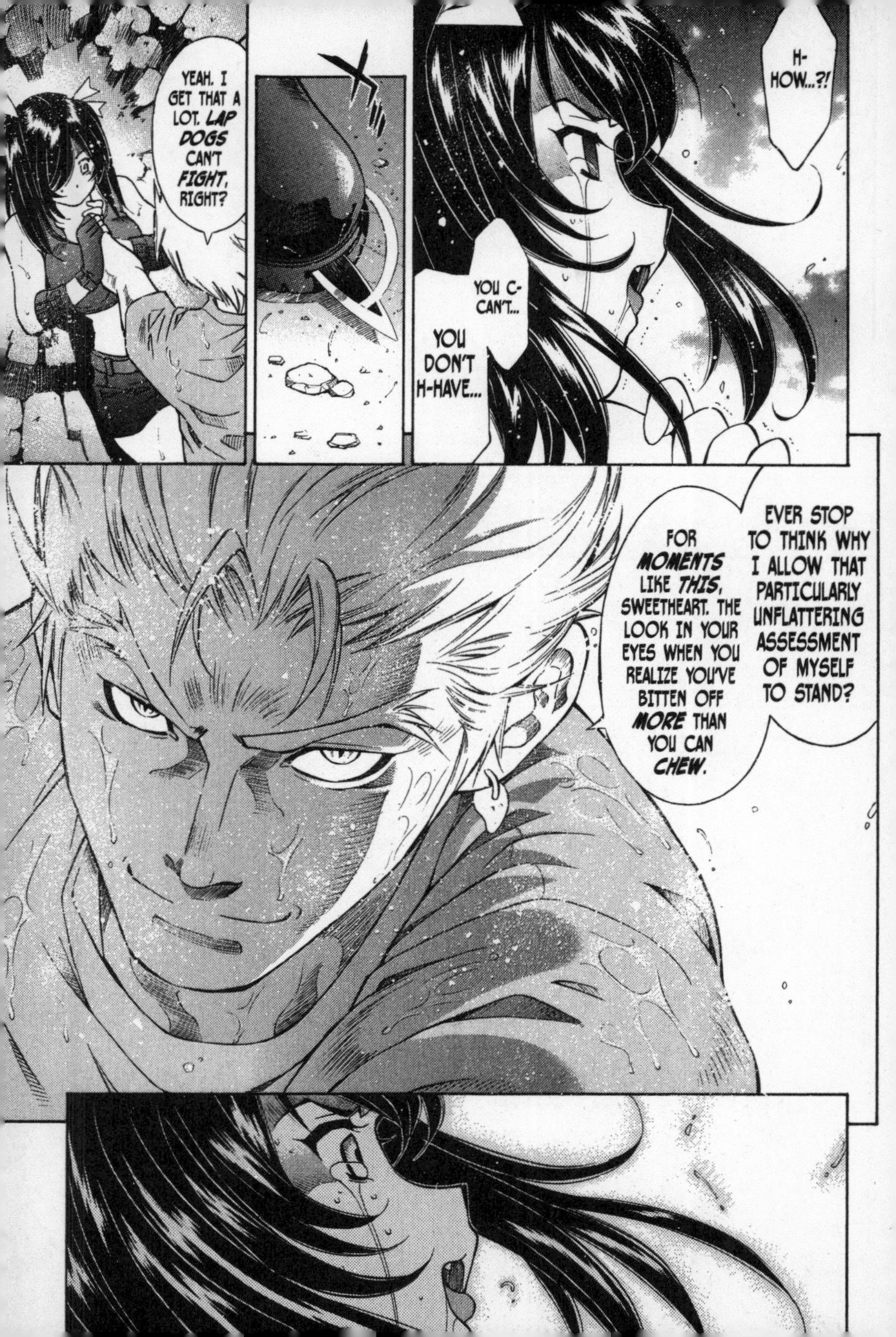
H-HOW...?!
YOU C-CAN'T...
YOU DON'T H-HAVE...
YEAH. I GET THAT A LOT. LAP DOGS CAN'T FIGHT, RIGHT?
EVER STOP TO THINK WHY I ALLOW THAT PARTICULARLY UNFLATTERING ASSESSMENT OF MYSELF TO STAND?
FOR MOMENTS LIKE THIS, SWEETHEART. THE LOOK IN YOUR EYES WHEN YOU REALIZE YOU'VE BITTEN OFF MORE THAN YOU CAN CHEW.

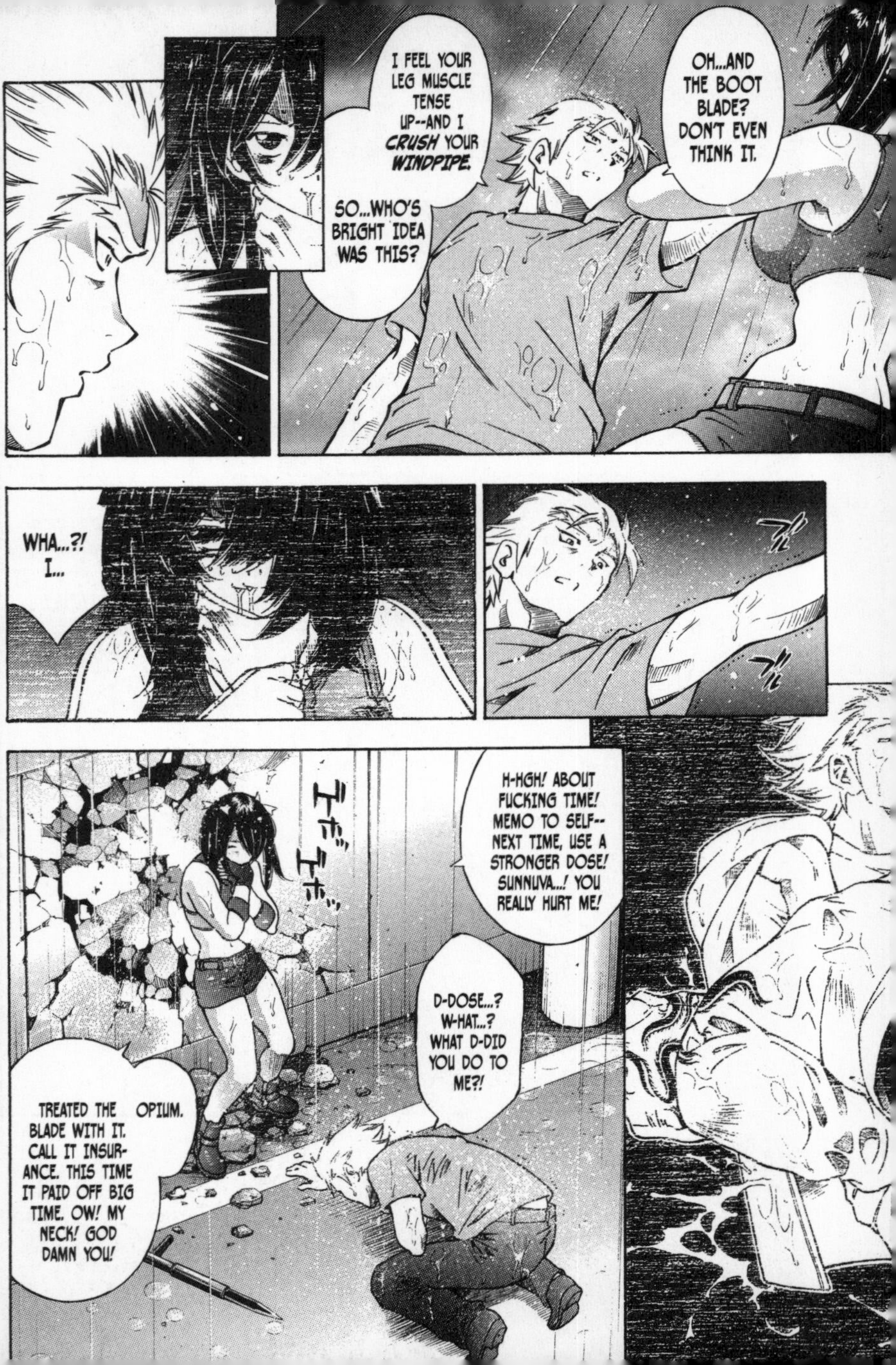

OH...AND THE BOOT BLADE? DON'T EVEN THINK IT.
I FEEL YOUR LEG MUSCLE TENSE UP--AND I *CRUSH* YOUR *WINDPIPE.*
SO...WHO'S BRIGHT IDEA WAS THIS?
WHA...?! I...
H-HGH! ABOUT FUCKING TIME! MEMO TO SELF--NEXT TIME, USE A STRONGER DOSE! SUNNUVA...! YOU REALLY HURT ME!
D-DOSE...? W-HAT...? WHAT D-DID YOU DO TO ME?!
OPIUM.
TREATED THE BLADE WITH IT. CALL IT INSURANCE. THIS TIME IT PAID OFF BIG TIME. OW! MY NECK! GOD DAMN YOU!

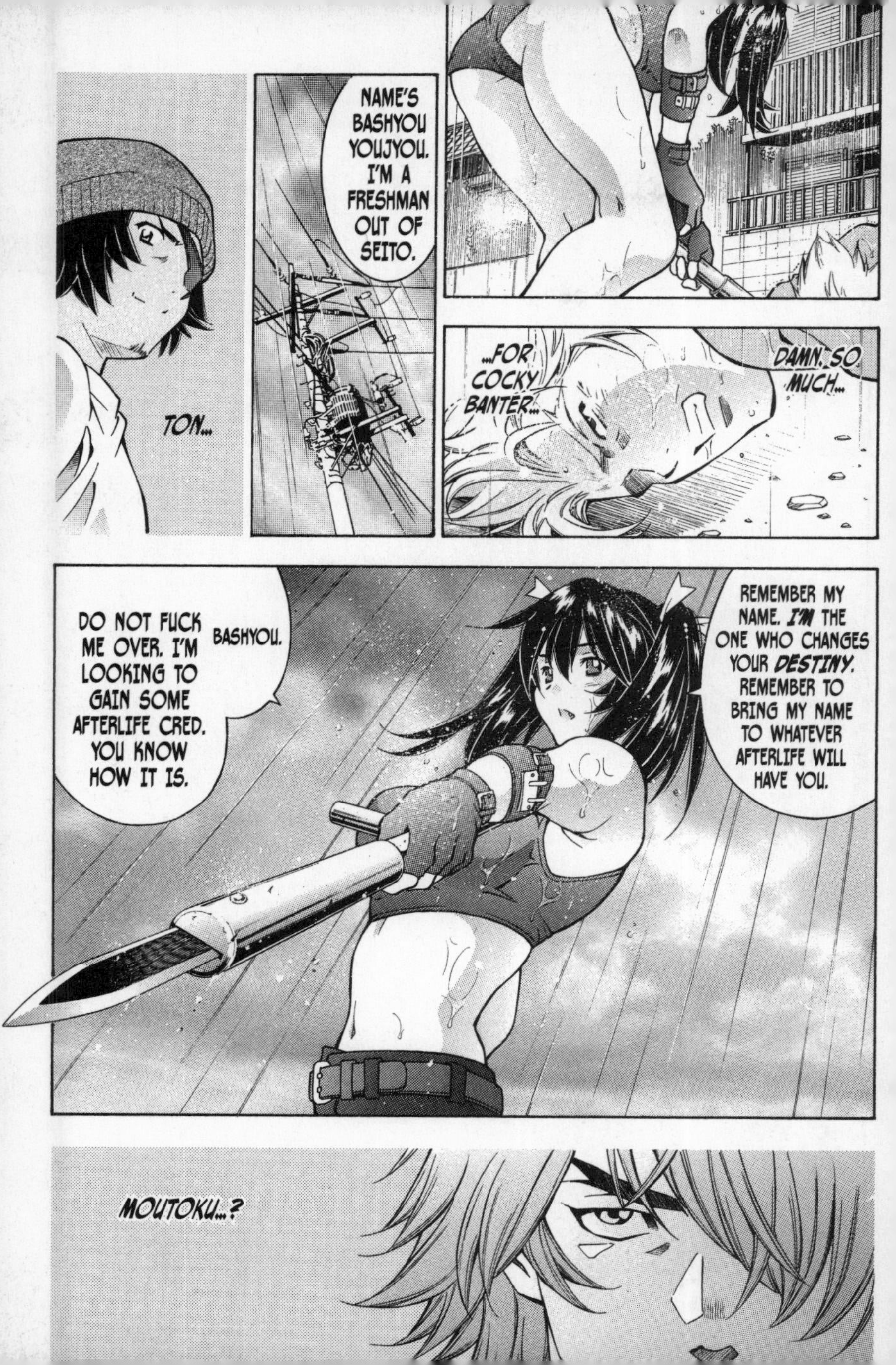
DAMN. SO MUCH...
...FOR COCKY BANTER...
NAME'S BASHYOU YOUJYOU. I'M A FRESHMAN OUT OF SEITO.
TON...
REMEMBER MY NAME. *I'M* THE ONE WHO CHANGES YOUR *DESTINY*. REMEMBER TO BRING MY NAME TO WHATEVER AFTERLIFE WILL HAVE YOU.
BASHYOU.
DO NOT FUCK ME OVER. I'M LOOKING TO GAIN SOME AFTERLIFE CRED. YOU KNOW HOW IT IS.
MOUTOKU...?

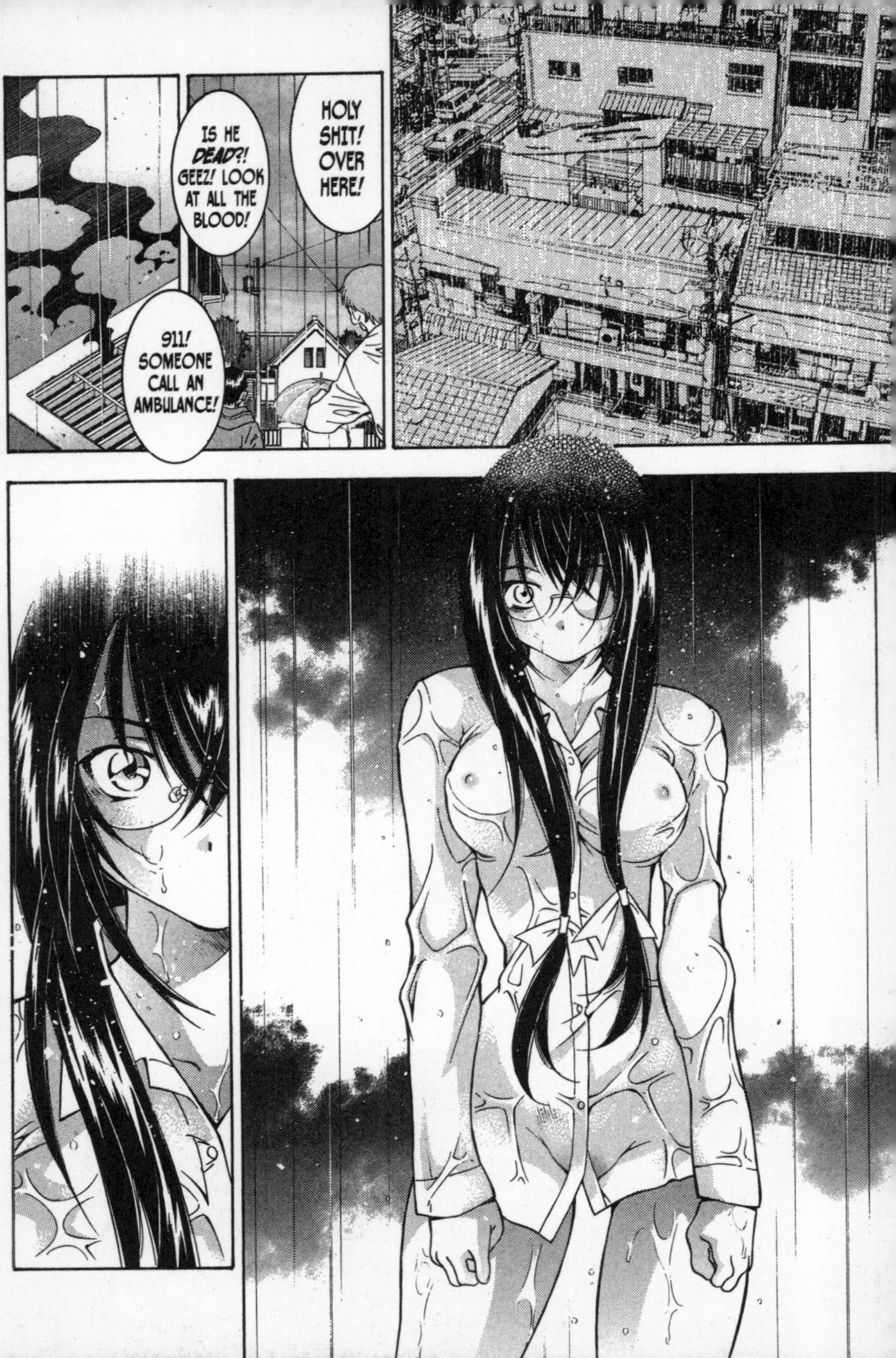
HOLY SHIT! OVER HERE!
IS HE DEAD?! GEEZ! LOOK AT ALL THE BLOOD!
911! SOMEONE CALL AN AMBULANCE!

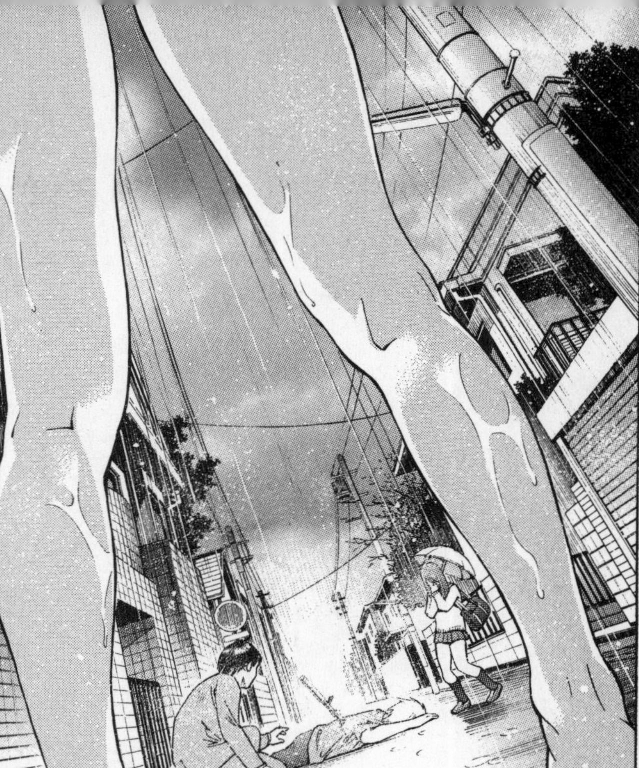
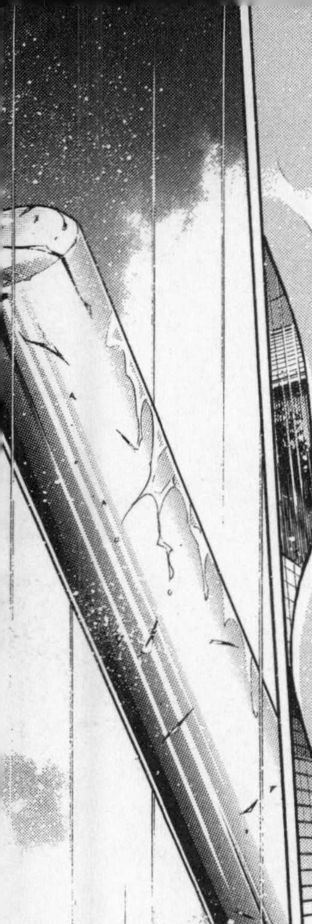
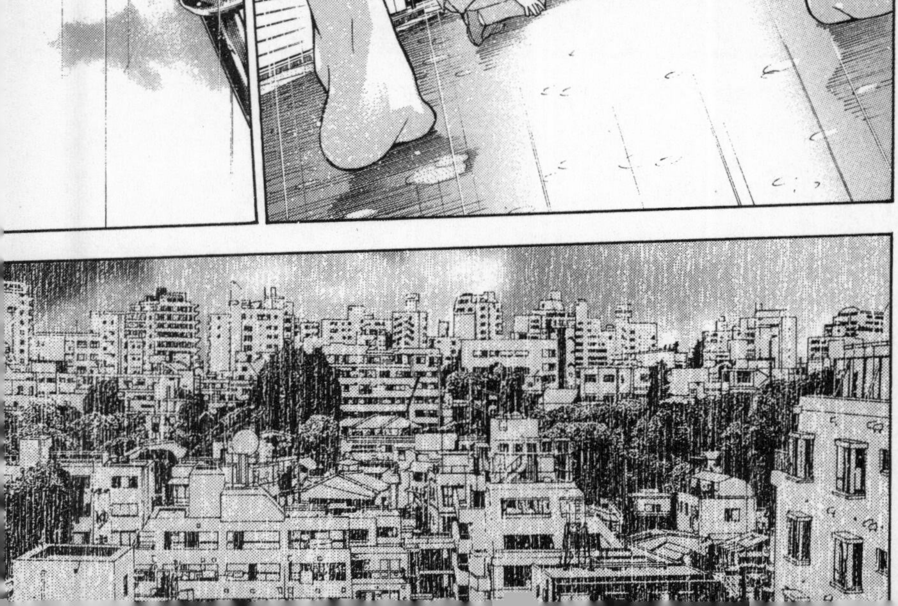

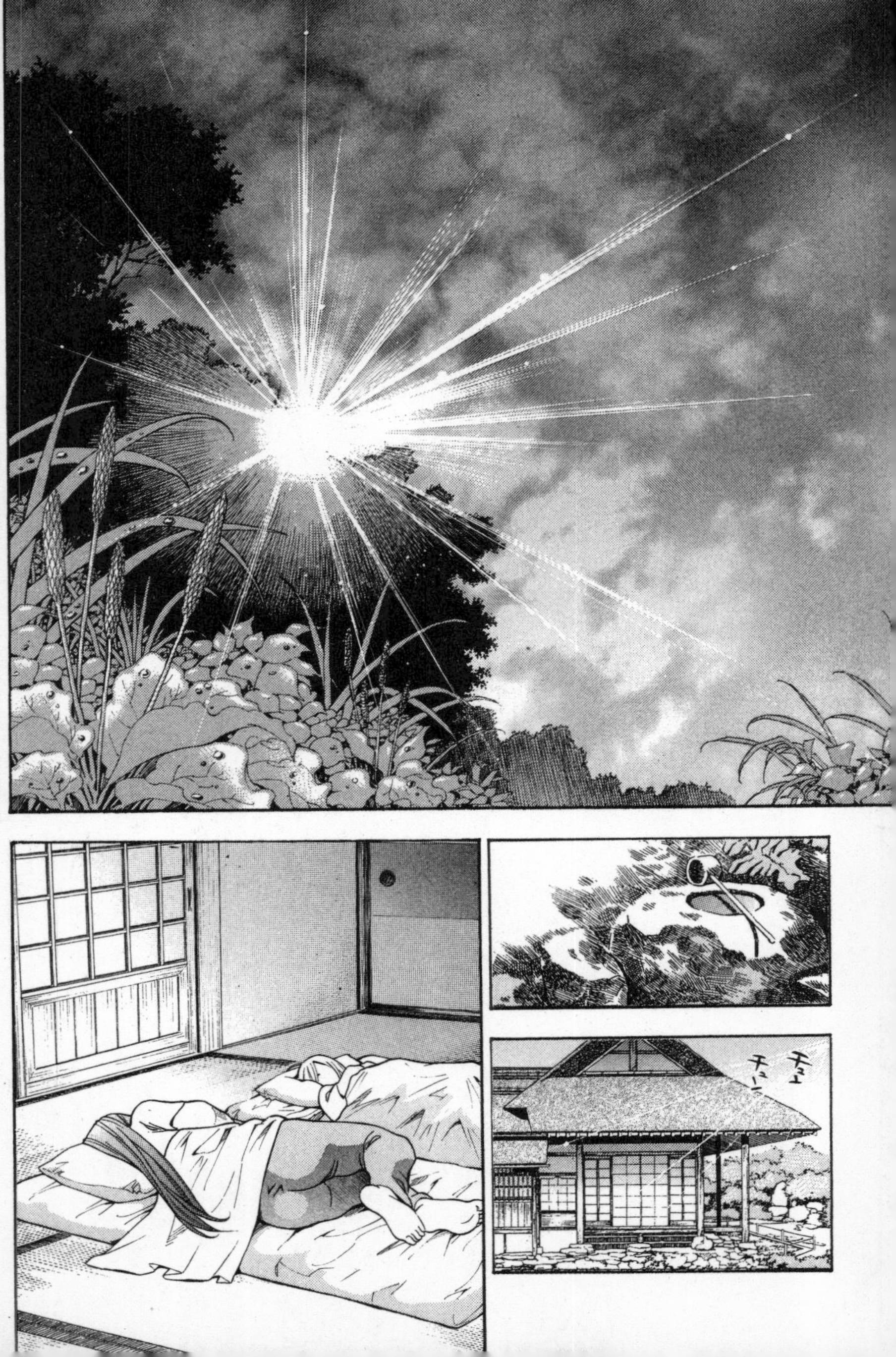
チュュ
チュ－ン

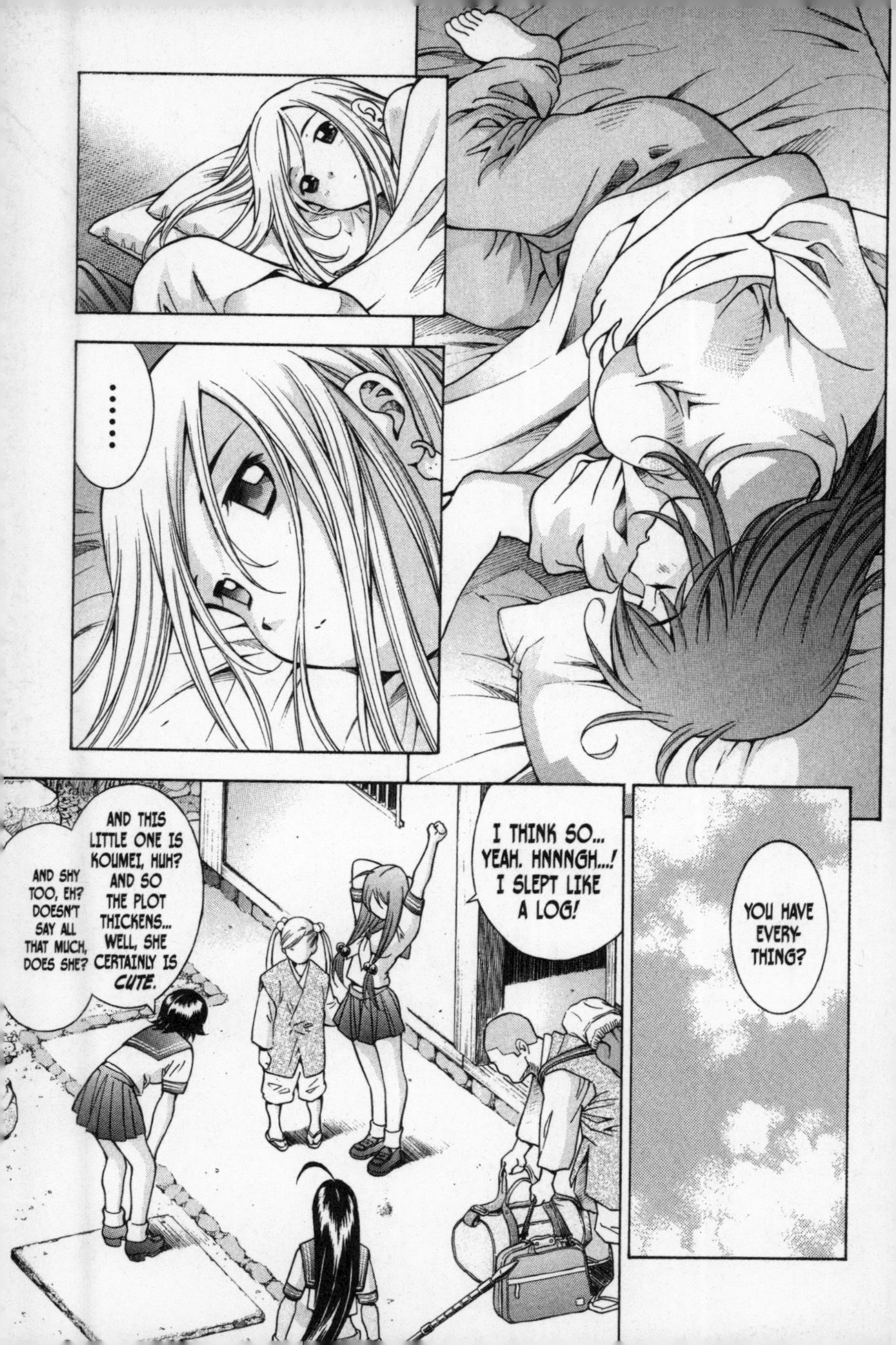
......
YOU HAVE EVERYTHING?
I THINK SO... YEAH. HNNNGH...! I SLEPT LIKE A LOG!
AND THIS LITTLE ONE IS KOUMEI, HUH? AND SO THE PLOT THICKENS... WELL, SHE CERTAINLY IS *CUTE*.
AND SHY TOO, EH? DOESN'T SAY ALL THAT MUCH, DOES SHE?

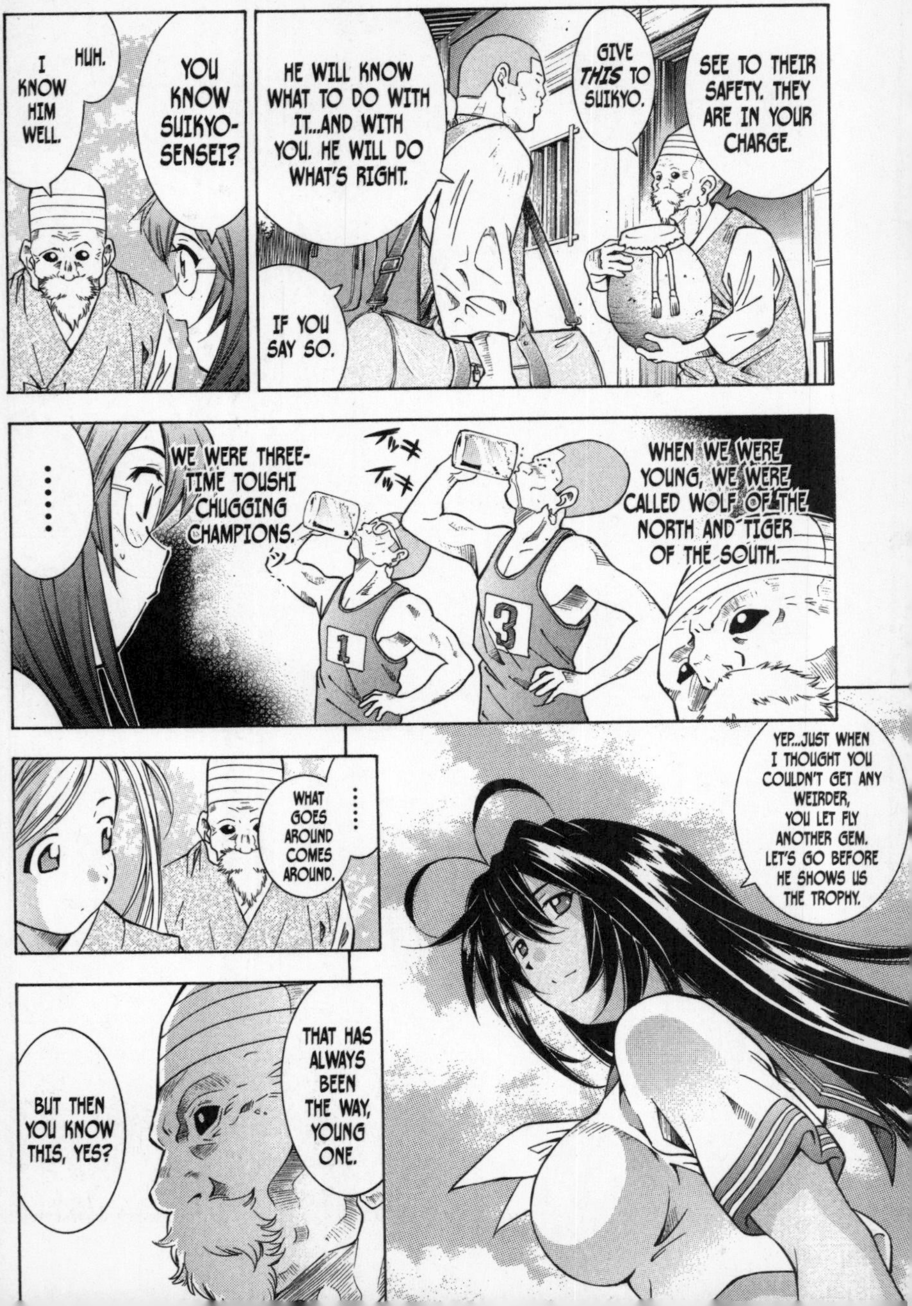
SEE TO THEIR SAFETY. THEY ARE IN YOUR CHARGE.
GIVE THIS TO SUIKYO.
HE WILL KNOW WHAT TO DO WITH IT...AND WITH YOU. HE WILL DO WHAT'S RIGHT.
IF YOU SAY SO.
YOU KNOW SUIKYO-SENSEI?
HUH.
I KNOW HIM WELL.
WHEN WE WERE YOUNG, WE WERE CALLED WOLF OF THE NORTH AND TIGER OF THE SOUTH.
WE WERE THREE-TIME TOUSHI CHUGGING CHAMPIONS.
......
YEP...JUST WHEN I THOUGHT YOU COULDN'T GET ANY WEIRDER, YOU LET FLY ANOTHER GEM. LET'S GO BEFORE HE SHOWS US THE TROPHY.
......
WHAT GOES AROUND COMES AROUND.
THAT HAS ALWAYS BEEN THE WAY, YOUNG ONE.
BUT THEN YOU KNOW THIS, YES?

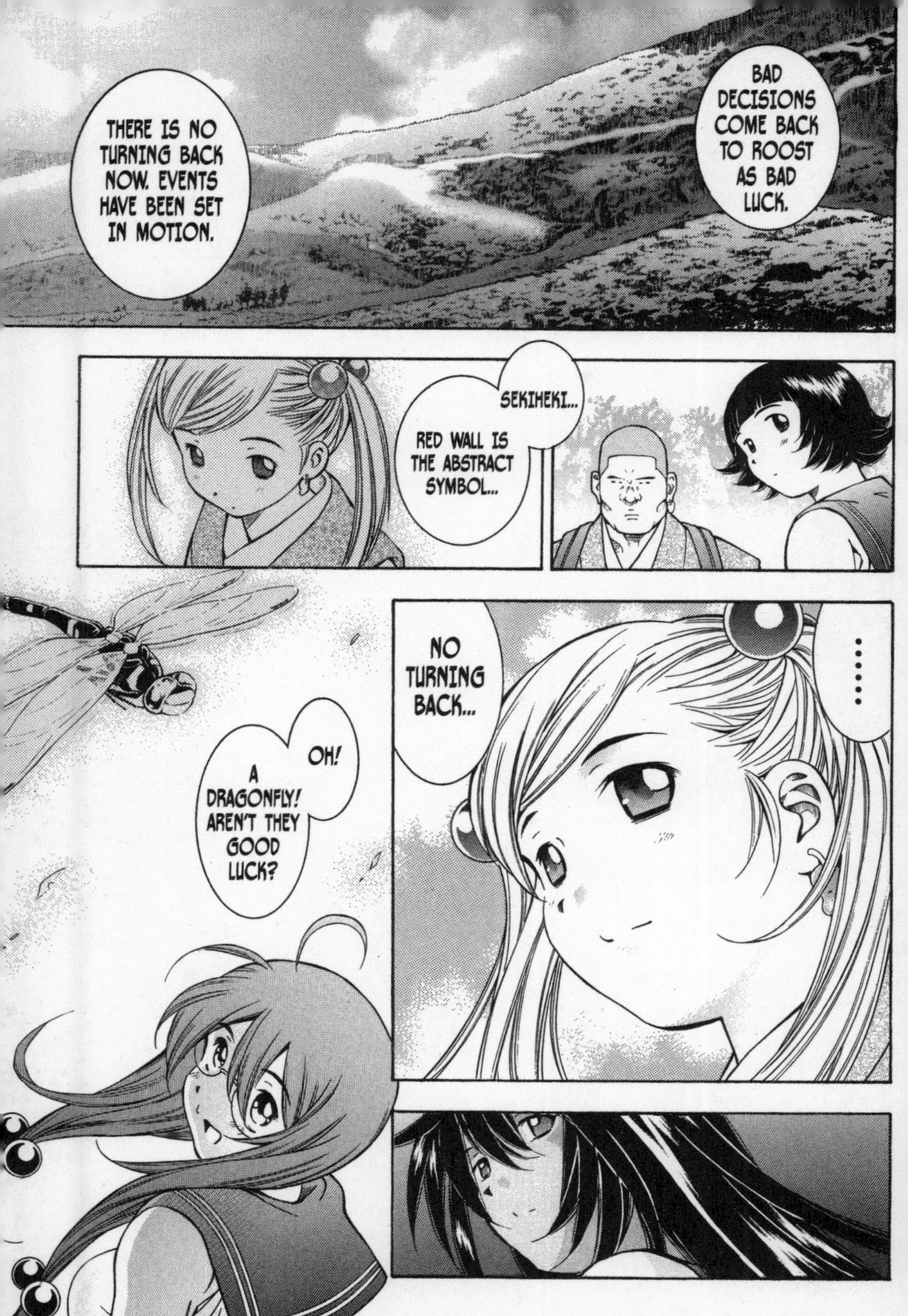
BAD DECISIONS COME BACK TO ROOST AS BAD LUCK.
THERE IS NO TURNING BACK NOW. EVENTS HAVE BEEN SET IN MOTION.
SEKIHEKI...
RED WALL IS THE ABSTRACT SYMBOL...
......
NO TURNING BACK...
OH!
A DRAGONFLY! AREN'T THEY GOOD LUCK?

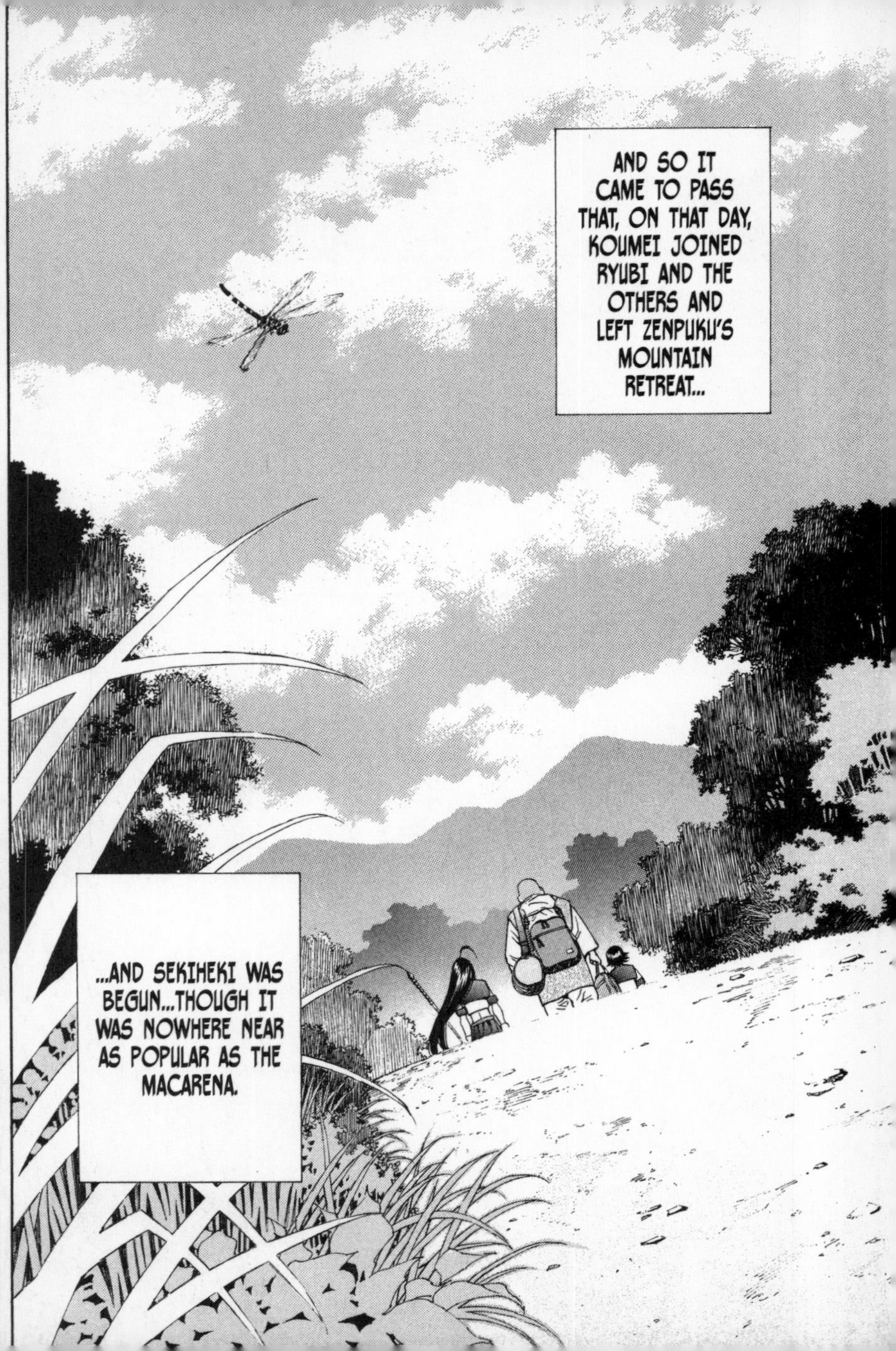
AND SO IT CAME TO PASS THAT, ON THAT DAY, KOUMEI JOINED RYUBI AND THE OTHERS AND LEFT ZENPUKU'S MOUNTAIN RETREAT...
...AND SEKIHEKI WAS BEGUN...THOUGH IT WAS NOWHERE NEAR AS POPULAR AS THE MACARENA.

051

ORDER

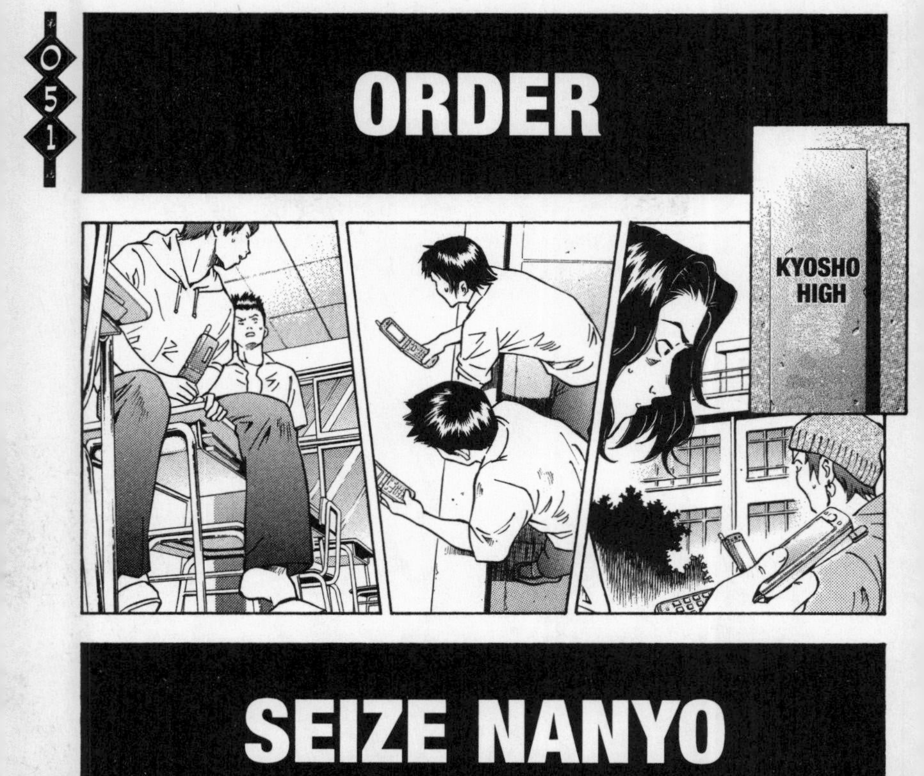
KYOSHO HIGH

SEIZE NANYO

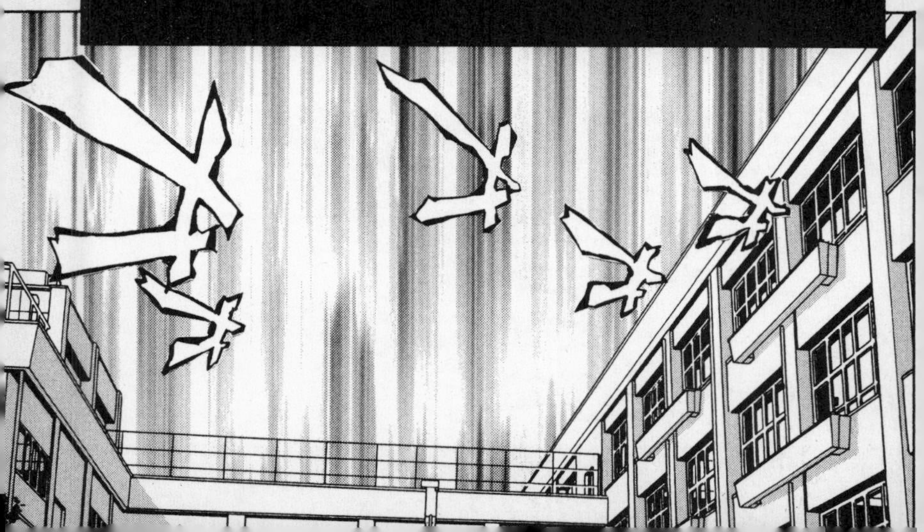

第051話

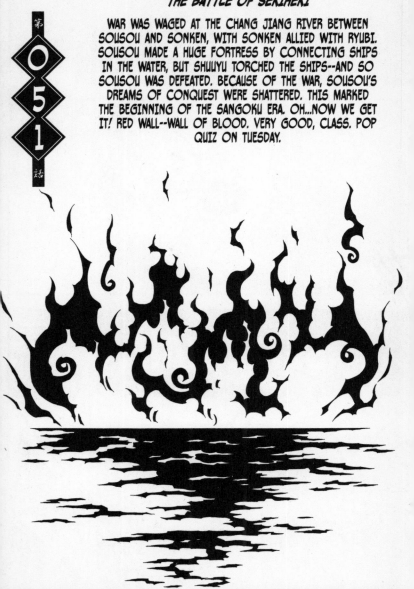

THE BATTLE OF SEKIHEKI

WAR WAS WAGED AT THE CHANG JIANG RIVER BETWEEN SOUSOU AND SONKEN, WITH SONKEN ALLIED WITH RYUBI. SOUSOU MADE A HUGE FORTRESS BY CONNECTING SHIPS IN THE WATER, BUT SHUUYU TORCHED THE SHIPS--AND SO SOUSOU WAS DEFEATED. BECAUSE OF THE WAR, SOUSOU'S DREAMS OF CONQUEST WERE SHATTERED. THIS MARKED THE BEGINNING OF THE SANGOKU ERA. OH...NOW WE GET IT! RED WALL--WALL OF BLOOD. VERY GOOD, CLASS. POP QUIZ ON TUESDAY.

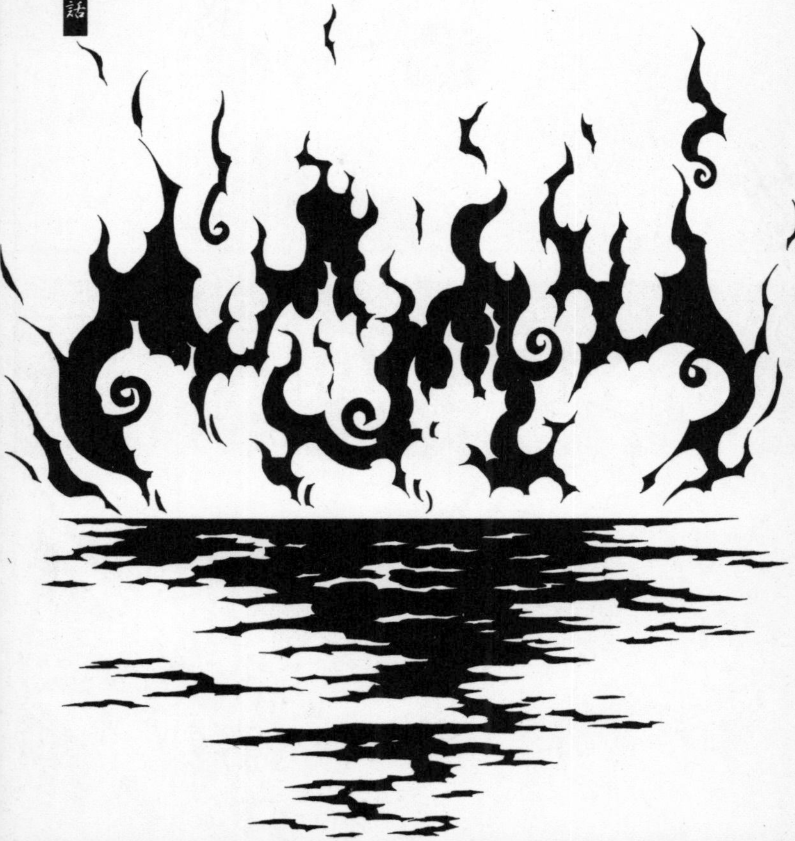

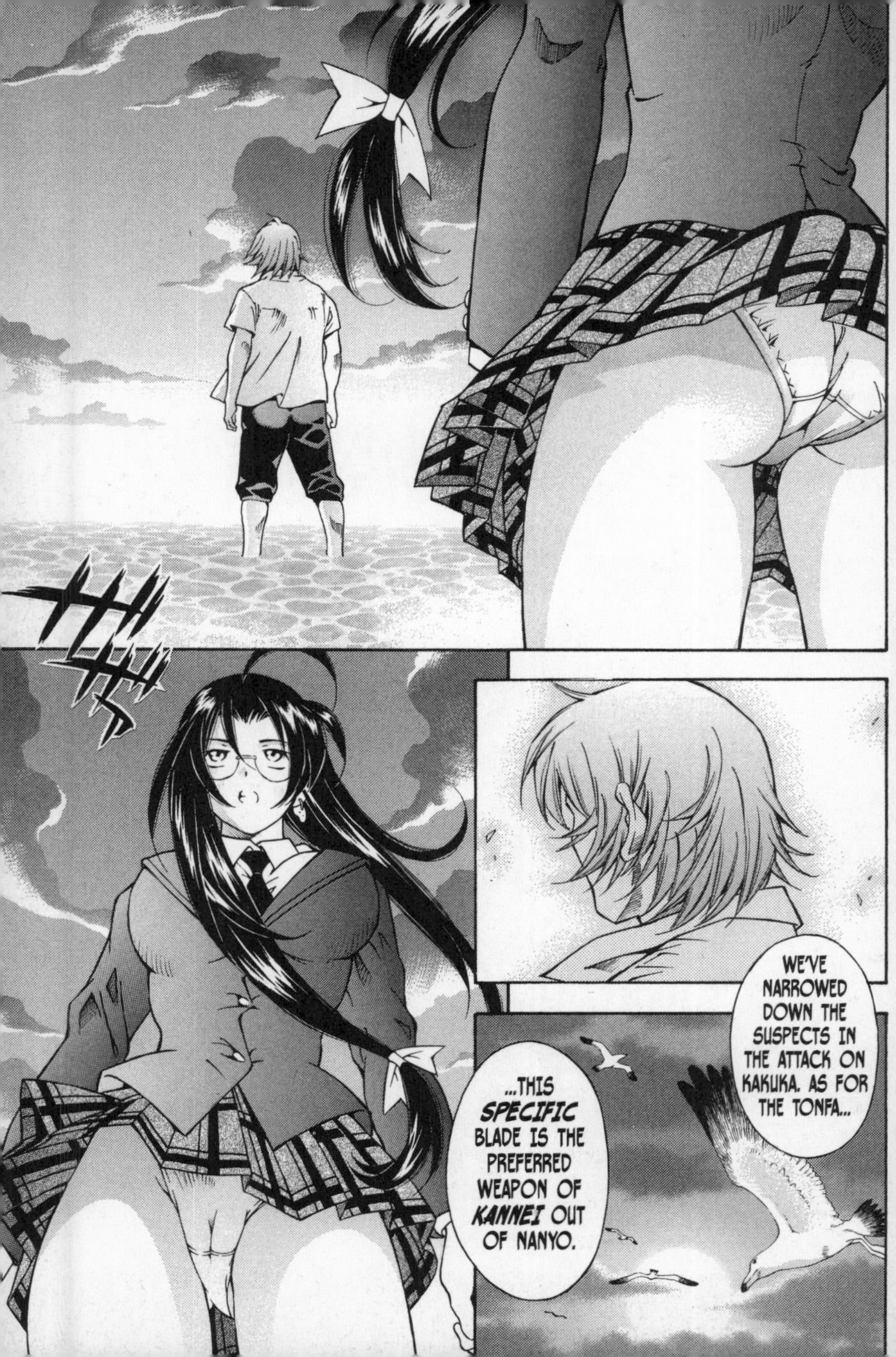
WE'VE NARROWED DOWN THE SUSPECTS IN THE ATTACK ON KAKUKA. AS FOR THE TONFA...
...THIS *SPECIFIC* BLADE IS THE PREFERRED WEAPON OF *KANNEI* OUT OF NANYO.

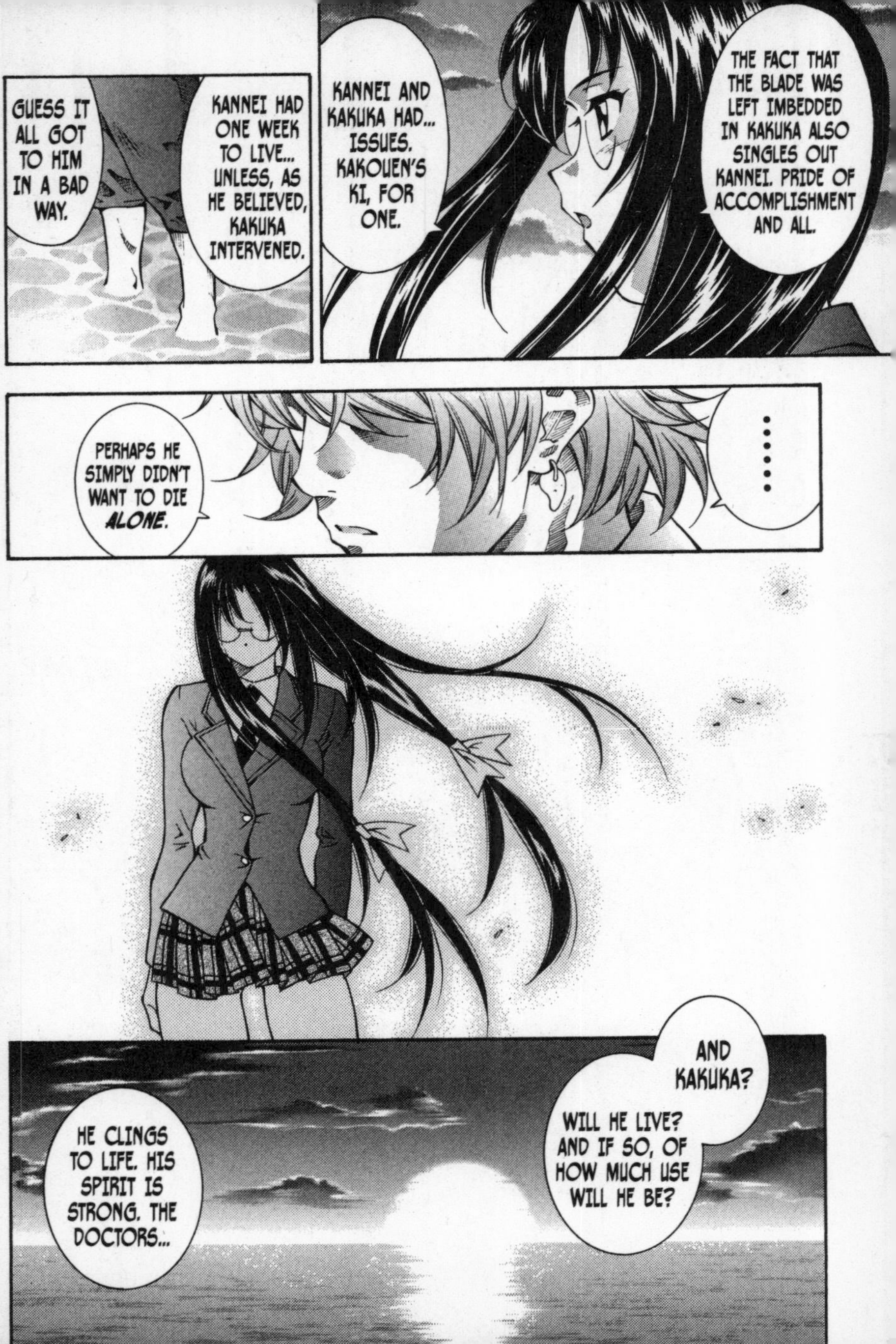
THE FACT THAT THE BLADE WAS LEFT IMBEDDED IN KAKUKA ALSO SINGLES OUT KANNEI. PRIDE OF ACCOMPLISHMENT AND ALL.
KANNEI AND KAKUKA HAD... ISSUES. KAKOUEN'S KI, FOR ONE.
KANNEI HAD ONE WEEK TO LIVE... UNLESS, AS HE BELIEVED, KAKUKA INTERVENED.
GUESS IT ALL GOT TO HIM IN A BAD WAY.
......
PERHAPS HE SIMPLY DIDN'T WANT TO DIE *ALONE*.
AND KAKUKA?
WILL HE LIVE? AND IF SO, OF HOW MUCH USE WILL HE BE?
HE CLINGS TO LIFE. HIS SPIRIT IS STRONG. THE DOCTORS...

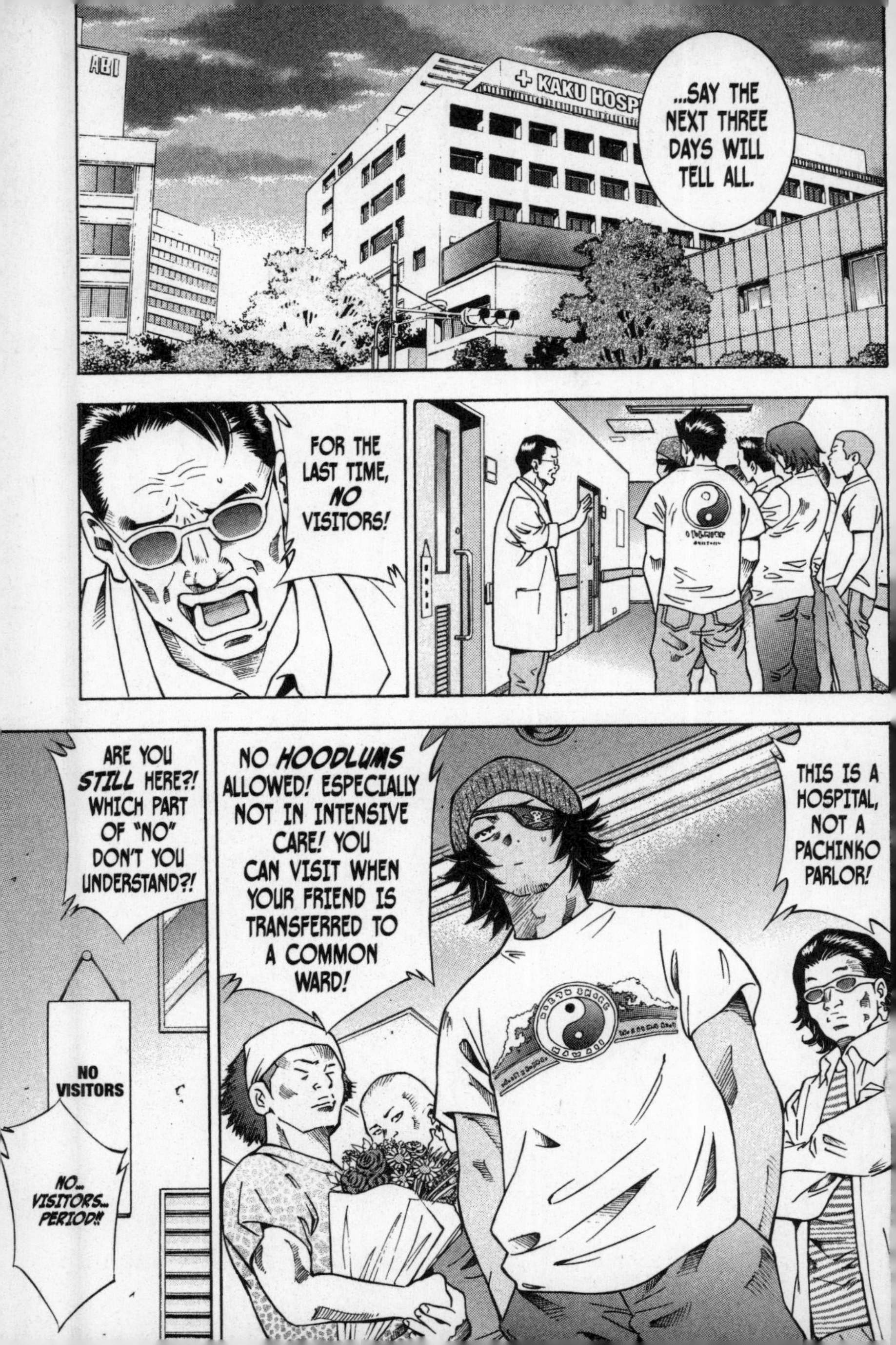
...SAY THE NEXT THREE DAYS WILL TELL ALL.
FOR THE LAST TIME, *NO* VISITORS!
THIS IS A HOSPITAL, NOT A PACHINKO PARLOR!
NO ***HOODLUMS*** ALLOWED! ESPECIALLY NOT IN INTENSIVE CARE! YOU CAN VISIT WHEN YOUR FRIEND IS TRANSFERRED TO A COMMON WARD!
ARE YOU ***STILL*** HERE?! WHICH PART OF "NO" DON'T YOU UNDERSTAND?!
NO VISITORS
NO... VISITORS... PERIOD!!

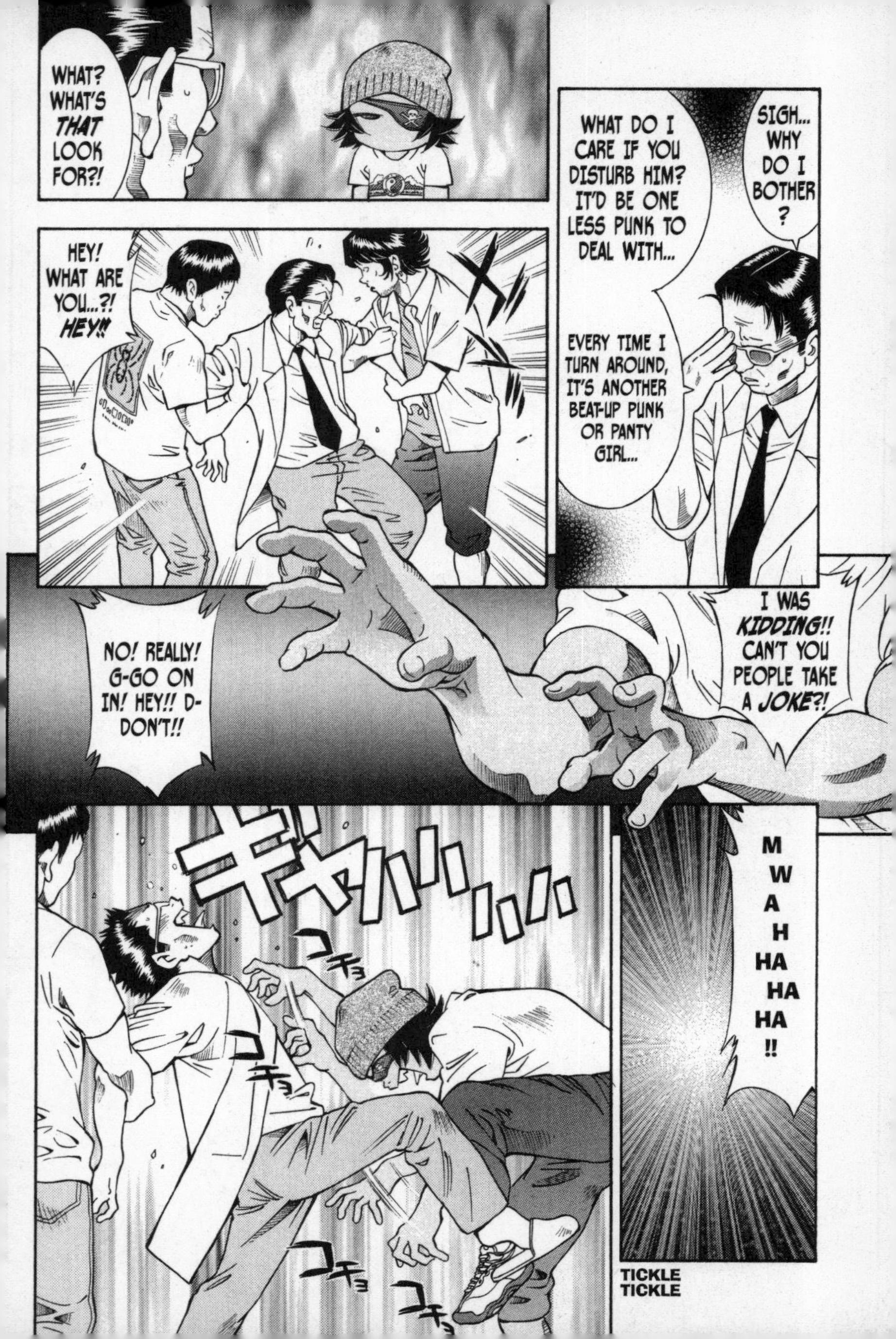
SIGH... WHY DO I BOTHER?
WHAT DO I CARE IF YOU DISTURB HIM? IT'D BE ONE LESS PUNK TO DEAL WITH...
EVERY TIME I TURN AROUND, IT'S ANOTHER BEAT-UP PUNK OR PANTY GIRL...
WHAT? WHAT'S *THAT* LOOK FOR?!
HEY! WHAT ARE YOU...?! ***HEY!!***
I WAS ***KIDDING!!*** CAN'T YOU PEOPLE TAKE A ***JOKE?!***
NO! REALLY! G-GO ON IN! HEY!! D-DON'T!!
MWAHAHAHAHA!!
TICKLE TICKLE
ギャハハハ
コチョ
コチョ
コチョ
コチョ

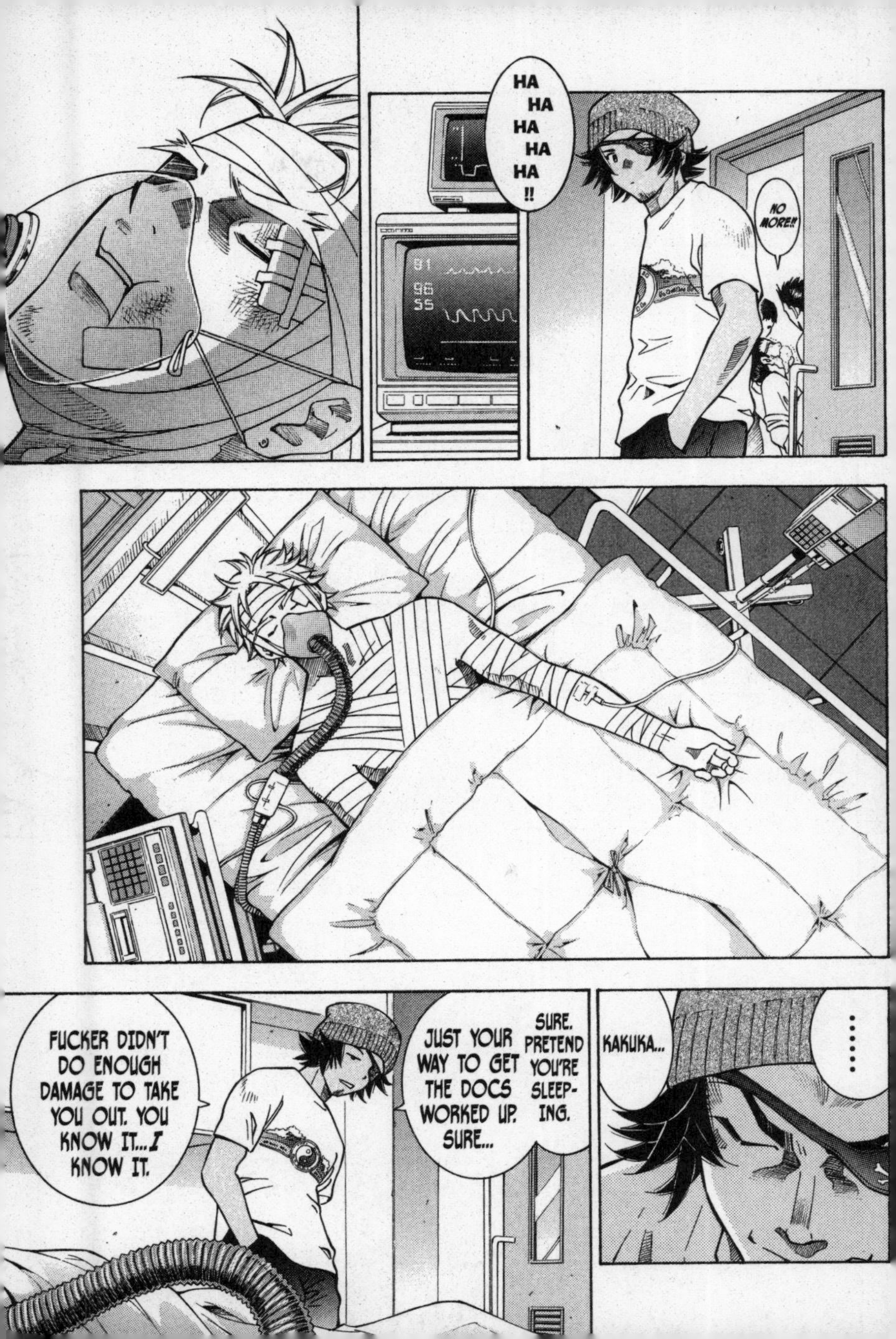
NO MORE!!
HA HA HA HA HA !!
......
KAKUKA...
SURE. PRETEND YOU'RE SLEEP-ING.
JUST YOUR WAY TO GET THE DOCS WORKED UP. SURE...
FUCKER DIDN'T DO ENOUGH DAMAGE TO TAKE YOU OUT. YOU KNOW IT...I KNOW IT.

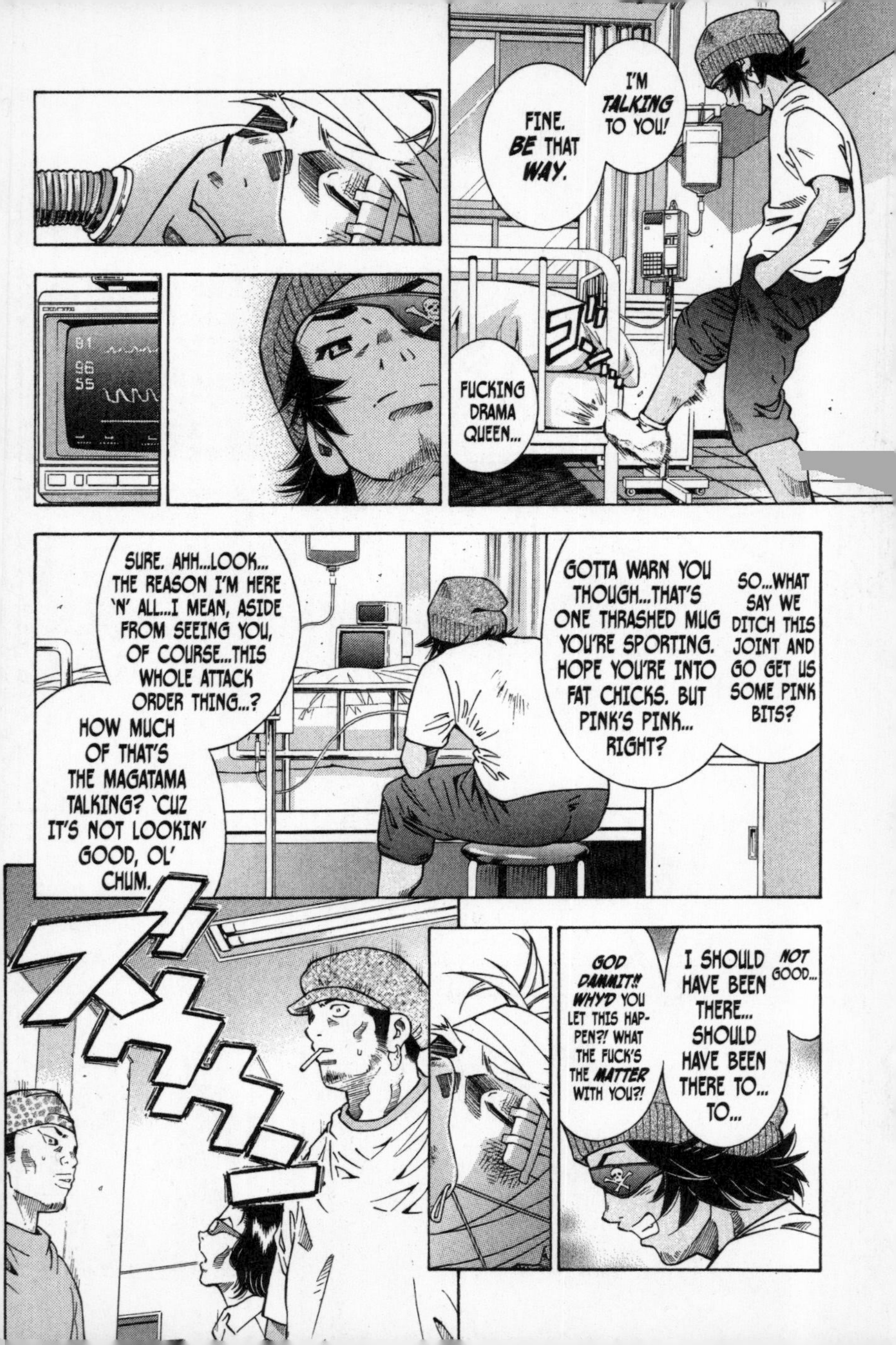
I'M TALKING TO YOU!
FINE. BE THAT WAY.
FUCKING DRAMA QUEEN...
SO...WHAT SAY WE DITCH THIS JOINT AND GO GET US SOME PINK BITS?
GOTTA WARN YOU THOUGH...THAT'S ONE THRASHED MUG YOU'RE SPORTING. HOPE YOU'RE INTO FAT CHICKS. BUT PINK'S PINK... RIGHT?
SURE. AHH...LOOK... THE REASON I'M HERE 'N' ALL...I MEAN, ASIDE FROM SEEING YOU, OF COURSE...THIS WHOLE ATTACK ORDER THING...?
HOW MUCH OF THAT'S THE MAGATAMA TALKING? 'CUZ IT'S NOT LOOKIN' GOOD, OL' CHUM.
NOT GOOD...
I SHOULD HAVE BEEN THERE... SHOULD HAVE BEEN THERE TO... TO...
GOD DAMMIT!! WHY'D YOU LET THIS HAP-PEN?! WHAT THE FUCK'S THE MATTER WITH YOU?!

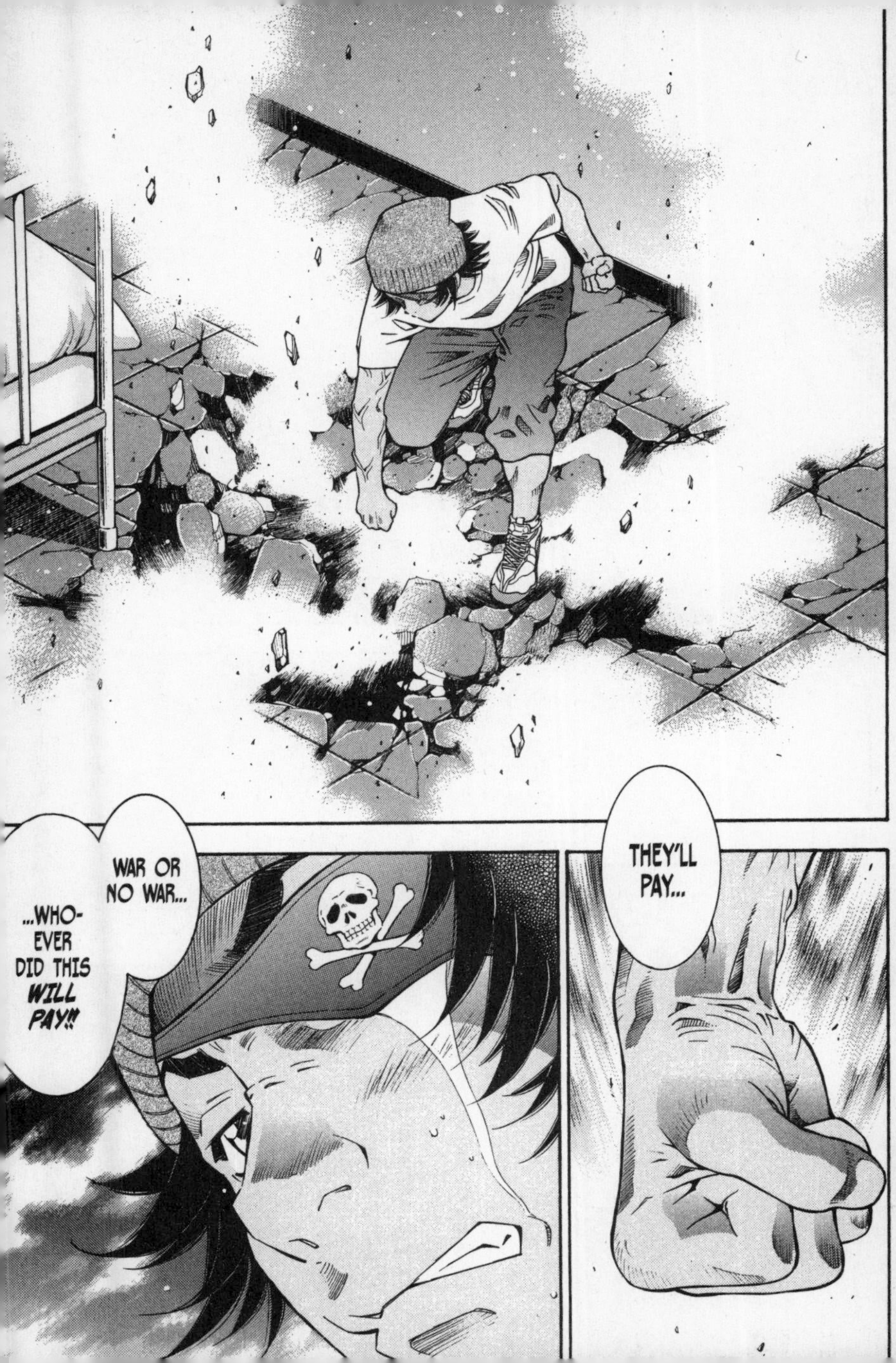
THEY'LL PAY...
WAR OR NO WAR...
...WHO-EVER DID THIS ***WILL PAY!!***

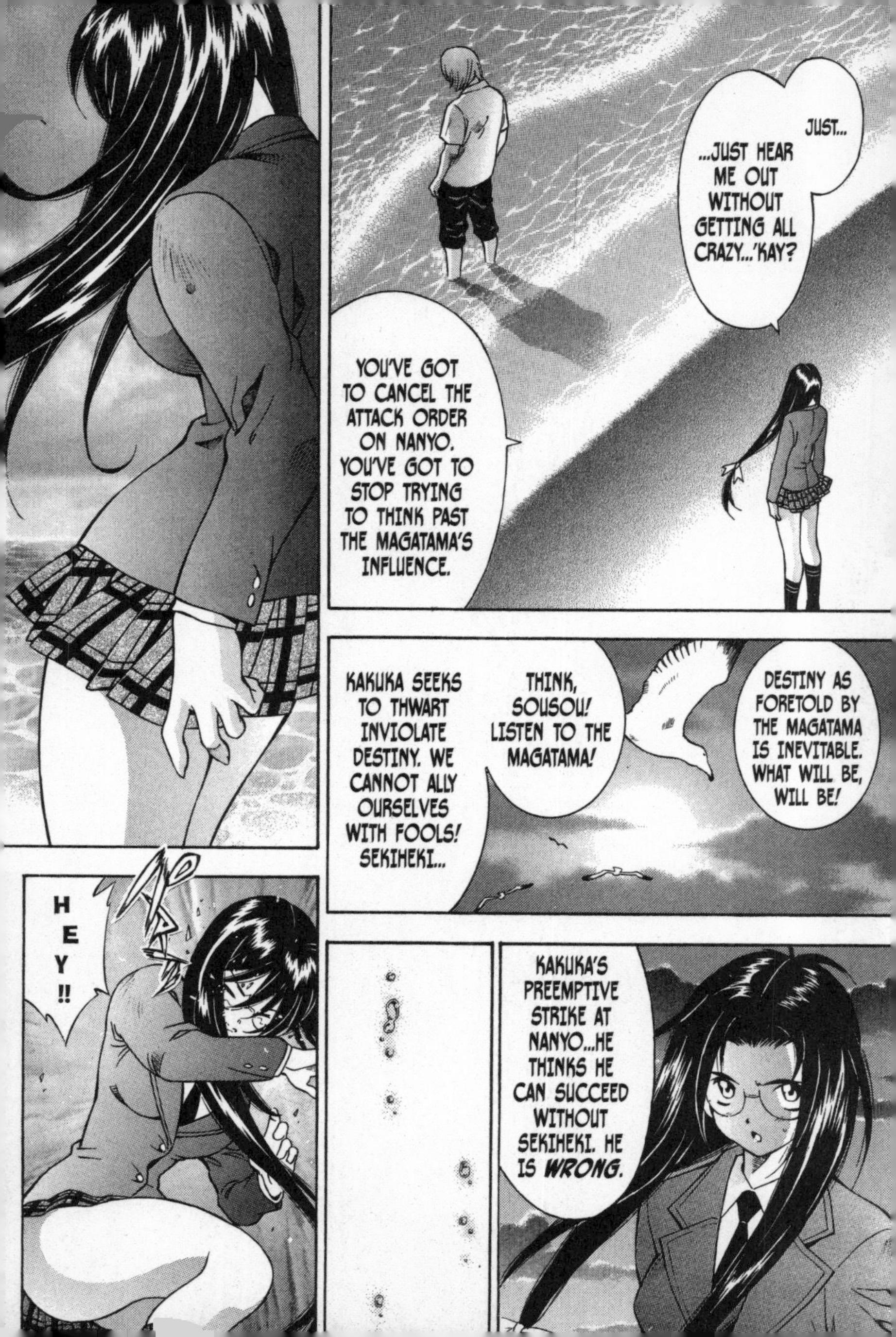
JUST... ...JUST HEAR ME OUT WITHOUT GETTING ALL CRAZY...'KAY?
YOU'VE GOT TO CANCEL THE ATTACK ORDER ON NANYO. YOU'VE GOT TO STOP TRYING TO THINK PAST THE MAGATAMA'S INFLUENCE.
DESTINY AS FORETOLD BY THE MAGATAMA IS INEVITABLE. WHAT WILL BE, WILL BE!
THINK, SOUSOU! LISTEN TO THE MAGATAMA!
KAKUKA SEEKS TO THWART INVIOLATE DESTINY. WE CANNOT ALLY OURSELVES WITH FOOLS! SEKIHEKI...
KAKUKA'S PREEMPTIVE STRIKE AT NANYO...HE THINKS HE CAN SUCCEED WITHOUT SEKIHEKI. HE IS ***WRONG***.
HEY!!

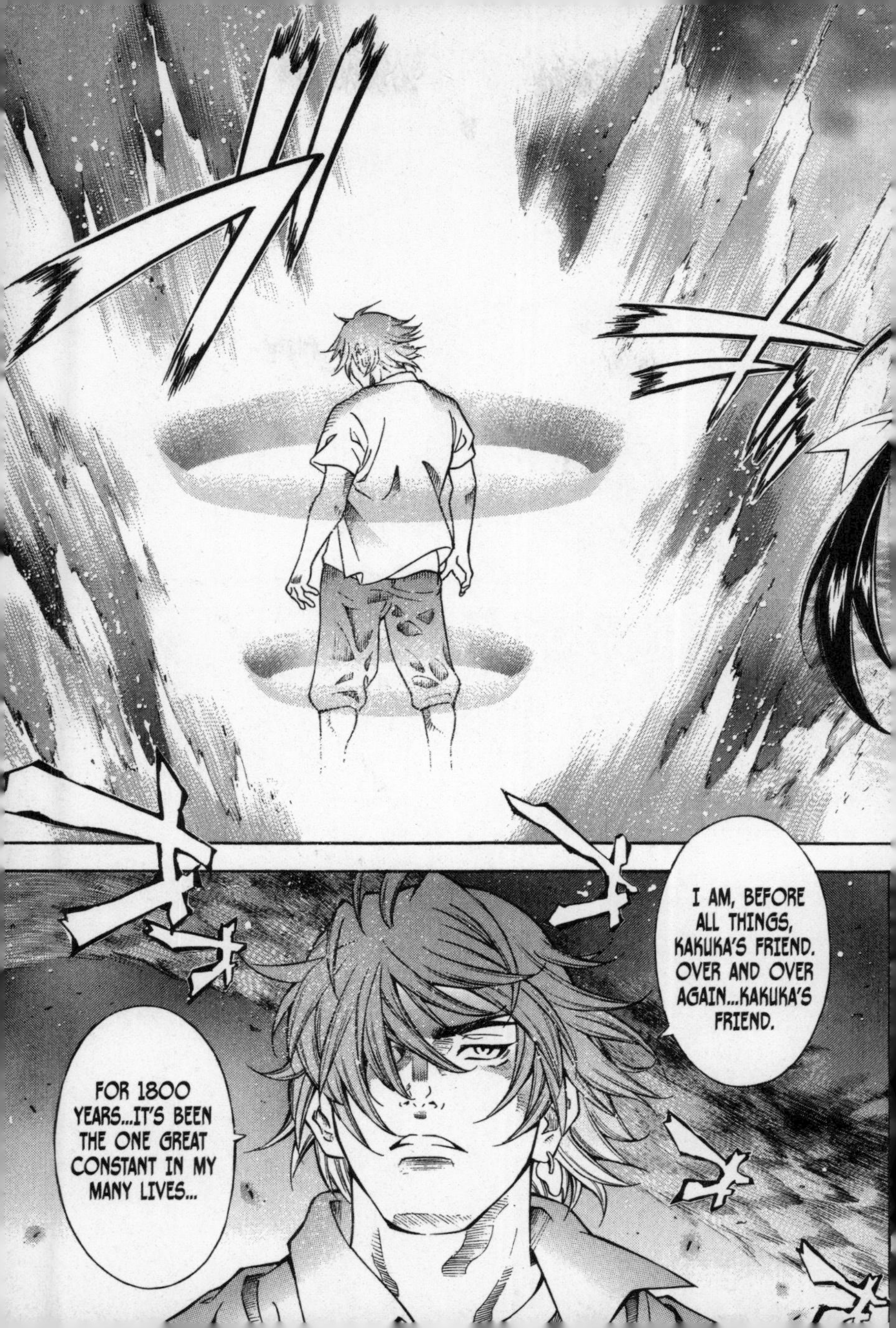
I AM, BEFORE ALL THINGS, KAKUKA'S FRIEND. OVER AND OVER AGAIN...KAKUKA'S FRIEND.
FOR 1800 YEARS...IT'S BEEN THE ONE GREAT CONSTANT IN MY MANY LIVES...

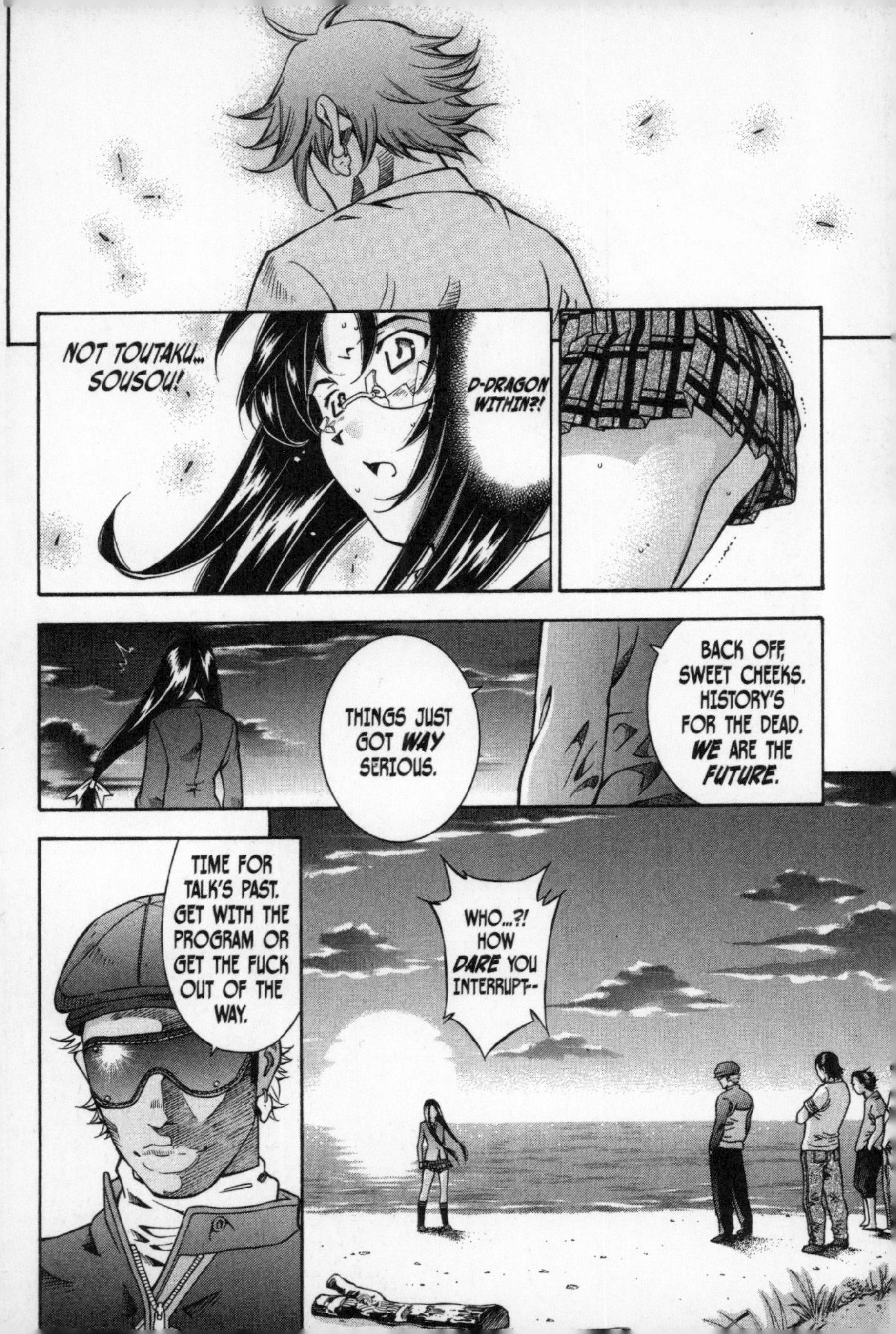
D-DRAGON WITHIN?!
NOT TOUTAKU... SOUSOU!
BACK OFF, SWEET CHEEKS. HISTORY'S FOR THE DEAD. WE ARE THE FUTURE.
THINGS JUST GOT WAY SERIOUS.
WHO...?! HOW DARE YOU INTERRUPT--
TIME FOR TALK'S PAST. GET WITH THE PROGRAM OR GET THE FUCK OUT OF THE WAY.

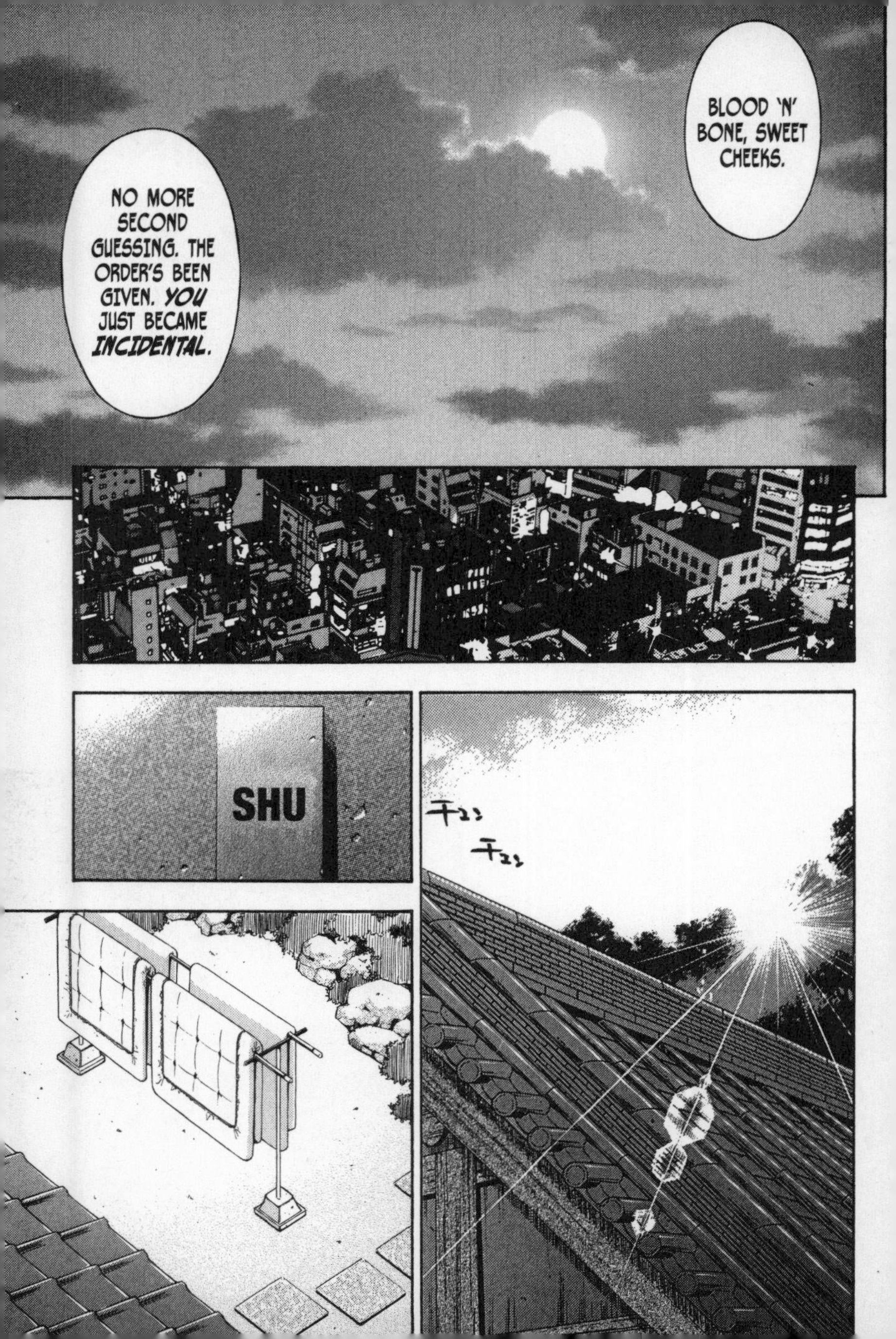
BLOOD 'N' BONE, SWEET CHEEKS.
NO MORE SECOND GUESSING. THE ORDER'S BEEN GIVEN. *YOU* JUST BECAME ***INCIDENTAL***.
SHU

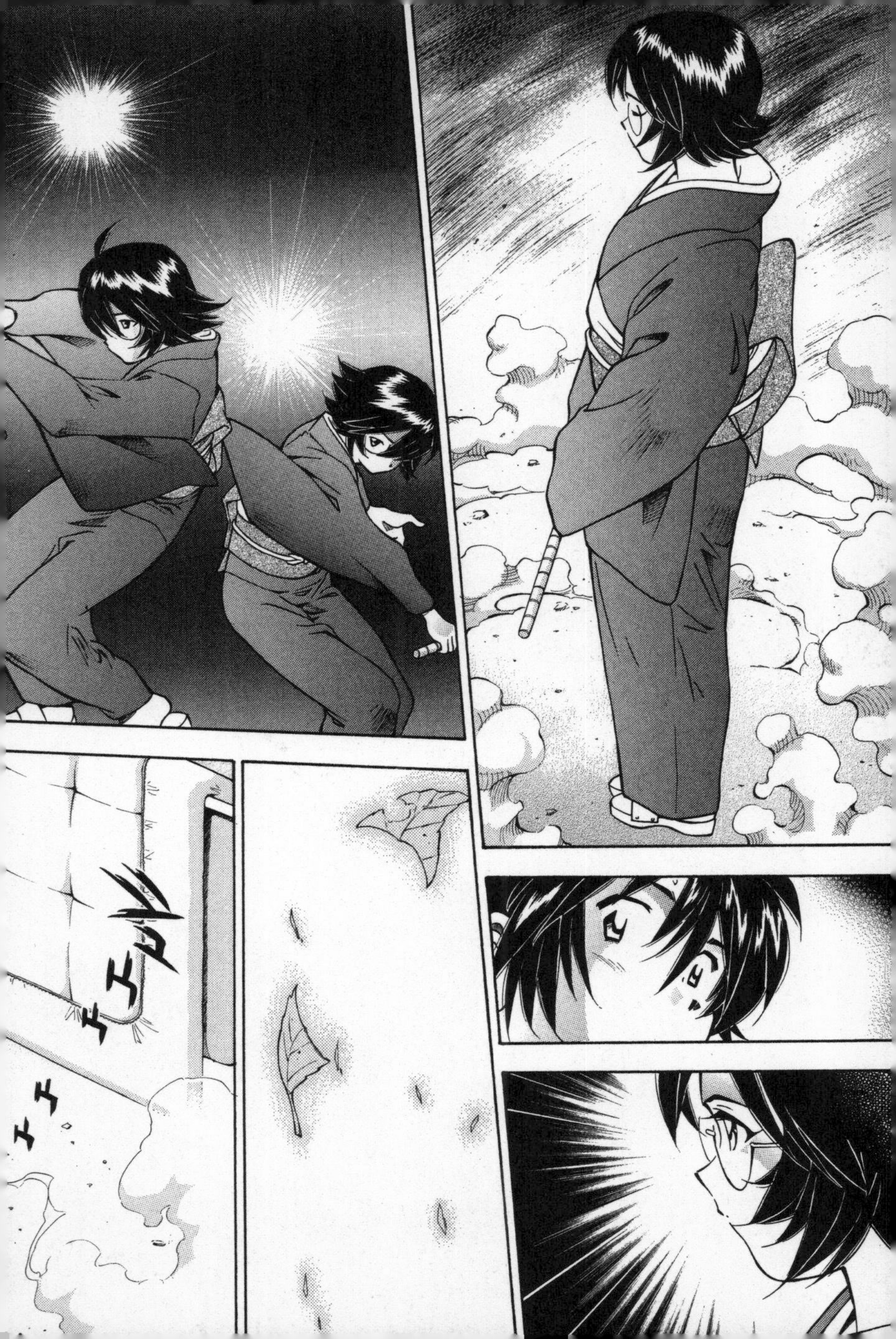

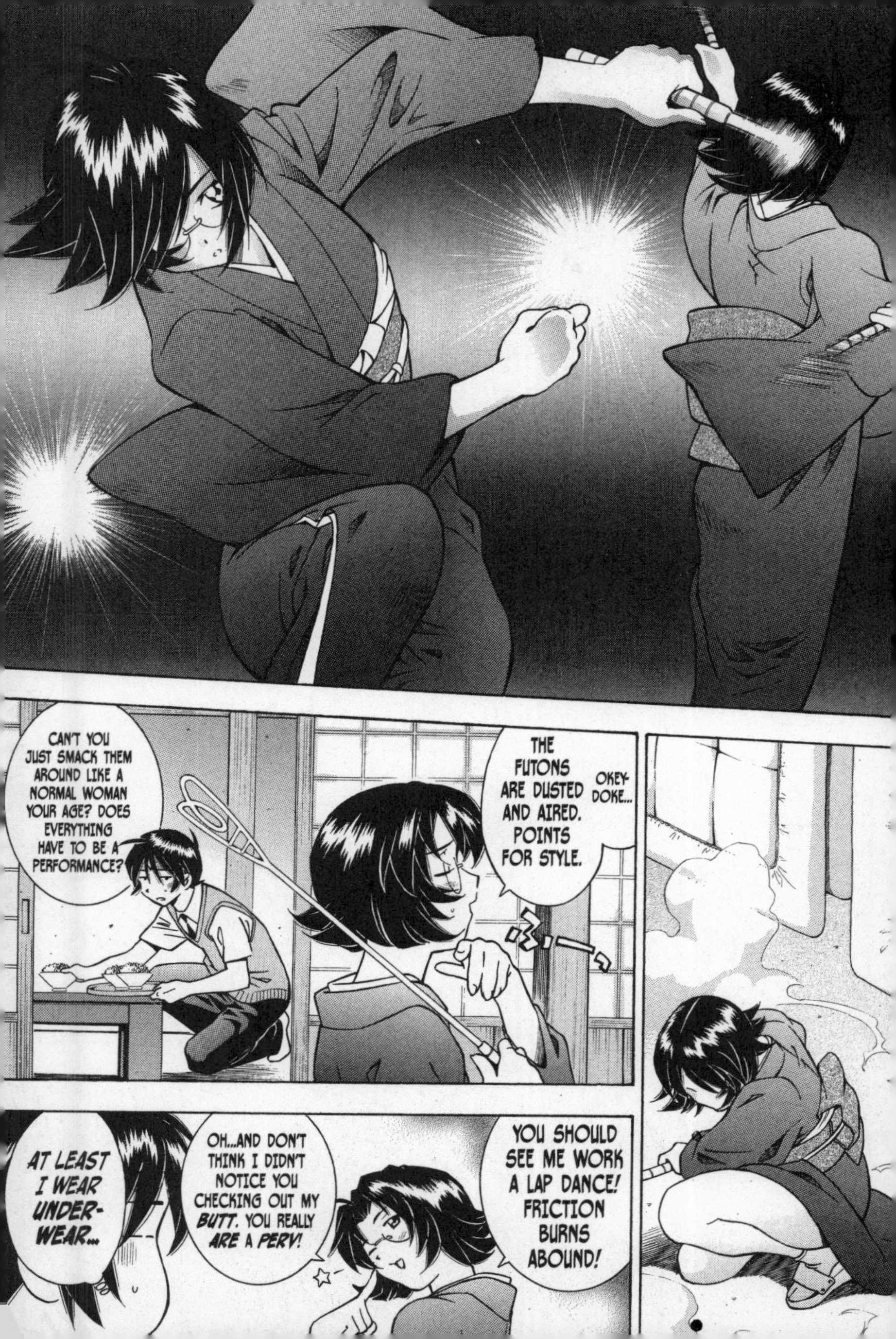
THE FUTONS ARE DUSTED AND AIRED. POINTS FOR STYLE.
OKEY-DOKE...
CAN'T YOU JUST SMACK THEM AROUND LIKE A NORMAL WOMAN YOUR AGE? DOES EVERYTHING HAVE TO BE A PERFORMANCE?
YOU SHOULD SEE ME WORK A LAP DANCE! FRICTION BURNS ABOUND!
OH...AND DON'T THINK I DIDN'T NOTICE YOU CHECKING OUT MY BUTT. YOU REALLY ARE A PERV!
AT LEAST I WEAR UNDER-WEAR...

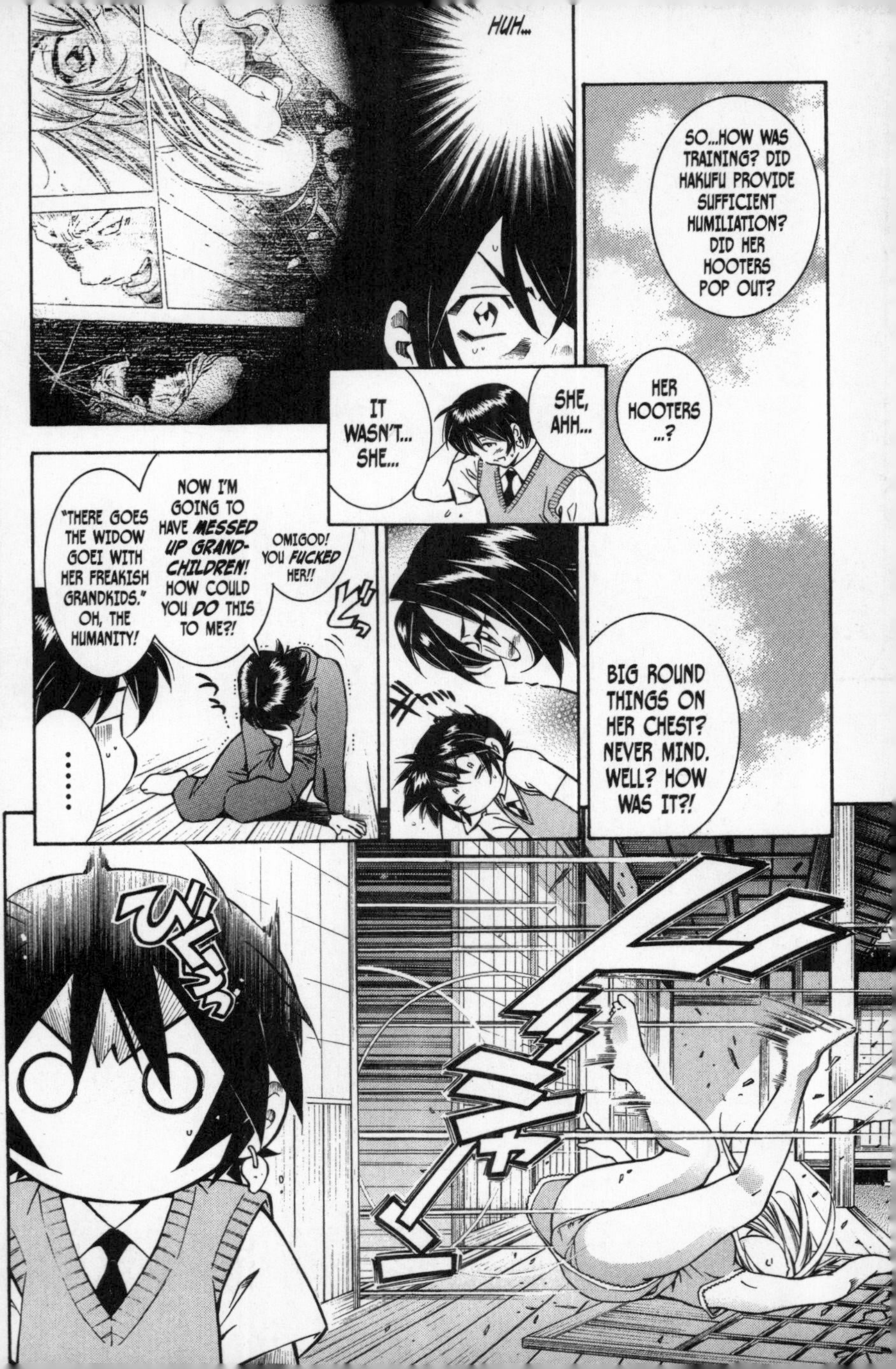
SO...HOW WAS TRAINING? DID HAKUFU PROVIDE SUFFICIENT HUMILIATION? DID HER HOOTERS POP OUT?
HUH...
HER HOOTERS ...?
SHE, AHH...
IT WASN'T... SHE...
BIG ROUND THINGS ON HER CHEST? NEVER MIND. WELL? HOW WAS IT?!
OMIGOD! YOU FUCKED HER!!
NOW I'M GOING TO HAVE MESSED UP GRAND-CHILDREN! HOW COULD YOU DO THIS TO ME?!
"THERE GOES THE WIDOW GOEI WITH HER FREAKISH GRANDKIDS." OH, THE HUMANITY!
......

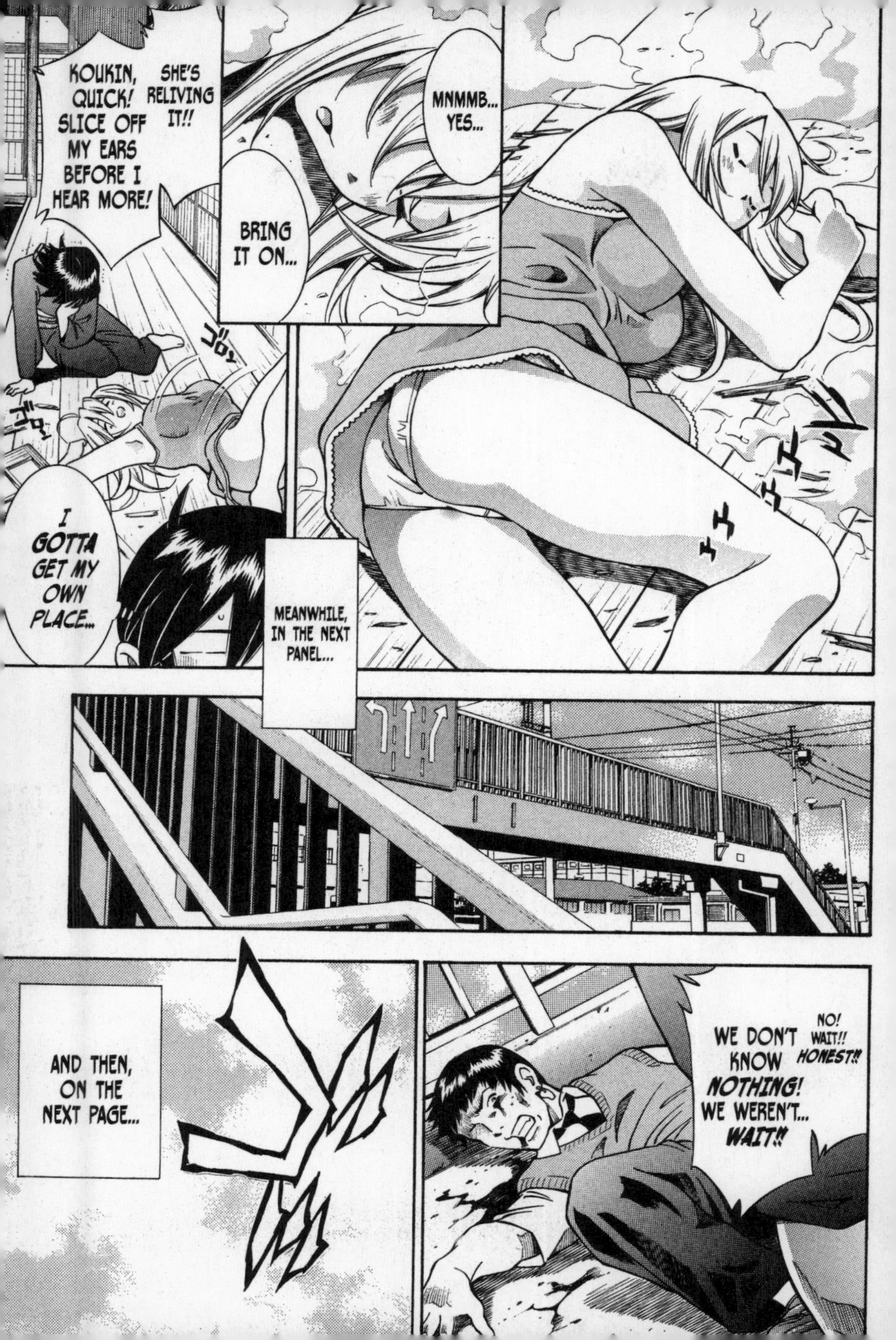
MNMMB... YES...
BRING IT ON...
SHE'S RELIVING IT!!
KOUKIN, QUICK! SLICE OFF MY EARS BEFORE I HEAR MORE!
I GOTTA GET MY OWN PLACE...
MEANWHILE, IN THE NEXT PANEL...
NO! WAIT!! HONEST!!
WE DON'T KNOW NOTHING! WE WEREN'T... WAIT!!
AND THEN, ON THE NEXT PAGE...

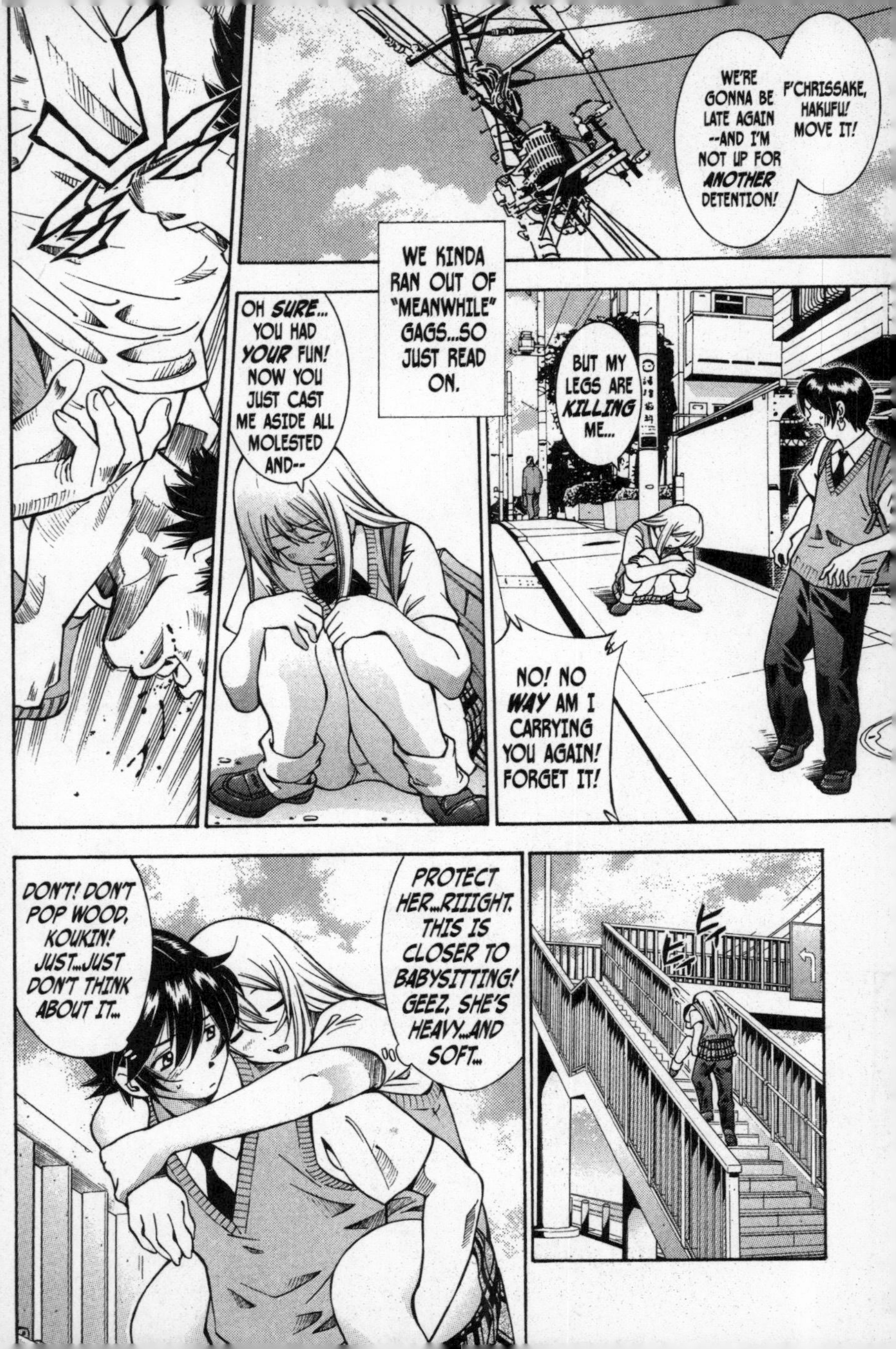
F'CHRISSAKE, HAKUFU! MOVE IT!
WE'RE GONNA BE LATE AGAIN --AND I'M NOT UP FOR ANOTHER DETENTION!
BUT MY LEGS ARE KILLING ME...
NO! NO WAY AM I CARRYING YOU AGAIN! FORGET IT!
WE KINDA RAN OUT OF "MEANWHILE" GAGS...SO JUST READ ON.
OH SURE... YOU HAD YOUR FUN! NOW YOU JUST CAST ME ASIDE ALL MOLESTED AND--
PROTECT HER...RIIIGHT. THIS IS CLOSER TO BABYSITTING! GEEZ, SHE'S HEAVY...AND SOFT...
DON'T! DON'T POP WOOD, KOUKIN! JUST...JUST DON'T THINK ABOUT IT...

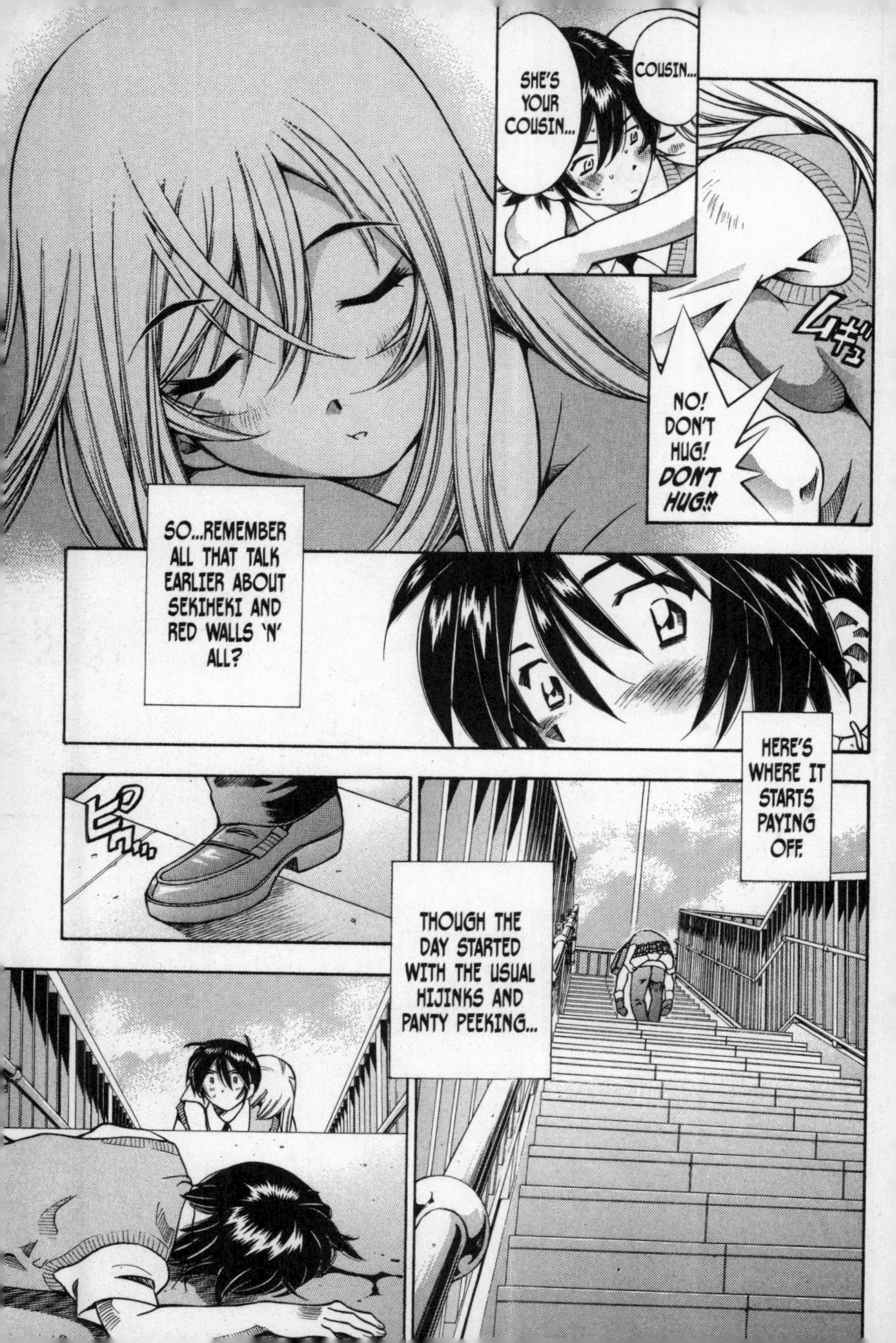
COUSIN...
SHE'S YOUR COUSIN...
ムギュ
NO! DON'T HUG! *DON'T HUG!!*
SO...REMEMBER ALL THAT TALK EARLIER ABOUT SEKIHEKI AND RED WALLS 'N' ALL?
HERE'S WHERE IT STARTS PAYING OFF.
THOUGH THE DAY STARTED WITH THE USUAL HIJINKS AND PANTY PEEKING...

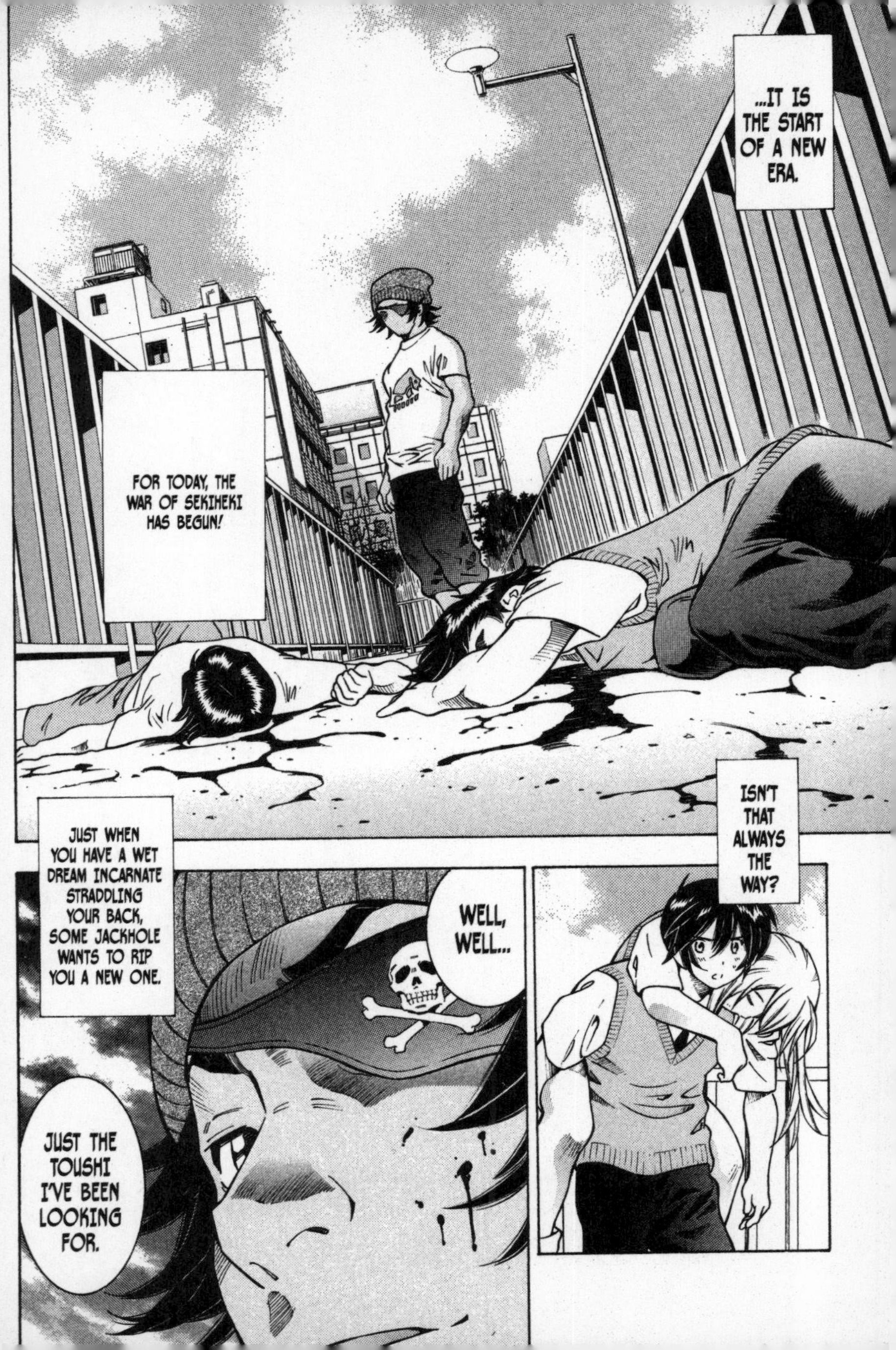
...IT IS THE START OF A NEW ERA.
FOR TODAY, THE WAR OF SEKIHEKI HAS BEGUN!
ISN'T THAT ALWAYS THE WAY?
JUST WHEN YOU HAVE A WET DREAM INCARNATE STRADDLING YOUR BACK, SOME JACKHOLE WANTS TO RIP YOU A NEW ONE.
WELL, WELL...
JUST THE TOUSHI I'VE BEEN LOOKING FOR.

一騎当千

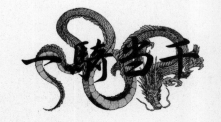

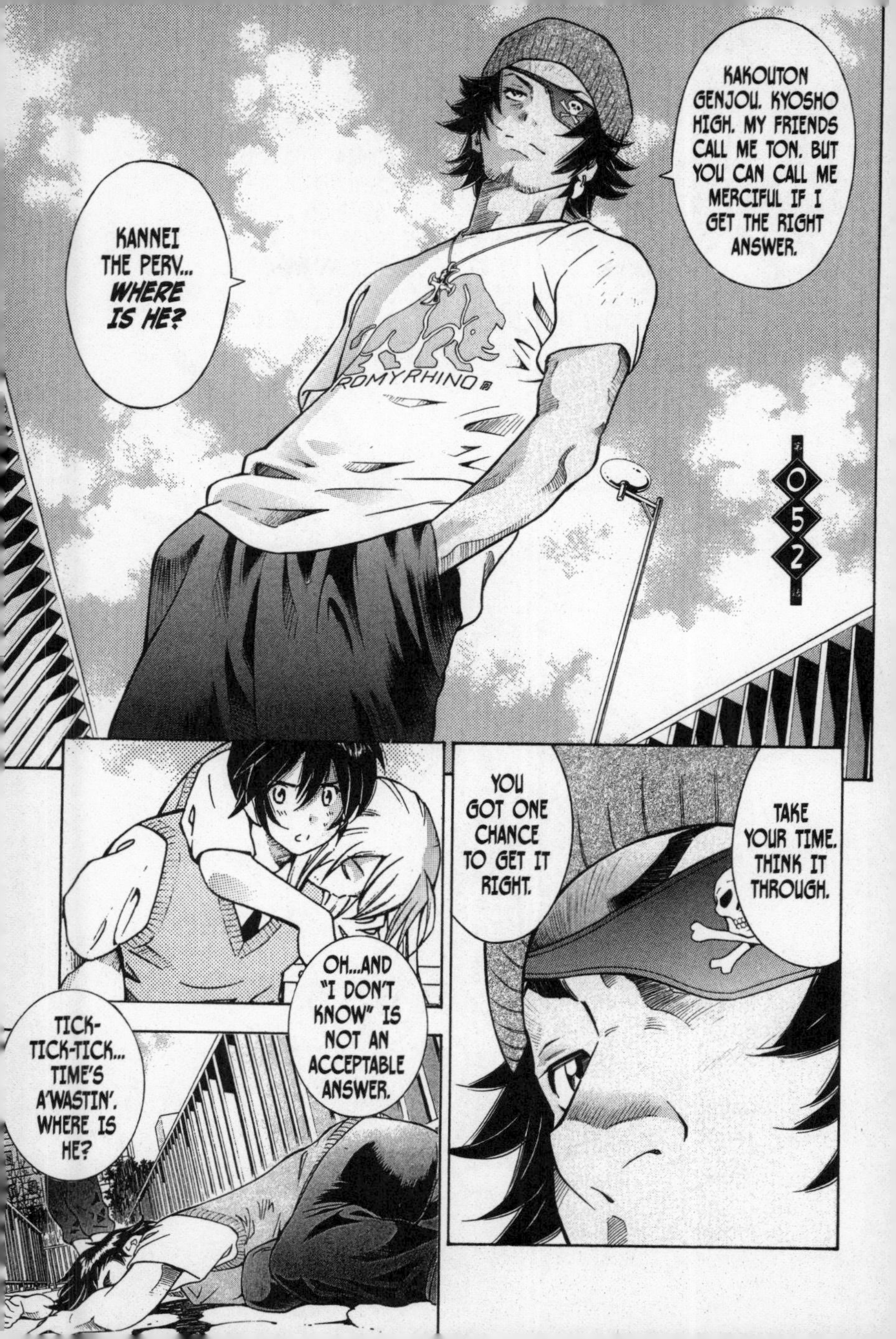
KAKOUTON GENJOU. KYOSHO HIGH. MY FRIENDS CALL ME TON. BUT YOU CAN CALL ME MERCIFUL IF I GET THE RIGHT ANSWER.
052
KANNEI THE PERV... *WHERE IS HE?*
TAKE YOUR TIME. THINK IT THROUGH.
YOU GOT ONE CHANCE TO GET IT RIGHT.
OH...AND "I DON'T KNOW" IS NOT AN ACCEPTABLE ANSWER.
TICK-TICK-TICK... TIME'S A'WASTIN'. WHERE IS HE?

第052話

UGAN TRIBE

A NOMADIC PEOPLE WHO LIVED IN NORTHERN CHINA'S UGAN MOUNTAINS. THEIR COMBAT PROWESS AND HORSEMANSHIP WERE WELL-KNOWN THROUGHOUT CHINA. SOUSOU, WHO FEARED THEM AS MUCH AS HE DESIRED TO CONTROL THEM, ATTACKED THEM WITH AN ARMY FIFTY THOUSAND DEEP. THE CONQUERED UGAN WERE THEN PLACED UNDER THE PUPPET RULE OF CHOURYOU. THOUGH WHY ANYONE WOULD LISTEN TO A PUPPET IS BEYOND US.

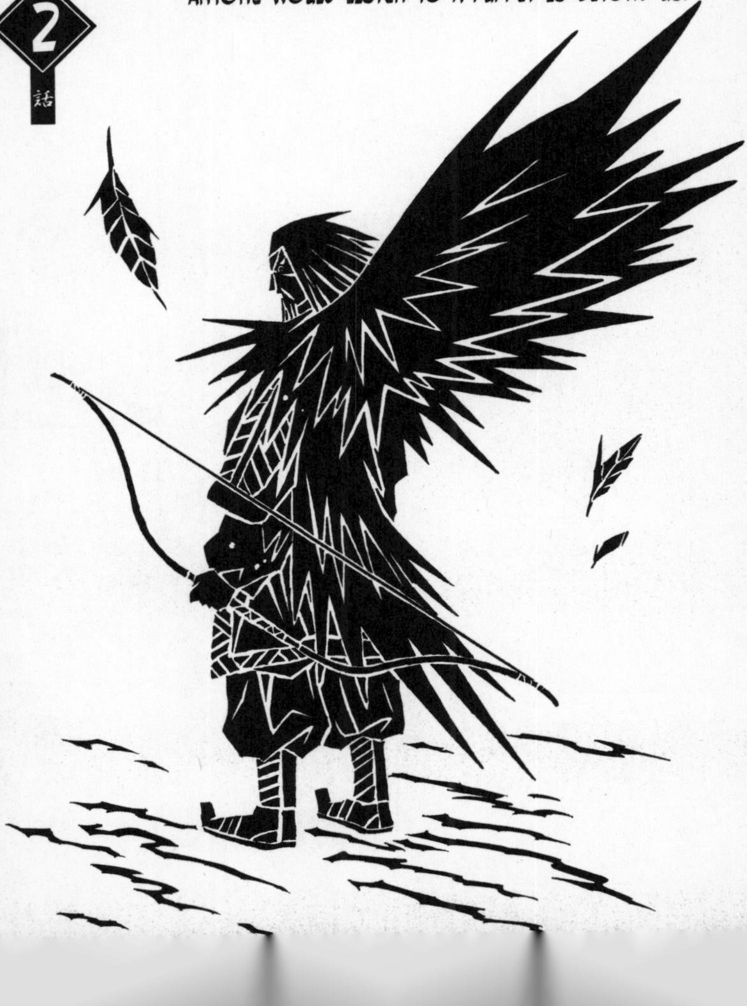

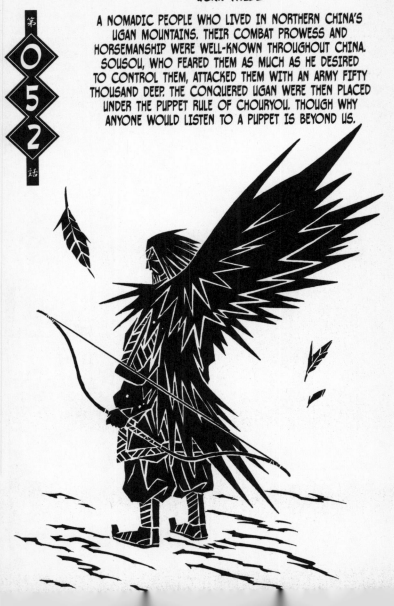

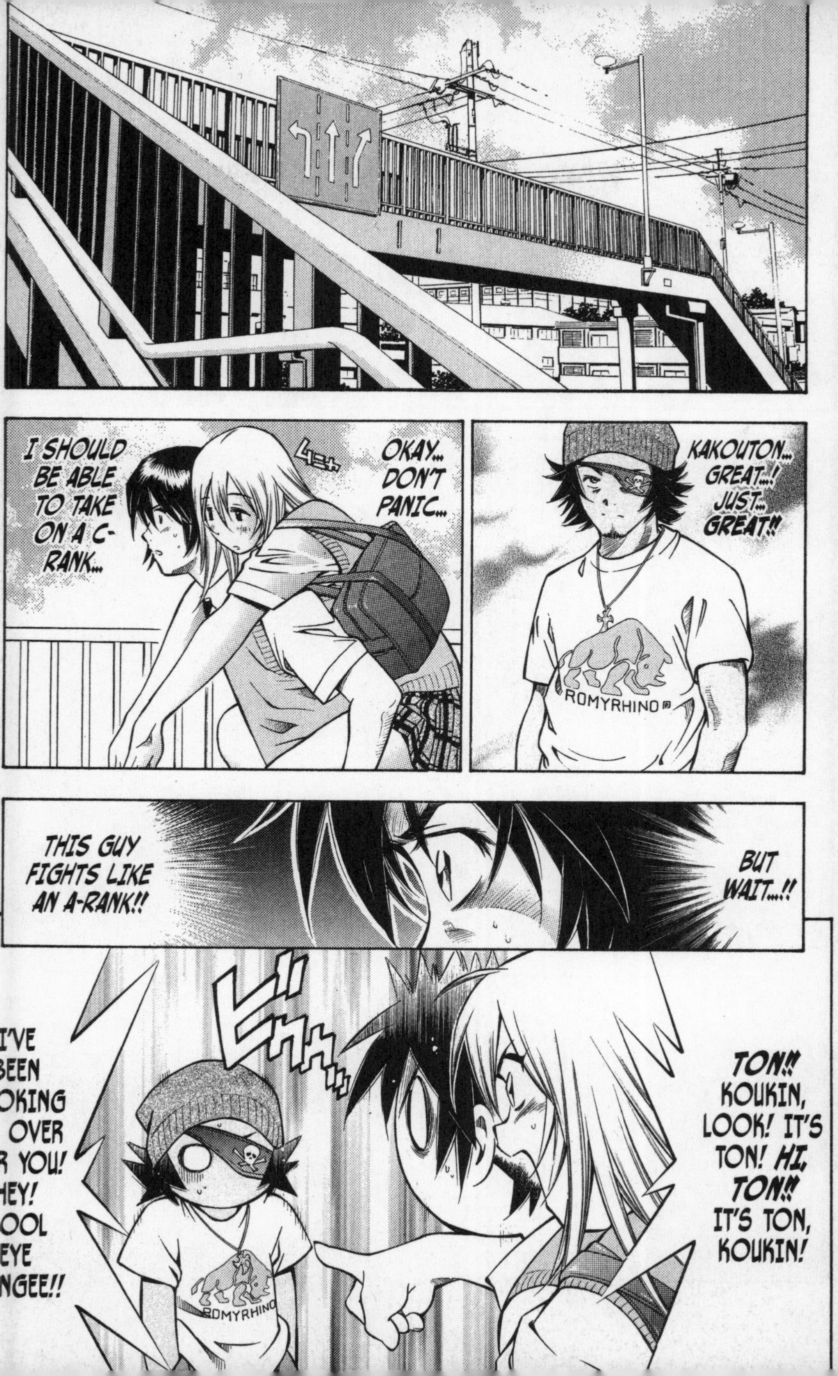
KAKOUTON... GREAT...! JUST... GREAT!!
OKAY... DON'T PANIC...
I SHOULD BE ABLE TO TAKE ON A C-RANK...
BUT WAIT...!!
THIS GUY FIGHTS LIKE AN A-RANK!!
TON!! KOUKIN, LOOK! IT'S TON! HI, TON!! IT'S TON, KOUKIN!
I'VE BEEN LOOKING ALL OVER FOR YOU! HEY! COOL EYE THINGEE!!
ROMYRHINO

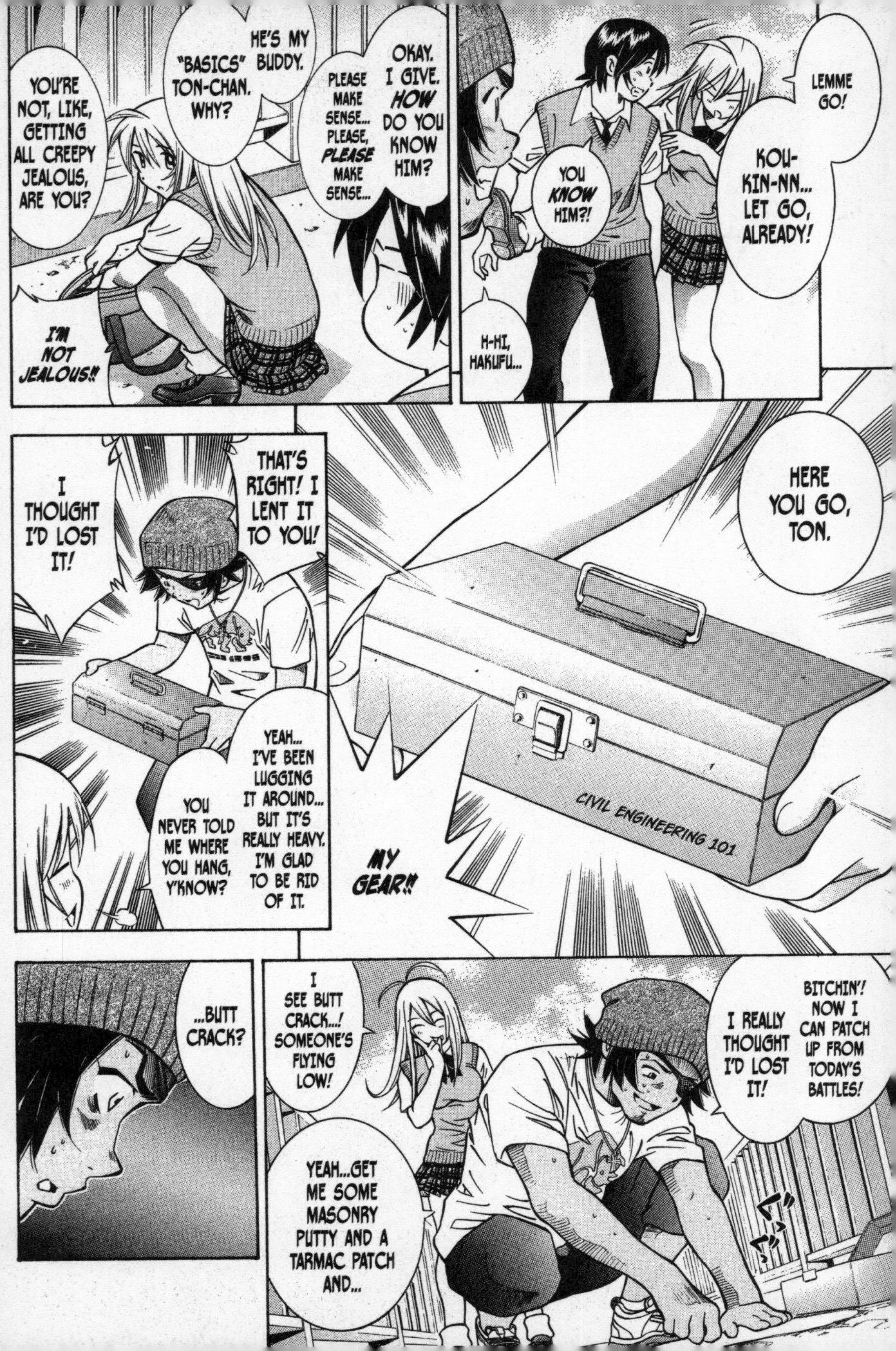
LEMME GO!
KOU-KIN-NN... LET GO, ALREADY!
YOU KNOW HIM?!
H-HI, HAKUFU...
OKAY. I GIVE. HOW DO YOU KNOW HIM?
PLEASE MAKE SENSE... PLEASE, PLEASE MAKE SENSE...
HE'S MY BUDDY.
"BASICS" TON-CHAN. WHY?
YOU'RE NOT, LIKE, GETTING ALL CREEPY JEALOUS, ARE YOU?
I'M NOT JEALOUS!!
HERE YOU GO, TON.
CIVIL ENGINEERING 101
MY GEAR!!
THAT'S RIGHT! I LENT IT TO YOU!
I THOUGHT I'D LOST IT!
YEAH... I'VE BEEN LUGGING IT AROUND... BUT IT'S REALLY HEAVY. I'M GLAD TO BE RID OF IT.
YOU NEVER TOLD ME WHERE YOU HANG, Y'KNOW?
BITCHIN'! NOW I CAN PATCH UP FROM TODAY'S BATTLES!
I REALLY THOUGHT I'D LOST IT!
I SEE BUTT CRACK...! SOMEONE'S FLYING LOW!
YEAH...GET ME SOME MASONRY PUTTY AND A TARMAC PATCH AND...
...BUTT CRACK?

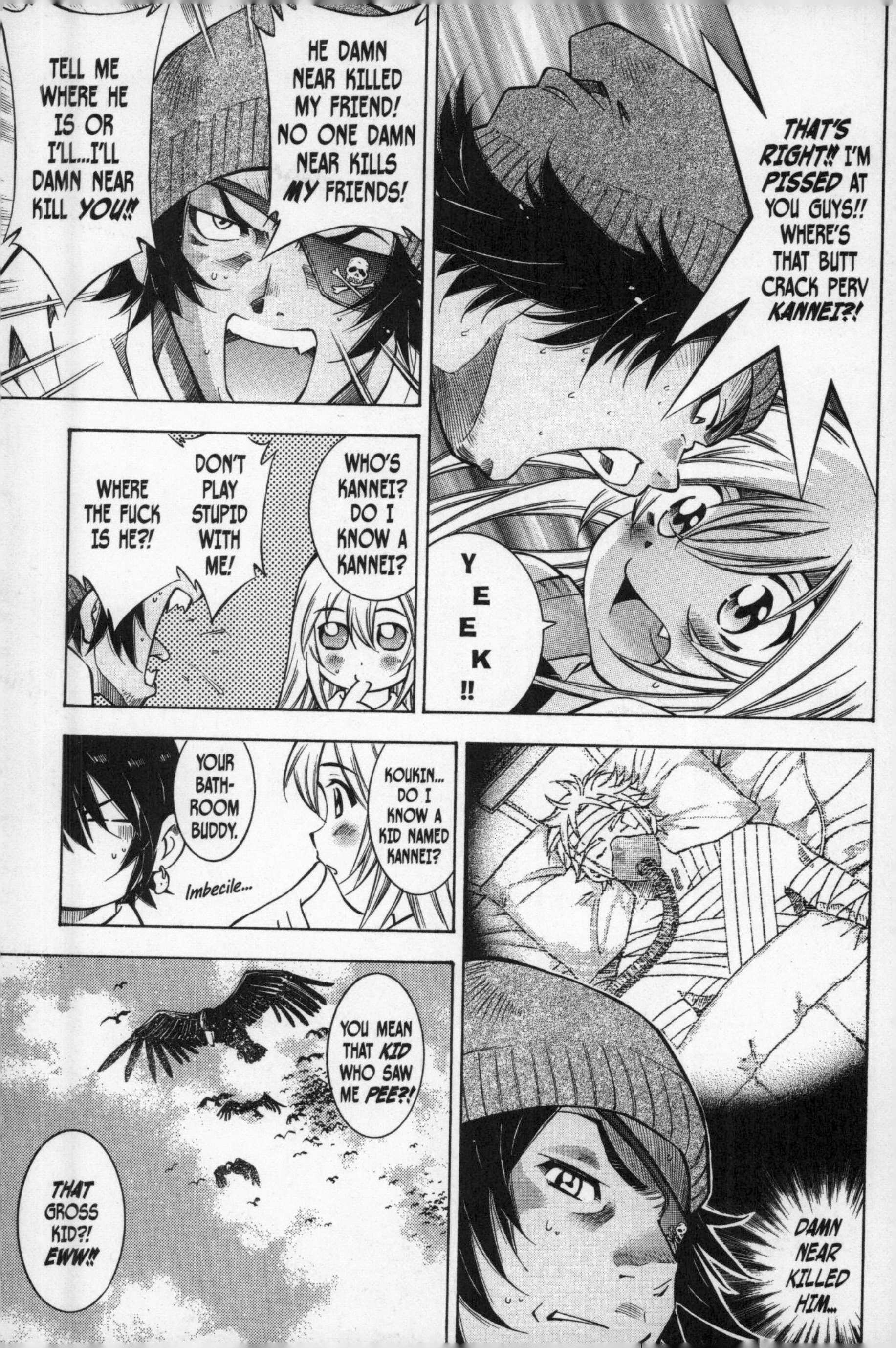
THAT'S RIGHT!! I'M PISSED AT YOU GUYS!! WHERE'S THAT BUTT CRACK PERV KANNEI?!
YEEK!!
HE DAMN NEAR KILLED MY FRIEND! NO ONE DAMN NEAR KILLS MY FRIENDS!
TELL ME WHERE HE IS OR I'LL...I'LL DAMN NEAR KILL YOU!!
WHO'S KANNEI? DO I KNOW A KANNEI?
DON'T PLAY STUPID WITH ME!
WHERE THE FUCK IS HE?!
DAMN NEAR KILLED HIM...
KOUKIN... DO I KNOW A KID NAMED KANNEI?
YOUR BATH-ROOM BUDDY.
Imbecile...
YOU MEAN THAT KID WHO SAW ME PEE?!
THAT GROSS KID?! EWW!!

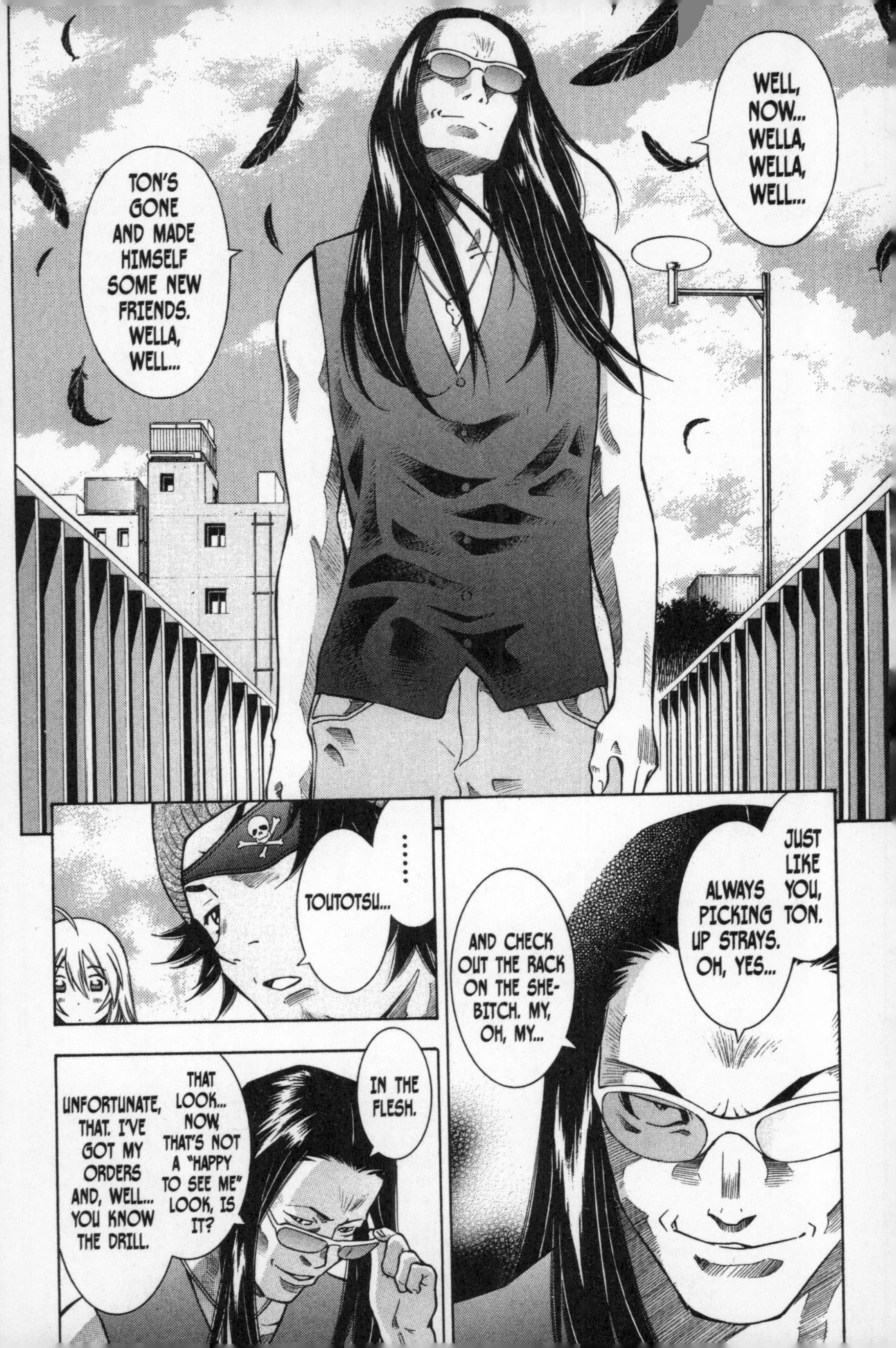
WELL, NOW... WELLA, WELLA, WELL...
TON'S GONE AND MADE HIMSELF SOME NEW FRIENDS. WELLA, WELL...
JUST LIKE YOU, TON.
ALWAYS PICKING UP STRAYS. OH, YES...
AND CHECK OUT THE RACK ON THE SHE-BITCH. MY, OH, MY...
......
TOUTOTSU...
IN THE FLESH.
THAT LOOK... NOW, THAT'S NOT A "HAPPY TO SEE ME" LOOK, IS IT?
UNFORTUNATE, THAT. I'VE GOT MY ORDERS AND, WELL... YOU KNOW THE DRILL.

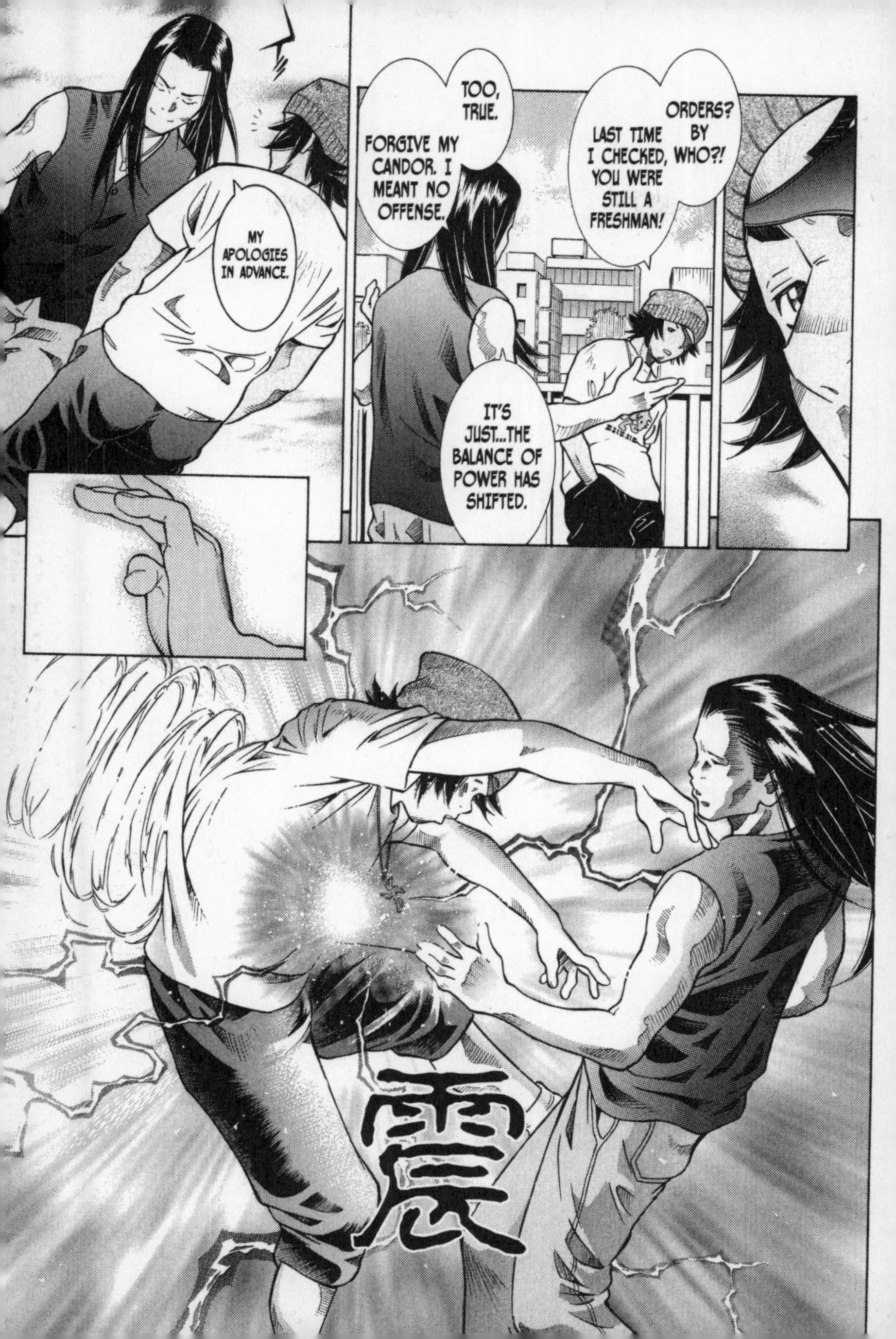
ORDERS? BY WHO?!
LAST TIME I CHECKED, YOU WERE STILL A FRESHMAN!
TOO, TRUE.
FORGIVE MY CANDOR. I MEANT NO OFFENSE.
IT'S JUST...THE BALANCE OF POWER HAS SHIFTED.
MY APOLOGIES IN ADVANCE.
震

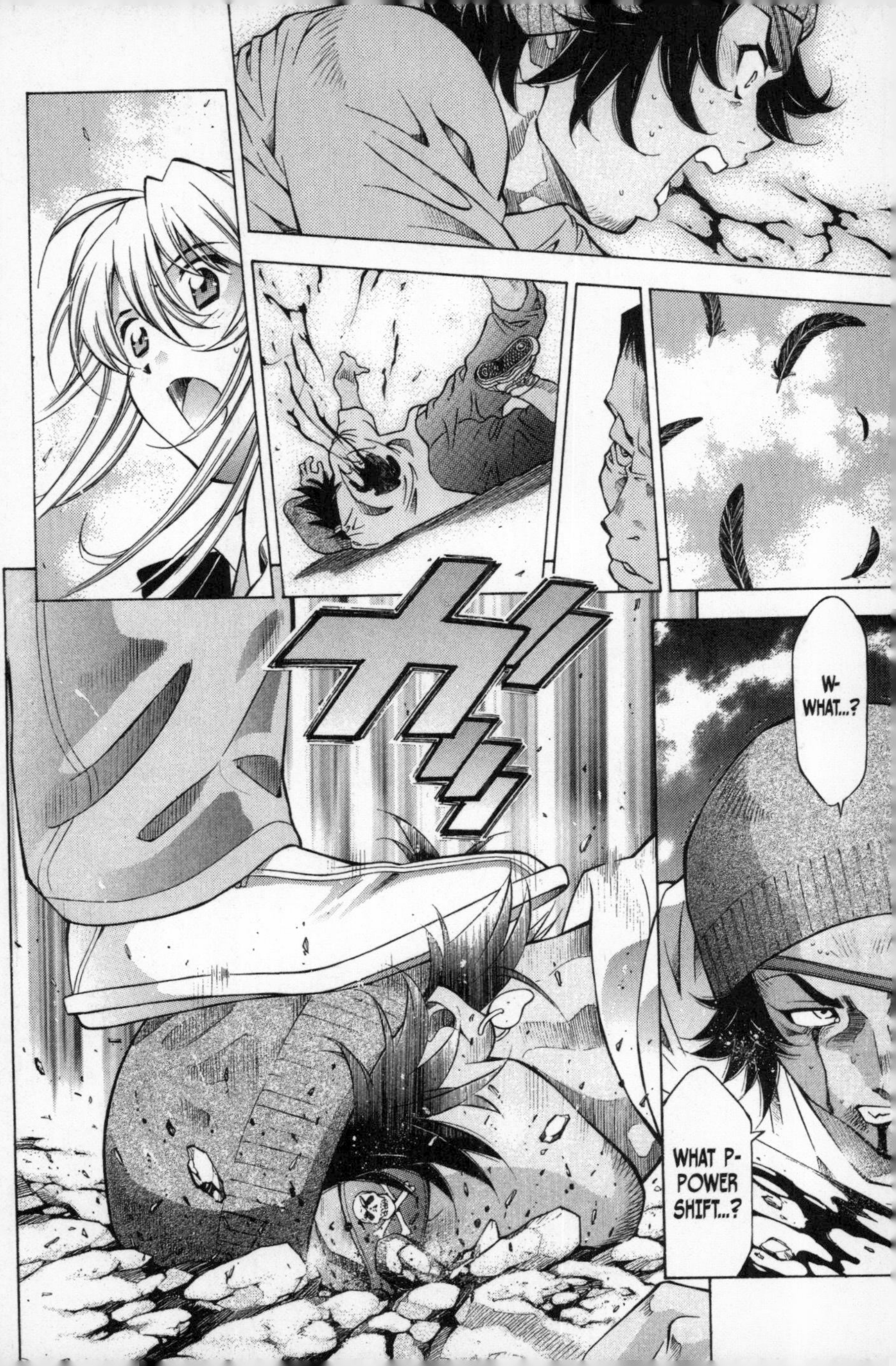
W-
WHAT...?
WHAT P-
POWER
SHIFT...?

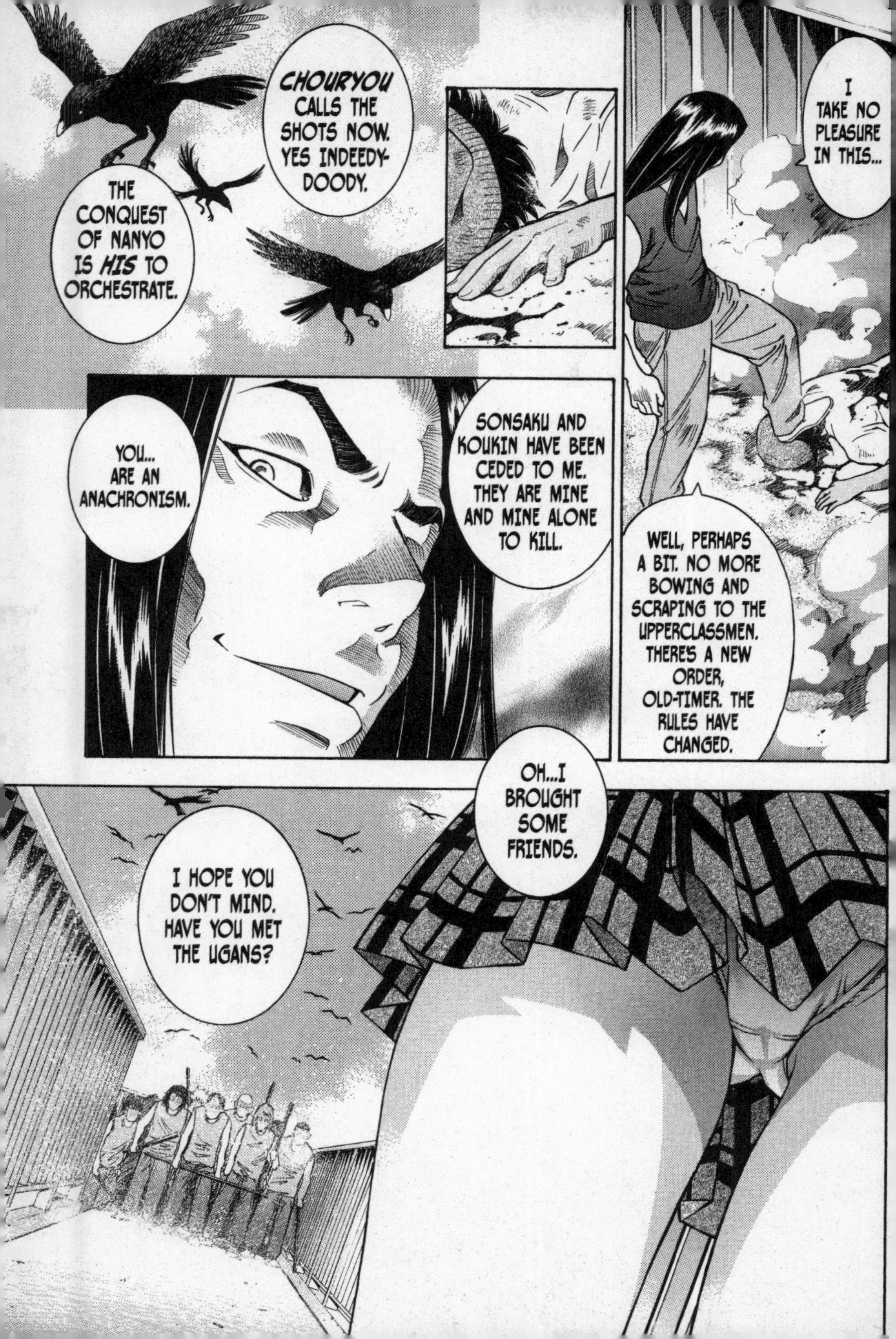
I TAKE NO PLEASURE IN THIS...
WELL, PERHAPS A BIT. NO MORE BOWING AND SCRAPING TO THE UPPERCLASSMEN. THERE'S A NEW ORDER, OLD-TIMER. THE RULES HAVE CHANGED.
CHOURYOU CALLS THE SHOTS NOW. YES INDEEDY-DOODY.
THE CONQUEST OF NANYO IS *HIS* TO ORCHESTRATE.
SONSAKU AND KOUKIN HAVE BEEN CEDED TO ME. THEY ARE MINE AND MINE ALONE TO KILL.
YOU... ARE AN ANACHRONISM.
OH...I BROUGHT SOME FRIENDS.
I HOPE YOU DON'T MIND. HAVE YOU MET THE UGANS?

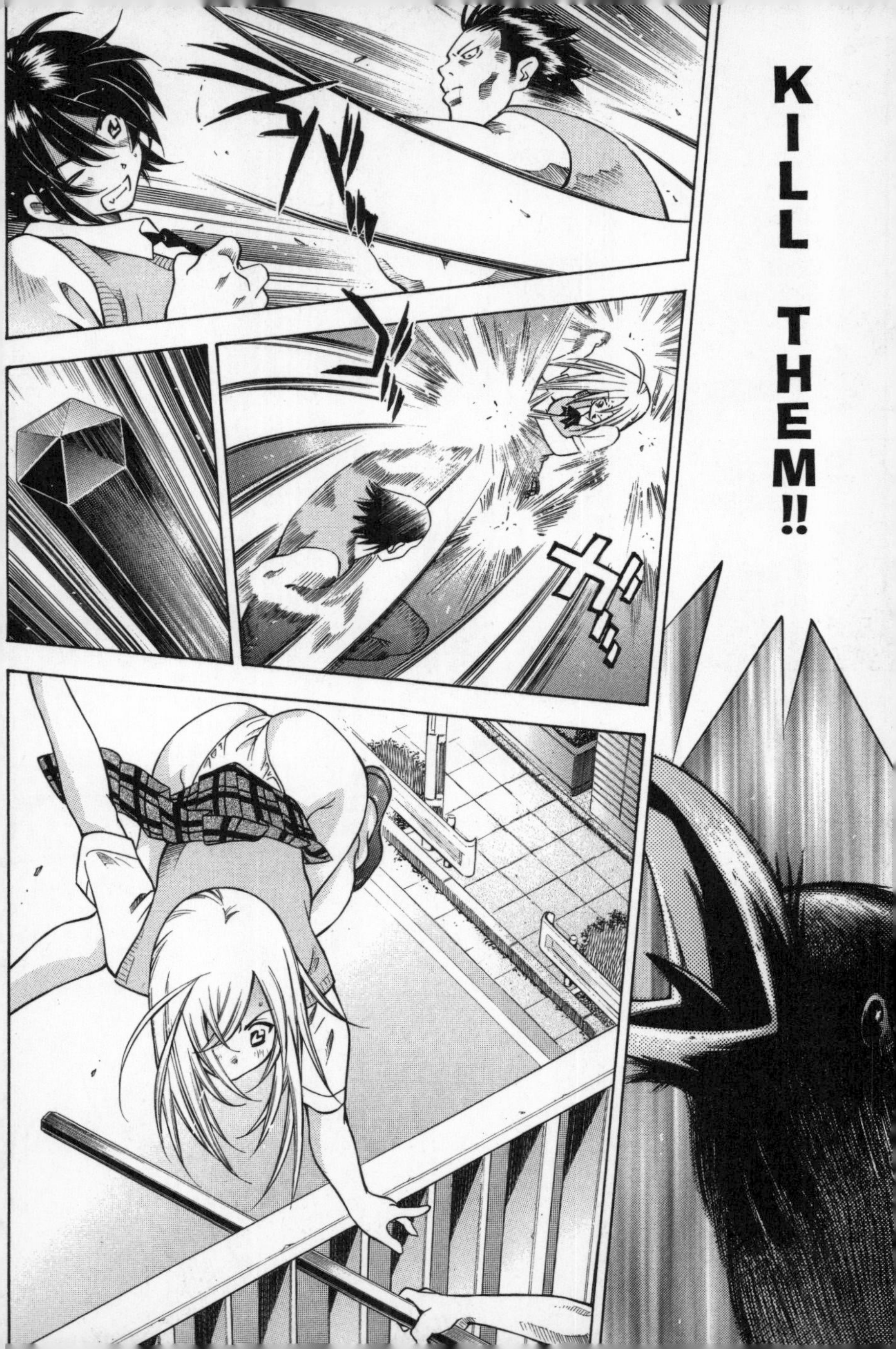
KILL THEM!!

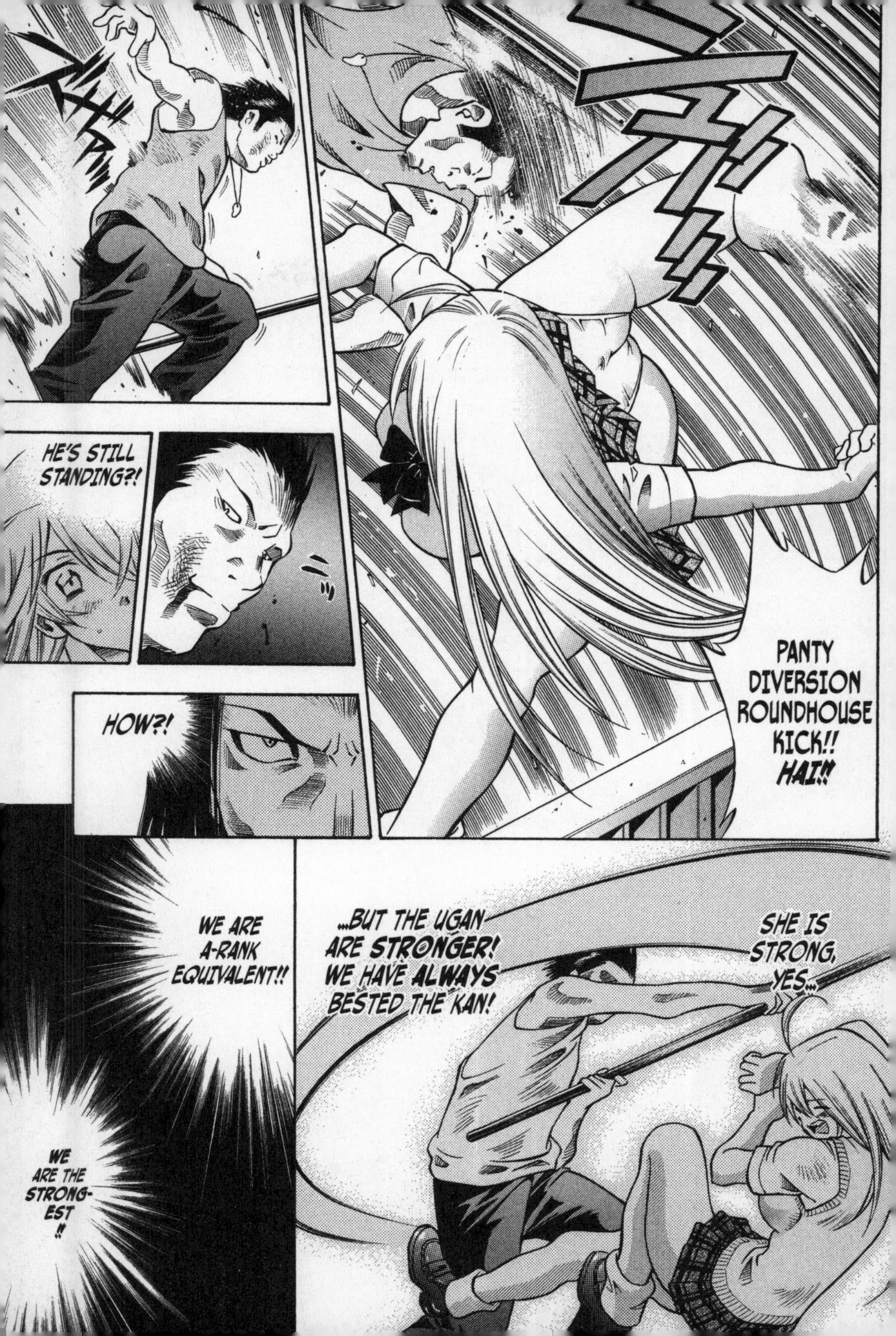
PANTY DIVERSION ROUNDHOUSE KICK!! HAI!!
HE'S STILL STANDING?!
HOW?!
SHE IS STRONG, YES...
...BUT THE UGAN ARE STRONGER! WE HAVE ALWAYS BESTED THE KAN!
WE ARE A-RANK EQUIVALENT!!
WE ARE THE STRONGEST!!

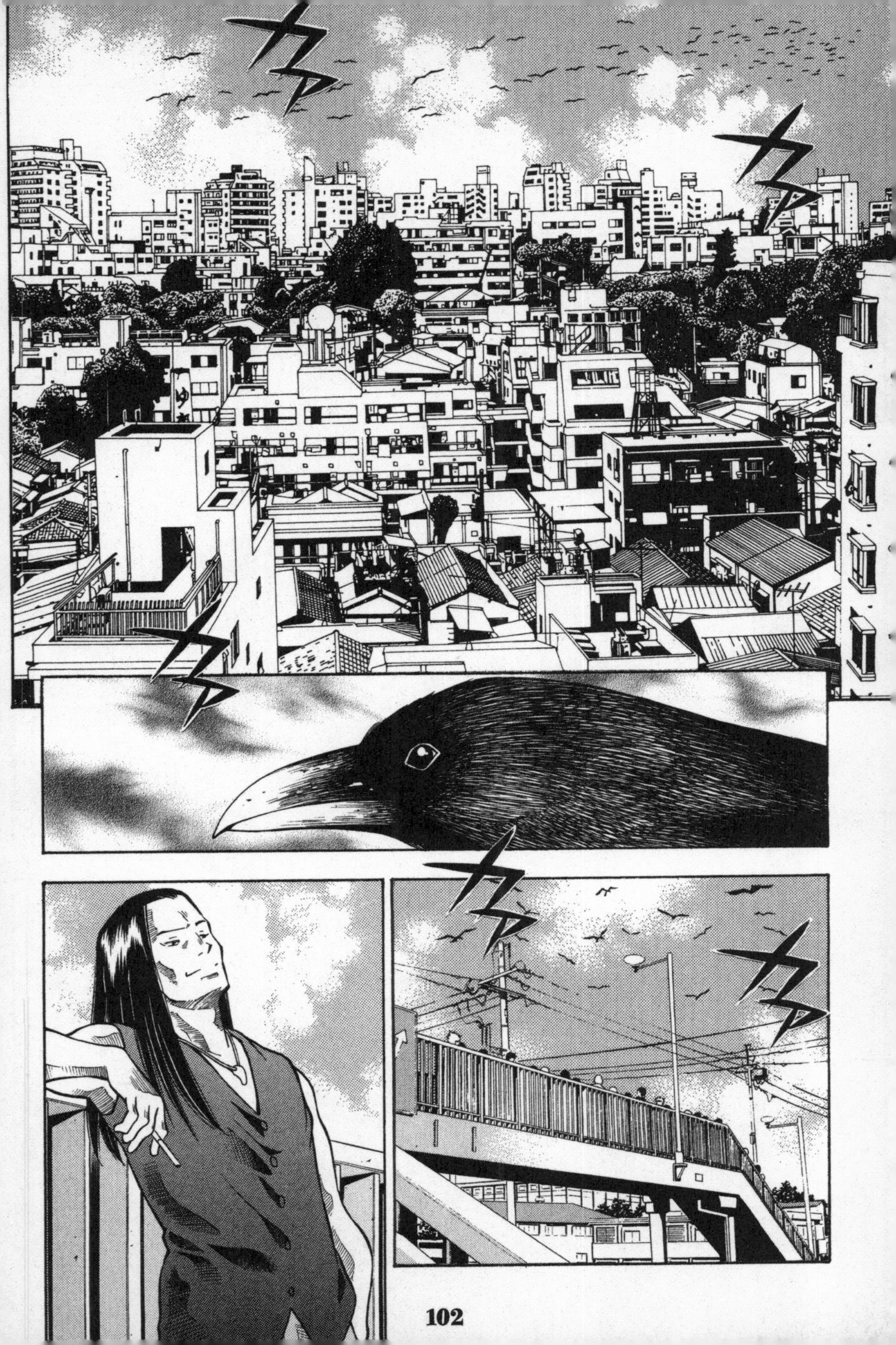
カァ
カァ
カァ
カァ
カァ

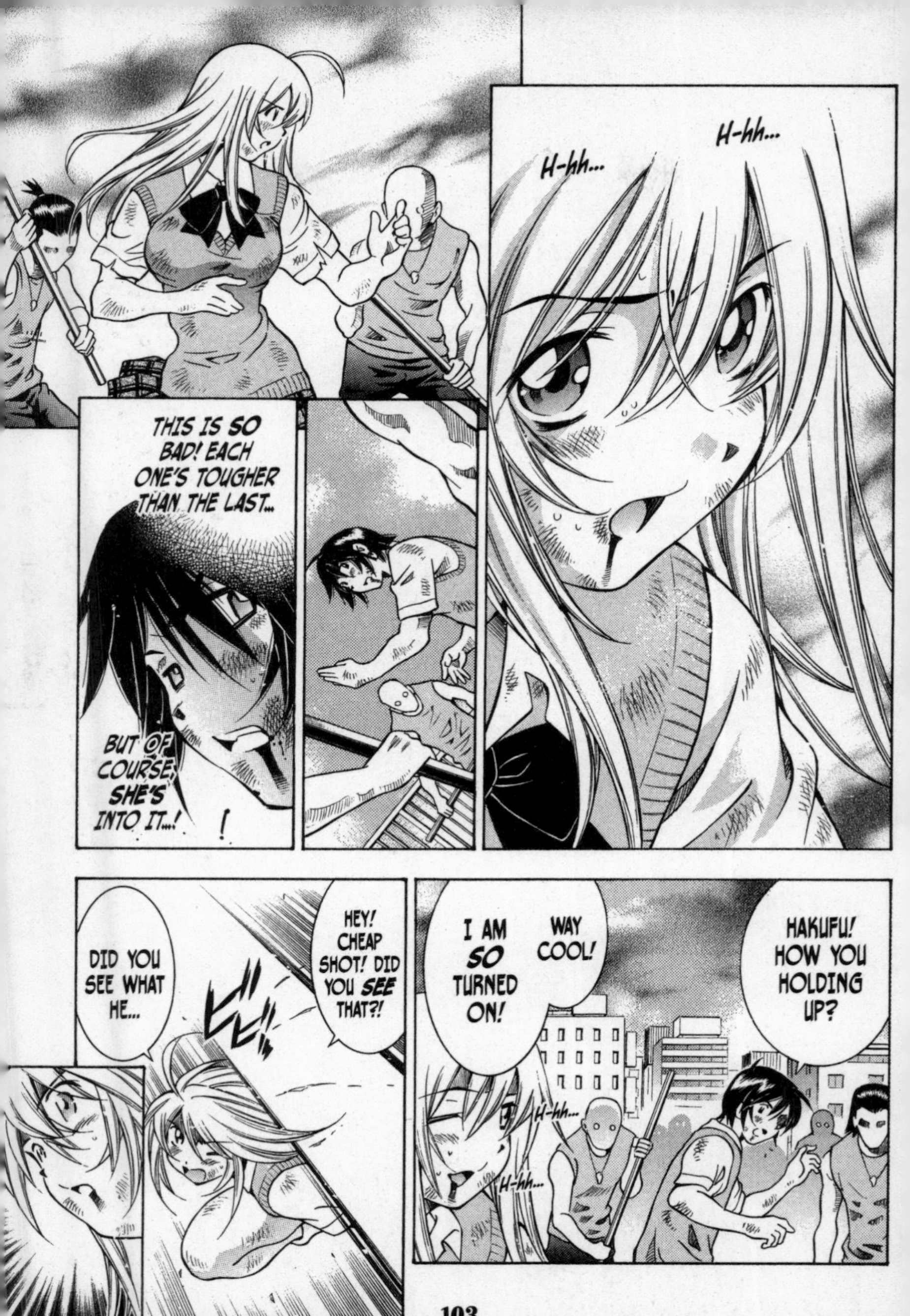
H-hh...
H-hh...
THIS IS SO BAD! EACH ONE'S TOUGHER THAN THE LAST...
BUT OF COURSE, SHE'S INTO IT...!
!
HAKUFU! HOW YOU HOLDING UP?
WAY COOL!
I AM SO TURNED ON!
H-hh...
H-hh...
HEY! CHEAP SHOT! DID YOU SEE THAT?!
DID YOU SEE WHAT HE...

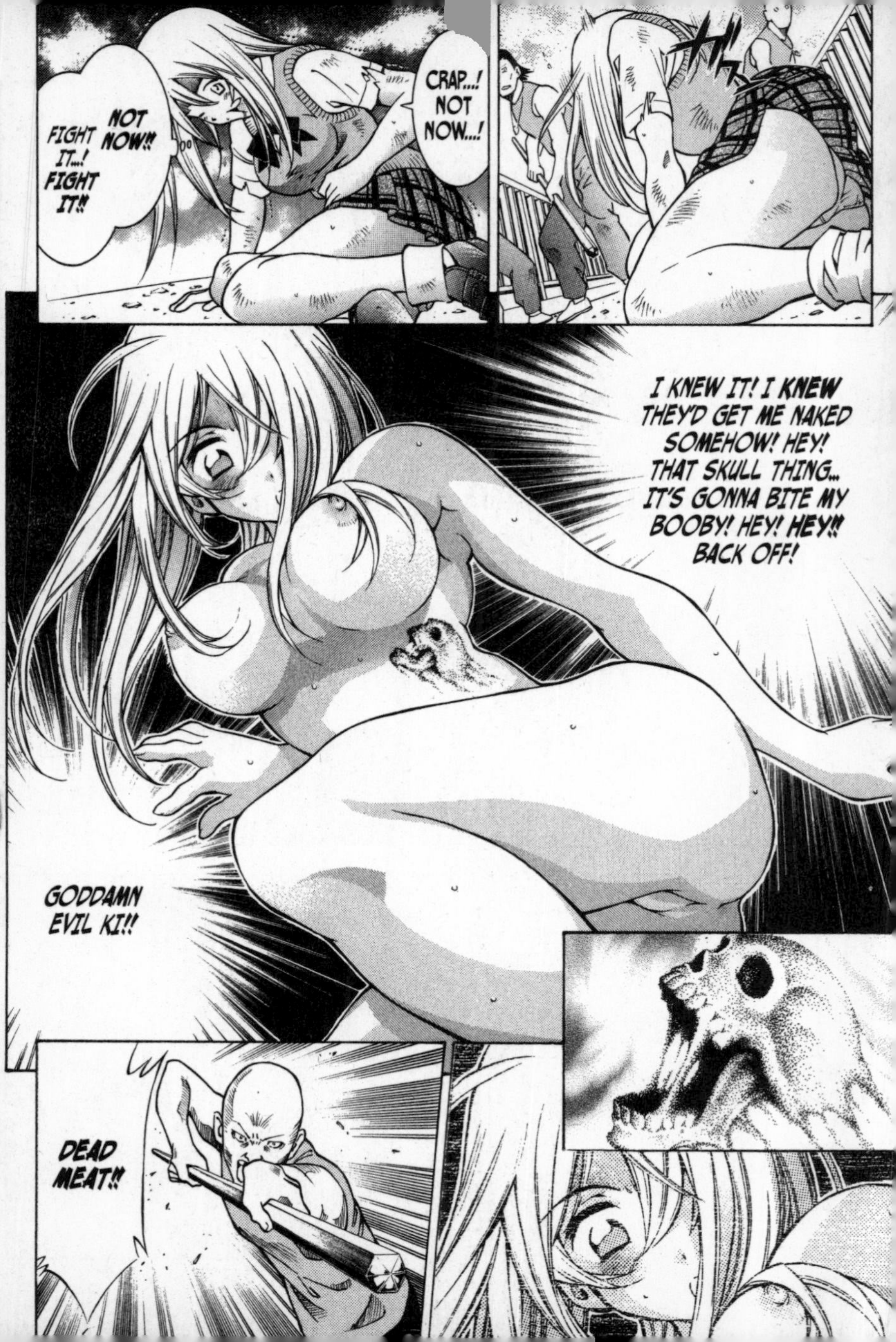
CRAP...! NOT NOW...!
NOT NOW!! FIGHT IT...! FIGHT IT!!
I KNEW IT! I KNEW THEY'D GET ME NAKED SOMEHOW! HEY! THAT SKULL THING... IT'S GONNA BITE MY BOOBY! HEY! HEY!! BACK OFF!
GODDAMN EVIL KI!!
DEAD MEAT!!

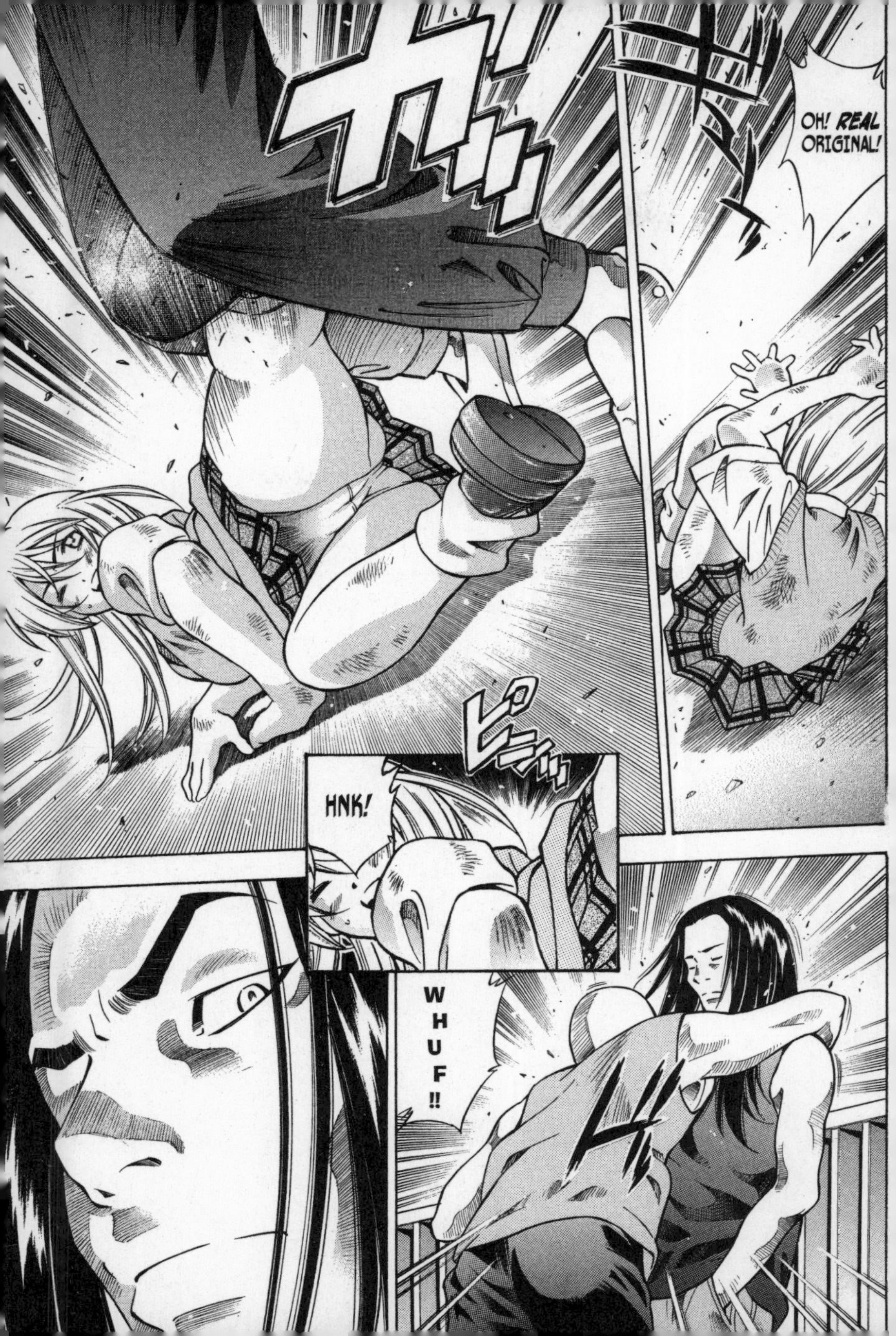
OH! REAL ORIGINAL!
HNK!
WHUF!!

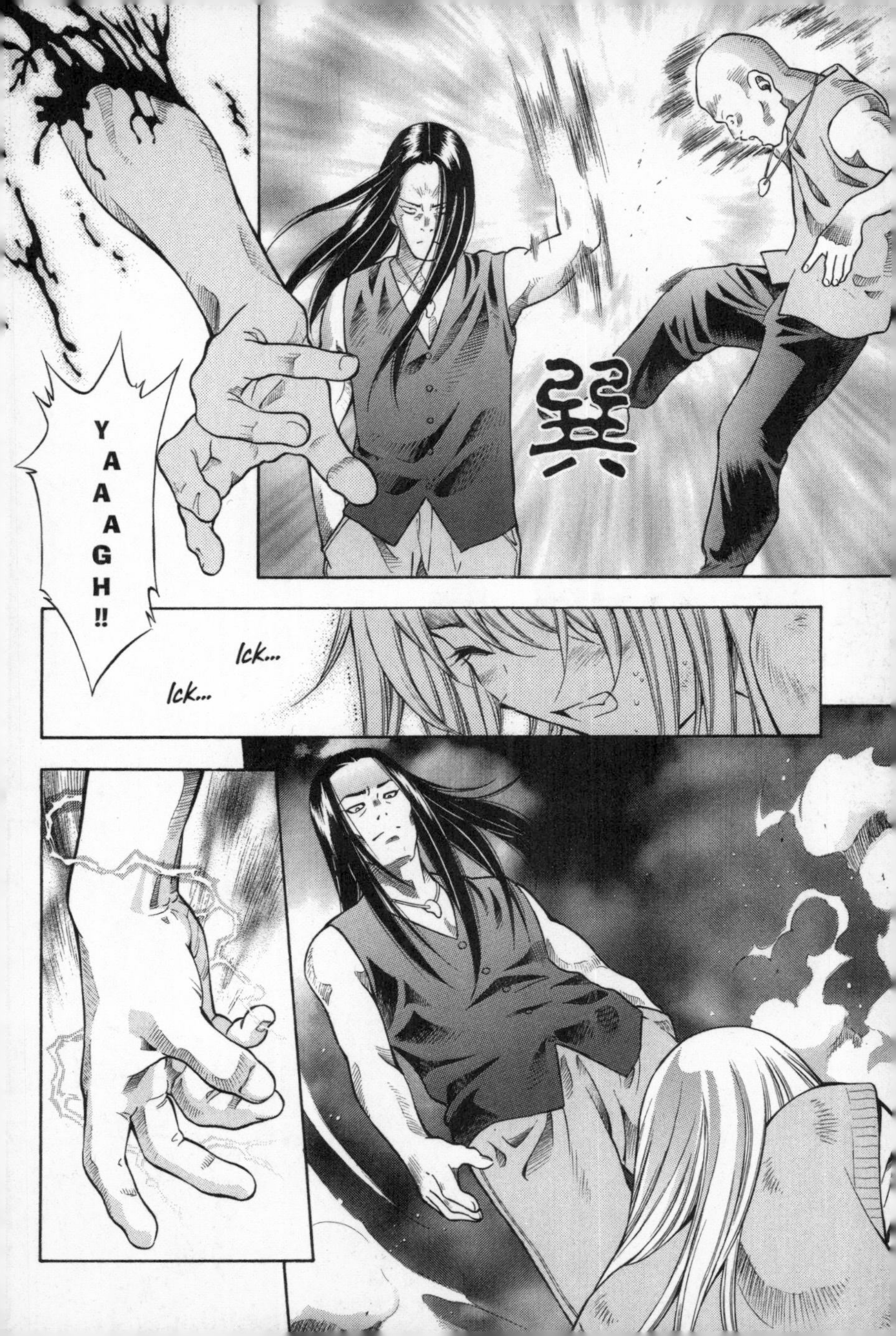
YAAAGH!!
Ick...
Ick...

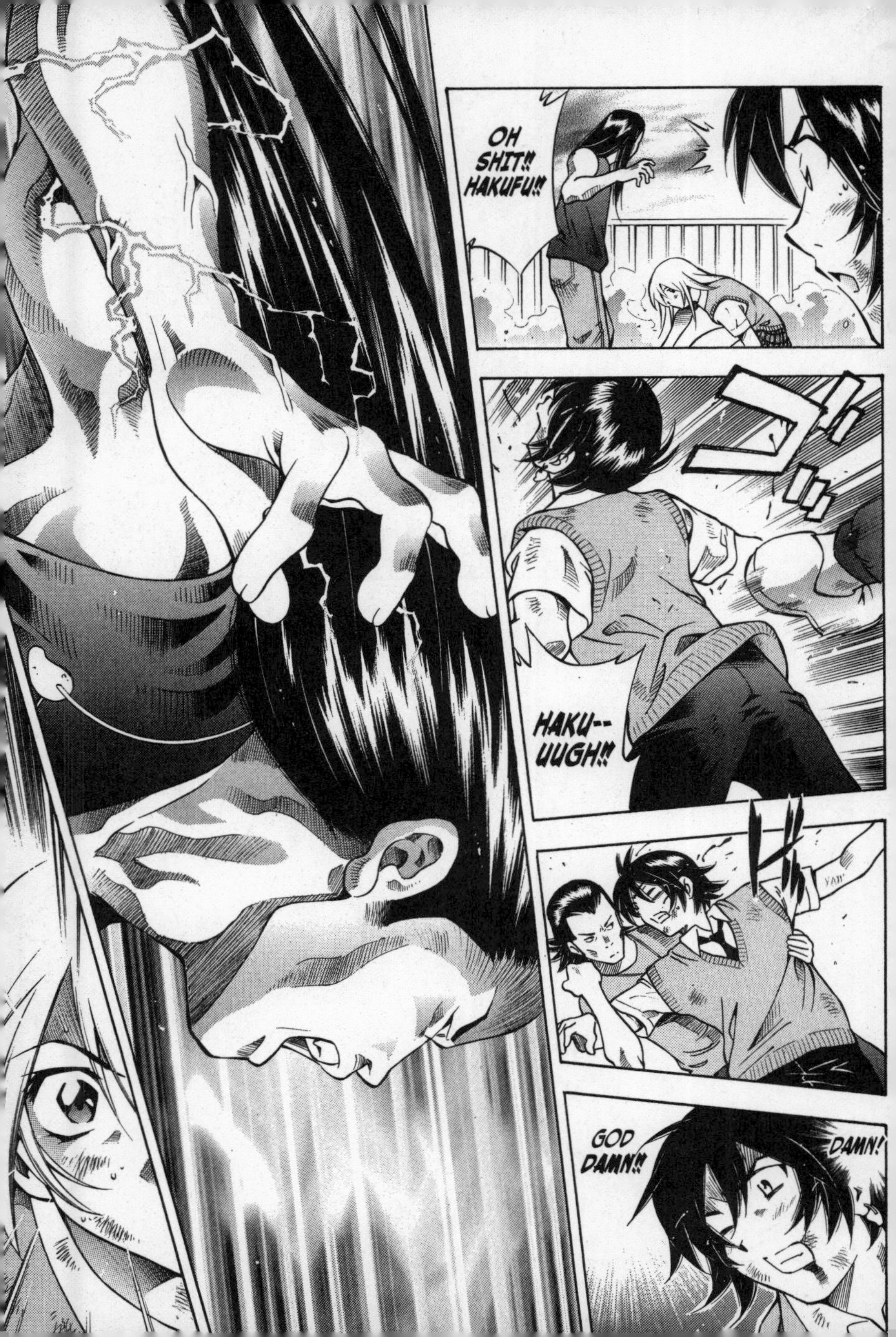
OH SHIT!! HAKUFU!!
HAKU-- UUGH!!
DAMN!
GOD DAMN!!

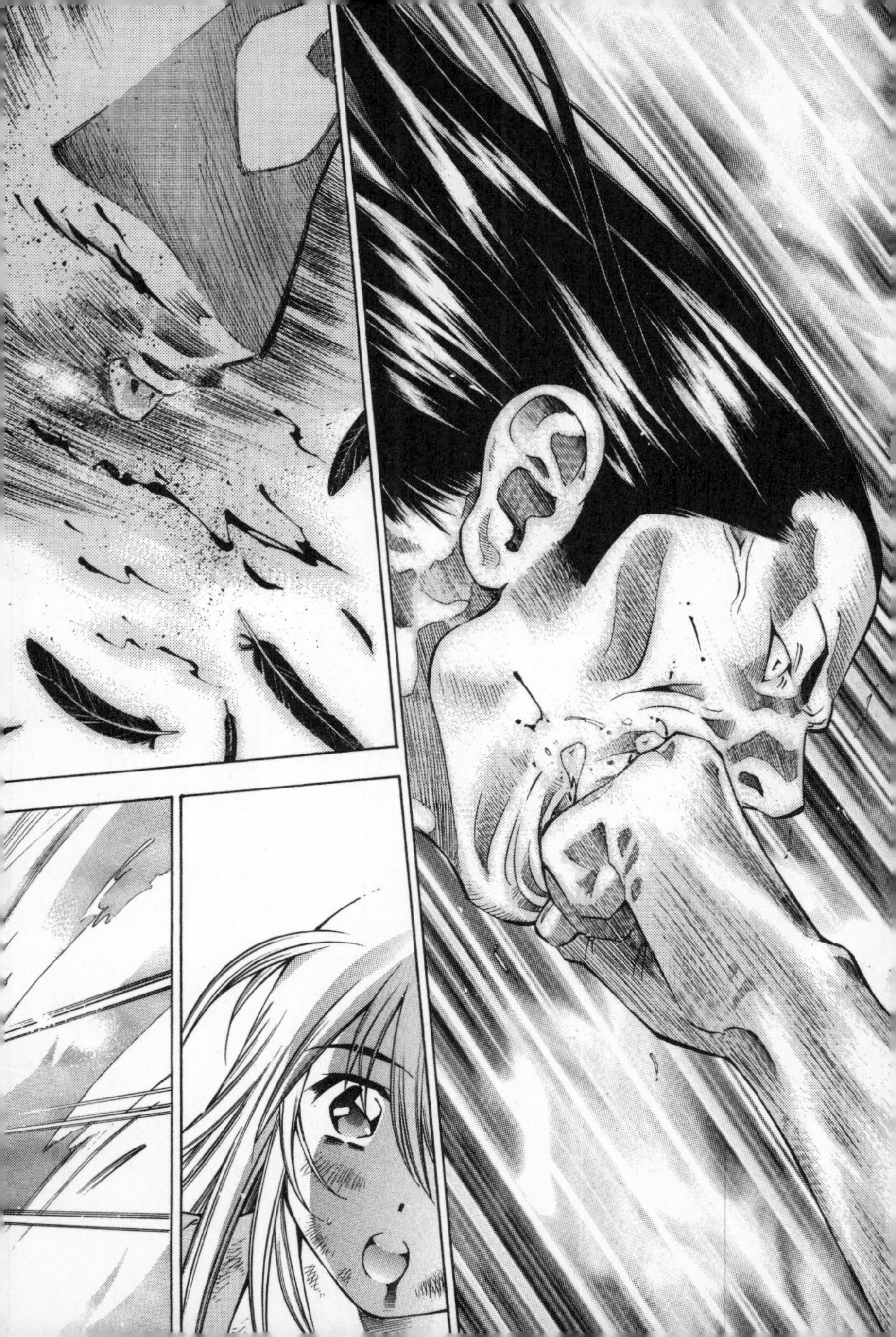

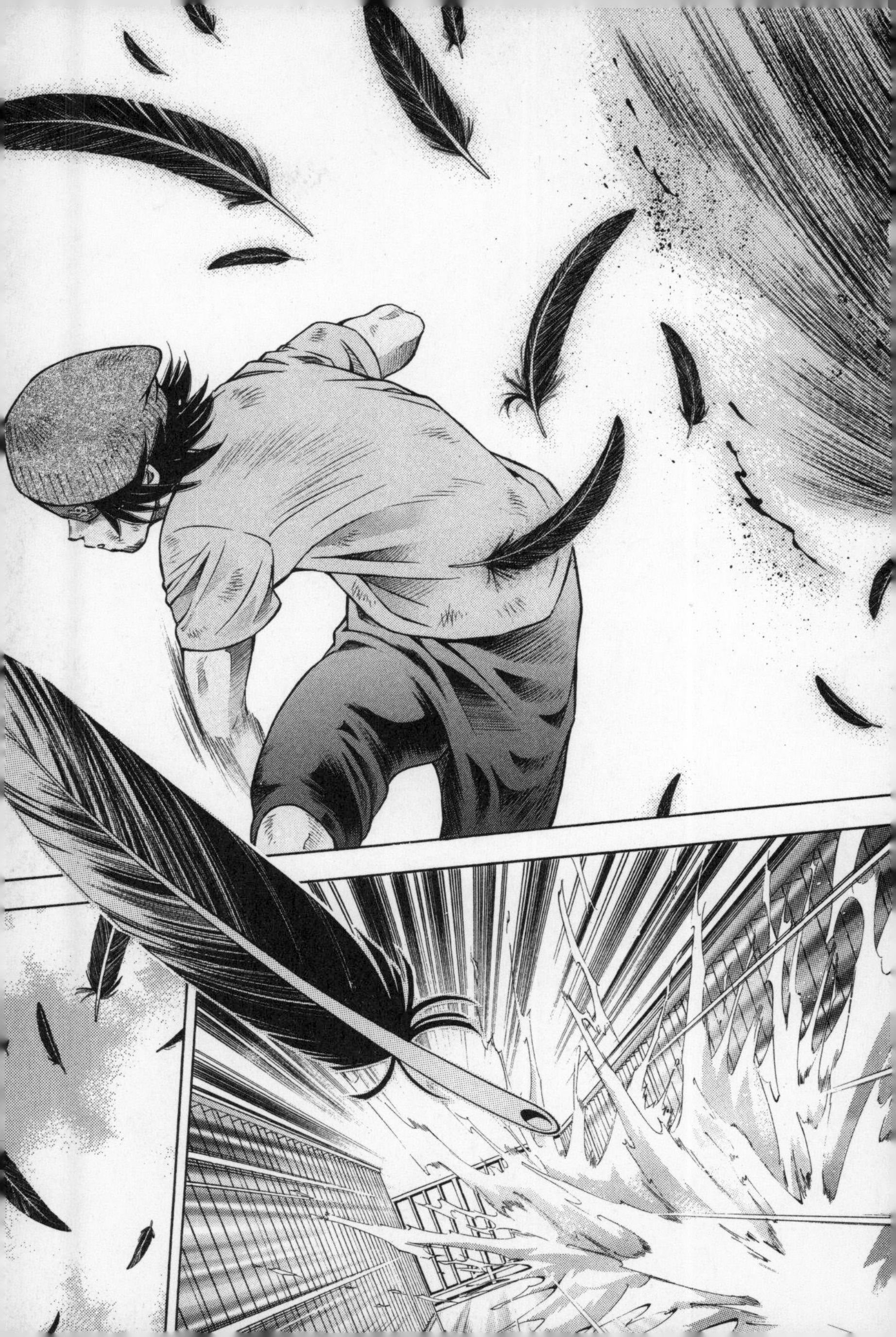

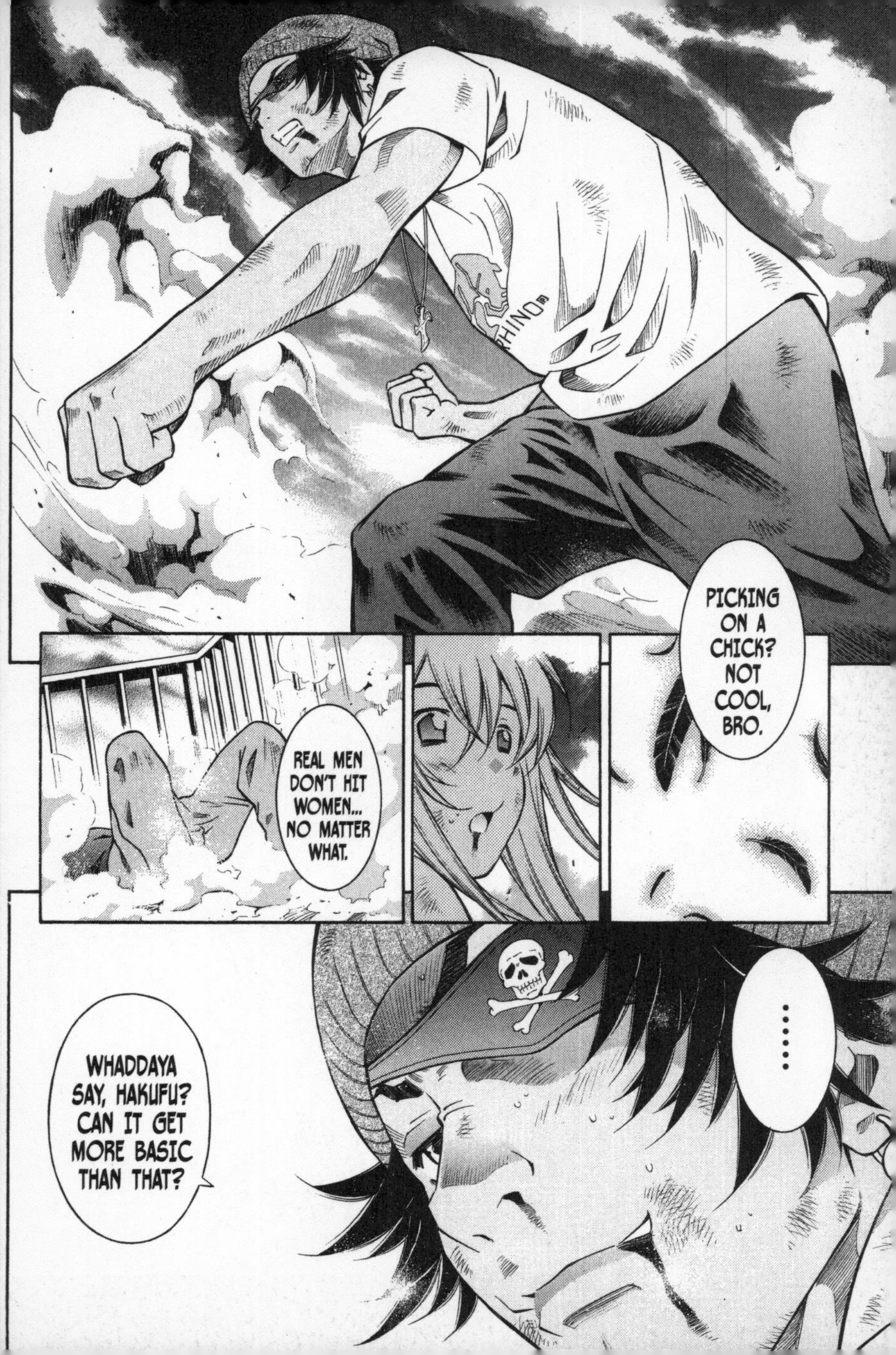
PICKING ON A CHICK? NOT COOL, BRO.
REAL MEN DON'T HIT WOMEN... NO MATTER WHAT.
......
WHADDAYA SAY, HAKUFU? CAN IT GET MORE BASIC THAN THAT?

ENJUTSU KOURO

THE SON OF ENHOU AND COUSIN TO ENSHOU.
AS GOVERNOR OF NANYO, ENJUTSU PARTICIPATED
IN THE ANTI-TOUTAKU ALLIANCE. HE LATER ACCEDED
AND CALLED HIMSELF EMPEROR, CITING GYOKUJI
OF DENKOKU (A.K.A. I'M THE GOVERNOR, NYAH,
NYAH, NYAH). IN THIS HE WAS BACKED BY SONKEN.
HOWEVER, DUE TO HIS HEDONISTIC LIFESTYLE,
ENJUTSU WAS ULTIMATELY ABANDONED BY HIS FOL-
LOWERS. SHORT FORM: HE WAS A SELFISH DICK.

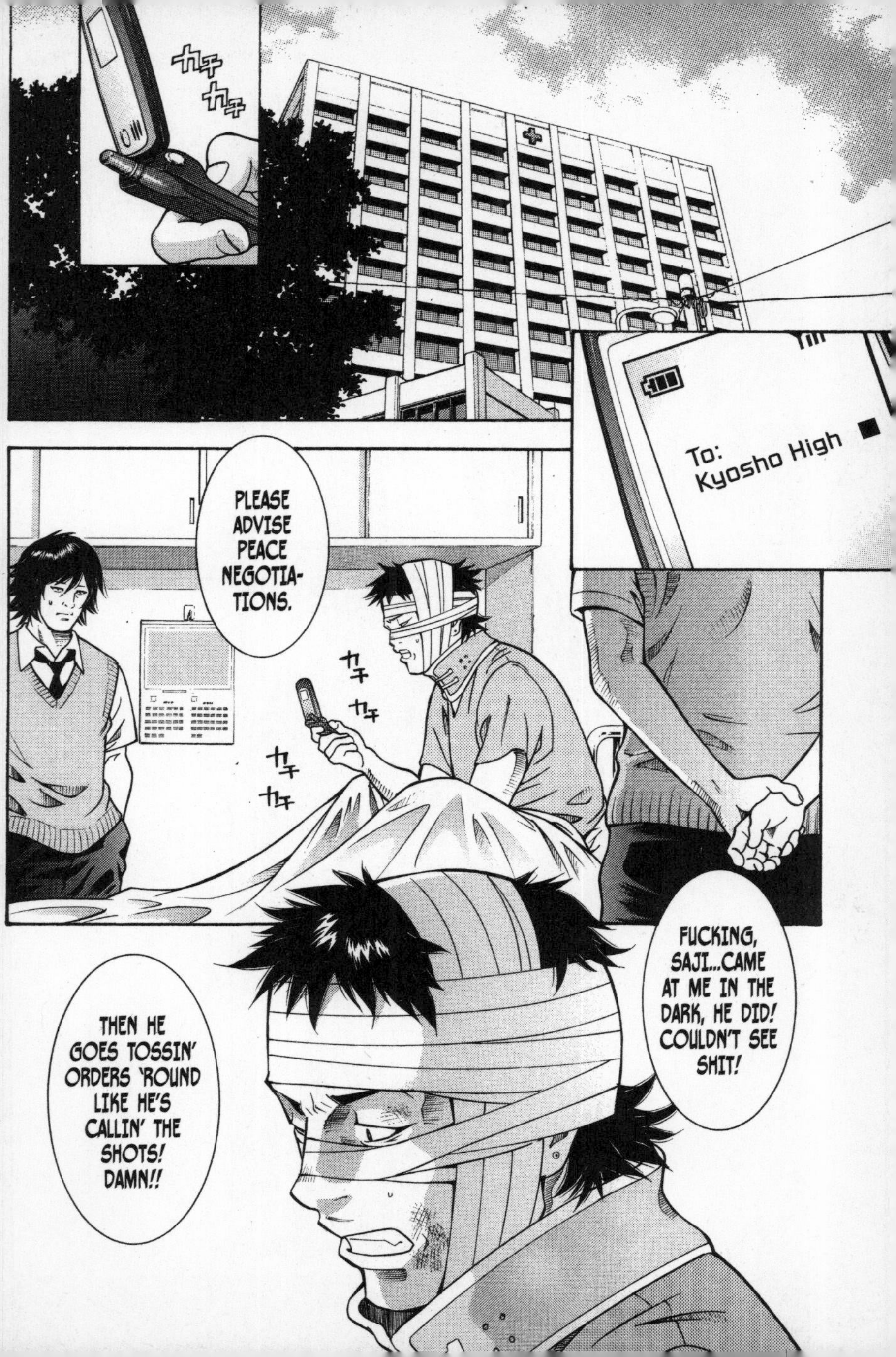
カチ
カチ
To:
Kyosho High
PLEASE ADVISE PEACE NEGOTIA-TIONS.
カチ
カチ
カチ
カチ
FUCKING, SAJI...CAME AT ME IN THE DARK, HE DID! COULDN'T SEE SHIT!
THEN HE GOES TOSSIN' ORDERS 'ROUND LIKE HE'S CALLIN' THE SHOTS! DAMN!!

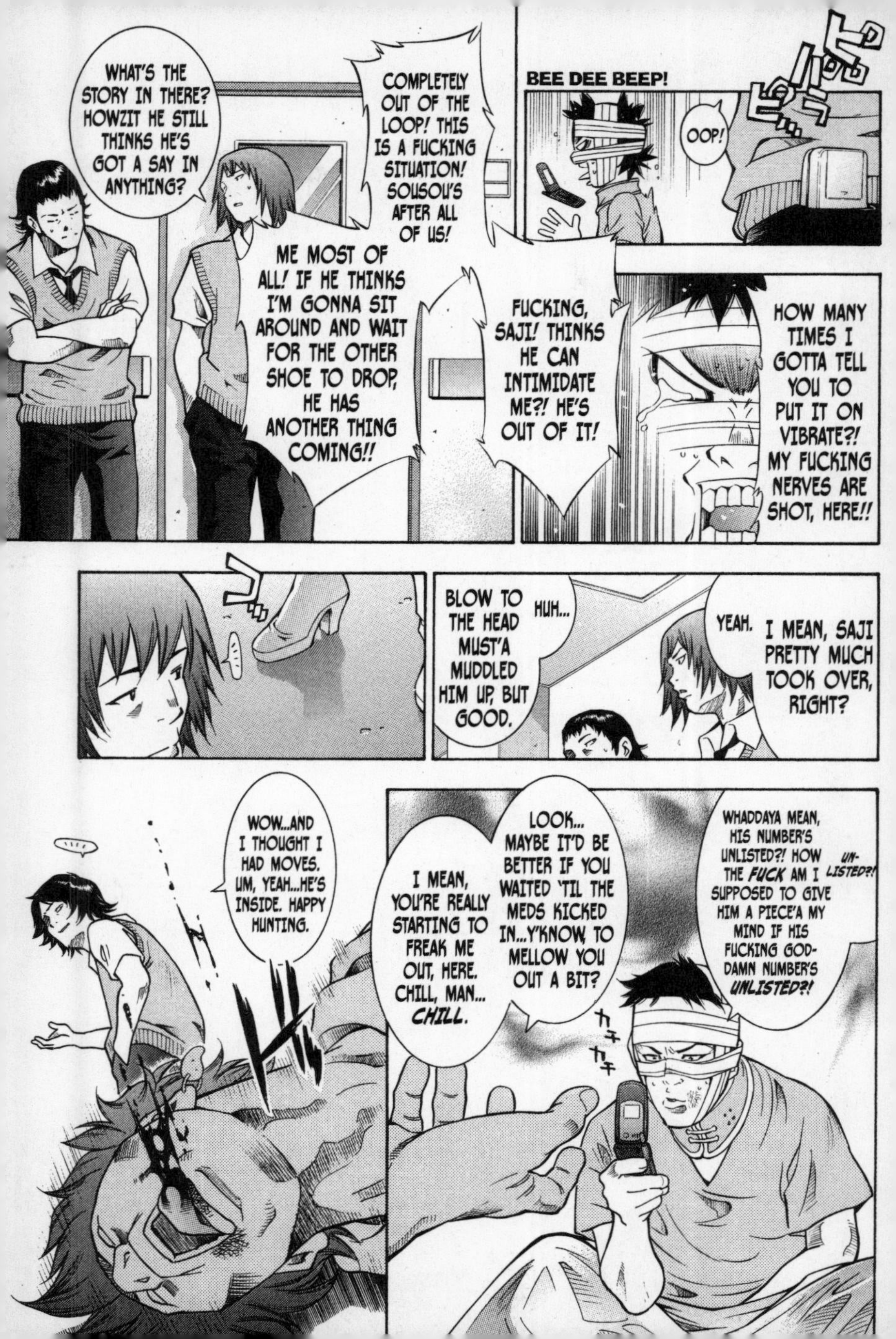
BEE DEE BEEP!
OOP!
HOW MANY TIMES I GOTTA TELL YOU TO PUT IT ON VIBRATE?! MY FUCKING NERVES ARE SHOT, HERE!!
COMPLETELY OUT OF THE LOOP! THIS IS A FUCKING SITUATION! SOUSOU'S AFTER ALL OF US!
ME MOST OF ALL! IF HE THINKS I'M GONNA SIT AROUND AND WAIT FOR THE OTHER SHOE TO DROP, HE HAS ANOTHER THING COMING!!
FUCKING, SAJI! THINKS HE CAN INTIMIDATE ME?! HE'S OUT OF IT!
WHAT'S THE STORY IN THERE? HOWZIT HE STILL THINKS HE'S GOT A SAY IN ANYTHING?
YEAH. I MEAN, SAJI PRETTY MUCH TOOK OVER, RIGHT?
HUH...
BLOW TO THE HEAD MUST'A MUDDLED HIM UP, BUT GOOD.
WHADDAYA MEAN, HIS NUMBER'S UNLISTED?! HOW THE *FUCK* AM I SUPPOSED TO GIVE HIM A PIECE'A MY MIND IF HIS FUCKING GOD-DAMN NUMBER'S *UNLISTED?!*
UN-LISTED?!
LOOK... MAYBE IT'D BE BETTER IF YOU WAITED 'TIL THE MEDS KICKED IN...Y'KNOW, TO MELLOW YOU OUT A BIT?
I MEAN, YOU'RE REALLY STARTING TO FREAK ME OUT, HERE. CHILL, MAN... ***CHILL***.
WOW...AND I THOUGHT I HAD MOVES. UM, YEAH...HE'S INSIDE. HAPPY HUNTING.

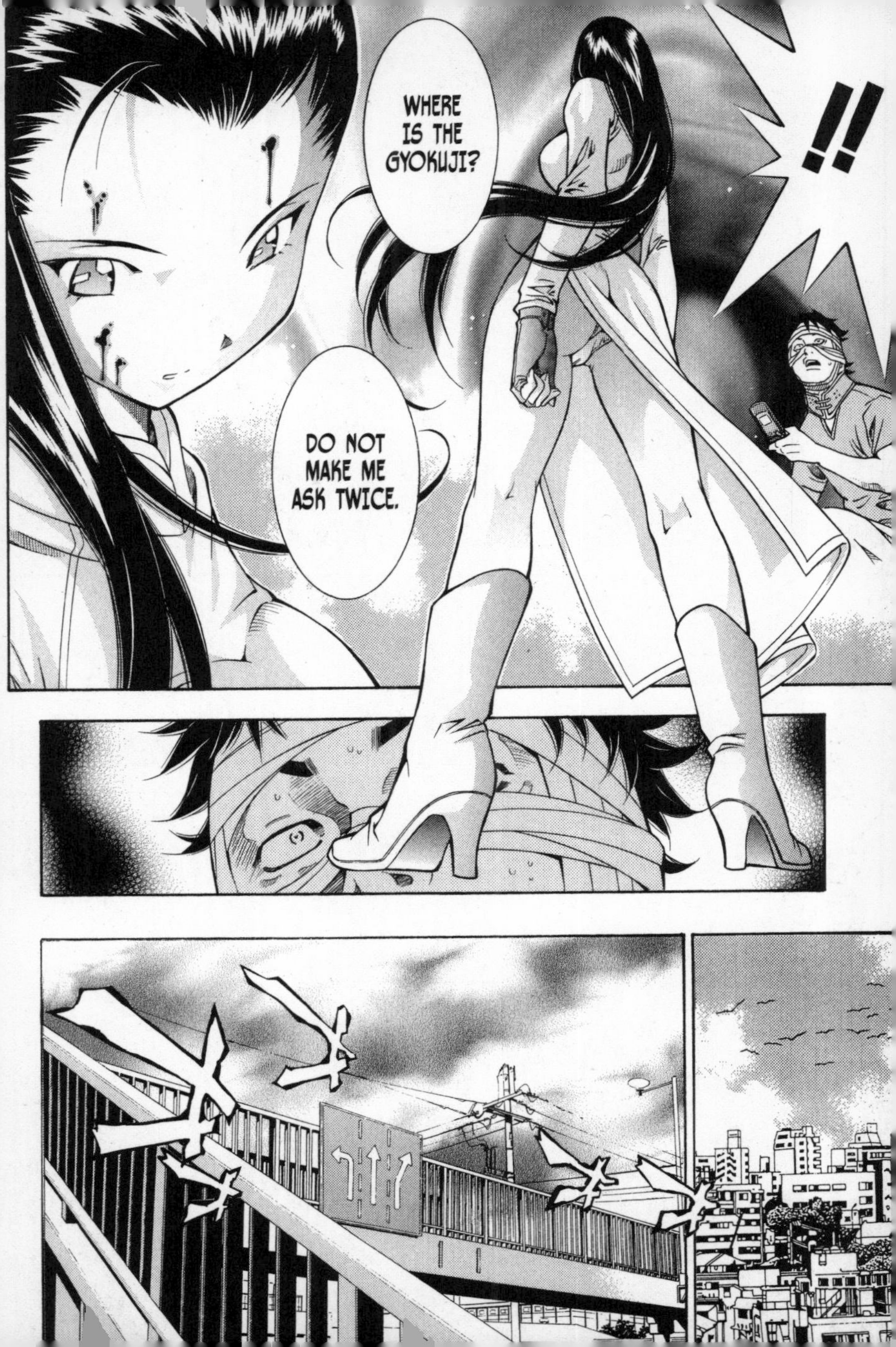
!!
WHERE IS THE GYOKUJI?
DO NOT MAKE ME ASK TWICE.

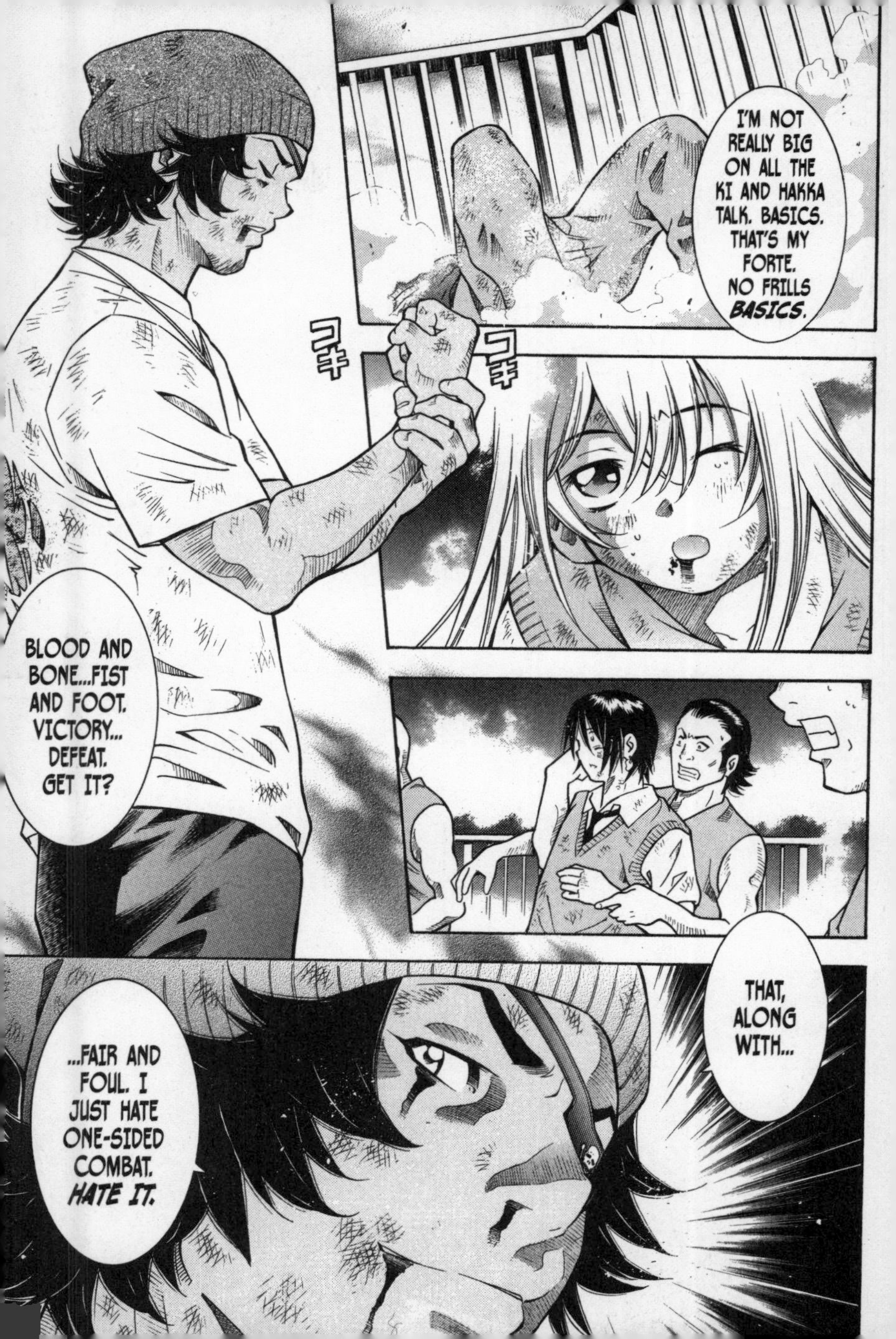
I'M NOT REALLY BIG ON ALL THE KI AND HAKKA TALK. BASICS. THAT'S MY FORTE. NO FRILLS *BASICS*.
コキ
コキ
BLOOD AND BONE...FIST AND FOOT. VICTORY... DEFEAT. GET IT?
THAT, ALONG WITH...
...FAIR AND FOUL. I JUST HATE ONE-SIDED COMBAT. *HATE IT.*

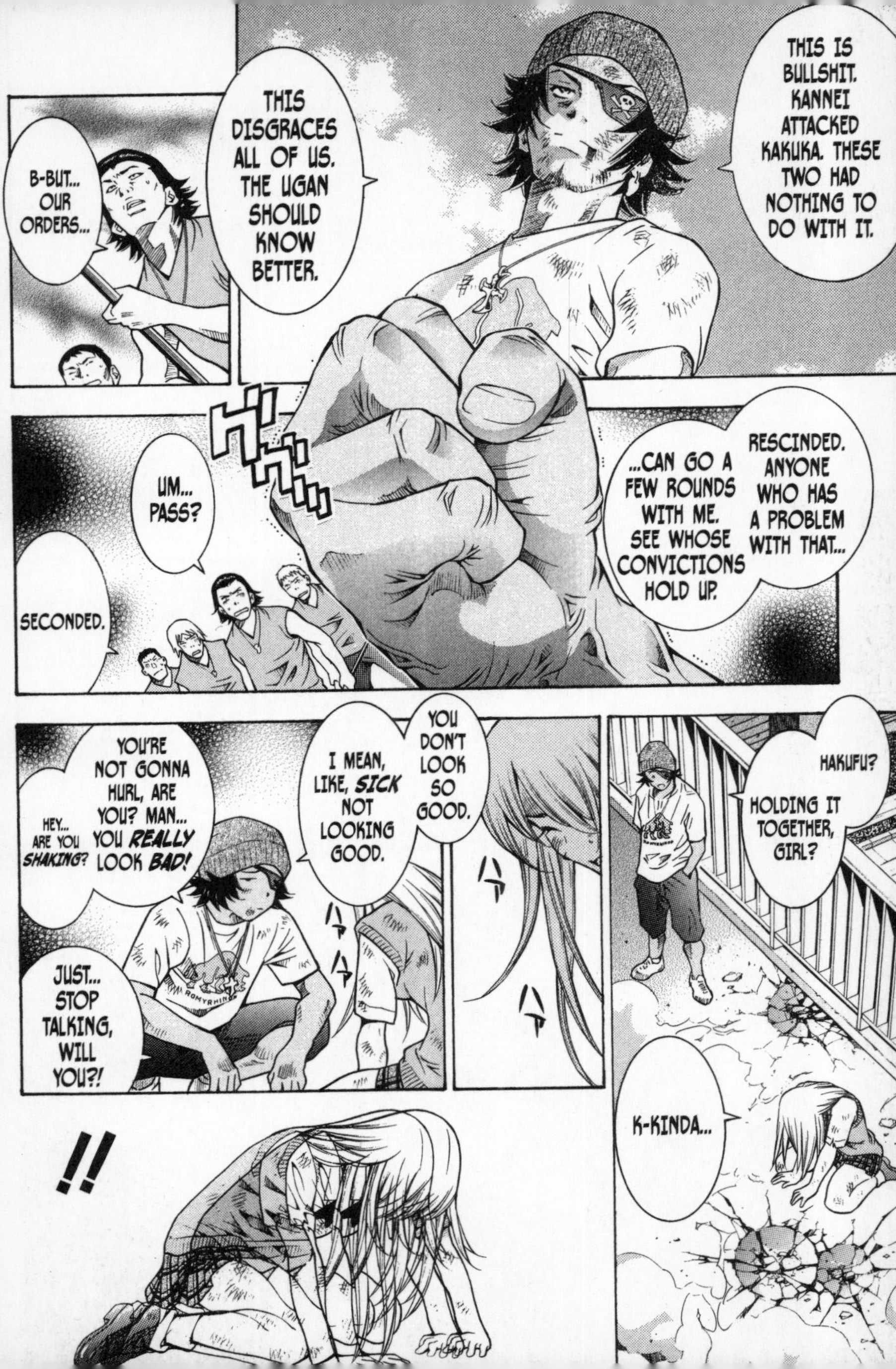
THIS IS BULLSHIT. KANNEI ATTACKED KAKUKA. THESE TWO HAD NOTHING TO DO WITH IT.
THIS DISGRACES ALL OF US. THE UGAN SHOULD KNOW BETTER.
B-BUT... OUR ORDERS...
RESCINDED. ANYONE WHO HAS A PROBLEM WITH THAT...
...CAN GO A FEW ROUNDS WITH ME. SEE WHOSE CONVICTIONS HOLD UP.
UM... PASS?
SECONDED.
HAKUFU?
HOLDING IT TOGETHER, GIRL?
K-KINDA...
YOU DON'T LOOK SO GOOD.
I MEAN, LIKE, *SICK* NOT LOOKING GOOD.
ハァ
ハァ
YOU'RE NOT GONNA HURL, ARE YOU? MAN... YOU *REALLY* LOOK *BAD!*
HEY... ARE YOU *SHAKING?*
JUST... STOP TALKING, WILL YOU?!
!!

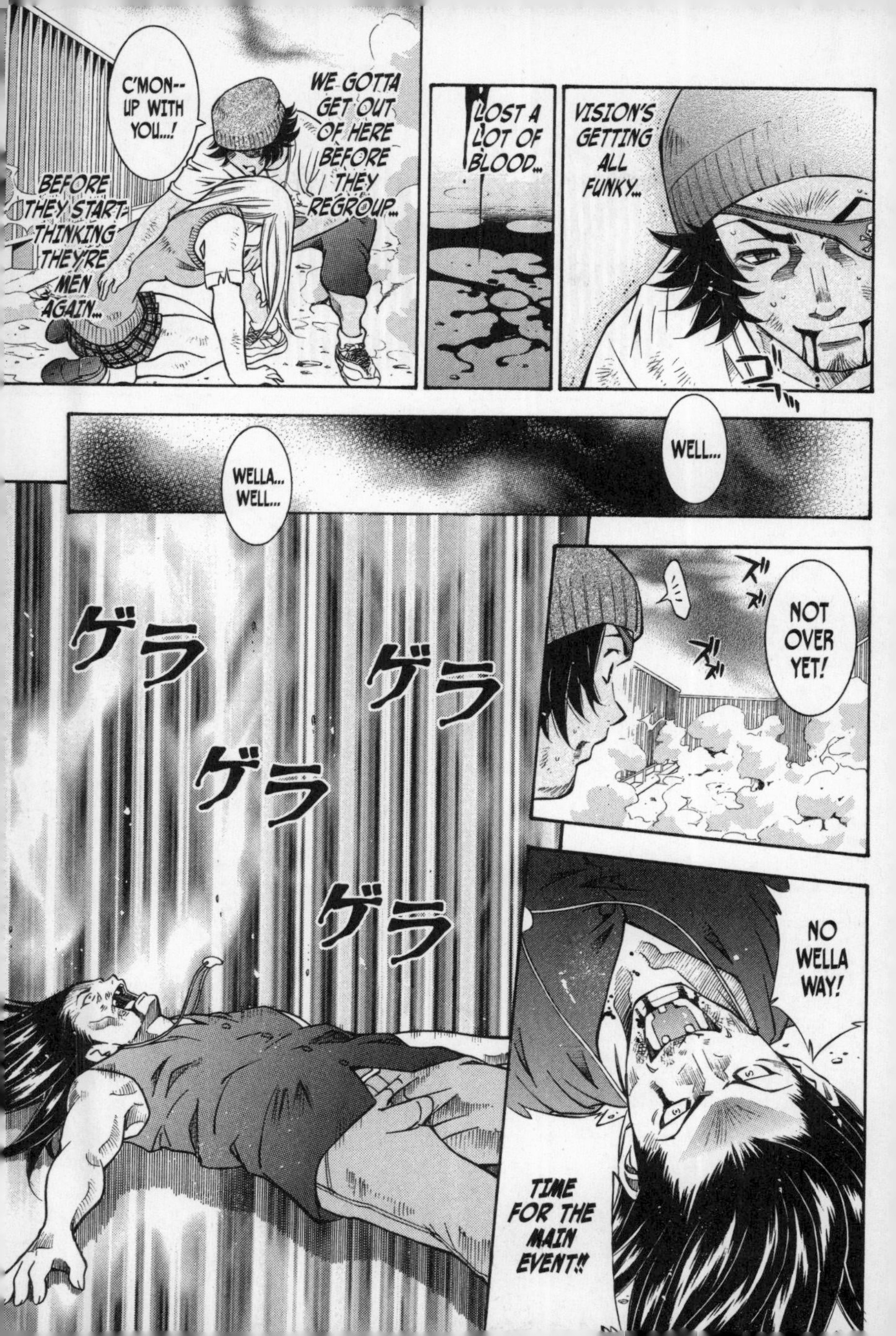
VISION'S GETTING ALL FUNKY...
LOST A LOT OF BLOOD...
WE GOTTA GET OUT OF HERE BEFORE THEY REGROUP...
C'MON-- UP WITH YOU...!
BEFORE THEY START THINKING THEY'RE MEN AGAIN...
WELL...
WELLA... WELL...
NOT OVER YET!
ズズ
ズズ
NO WELLA WAY!
TIME FOR THE MAIN EVENT!!
ゲラ
ゲラ
ゲラ
ゲラ

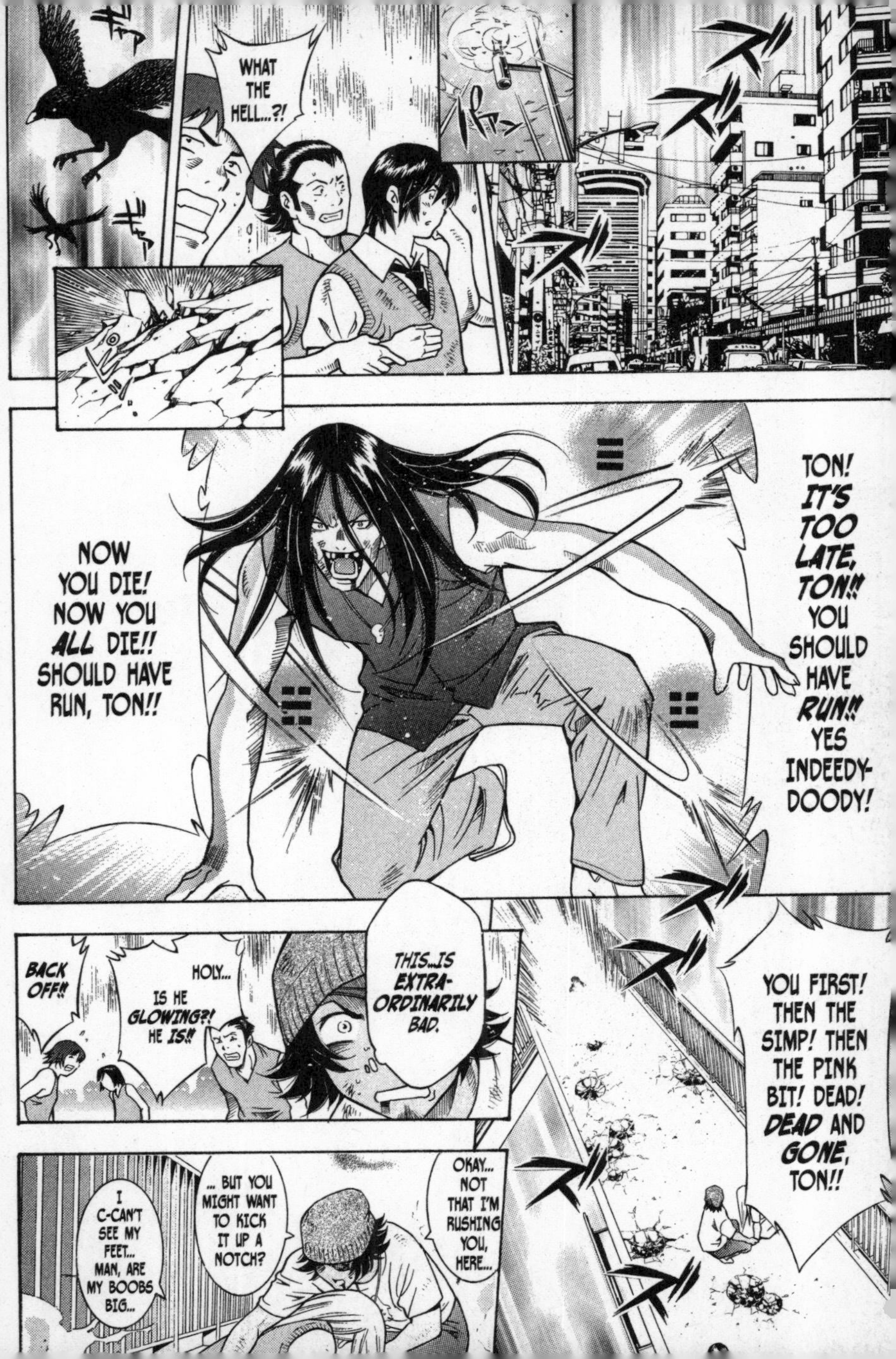
WHAT THE HELL...?!
TON! IT'S TOO LATE, TON!! YOU SHOULD HAVE RUN!! YES INDEEDY-DOODY!
NOW YOU DIE! NOW YOU ALL DIE!! SHOULD HAVE RUN, TON!!
YOU FIRST! THEN THE SIMP! THEN THE PINK BIT! DEAD! DEAD AND GONE, TON!!
THIS...IS EXTRA-ORDINARILY BAD.
HOLY... IS HE GLOWING?! HE IS!!
BACK OFF!!
OKAY... NOT THAT I'M RUSHING YOU, HERE...
... BUT YOU MIGHT WANT TO KICK IT UP A NOTCH?
I C-CAN'T SEE MY FEET... MAN, ARE MY BOOBS BIG...

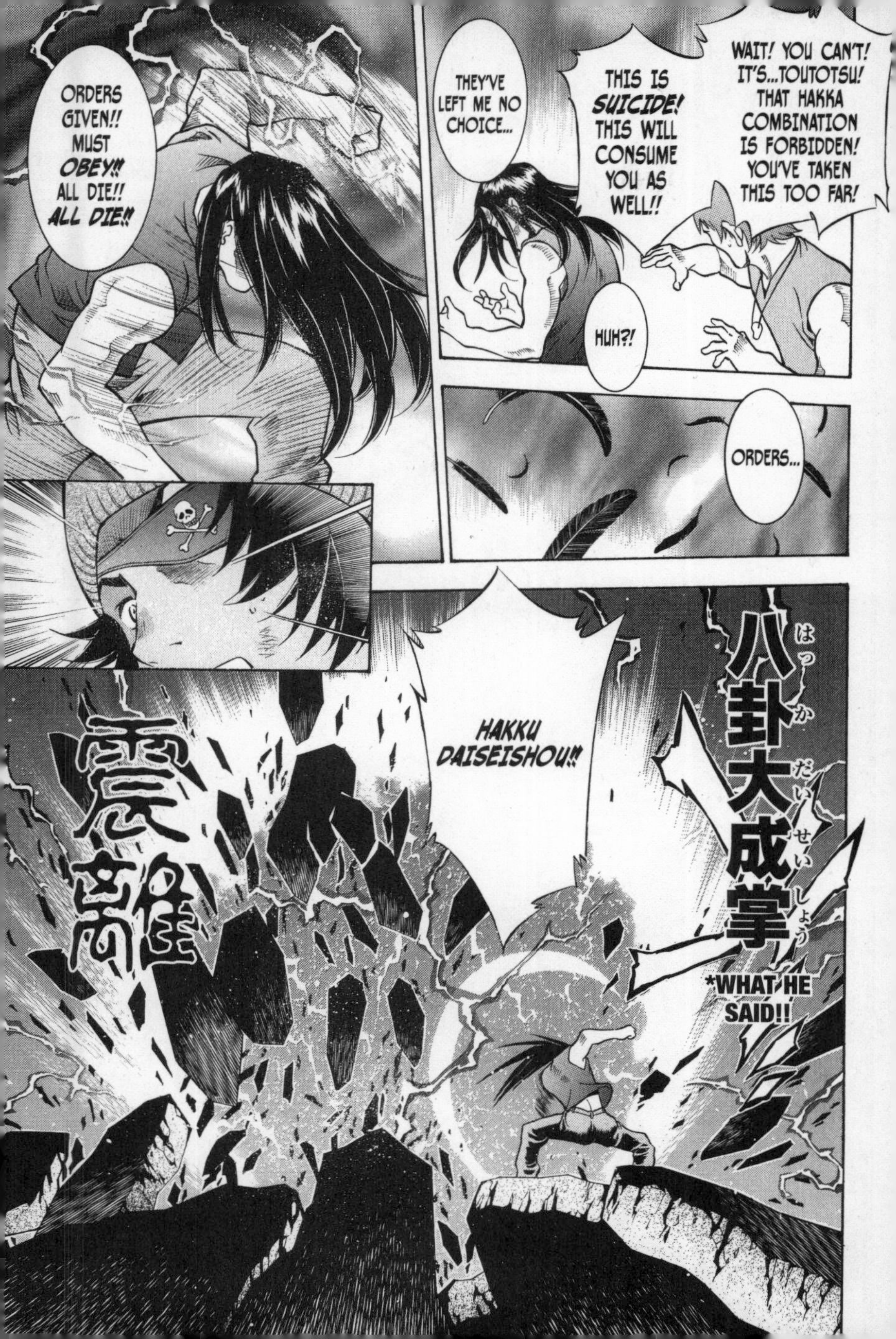
WAIT! YOU CAN'T! IT'S...TOUTOTSU! THAT HAKKA COMBINATION IS FORBIDDEN! YOU'VE TAKEN THIS TOO FAR!
THIS IS *SUICIDE!* THIS WILL CONSUME YOU AS WELL!!
THEY'VE LEFT ME NO CHOICE...
HUH?!
ORDERS...
ORDERS GIVEN!! MUST *OBEY!!* ALL DIE!! *ALL DIE!!*
八卦大成掌
はっかだいせいしょう
HAKKU DAISEISHOU!!
*WHAT HE SAID!!
震離

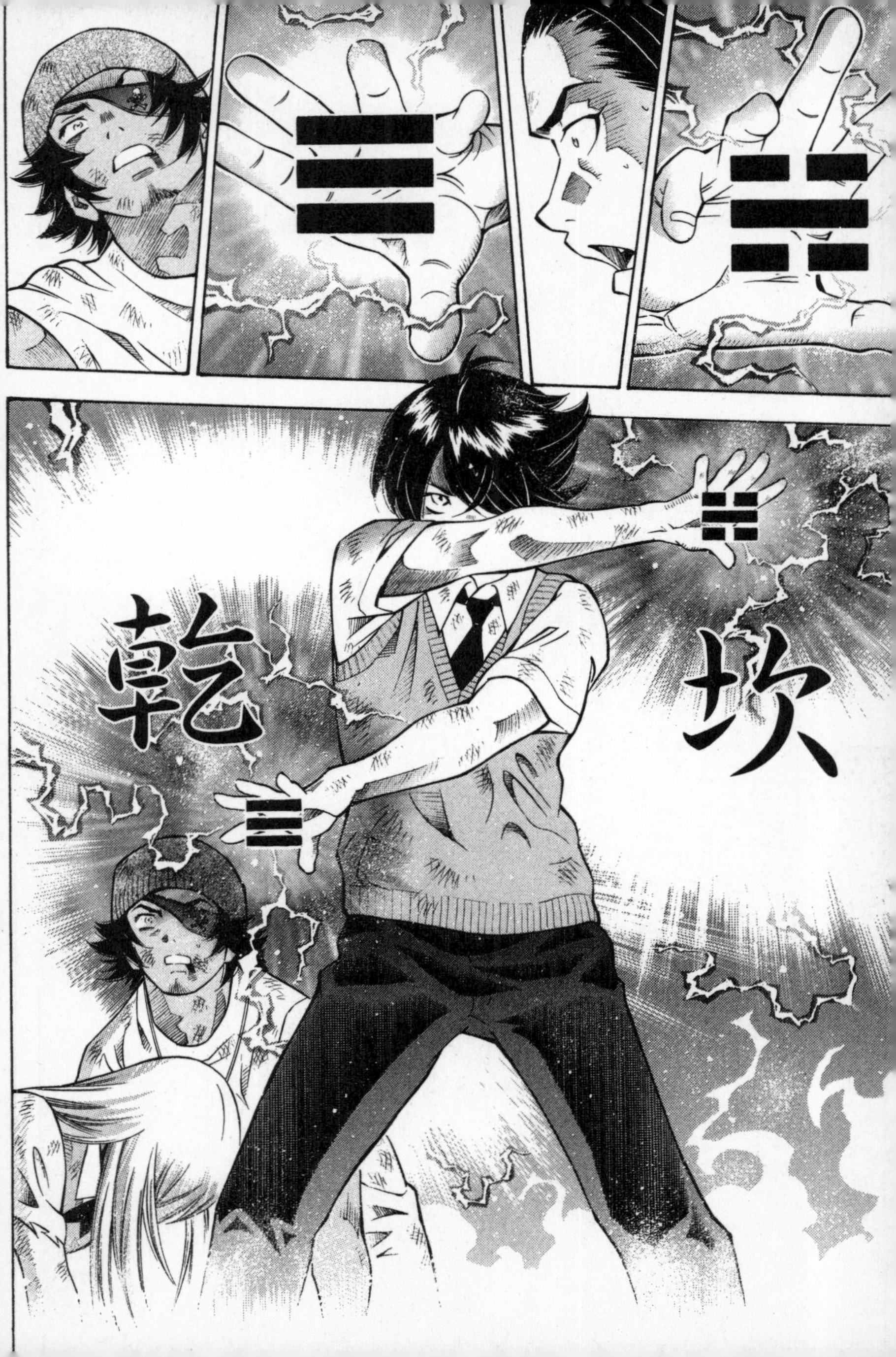
坎
乾

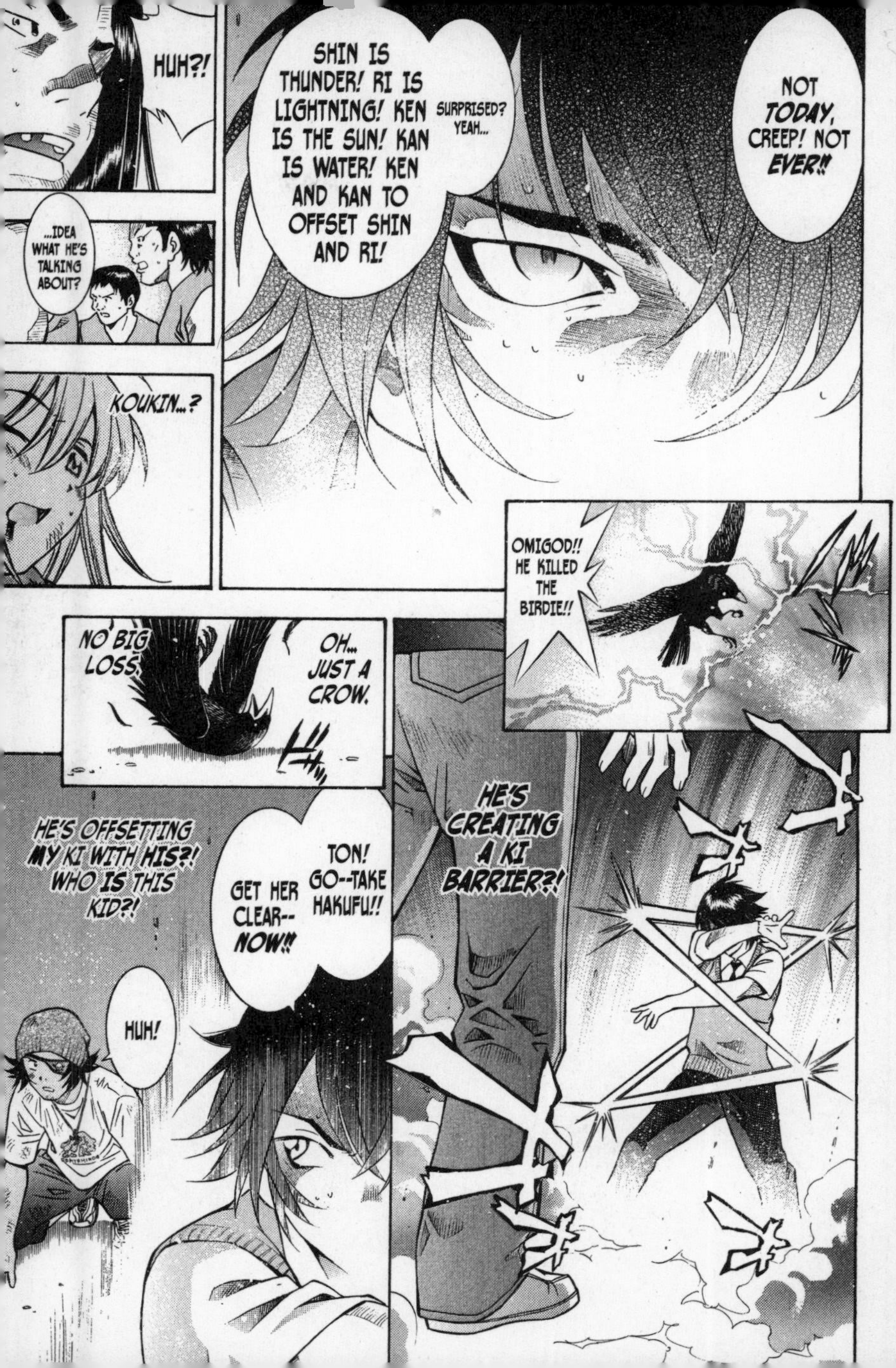
NOT TODAY, CREEP! NOT EVER!!
SURPRISED? YEAH...
SHIN IS THUNDER! RI IS LIGHTNING! KEN IS THE SUN! KAN IS WATER! KEN AND KAN TO OFFSET SHIN AND RI!
HUH?!
...IDEA WHAT HE'S TALKING ABOUT?
KOUKIN...?
OMIGOD!! HE KILLED THE BIRDIE!!
OH... JUST A CROW.
NO BIG LOSS.
HE'S CREATING A KI BARRIER?!
TON! GO--TAKE HAKUFU!!
GET HER CLEAR-- NOW!!
HE'S OFFSETTING MY KI WITH HIS?! WHO IS THIS KID?!
HUH!

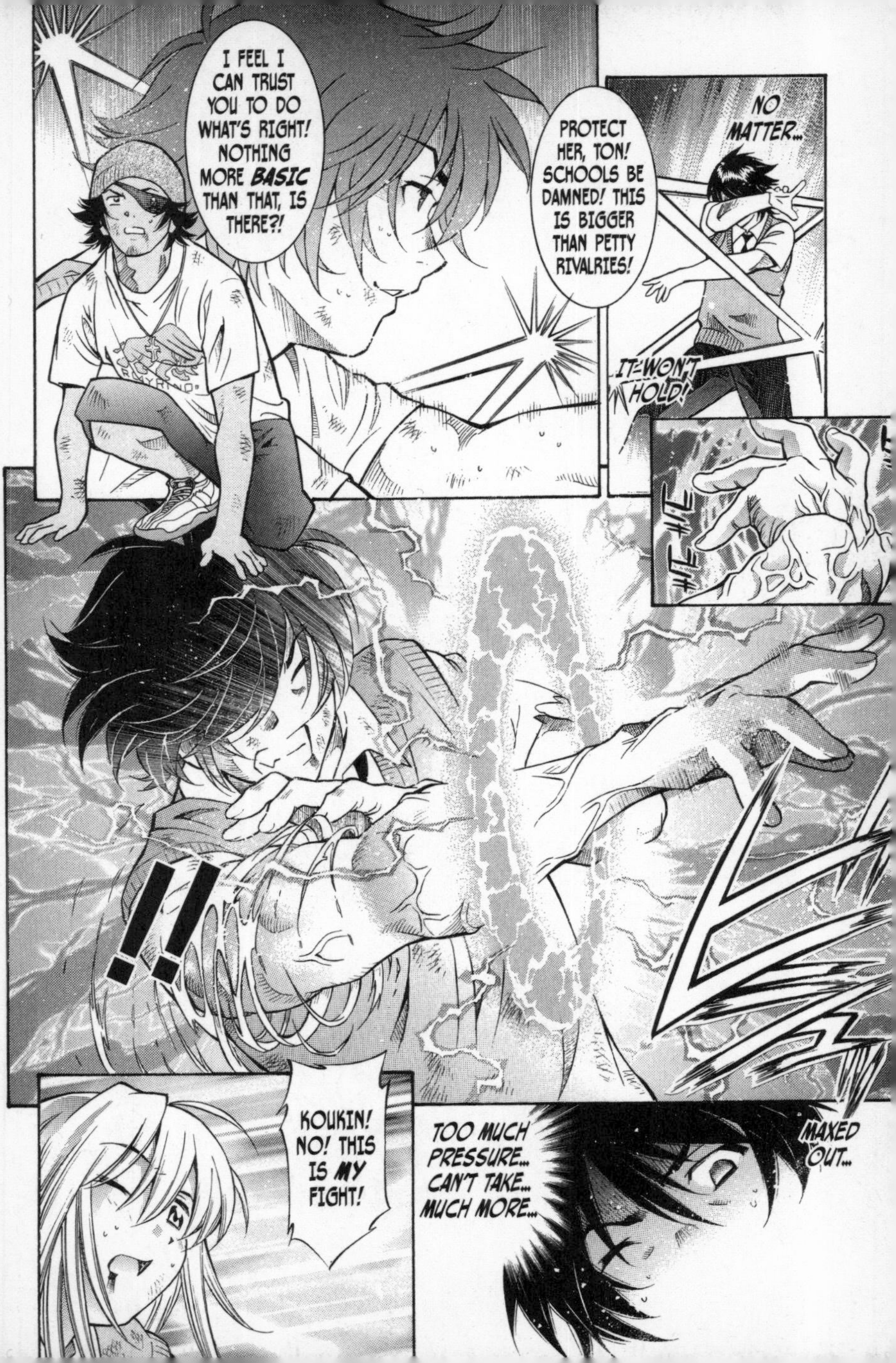
NO MATTER...
IT WON'T HOLD!
PROTECT HER, TON! SCHOOLS BE DAMNED! THIS IS BIGGER THAN PETTY RIVALRIES!
I FEEL I CAN TRUST YOU TO DO WHAT'S RIGHT! NOTHING MORE BASIC THAN THAT, IS THERE?!
!!
MAXED OUT...
TOO MUCH PRESSURE... CAN'T TAKE... MUCH MORE...
KOUKIN! NO! THIS IS MY FIGHT!

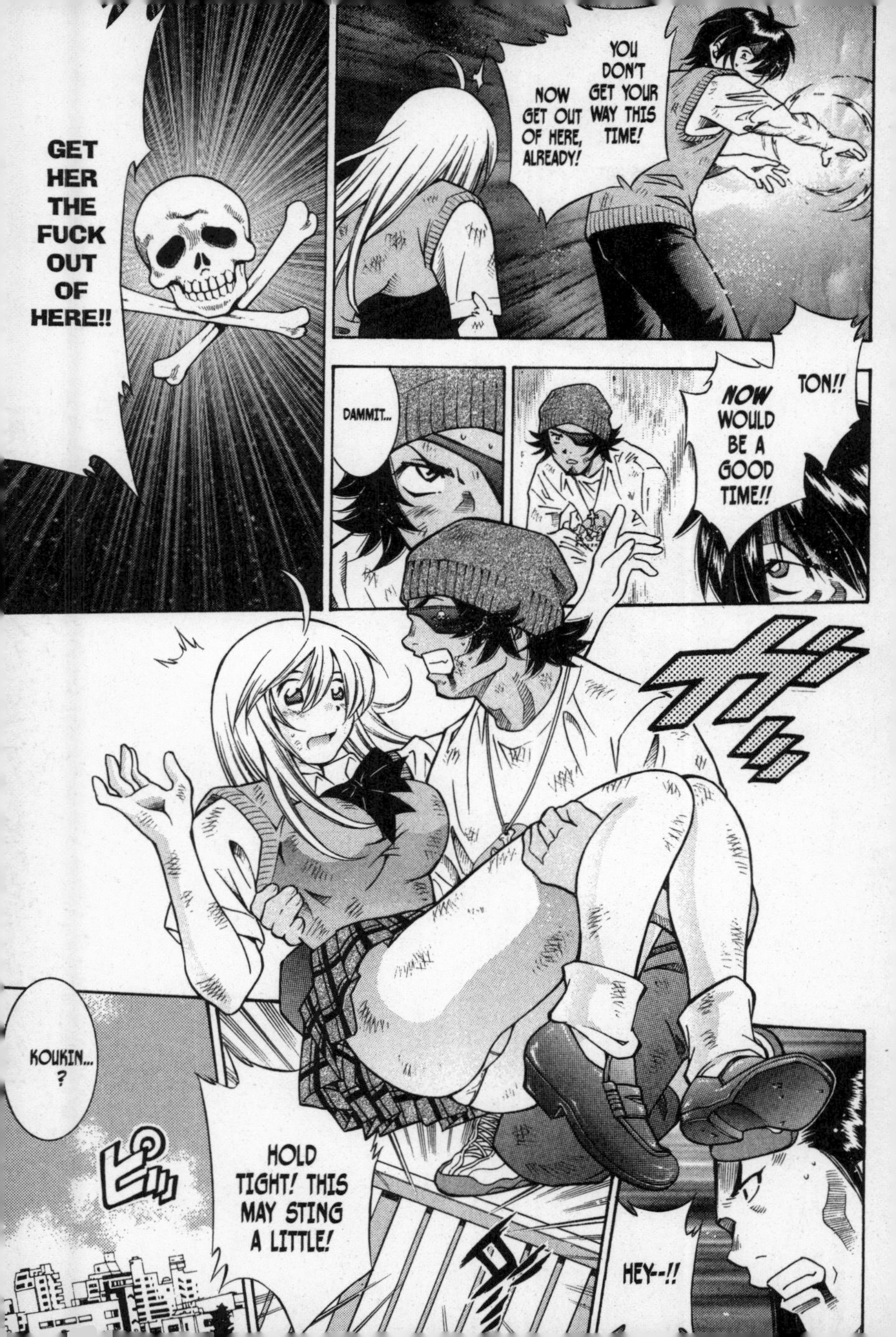

YOU DON'T GET YOUR WAY THIS TIME!
NOW GET OUT OF HERE, ALREADY!
TON!!
NOW WOULD BE A GOOD TIME!!
DAMMIT...
GET HER THE FUCK OUT OF HERE!!
HOLD TIGHT! THIS MAY STING A LITTLE!
HEY--!!
KOUKIN...?

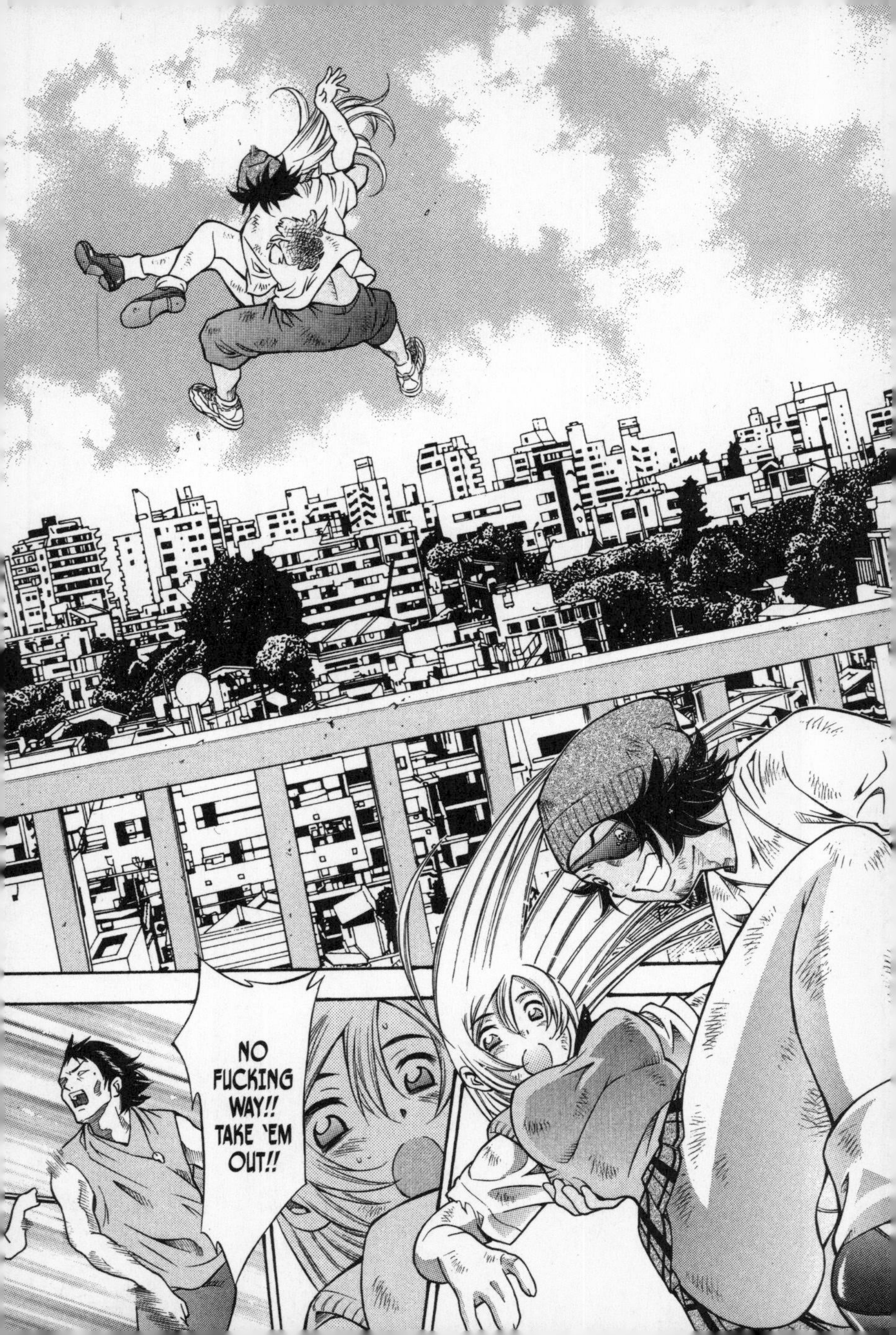
NO FUCKING WAY!! TAKE 'EM OUT!!

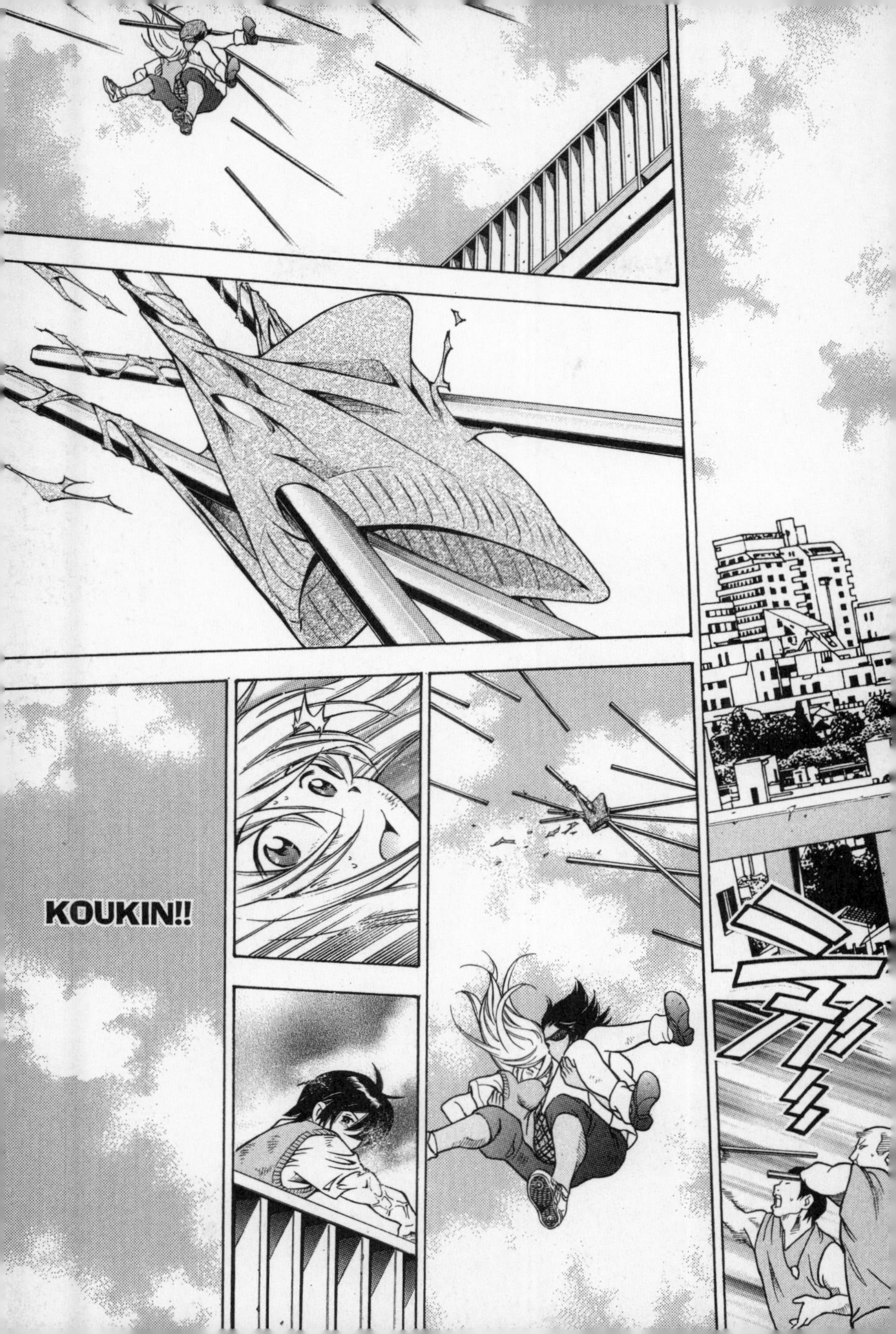
KOUKIN!!

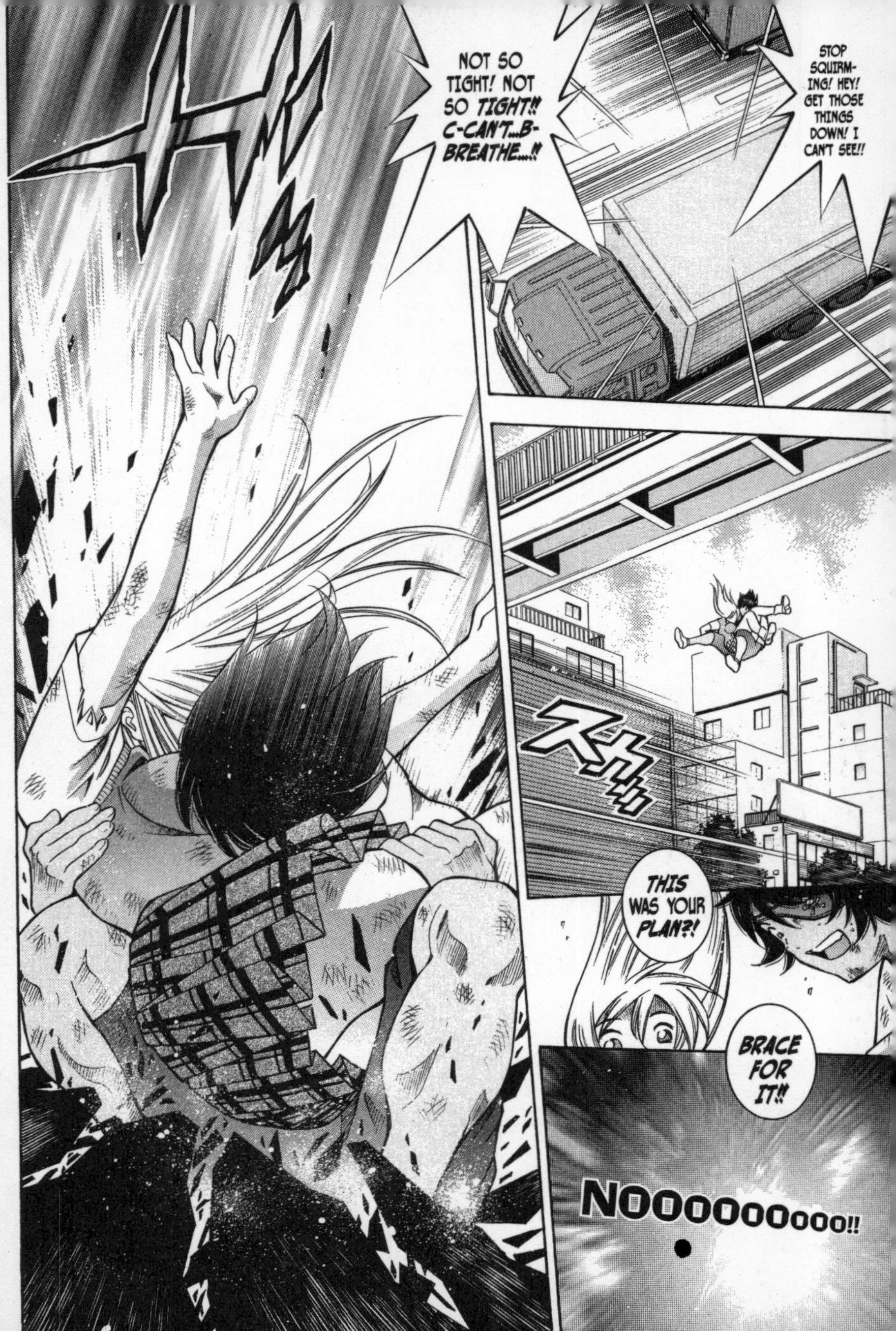
STOP SQUIRMING! HEY! GET THOSE THINGS DOWN! I CAN'T SEE!!
NOT SO TIGHT! NOT SO *TIGHT!!* *C-CAN'T...B-BREATHE...!!*
THIS WAS YOUR PLAN?!
BRACE FOR IT!!
NOOOOOOOO!!

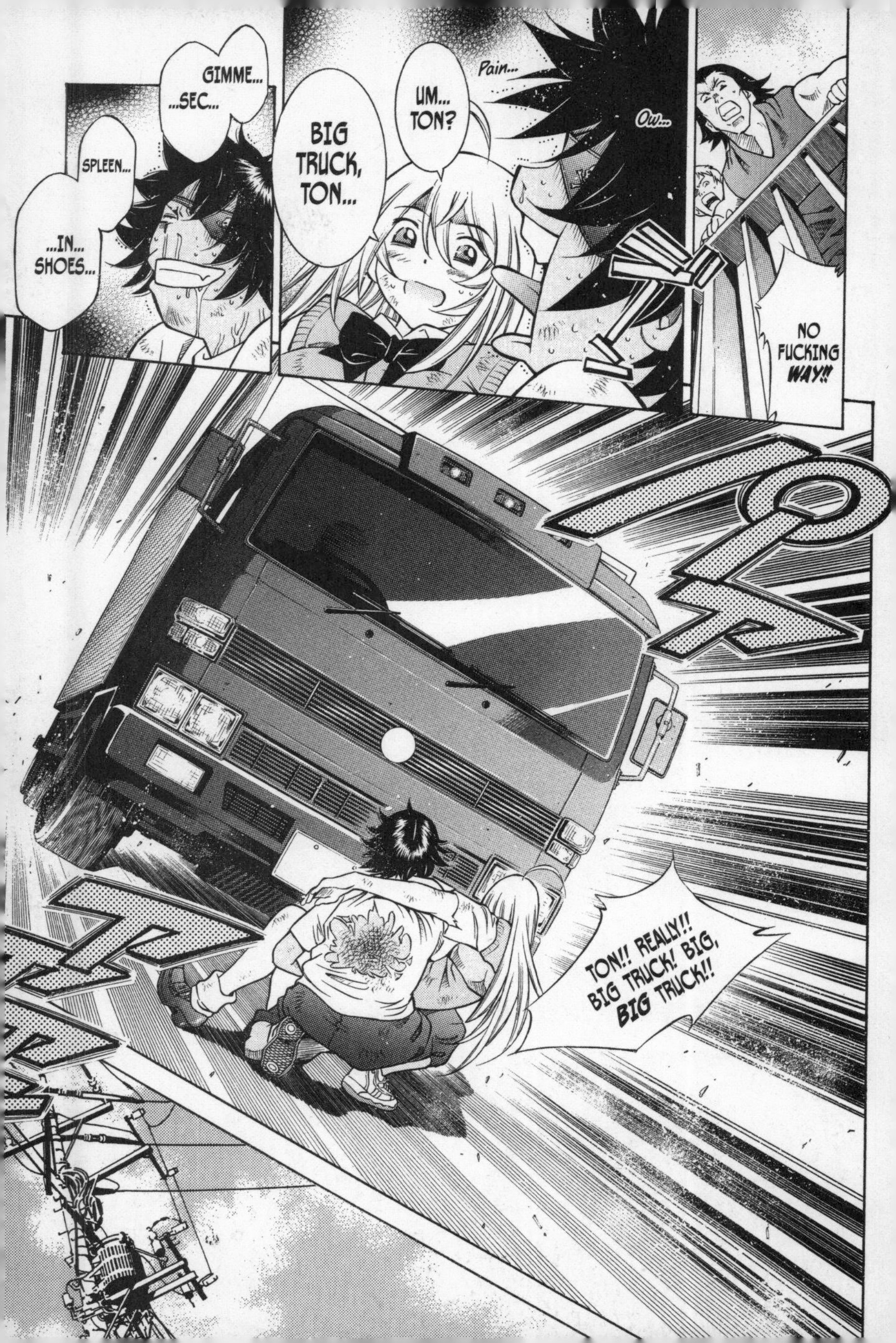
NO FUCKING WAY!!
Ow...
Pain...
UM... TON?
BIG TRUCK, TON...
GIMME... ...SEC...
SPLEEN...
...IN... SHOES...
TON!! REALLY!! BIG TRUCK! BIG, BIG TRUCK!!

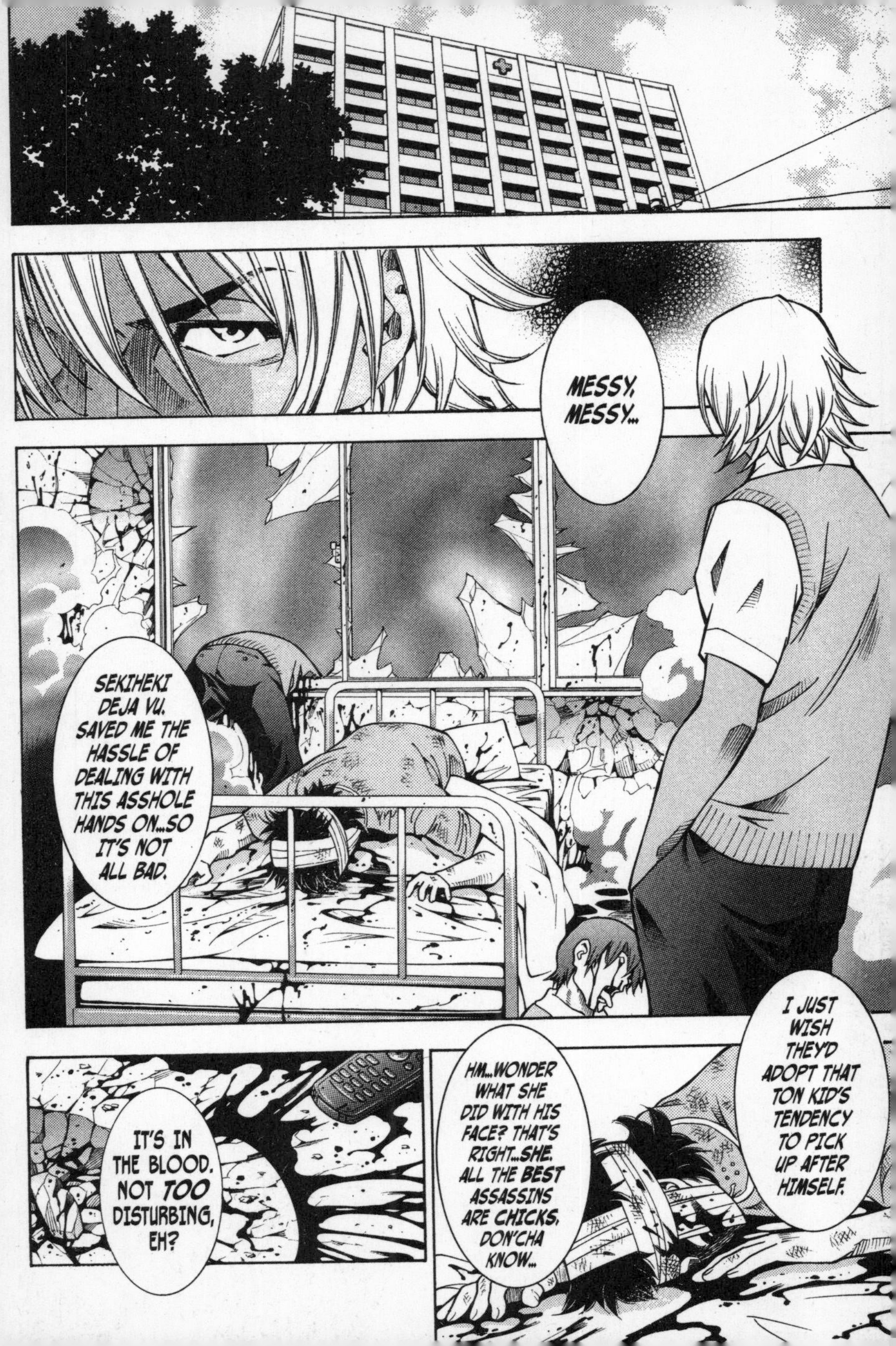
MESSY, MESSY...
SEKIHEKI DEJA VU. SAVED ME THE HASSLE OF DEALING WITH THIS ASSHOLE HANDS ON...SO IT'S NOT ALL BAD.
I JUST WISH THEY'D ADOPT THAT TON KID'S TENDENCY TO PICK UP AFTER HIMSELF.
HM...WONDER WHAT SHE DID WITH HIS FACE? THAT'S RIGHT...SHE. ALL THE BEST ASSASSINS ARE CHICKS. DON'CHA KNOW...
IT'S IN THE BLOOD. NOT TOO DISTURBING, EH?

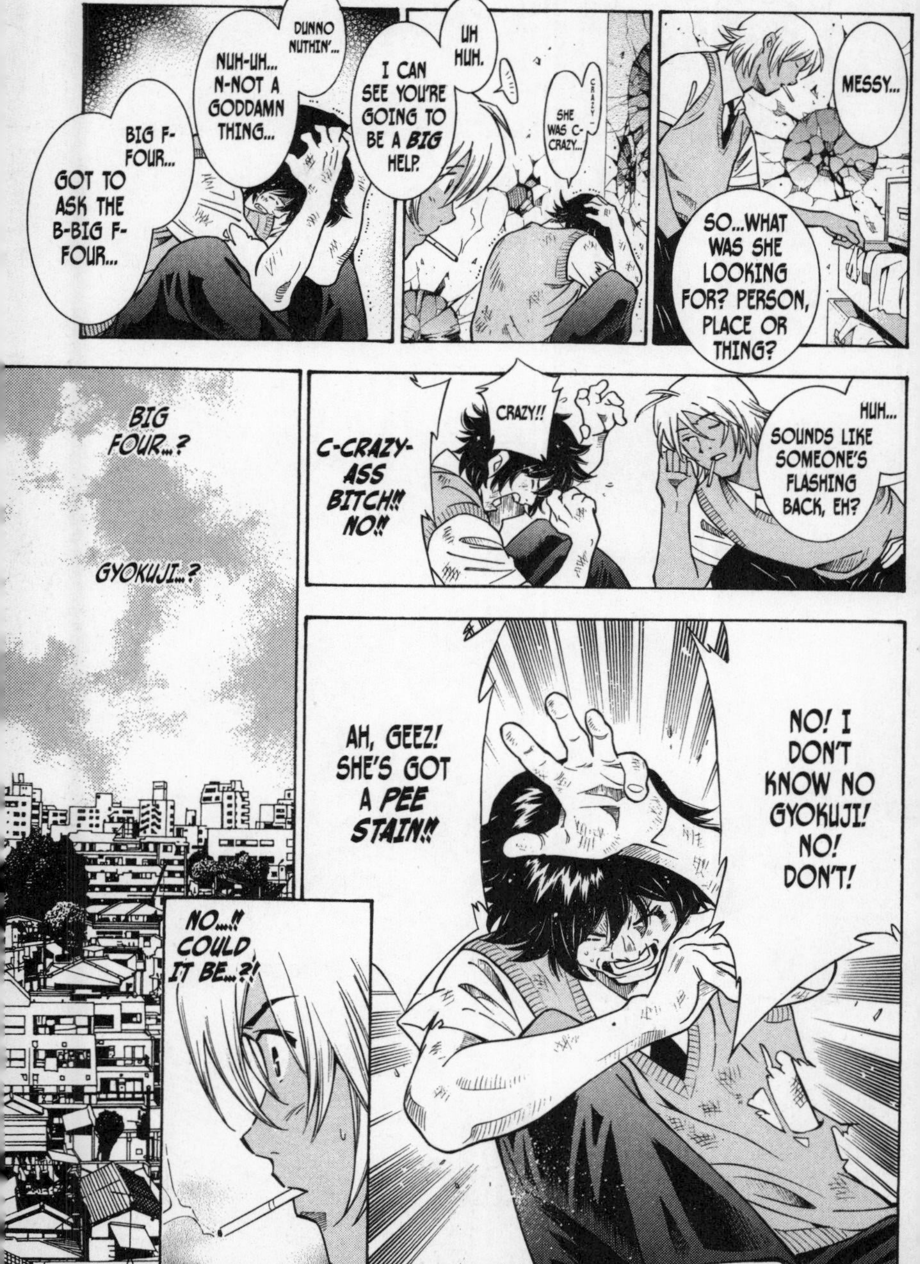
MESSY...
SO...WHAT WAS SHE LOOKING FOR? PERSON, PLACE OR THING?
UH HUH.
I CAN SEE YOU'RE GOING TO BE A *BIG* HELP.
SHE WAS C-CRAZY...
CRAZY...
DUNNO NUTHIN'...
NUH-UH... N-NOT A GODDAMN THING...
BIG F-FOUR...
GOT TO ASK THE B-BIG F-FOUR...
HUH... SOUNDS LIKE SOMEONE'S FLASHING BACK, EH?
CRAZY!!
C-CRAZY-ASS BITCH!! NO!!
NO! I DON'T KNOW NO GYOKUJI! NO! DON'T!
AH, GEEZ! SHE'S GOT A *PEE STAIN*!!
BIG FOUR...?
GYOKUJI...?
NO...!! COULD IT BE...?!

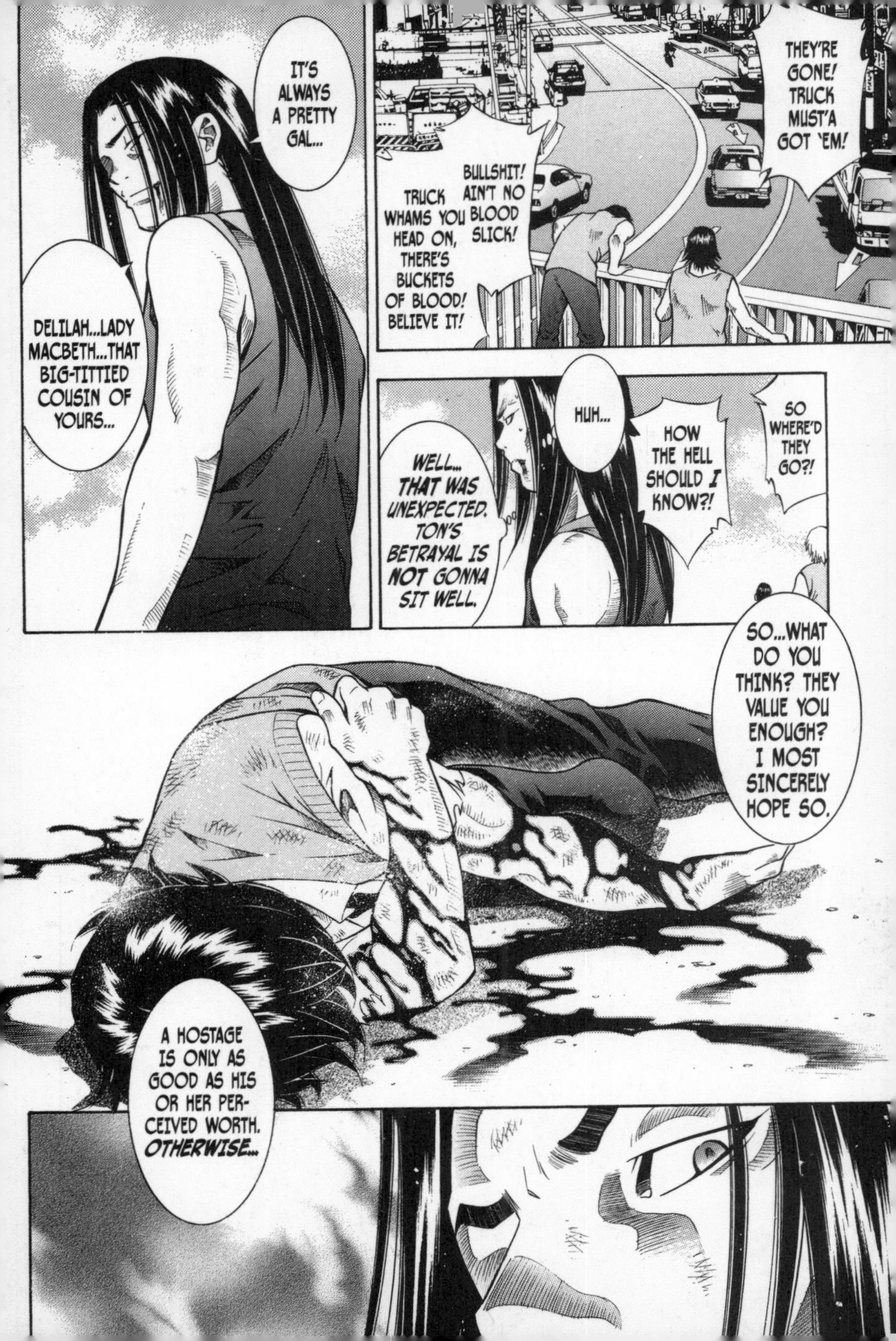
THEY'RE GONE! TRUCK MUST'A GOT 'EM!
BULLSHIT! AIN'T NO BLOOD SLICK!
TRUCK WHAMS YOU HEAD ON, THERE'S BUCKETS OF BLOOD! BELIEVE IT!
SO WHERE'D THEY GO?!
HOW THE HELL SHOULD I KNOW?!
HUH...
WELL... THAT WAS UNEXPECTED. TON'S BETRAYAL IS NOT GONNA SIT WELL.
IT'S ALWAYS A PRETTY GAL...
DELILAH...LADY MACBETH...THAT BIG-TITTIED COUSIN OF YOURS...
SO...WHAT DO YOU THINK? THEY VALUE YOU ENOUGH? I MOST SINCERELY HOPE SO.
A HOSTAGE IS ONLY AS GOOD AS HIS OR HER PERCEIVED WORTH. OTHERWISE...

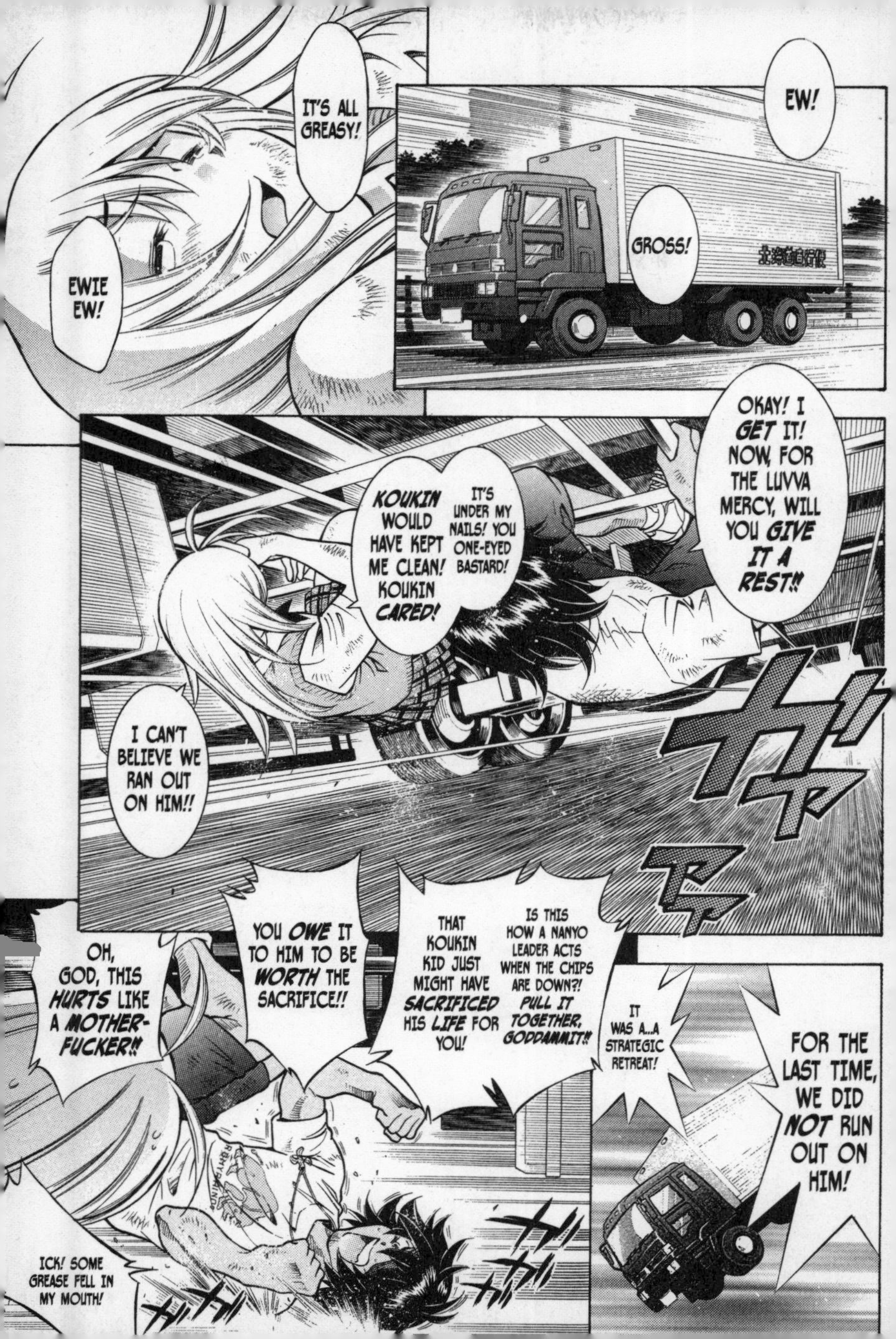
EW!
GROSS!
IT'S ALL GREASY!
EWIE EW!
OKAY! I GET IT! NOW, FOR THE LUVVA MERCY, WILL YOU GIVE IT A REST!!
IT'S UNDER MY NAILS! YOU ONE-EYED BASTARD!
KOUKIN WOULD HAVE KEPT ME CLEAN! KOUKIN CARED!
I CAN'T BELIEVE WE RAN OUT ON HIM!!
FOR THE LAST TIME, WE DID NOT RUN OUT ON HIM!
IT WAS A...A STRATEGIC RETREAT!
IS THIS HOW A NANYO LEADER ACTS WHEN THE CHIPS ARE DOWN?! PULL IT TOGETHER, GODDAMMIT!!
THAT KOUKIN KID JUST MIGHT HAVE SACRIFICED HIS LIFE FOR YOU!
YOU OWE IT TO HIM TO BE WORTH THE SACRIFICE!!
OH, GOD, THIS HURTS LIKE A MOTHER-FUCKER!!
ICK! SOME GREASE FELL IN MY MOUTH!

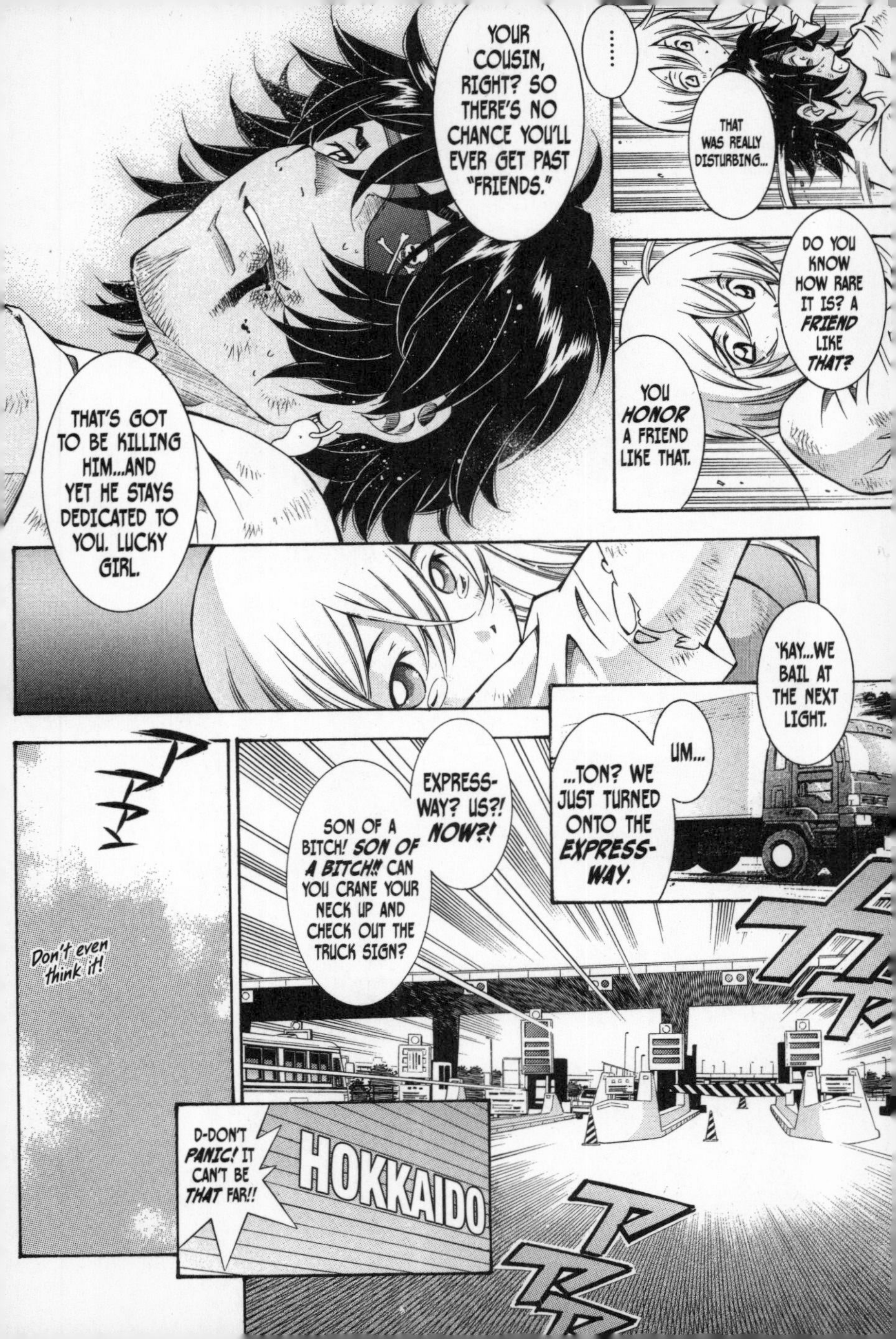
......
THAT WAS REALLY DISTURBING...
DO YOU KNOW HOW RARE IT IS? A *FRIEND* LIKE *THAT?*
YOU *HONOR* A FRIEND LIKE THAT.
YOUR COUSIN, RIGHT? SO THERE'S NO CHANCE YOU'LL EVER GET PAST "FRIENDS."
THAT'S GOT TO BE KILLING HIM...AND YET HE STAYS DEDICATED TO YOU. LUCKY GIRL.
'KAY...WE BAIL AT THE NEXT LIGHT.
UM...
...TON? WE JUST TURNED ONTO THE *EXPRESS-WAY*.
EXPRESS-WAY? US?! *NOW?!*
SON OF A BITCH! *SON OF A BITCH!!* CAN YOU CRANE YOUR NECK UP AND CHECK OUT THE TRUCK SIGN?
HOKKAIDO
D-DON'T *PANIC!* IT CAN'T BE *THAT* FAR!!
Don't even think it!

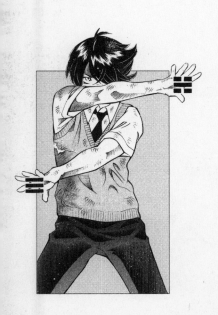

一騎当千

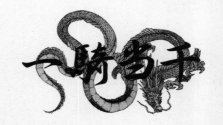

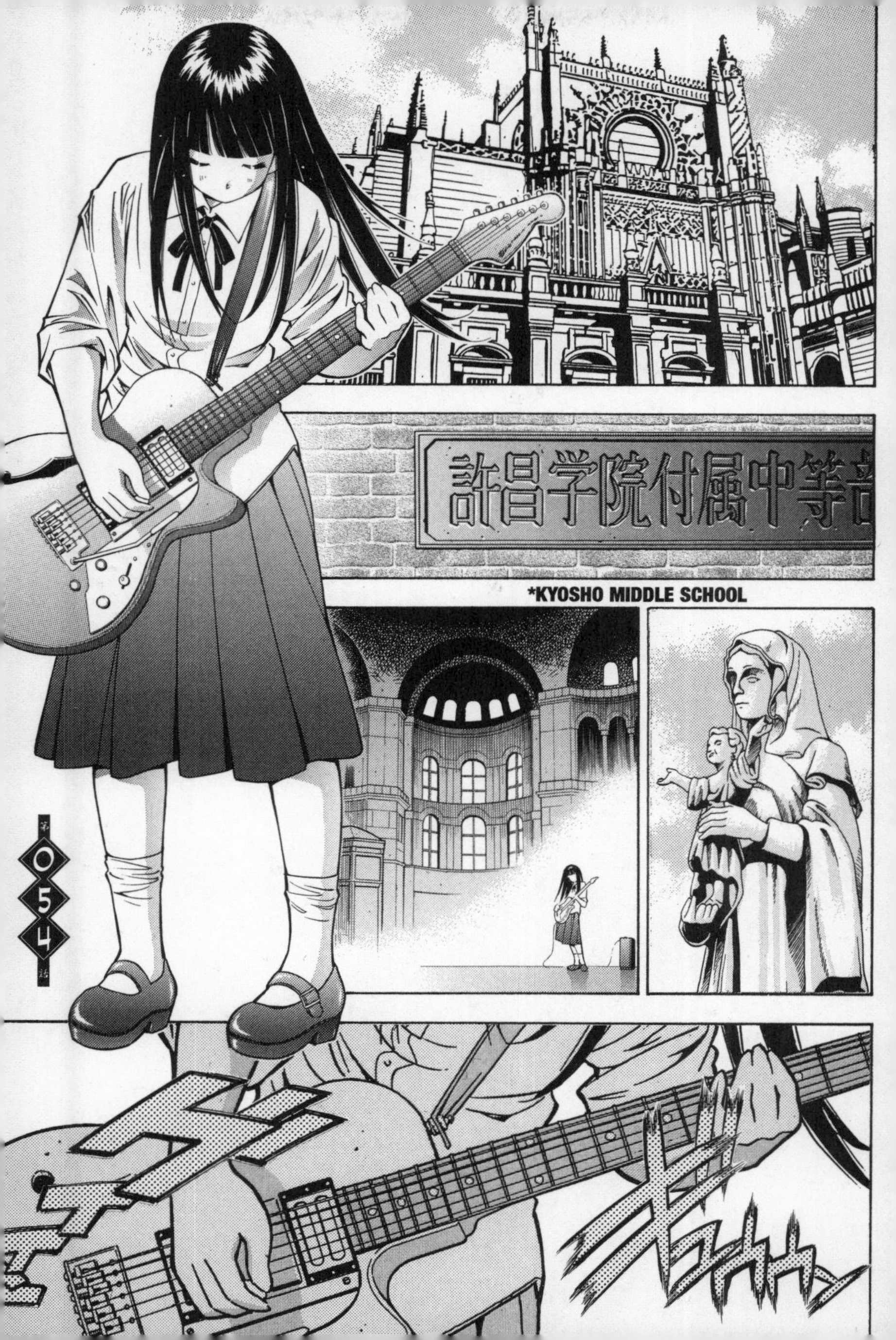

許昌学院付属中等
*KYOSHO MIDDLE SCHOOL
第054話

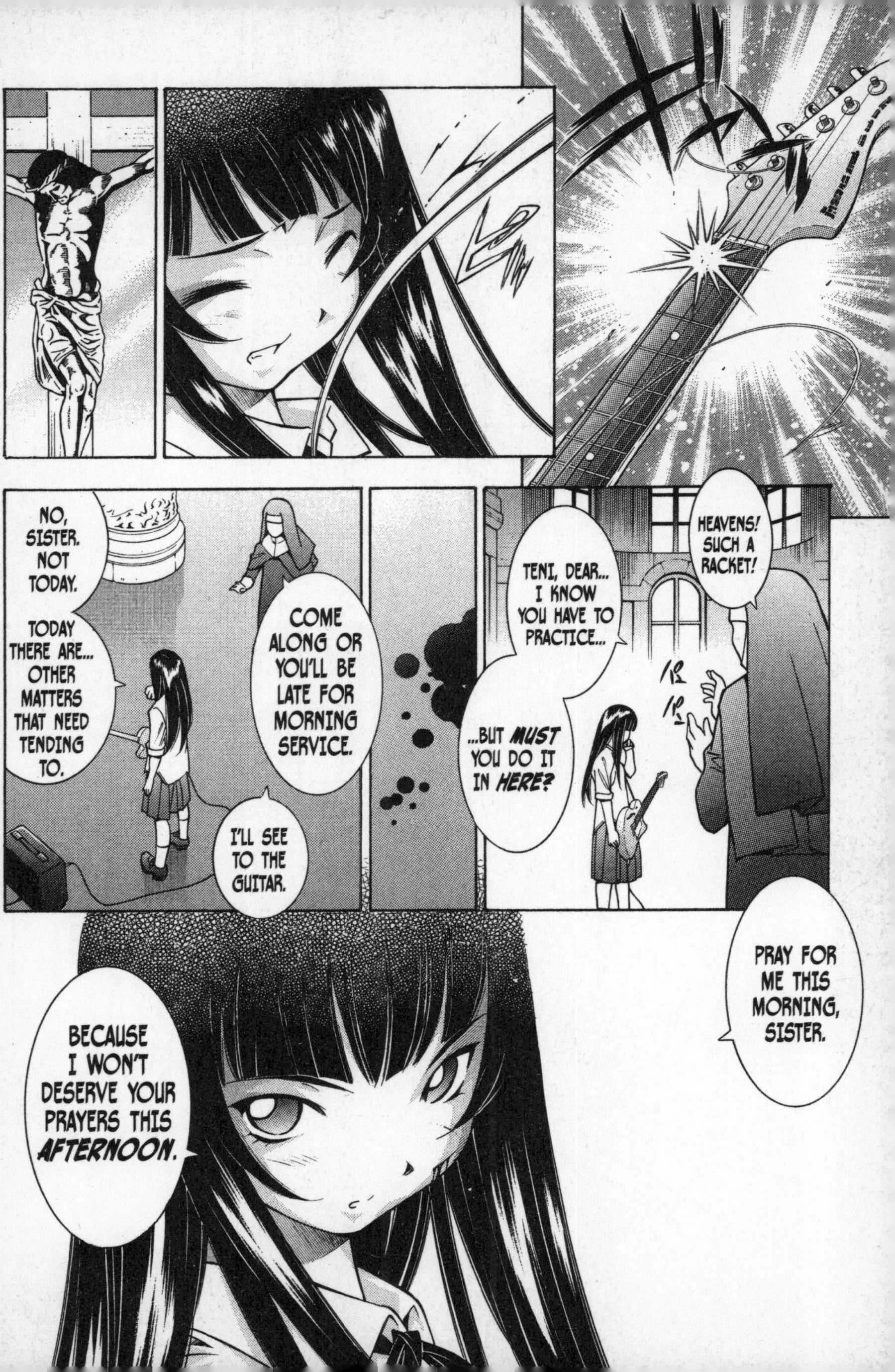
HEAVENS! SUCH A RACKET!
TENI, DEAR... I KNOW YOU HAVE TO PRACTICE...
...BUT *MUST* YOU DO IT IN *HERE?*
COME ALONG OR YOU'LL BE LATE FOR MORNING SERVICE.
NO, SISTER. NOT TODAY.
TODAY THERE ARE... OTHER MATTERS THAT NEED TENDING TO.
I'LL SEE TO THE GUITAR.
PRAY FOR ME THIS MORNING, SISTER.
BECAUSE I WON'T DESERVE YOUR PRAYERS THIS *AFTERNOON*.

第054話

TENI

HE WAS A LOOKER, NO DOUBT ABOUT IT. AND STRONG? BETCHER ASS! HIGH MORALS AND CHIVALRY ROUNDED OUT THE PACKAGE. SMALL WONDER HE WAS SOUSOU'S BODYGUARD OF CHOICE AND GO-TO GUY WHEN IT CAME TO BATTLE TACTICS. TENI'S WEAPON OF CHOICE WAS A SOUGEKI (ANCIENT CHINESE HALBERD) THAT WEIGHED IN AT 80 KIN (ABOUT 18KG). THE RANK AND FILE TROOPS ALWAYS REFERRED TO HIM AS "THE GREAT SOLDIER NAMED TENI WHO CARRIES A SOUGEKI WHICH WEIGHS 80 KIN." OR LARRY FOR SHORT.

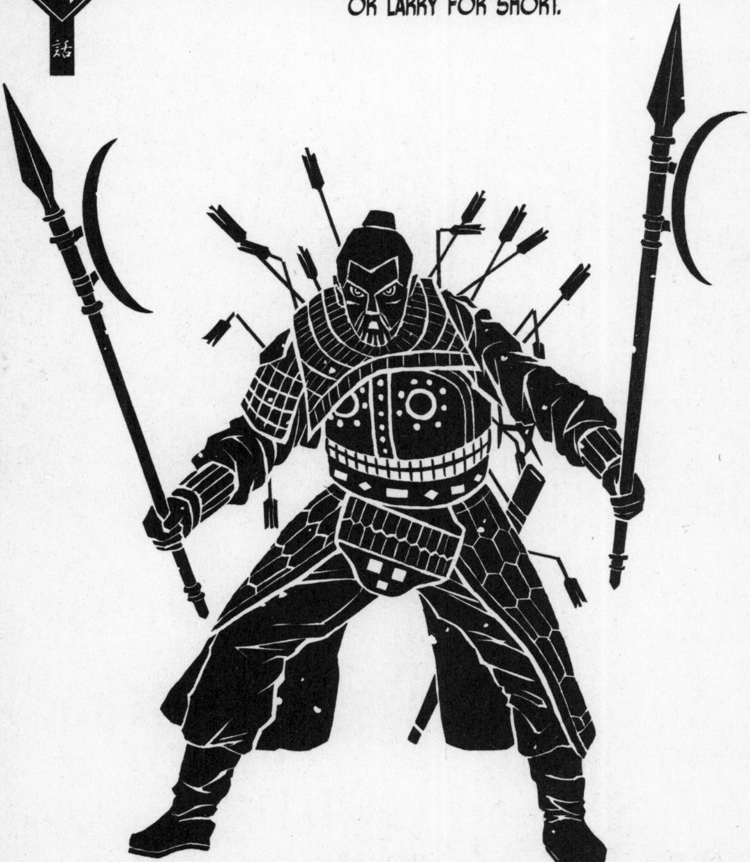

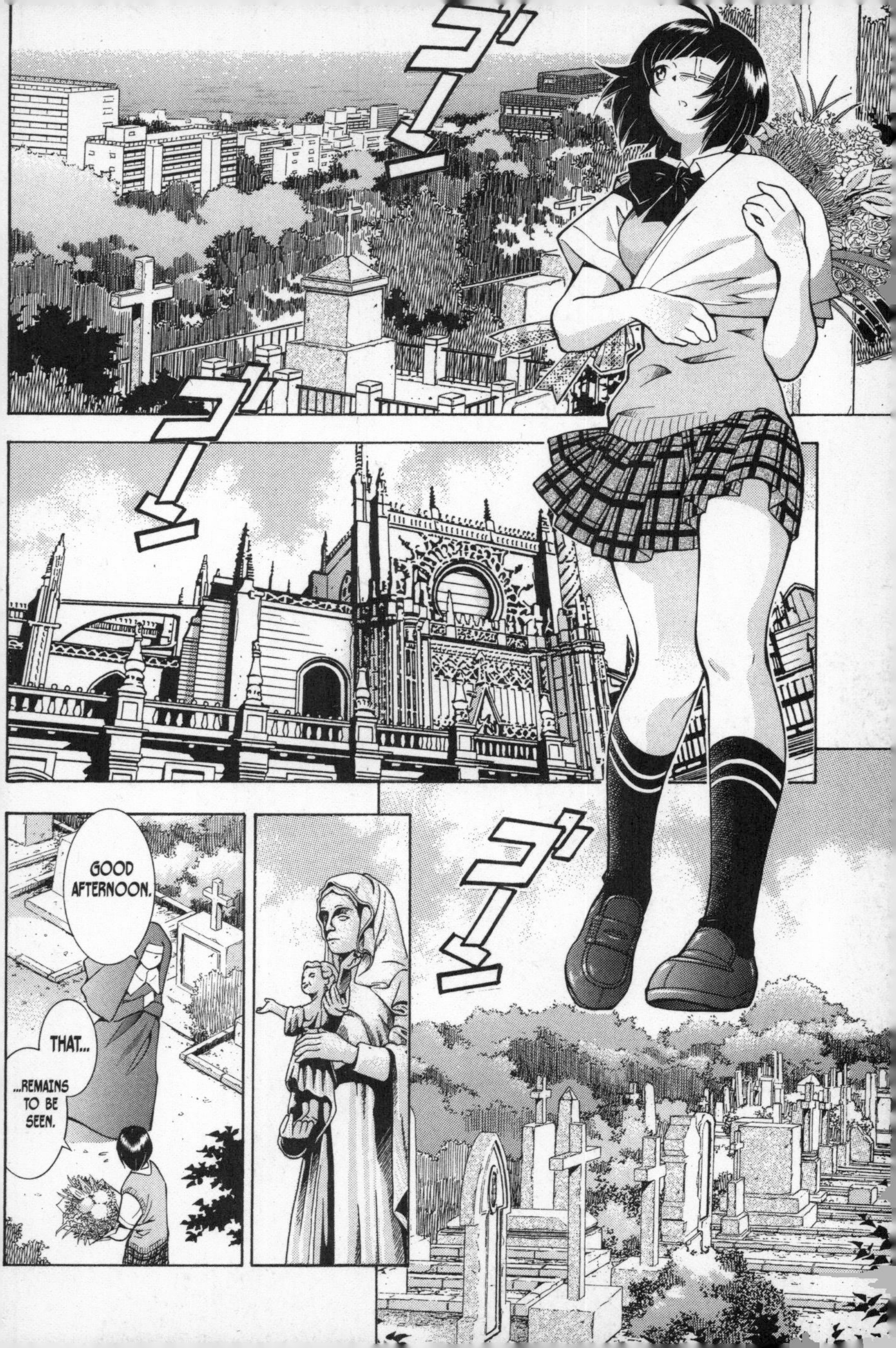
GOOD AFTERNOON.
THAT...
...REMAINS TO BE SEEN.

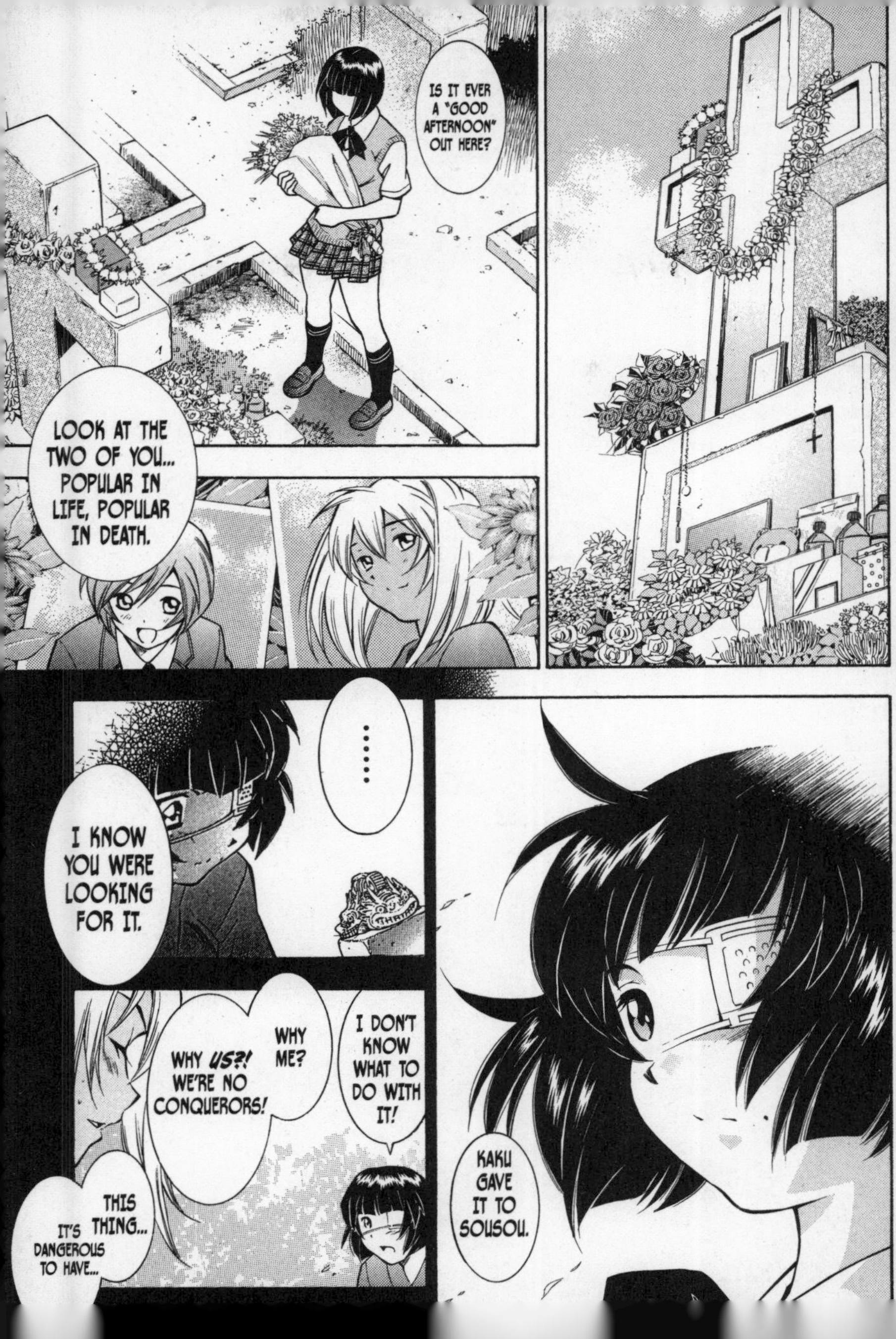
IS IT EVER A "GOOD AFTERNOON" OUT HERE?
LOOK AT THE TWO OF YOU... POPULAR IN LIFE, POPULAR IN DEATH.
KAKU GAVE IT TO SOUSOU.
......
I KNOW YOU WERE LOOKING FOR IT.
I DON'T KNOW WHAT TO DO WITH IT!
WHY ME?
WHY US?! WE'RE NO CONQUERORS!
THIS THING... IT'S DANGEROUS TO HAVE...

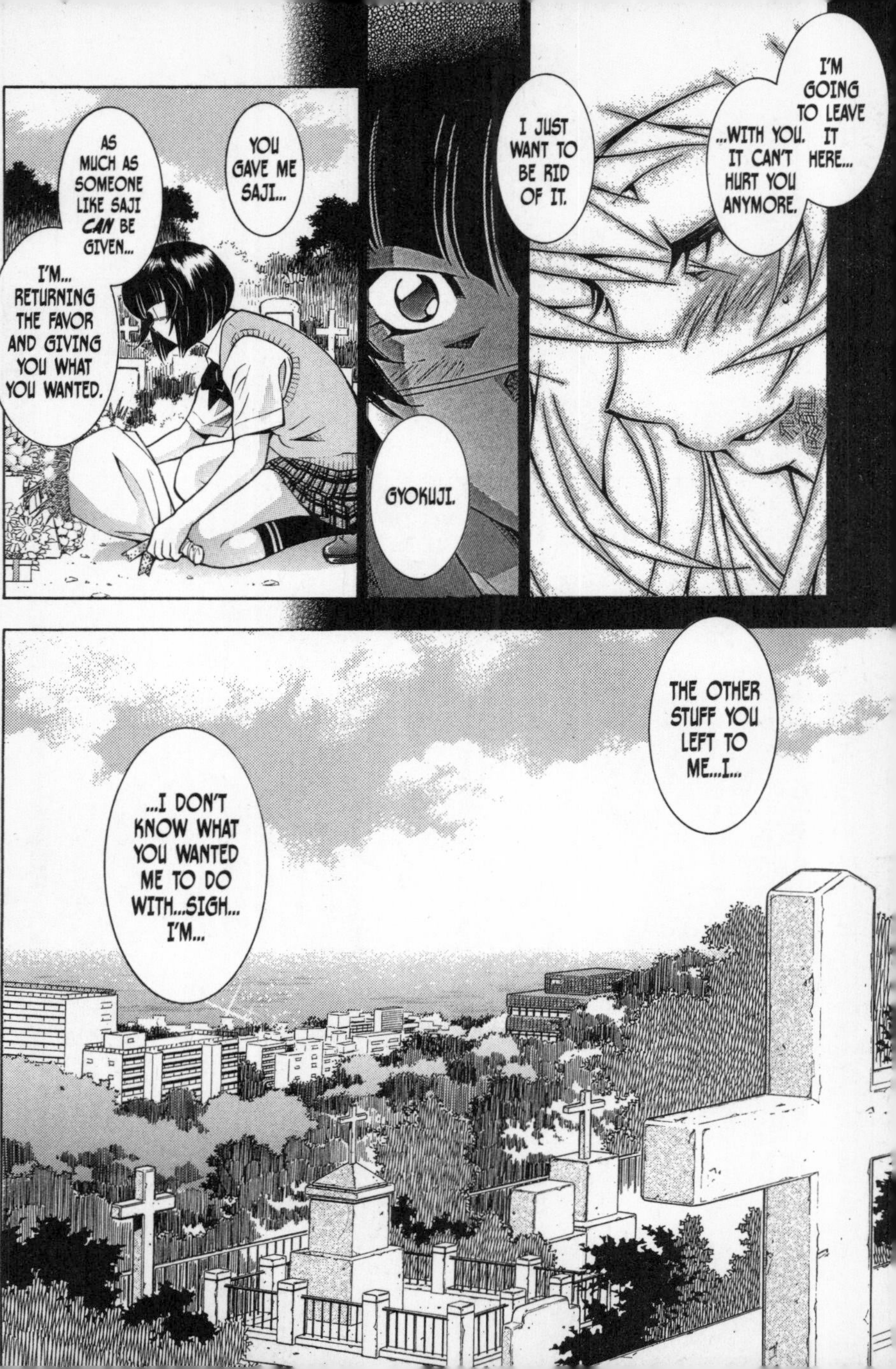
I'M GOING TO LEAVE IT HERE... ...WITH YOU. IT CAN'T HURT YOU ANYMORE.
I JUST WANT TO BE RID OF IT.
GYOKUJI.
YOU GAVE ME SAJI...
AS MUCH AS SOMEONE LIKE SAJI *CAN* BE GIVEN...
I'M... RETURNING THE FAVOR AND GIVING YOU WHAT YOU WANTED.
THE OTHER STUFF YOU LEFT TO ME...I...
...I DON'T KNOW WHAT YOU WANTED ME TO DO WITH...SIGH... I'M...

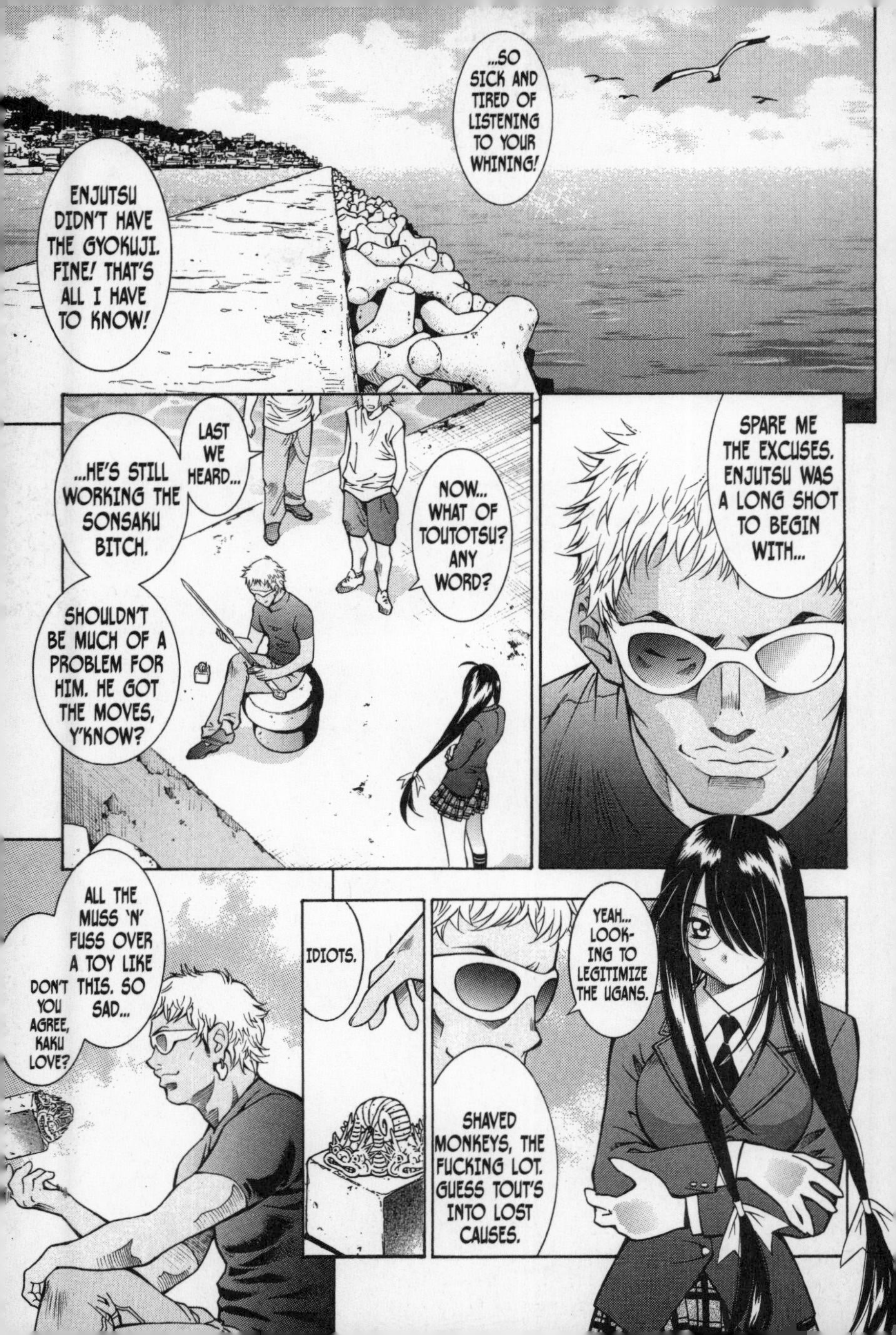
...SO SICK AND TIRED OF LISTENING TO YOUR WHINING!
ENJUTSU DIDN'T HAVE THE GYOKUJI. FINE! THAT'S ALL I HAVE TO KNOW!
SPARE ME THE EXCUSES. ENJUTSU WAS A LONG SHOT TO BEGIN WITH...
NOW... WHAT OF TOUTOTSU? ANY WORD?
LAST WE HEARD...
...HE'S STILL WORKING THE SONSAKU BITCH.
SHOULDN'T BE MUCH OF A PROBLEM FOR HIM. HE GOT THE MOVES, Y'KNOW?
YEAH... LOOK-ING TO LEGITIMIZE THE UGANS.
IDIOTS.
SHAVED MONKEYS, THE FUCKING LOT. GUESS TOUT'S INTO LOST CAUSES.
ALL THE MUSS 'N' FUSS OVER A TOY LIKE THIS. SO SAD...
DON'T YOU AGREE, KAKU LOVE?

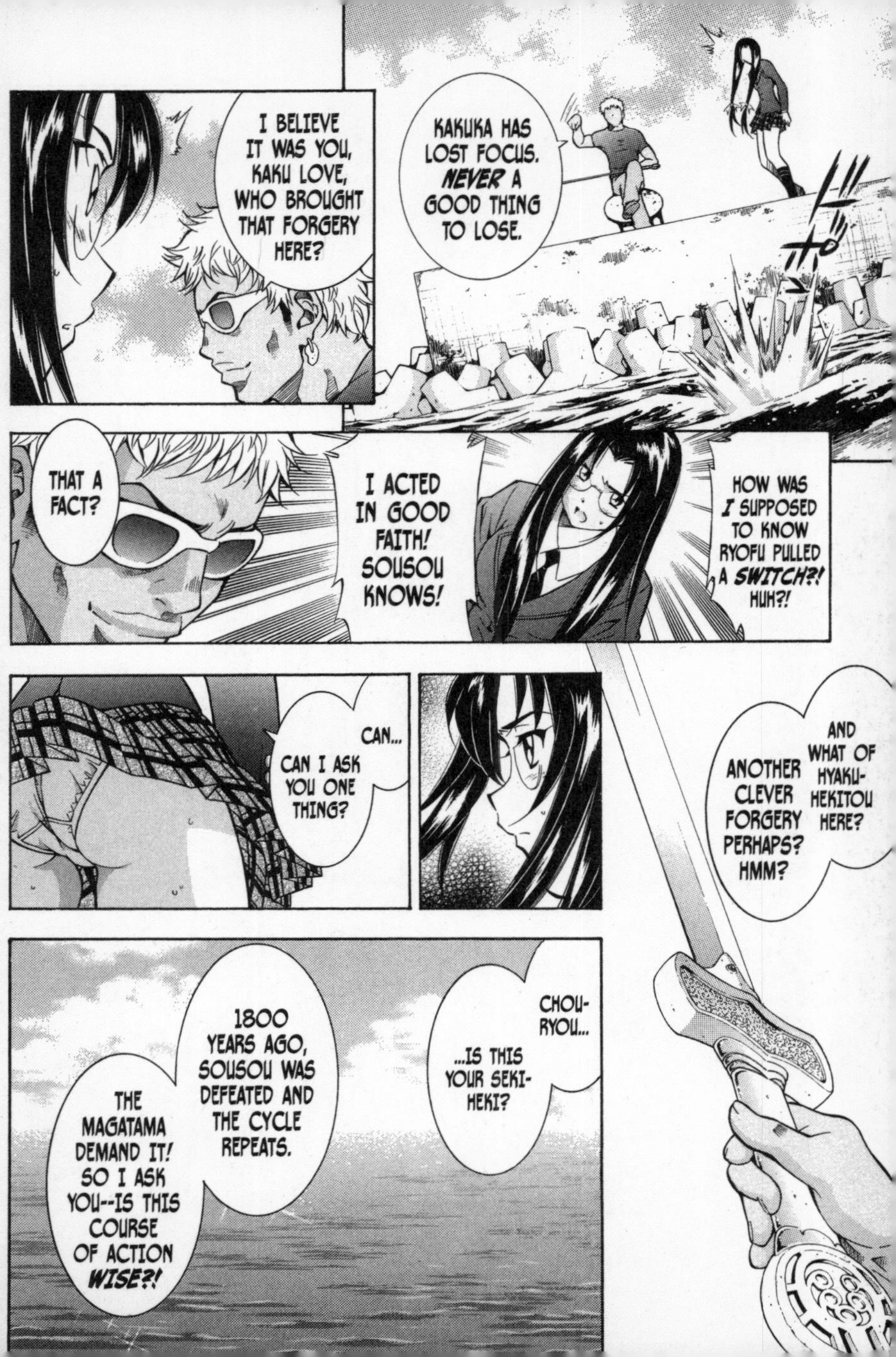
KAKUKA HAS LOST FOCUS. NEVER A GOOD THING TO LOSE.
I BELIEVE IT WAS YOU, KAKU LOVE, WHO BROUGHT THAT FORGERY HERE?
HOW WAS I SUPPOSED TO KNOW RYOFU PULLED A SWITCH?! HUH?!
I ACTED IN GOOD FAITH! SOUSOU KNOWS!
THAT A FACT?
AND WHAT OF HYAKU-HEKITOU HERE?
ANOTHER CLEVER FORGERY PERHAPS? HMM?
CAN...
CAN I ASK YOU ONE THING?
CHOU-RYOU...
...IS THIS YOUR SEKI-HEKI?
1800 YEARS AGO, SOUSOU WAS DEFEATED AND THE CYCLE REPEATS.
THE MAGATAMA DEMAND IT! SO I ASK YOU--IS THIS COURSE OF ACTION WISE?!

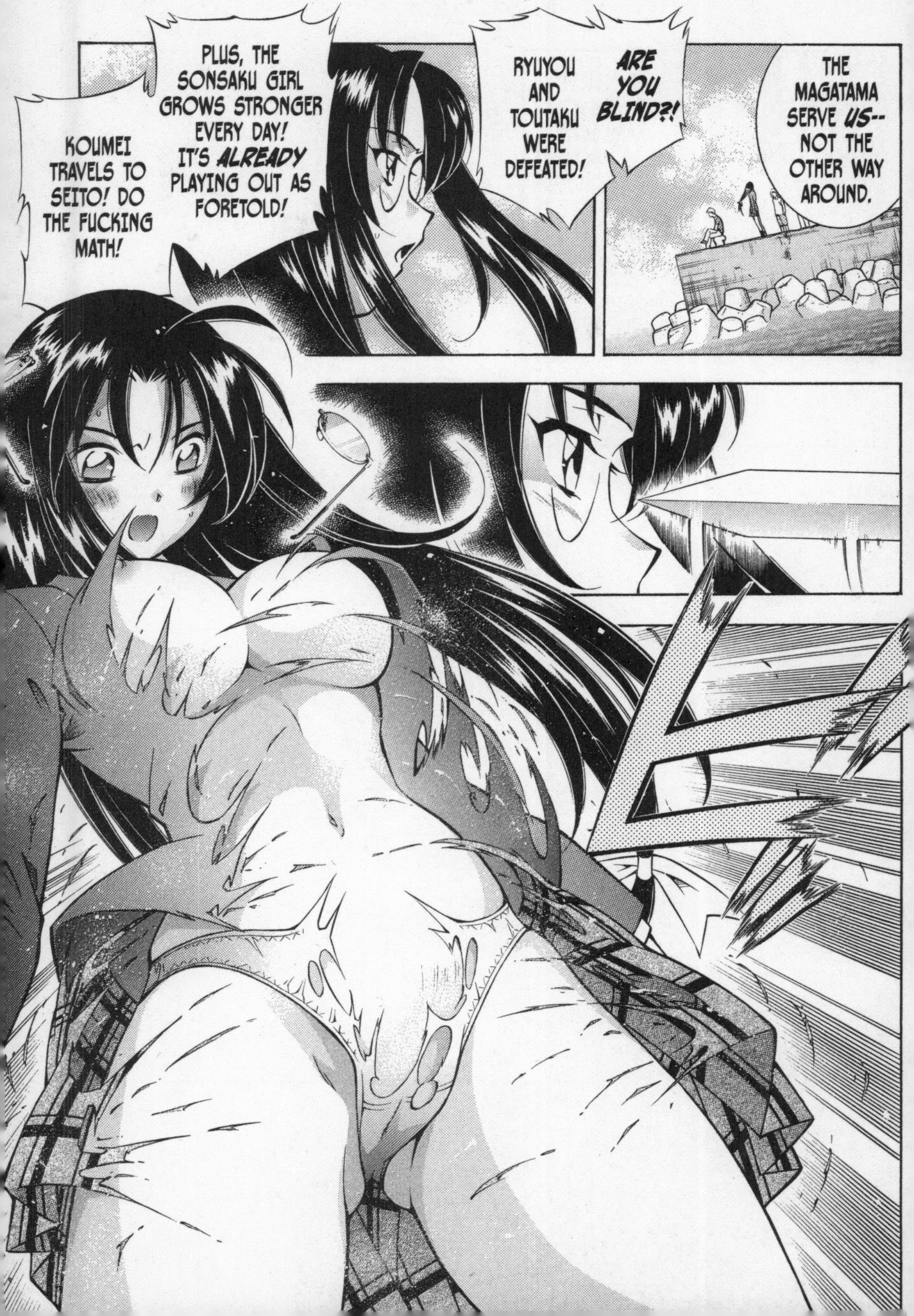
THE MAGATAMA SERVE *US*-- NOT THE OTHER WAY AROUND.
ARE YOU BLIND?!
RYUYOU AND TOUTAKU WERE DEFEATED!
PLUS, THE SONSAKU GIRL GROWS STRONGER EVERY DAY! IT'S *ALREADY* PLAYING OUT AS FORETOLD!
KOUMEI TRAVELS TO SEITO! DO THE FUCKING MATH!

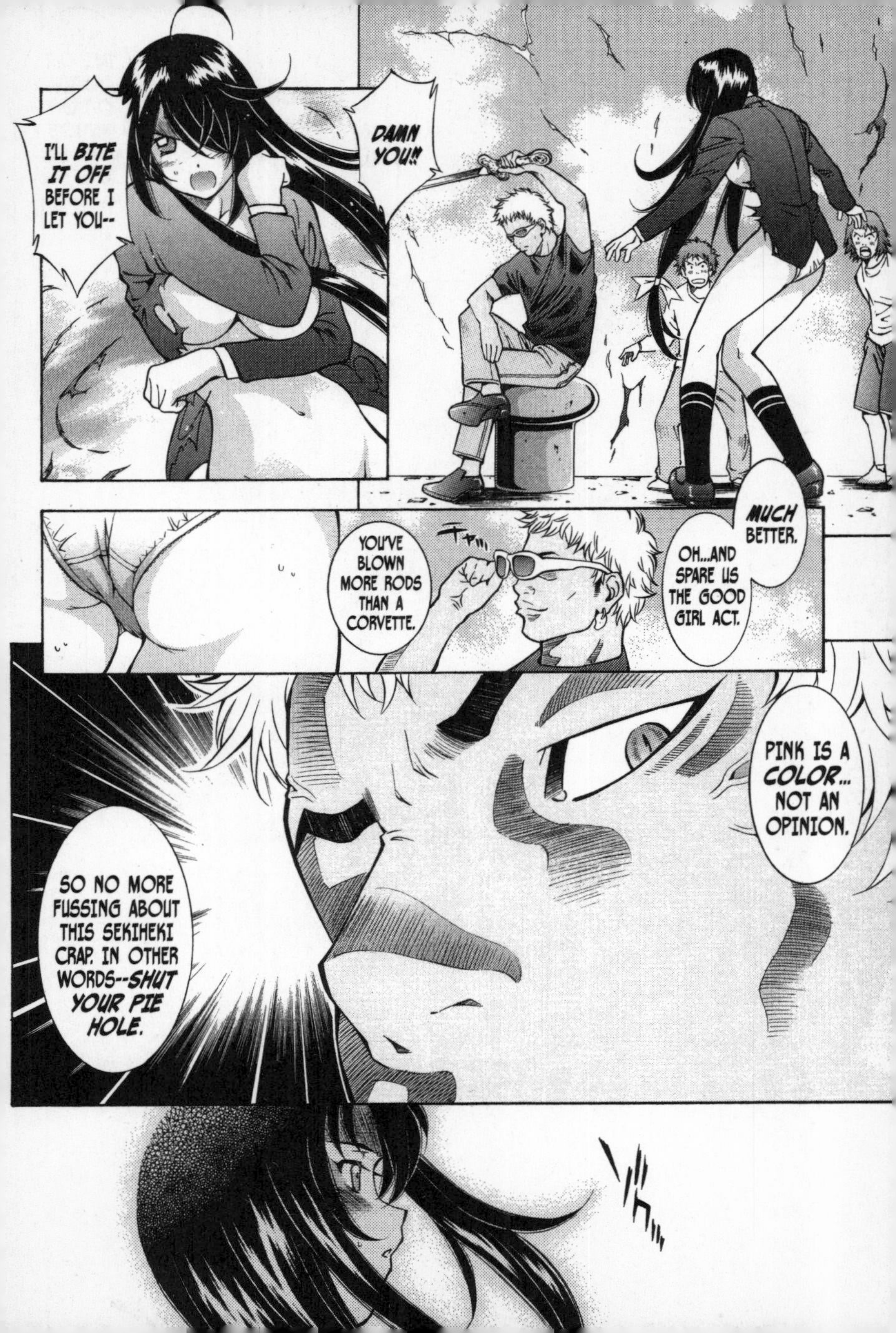
DAMN YOU!!
I'LL BITE IT OFF BEFORE I LET YOU--
MUCH BETTER.
OH...AND SPARE US THE GOOD GIRL ACT.
YOU'VE BLOWN MORE RODS THAN A CORVETTE.
PINK IS A COLOR... NOT AN OPINION.
SO NO MORE FUSSING ABOUT THIS SEKIHEKI CRAP. IN OTHER WORDS--SHUT YOUR PIE HOLE.

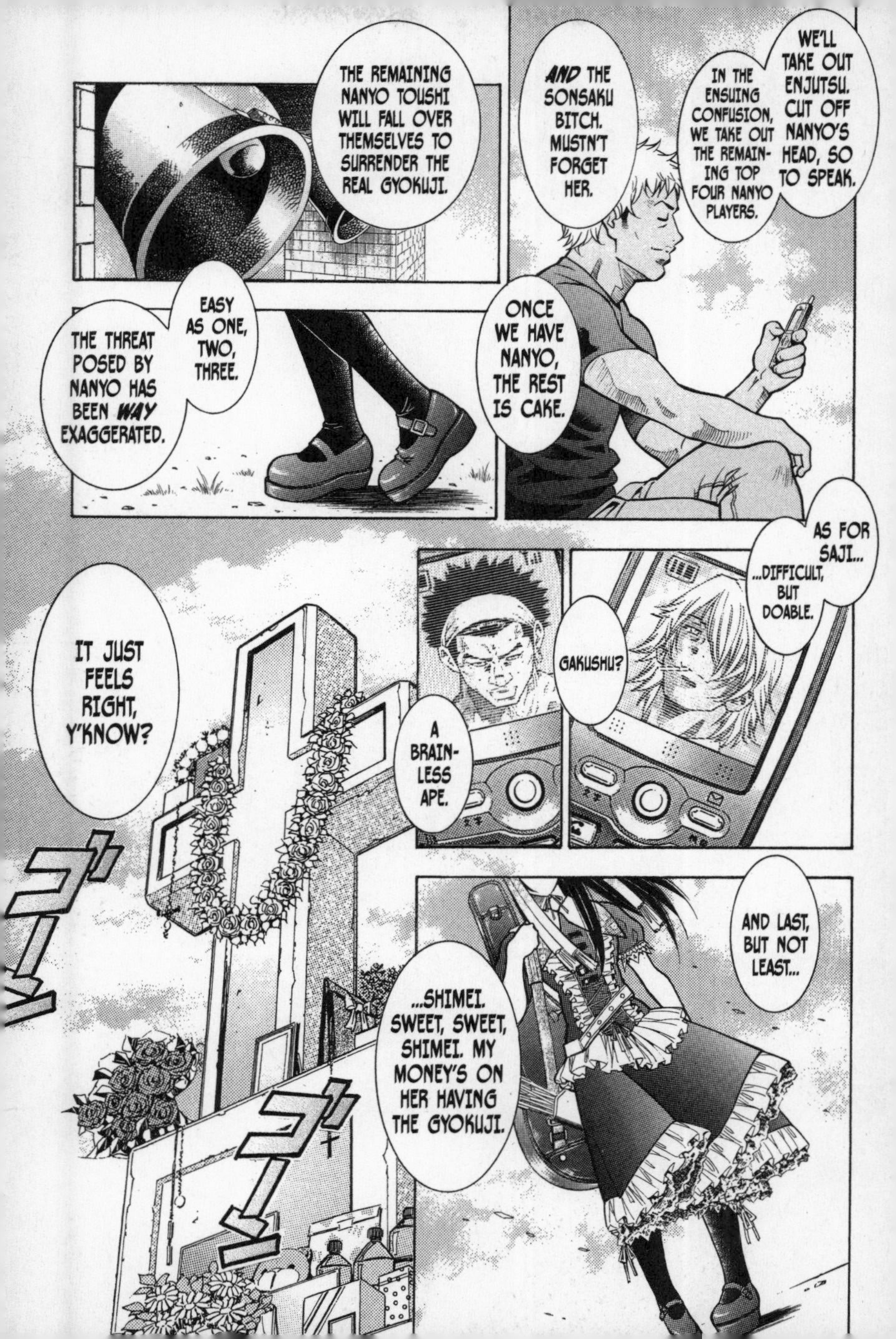
WE'LL TAKE OUT ENJUTSU. CUT OFF NANYO'S HEAD, SO TO SPEAK.
IN THE ENSUING CONFUSION, WE TAKE OUT THE REMAINING TOP FOUR NANYO PLAYERS.
AND THE SONSAKU BITCH. MUSTN'T FORGET HER.
THE REMAINING NANYO TOUSHI WILL FALL OVER THEMSELVES TO SURRENDER THE REAL GYOKUJI.
ONCE WE HAVE NANYO, THE REST IS CAKE.
EASY AS ONE, TWO, THREE.
THE THREAT POSED BY NANYO HAS BEEN WAY EXAGGERATED.
AS FOR SAJI...
...DIFFICULT, BUT DOABLE.
GAKUSHU?
A BRAINLESS APE.
AND LAST, BUT NOT LEAST...
...SHIMEI. SWEET, SWEET, SHIMEI. MY MONEY'S ON HER HAVING THE GYOKUJI.
IT JUST FEELS RIGHT, Y'KNOW?
ゴーン
ゴーン

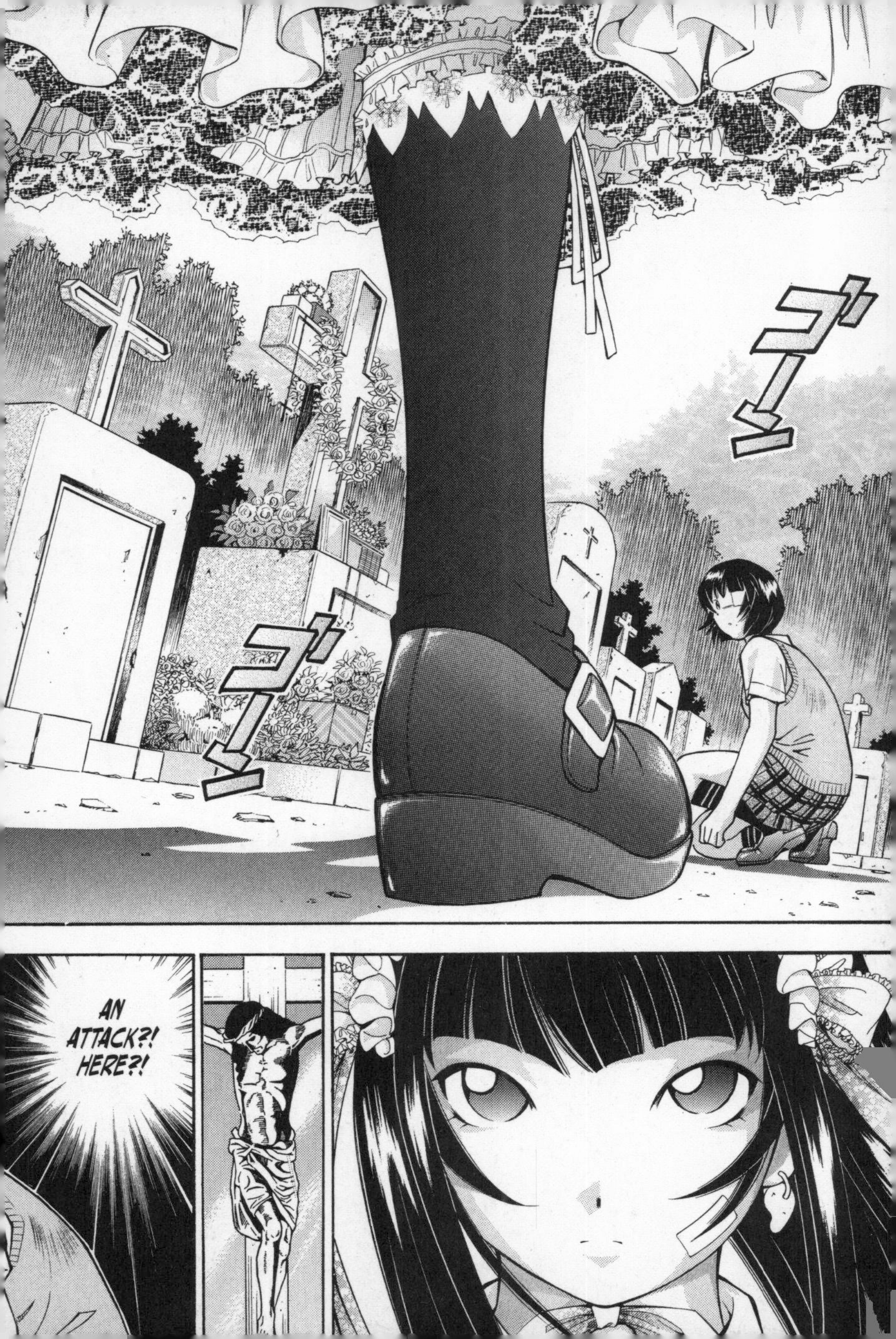
AN ATTACK?! HERE?!

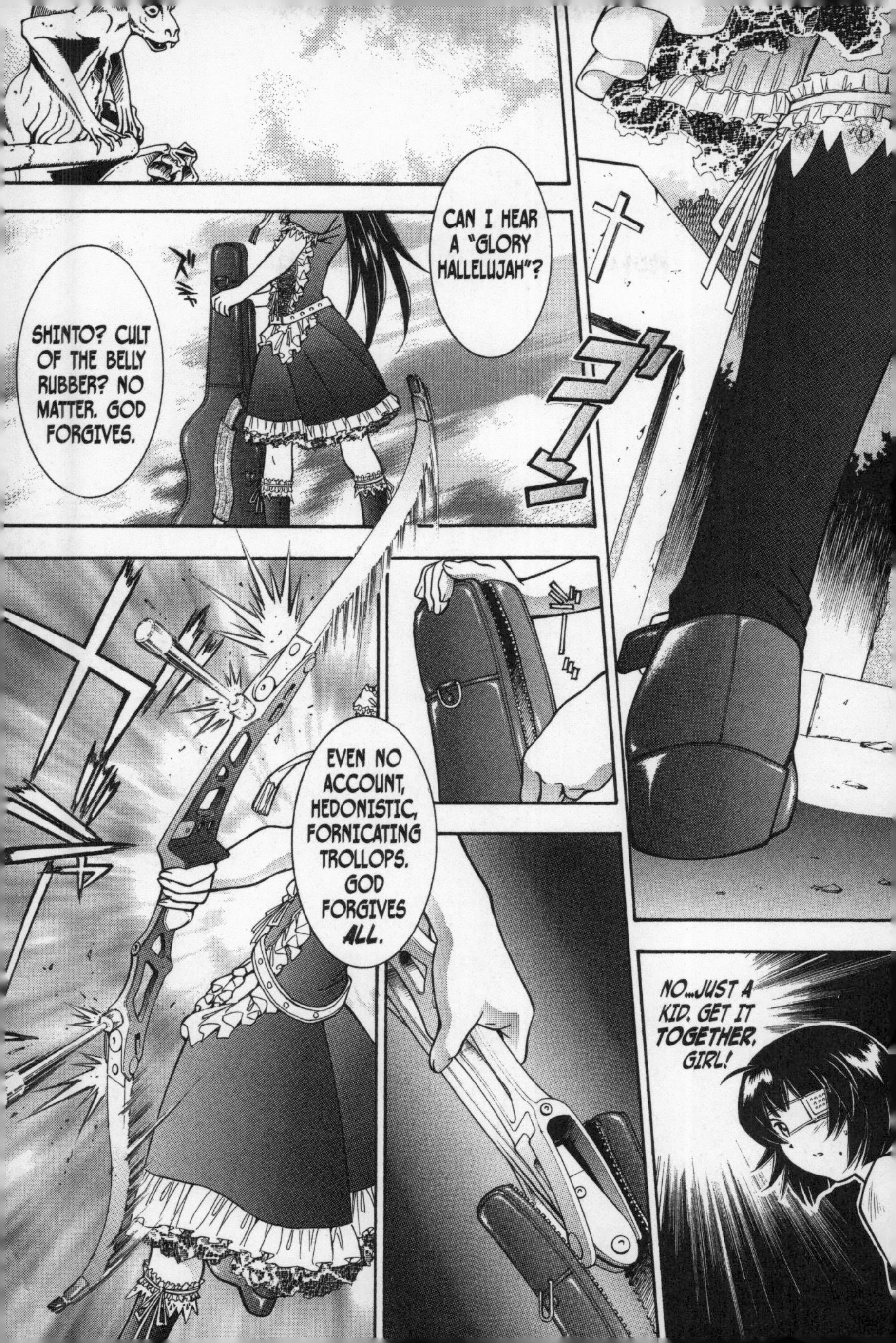
CAN I HEAR A "GLORY HALLELUJAH"?
SHINTO? CULT OF THE BELLY RUBBER? NO MATTER. GOD FORGIVES.
EVEN NO ACCOUNT, HEDONISTIC, FORNICATING TROLLOPS. GOD FORGIVES ALL.
NO...JUST A KID. GET IT TOGETHER, GIRL!

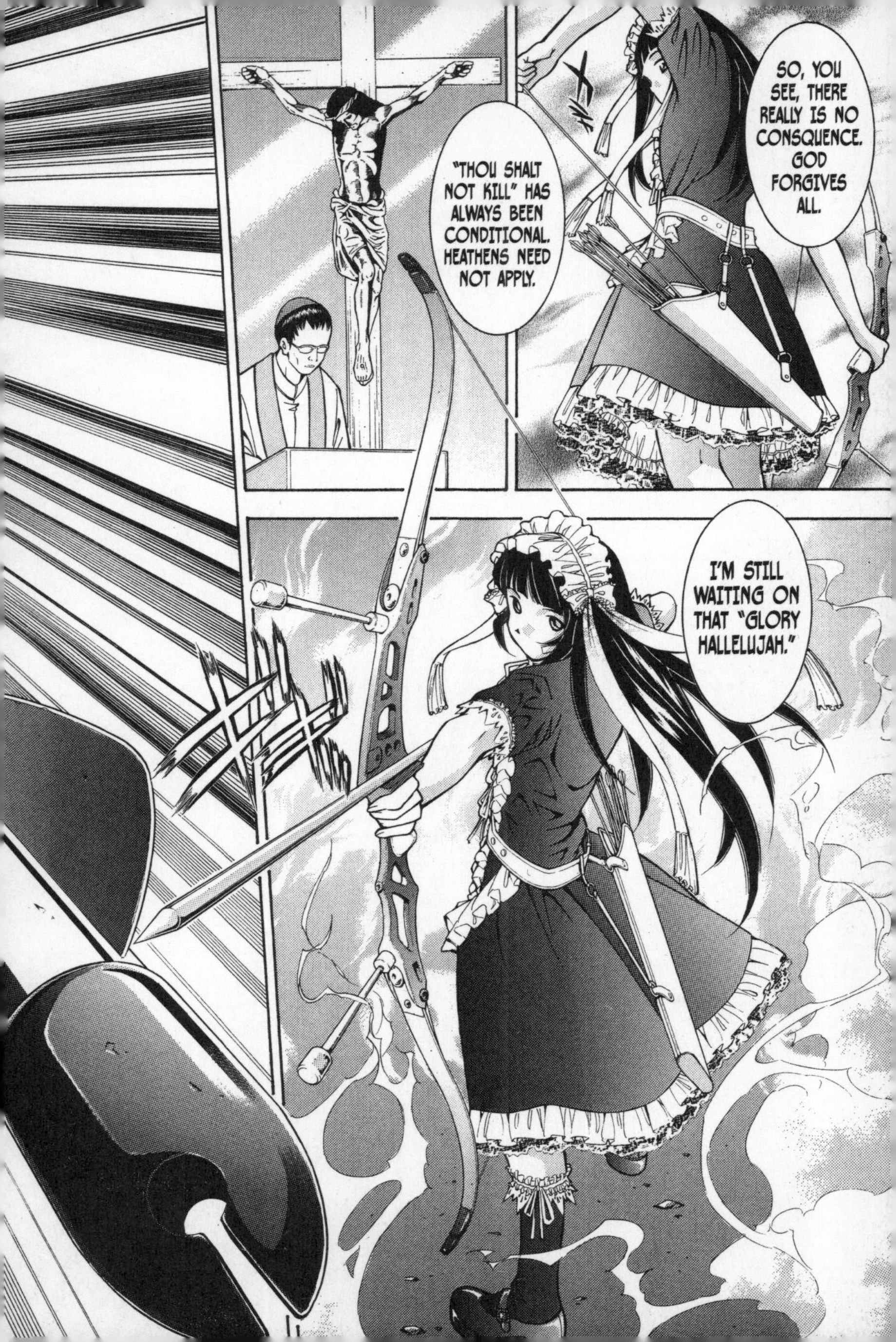
SO, YOU SEE, THERE REALLY IS NO CONSQUENCE. GOD FORGIVES ALL.
"THOU SHALT NOT KILL" HAS ALWAYS BEEN CONDITIONAL. HEATHENS NEED NOT APPLY.
I'M STILL WAITING ON THAT "GLORY HALLELUJAH."

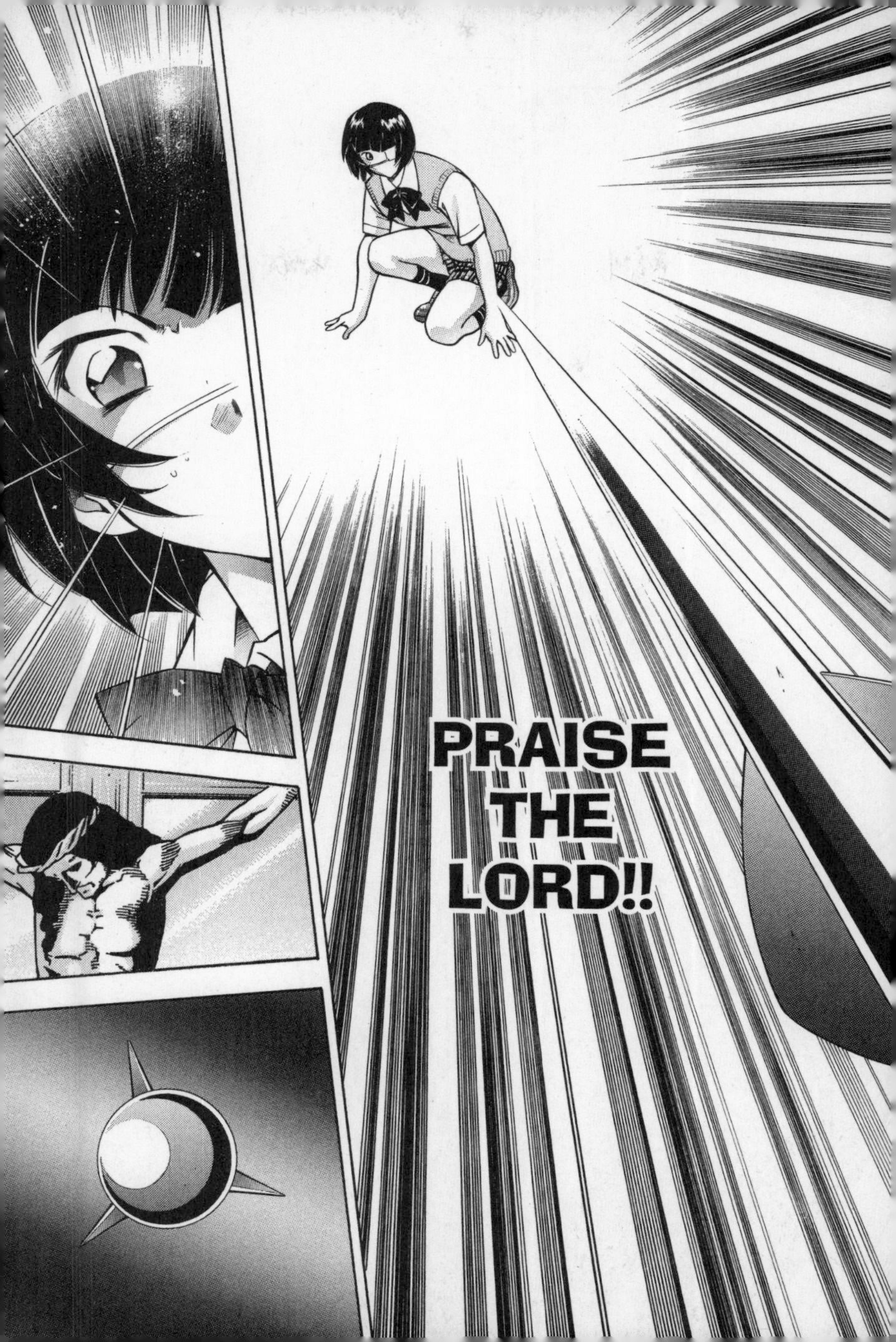
PRAISE THE LORD!!

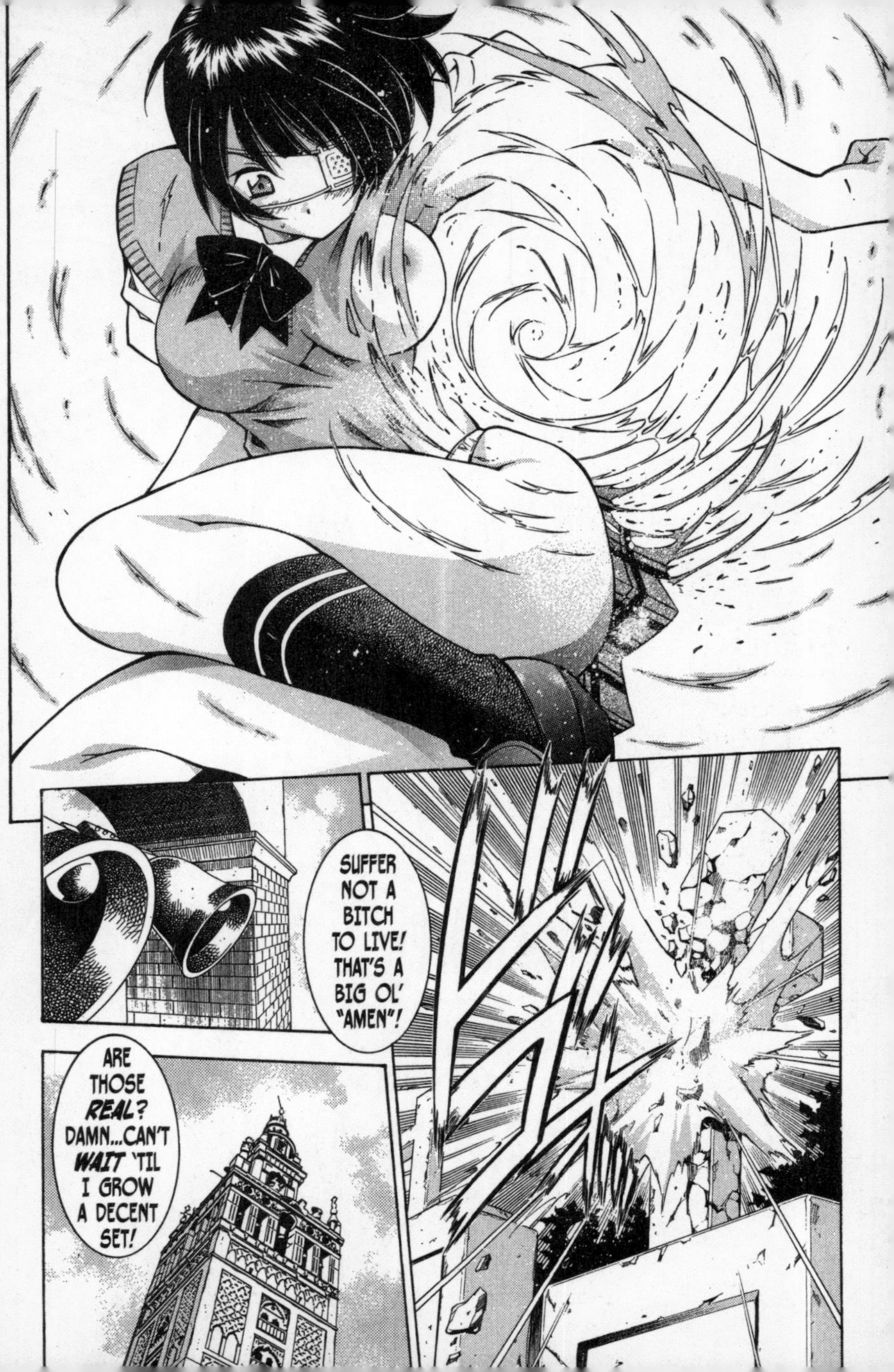
SUFFER NOT A BITCH TO LIVE! THAT'S A BIG OL' "AMEN"!
ARE THOSE ***REAL***? DAMN...CAN'T ***WAIT*** 'TIL I GROW A DECENT SET!

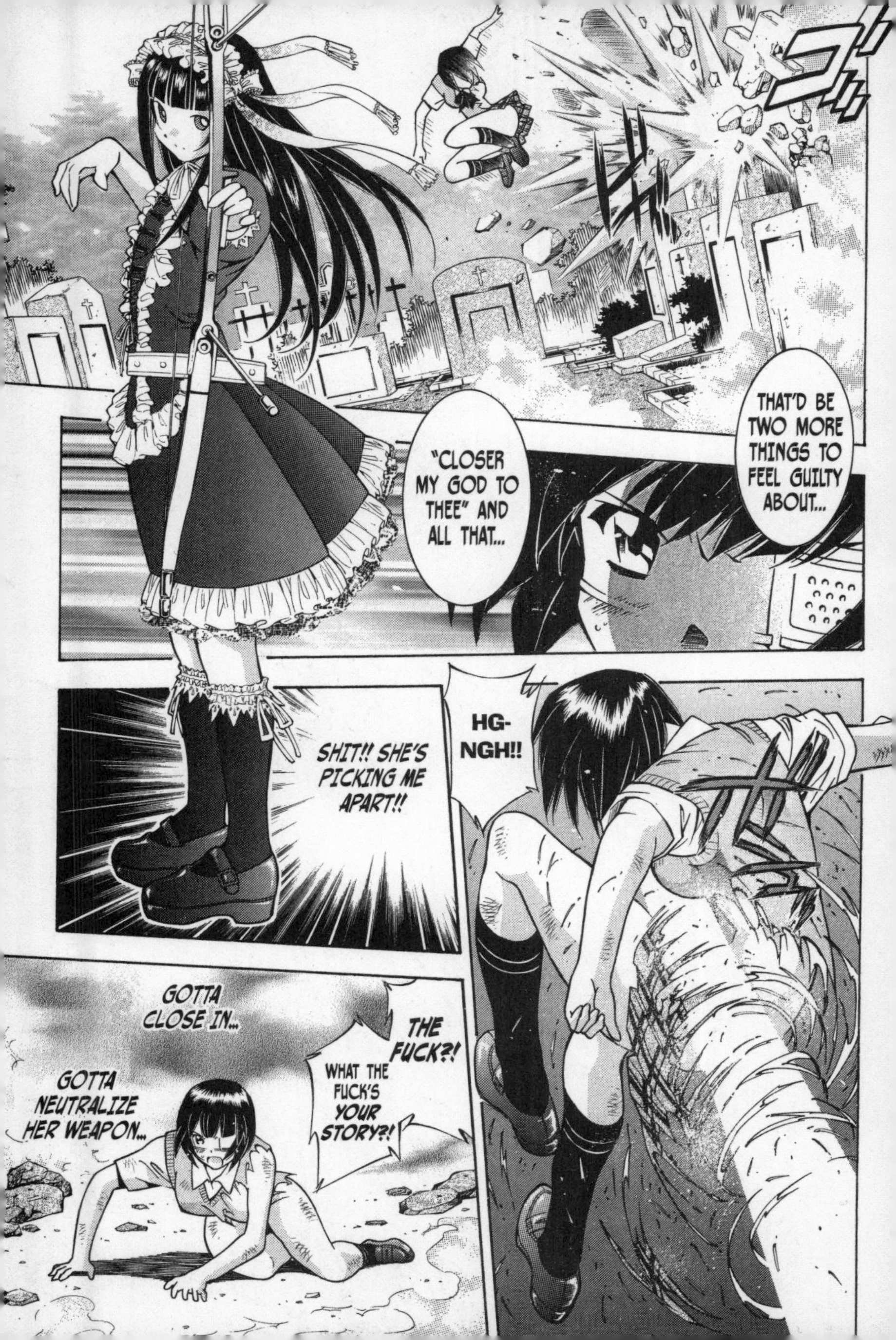
THAT'D BE TWO MORE THINGS TO FEEL GUILTY ABOUT...
"CLOSER MY GOD TO THEE" AND ALL THAT...
HG-NGH!!
SHIT!! SHE'S PICKING ME APART!!
THE FUCK?!
WHAT THE FUCK'S YOUR STORY?!
GOTTA CLOSE IN...
GOTTA NEUTRALIZE HER WEAPON...

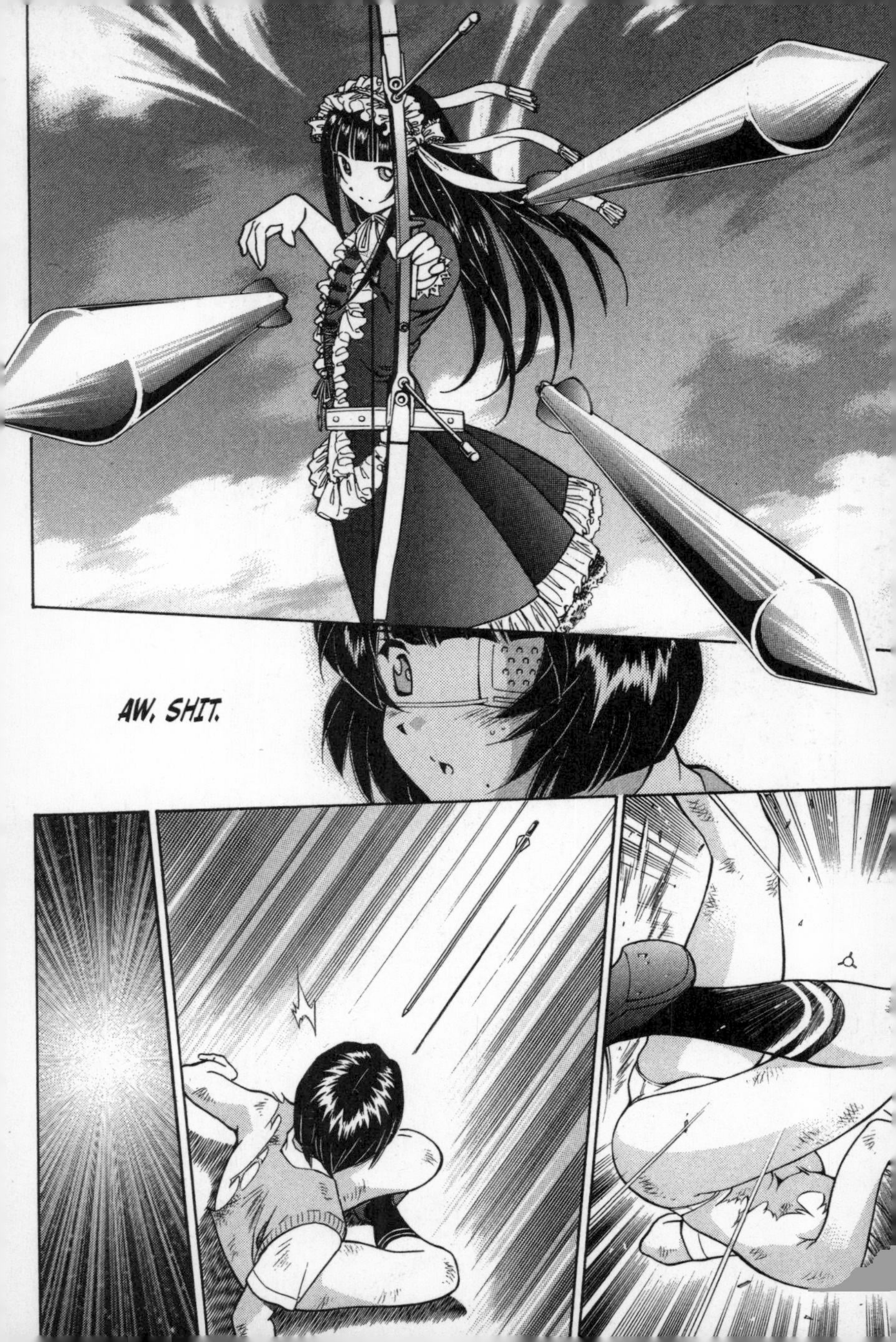
AW, SHIT.

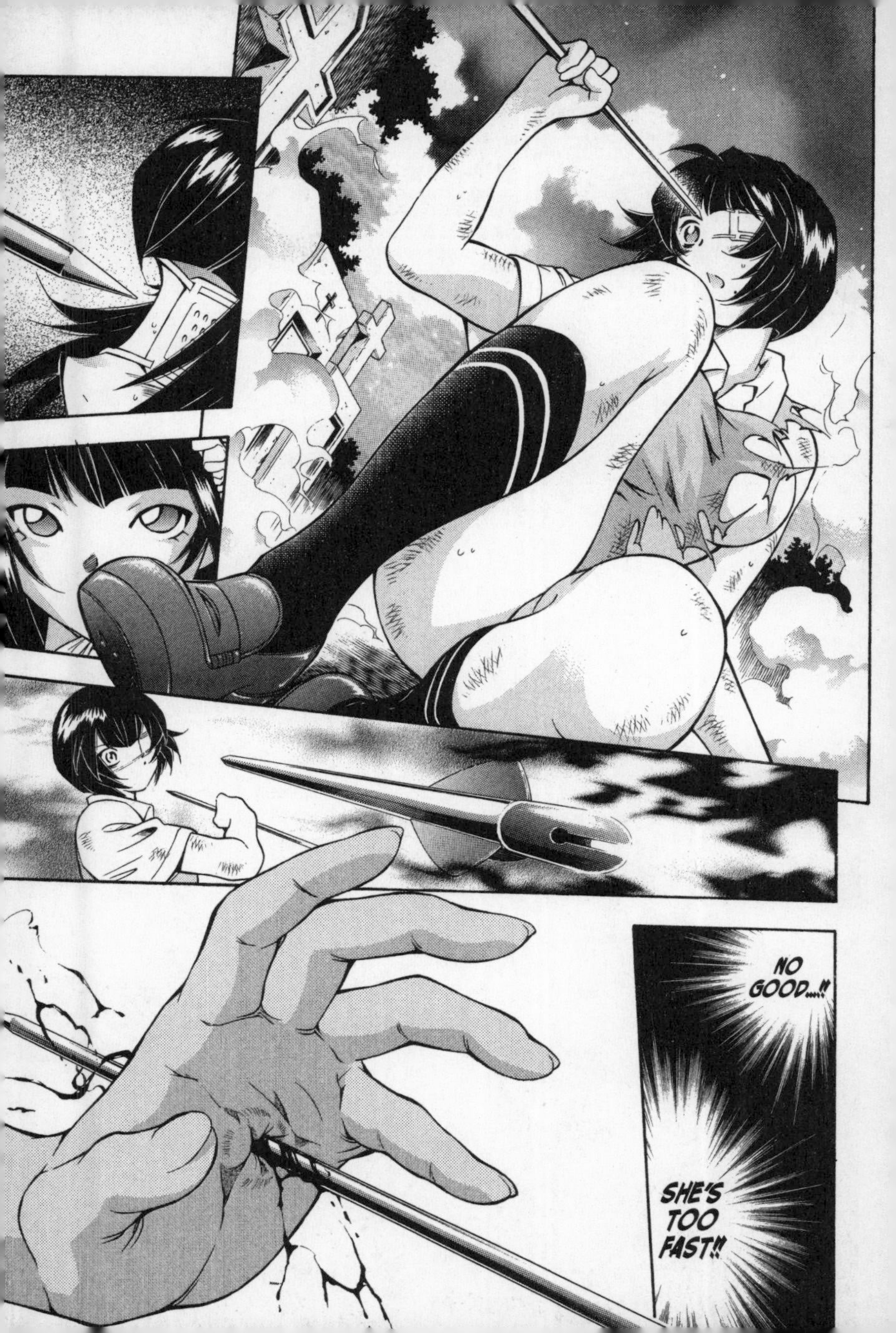
NO GOOD...!!
SHE'S TOO FAST!!

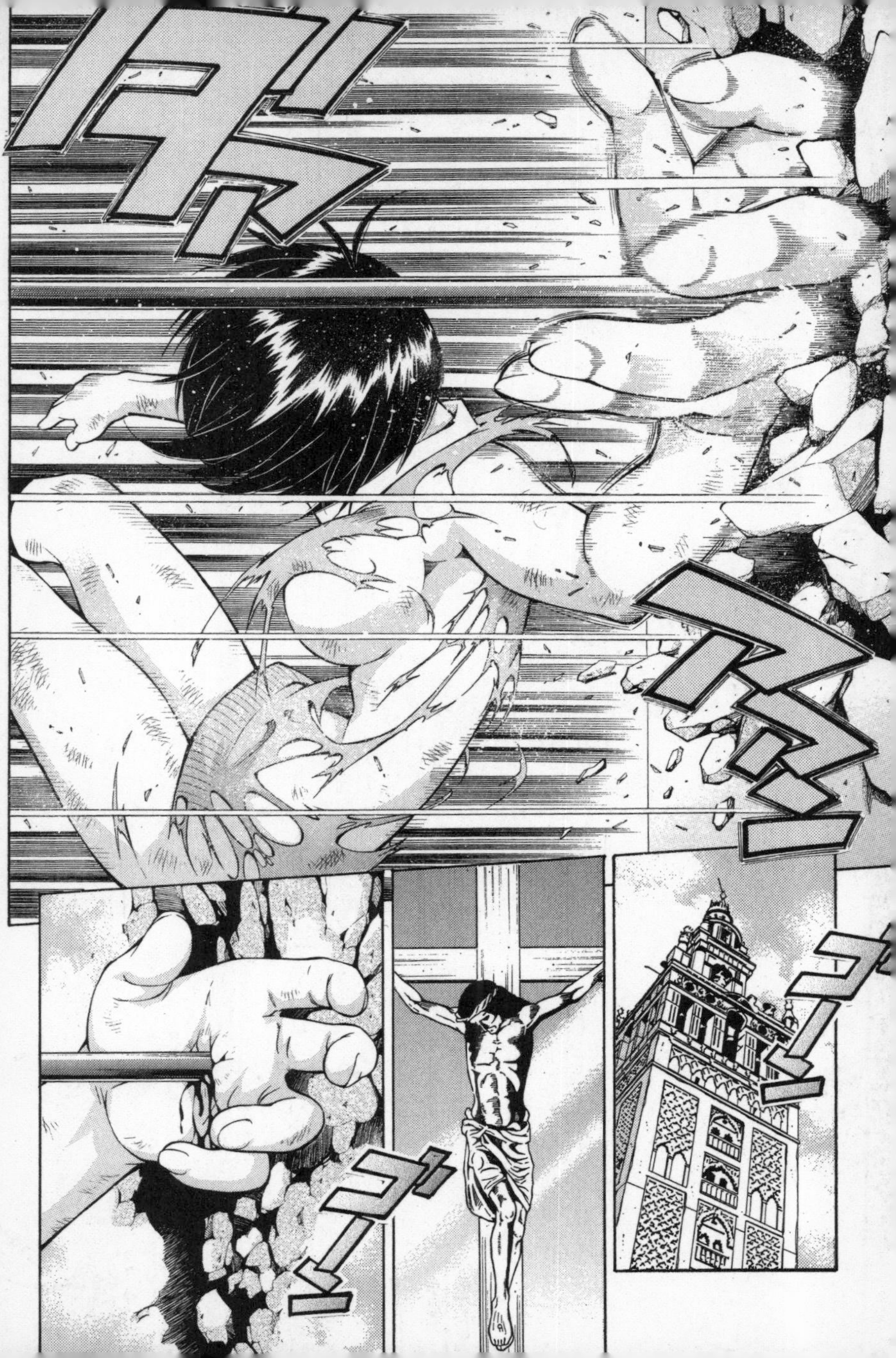

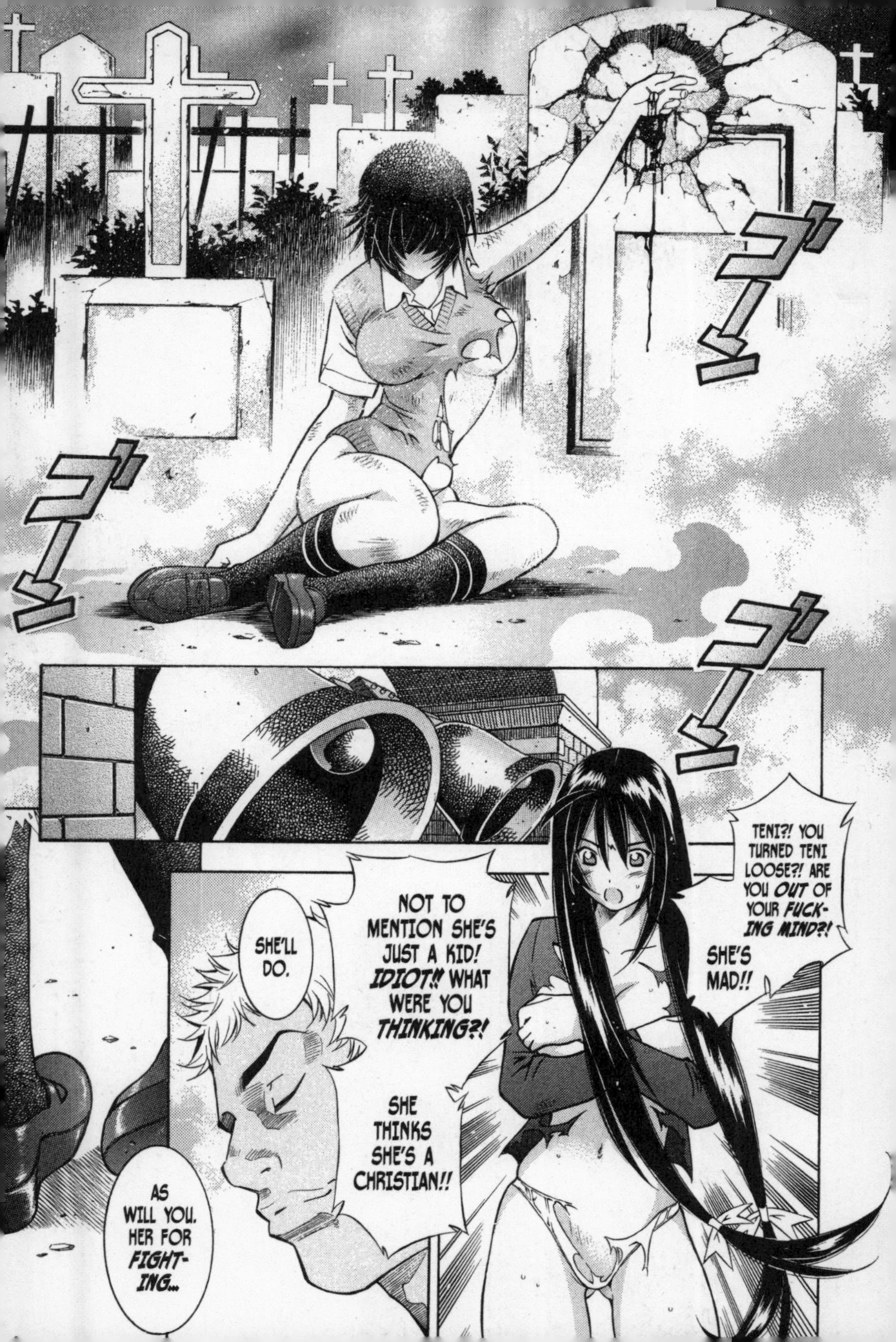
TENI?! YOU TURNED TENI LOOSE?! ARE YOU *OUT* OF YOUR *FUCKING MIND?!*
SHE'S MAD!!
NOT TO MENTION SHE'S JUST A KID! *IDIOT!!* WHAT WERE YOU *THINKING?!*
SHE THINKS SHE'S A CHRISTIAN!!
SHE'LL DO.
AS WILL YOU. HER FOR *FIGHTING...*

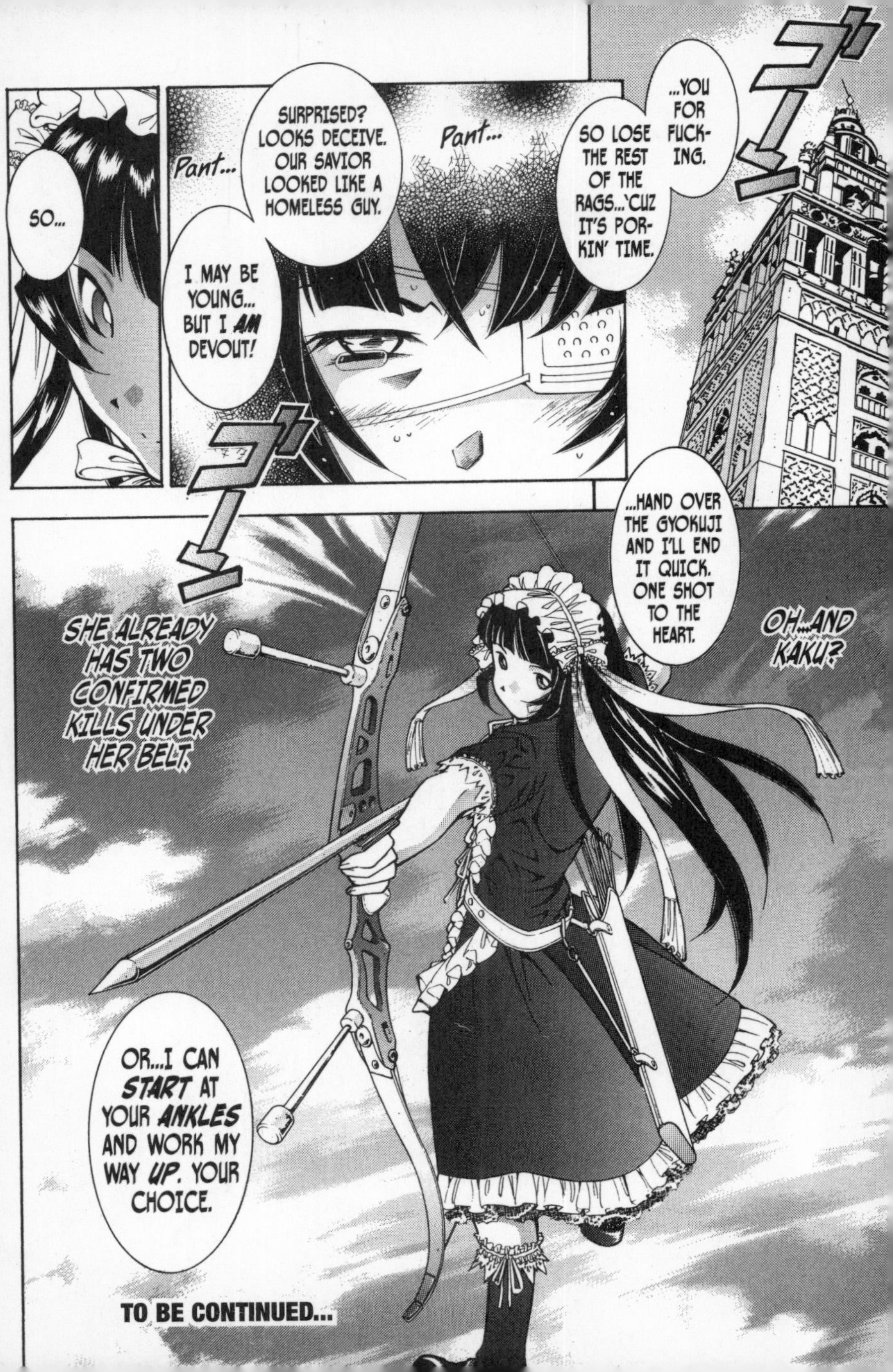
...YOU FOR FUCK-ING.
SO LOSE THE REST OF THE RAGS...'CUZ IT'S POR-KIN' TIME.
Pant...
SURPRISED? LOOKS DECEIVE. OUR SAVIOR LOOKED LIKE A HOMELESS GUY.
Pant...
I MAY BE YOUNG... BUT I AM DEVOUT!
SO...
OH...AND KAKU?
...HAND OVER THE GYOKUJI AND I'LL END IT QUICK. ONE SHOT TO THE HEART.
SHE ALREADY HAS TWO CONFIRMED KILLS UNDER HER BELT.
OR...I CAN START AT YOUR ANKLES AND WORK MY WAY UP. YOUR CHOICE.

TO BE CONTINUED...

A COLLECTION OF THE VARIOUS WOODCUT ARTWORK FOUND AT THE BEGINNING OF EACH BATTLE VIXENS CHAPTER.

XTRA

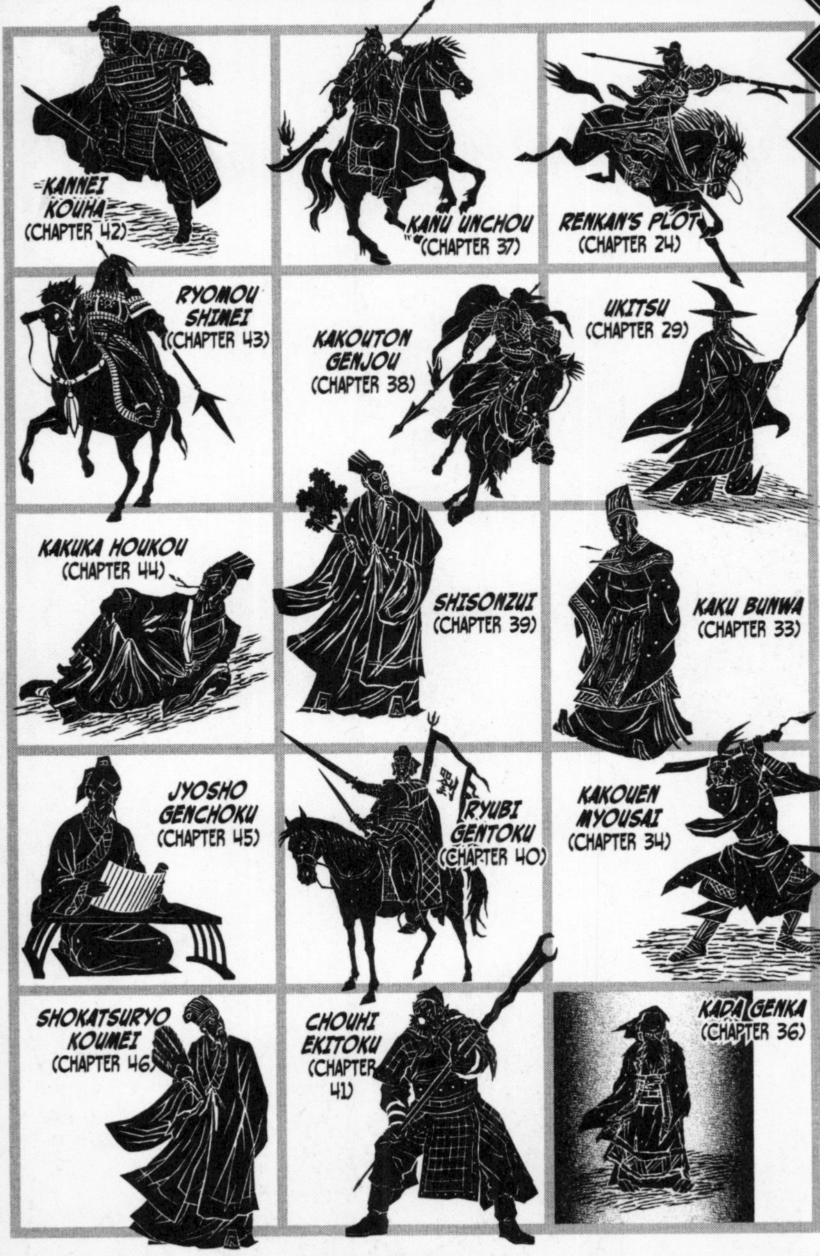

RENKAN'S PLOT (CHAPTER 24)
KANU UNCHOU (CHAPTER 37)
KANNEI KOUHA (CHAPTER 42)
UKITSU (CHAPTER 29)
KAKOUTON GENJOU (CHAPTER 38)
RYOMOU SHIMEI (CHAPTER 43)
KAKU BUNWA (CHAPTER 33)
SHISONZUI (CHAPTER 39)
KAKUKA HOUKOU (CHAPTER 44)
KAKOUEN MYOUSAI (CHAPTER 34)
RYUBI GENTOKU (CHAPTER 40)
JYOSHO GENCHOKU (CHAPTER 45)
KADA GENKA (CHAPTER 36)
CHOUHI EKITOKU (CHAPTER 41)
SHOKATSURYO KOUMEI (CHAPTER 46)

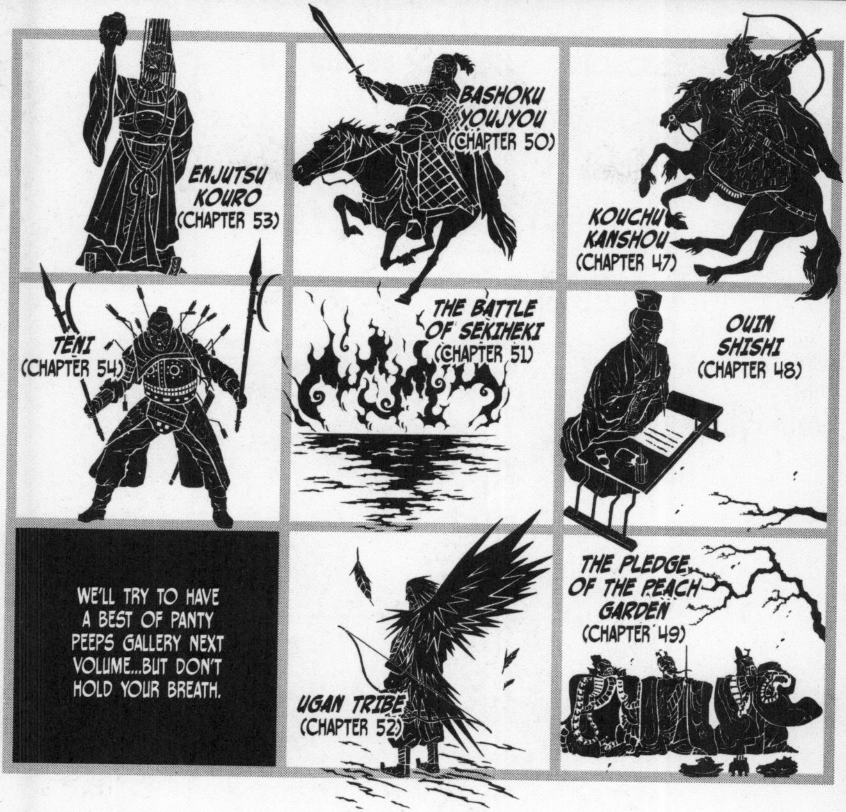
KOUCHU KANSHOU (CHAPTER 47)
BASHOKU YOUJYOU (CHAPTER 50)
ENJUTSU KOURO (CHAPTER 53)
OUIN SHISHI (CHAPTER 48)
THE BATTLE OF SEKIHEKI (CHAPTER 51)
TENI (CHAPTER 54)
THE PLEDGE OF THE PEACH GARDEN (CHAPTER 49)
UGAN TRIBE (CHAPTER 52)
WE'LL TRY TO HAVE A BEST OF PANTY PEEPS GALLERY NEXT VOLUME...BUT DON'T HOLD YOUR BREATH.

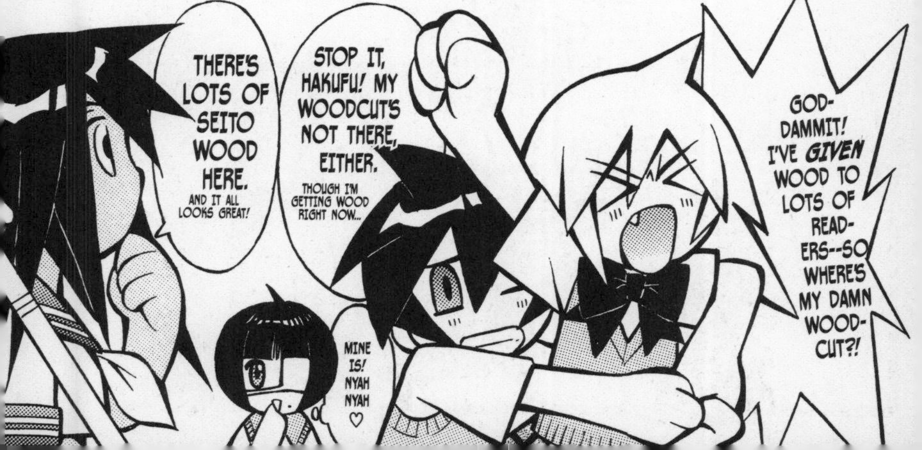
GOD-DAMMIT! I'VE *GIVEN* WOOD TO LOTS OF READ-ERS--SO WHERE'S MY DAMN WOOD-CUT?!
STOP IT, HAKUFU! MY WOODCUT'S NOT THERE, EITHER.
THOUGH I'M GETTING WOOD RIGHT NOW...
THERE'S LOTS OF SEITO WOOD HERE.
AND IT ALL LOOKS GREAT!
MINE IS! NYAH NYAH ♡

GANBARE!! STUDIO Y'S
TOKYO 24HR II

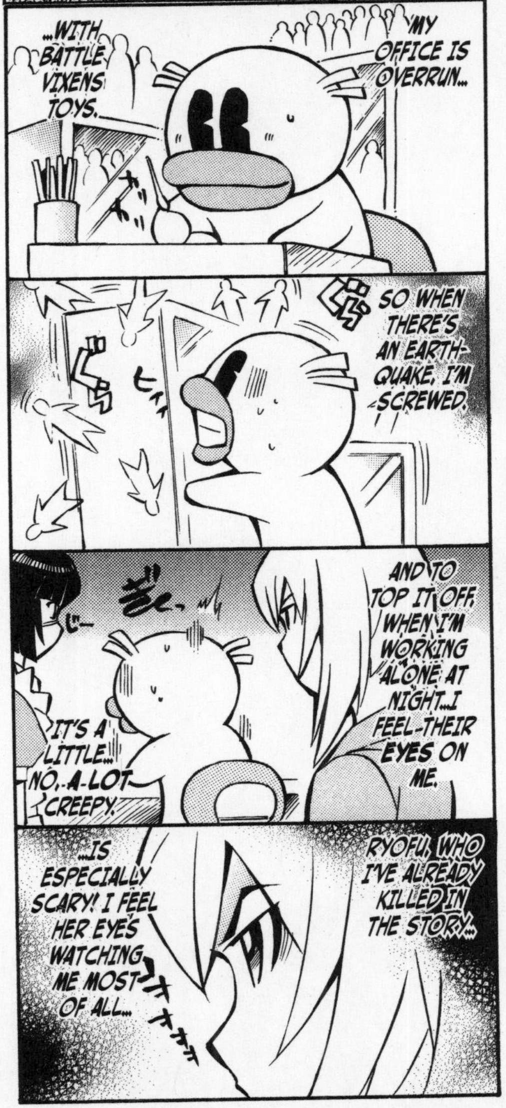
MY OFFICE IS OVERRUN...
...WITH BATTLE VIXENS TOYS.
SO WHEN THERE'S AN EARTH-QUAKE, I'M SCREWED.
AND TO TOP IT OFF, WHEN I'M WORKING ALONE AT NIGHT...I FEEL THEIR EYES ON ME.
IT'S A LITTLE... NO, A LOT CREEPY.
RYOFU, WHO I'VE ALREADY KILLED IN THE STORY...
...IS ESPECIALLY SCARY! I FEEL HER EYES WATCHING ME MOST OF ALL...

IN THE NEXT VOLUME OF

BATTLE VIXENS™

SHAFTED!

With the holy terror that is Teni closing in for the kill, can Shimei somehow fight back--or will she be penetrated by shaft after shaft until she's done for? And with Koukin being held hostage, Ton-chan is now Hakufu's protector but is he up to the challenge? Will the three-some survive? Or will it all just be an orgy of death?

Don't miss *Battle Vixens* volume 9!

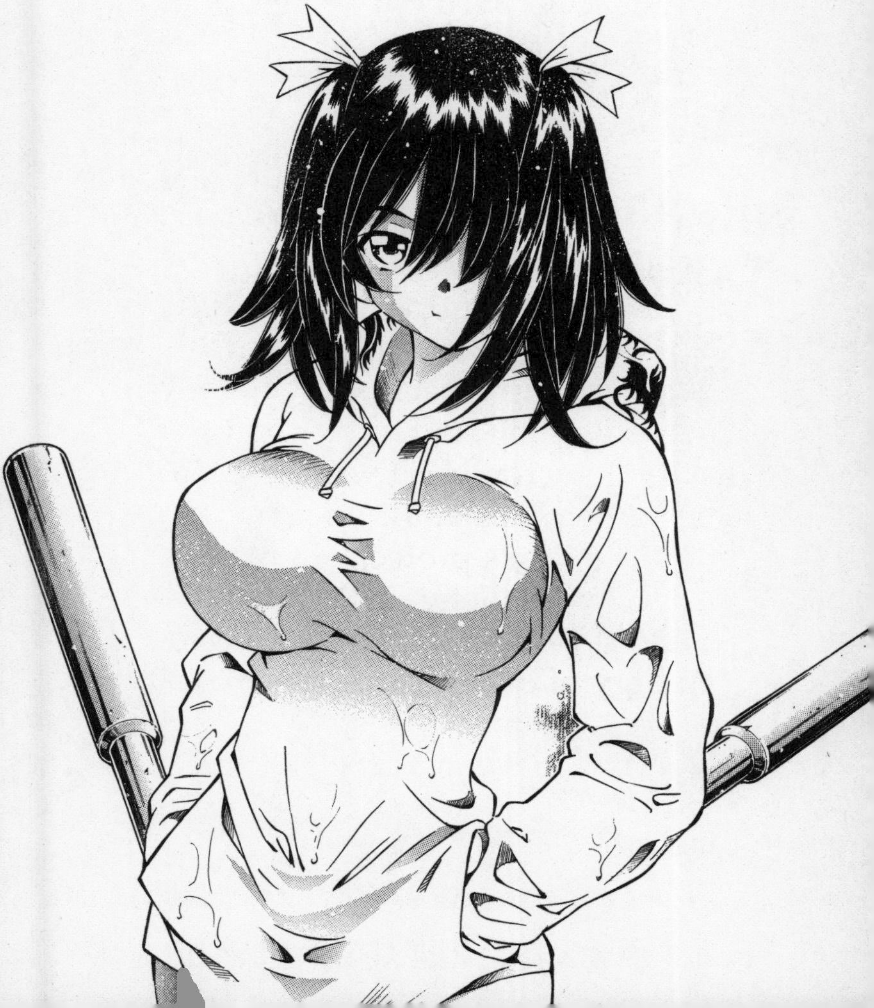

TOKYOPOP SHOP

WWW.TOKYOPOP.COM/SHOP

HOT NEWS!
Check out the TOKYOPOP SHOP!
The world's best collection of manga in English is now available online in one place!

GIRLS BRAVO

RIZELMINE

WAR ON FLESH

War on Flesh and other hot titles are available at the store that never closes!

- **LOOK FOR SPECIAL OFFERS**
- **PRE-ORDER UPCOMING RELEASES**
- **COMPLETE YOUR COLLECTIONS**

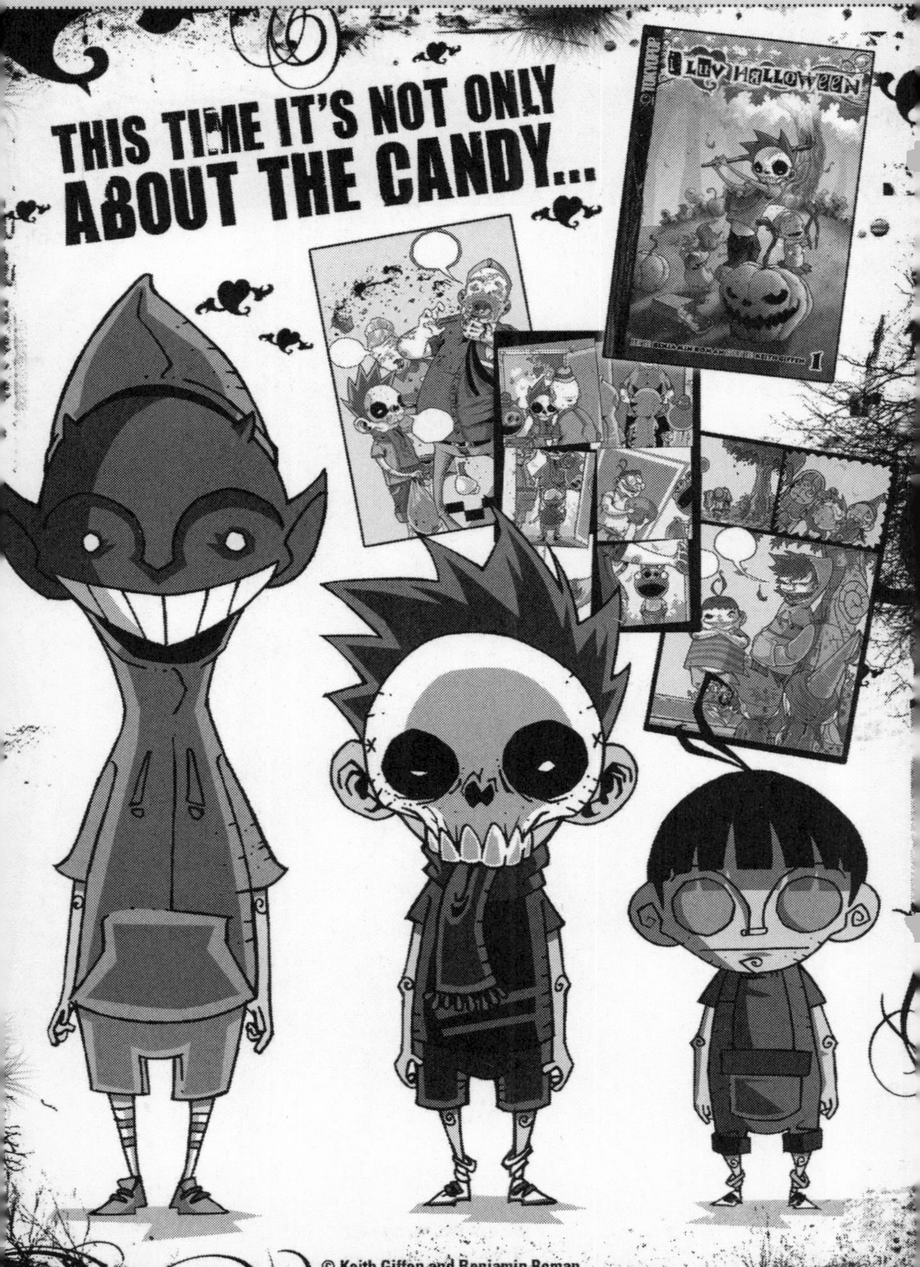
THIS TIME IT'S NOT ONLY
ABOUT THE CANDY...
I LUV HALLOWEEN
1

I LUV HALLOWEEN

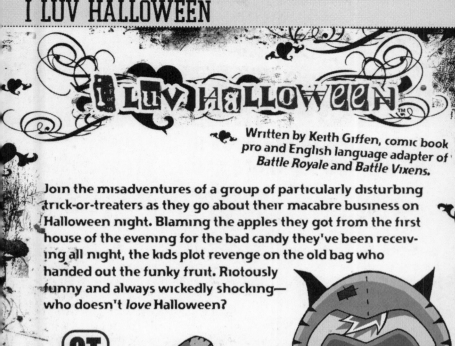

I LUV HALLOWEEN™

Written by Keith Giffen, comic book pro and English language adapter of *Battle Royale* and *Battle Vixens*.

Join the misadventures of a group of particularly disturbing trick-or-treaters as they go about their macabre business on Halloween night. Blaming the apples they got from the first house of the evening for the bad candy they've been receiving all night, the kids plot revenge on the old bag who handed out the funky fruit. Riotously funny and always wickedly shocking—who doesn't *love* Halloween?

OT
OLDER TEEN
AGE 16+

Preview the manga at:
www.TOKYOPOP.com/iluvhalloween

STOP!

This is the back of the book.
You wouldn't want to spoil a great ending!

This book is printed "manga-style," in the authentic Japanese right-to-left format. Since none of the artwork has been flipped or altered, readers get to experience the story just as the creator intended. You've been asking for it, so TOKYOPOP® delivered: authentic, hot-off-the-press, and far more fun!

DIRECTIONS

If this is your first time reading manga-style, here's a quick guide to help you understand how it works.

It's easy... just start in the top right panel and follow the numbers. Have fun, and look for more 100% authentic manga from TOKYOPOP®!